Inventing the Silent Majority in Western Europe and the United States

Inventing the Silent Majority in Western Europe and the United States examines the unprecedented mobilization and transformation of conservative movements on both sides of the Atlantic during a pivotal period in postwar history. Convinced that "noisy minorities" had seized the agenda, conservatives in Western Europe and the United States began to project themselves under Nixon's popularized label of the "Silent Majority." The years between the early 1960s and the late 1970s witnessed the emergence of countless new political organizations that sought to defend the existing order against a perceived left-wing threat from the resurgence of a new, politically organized Christian right to the beginnings of a radicalized version of neoliberal economic policy. Bringing together new research by leading international scholars, this ground-breaking volume offers a unique framework for studying the phenomenon of conservative mobilization in comparative and transnational perspective.

Anna von der Goltz is Associate Professor of History at Georgetown University. Her research focuses on protest movements, with a recent emphasis on responses to political, social, and cultural change among center-right students in West Germany. Her first book, *Hindenburg: Power, Myth, and the Rise of the Nazis* (2009), won the Wiener Library's Fraenkel Prize in Contemporary History.

Britta Waldschmidt-Nelson is Professor of History at the University of Augsburg. Her main research areas are transatlantic relations, African-American studies, and religious history. Her previous publications include a history of Christian Science in Germany from 1894 to 2009 (2009) and the first German Malcolm X biography (2015), as well as several co-edited collections, among them *Europe and America: Cultures in Translation* (2006) and *The Transatlantic Sixties: Europe and the United States in the Counterculture Decade* (2013).

Publications of the German Historical Institute

Edited by

SIMONE LÄSSIG

with the assistance of David Lazar

The German Historical Institute is a center for advanced study and research whose purpose is to provide a permanent basis for scholarly cooperation among historians from the Federal Republic of Germany and the United States. The Institute conducts, promotes, and supports research into both American and German political, social, economic, and cultural history; into transatlantic migration, especially during the nineteenth and twentieth centuries; and into the history of international relations, with special emphasis on the roles played by the United States and Germany.

Recent Books in the Series:

Inventing the Silent Majority in Western Europe and the United States

Conservatism in the 1960s and 1970s

ANNA VON DER GOLTZ

Georgetown University, Washington, DC

BRITTA WALDSCHMIDT-NELSON

University of Augsburg

GERMAN HISTORICAL INSTITUTE

Washington, D.C.

and

 CAMBRIDGE
UNIVERSITY PRESS

CAMBRIDGE
UNIVERSITY PRESS

University Printing House, Cambridge CB2 8BS, United Kingdom

One Liberty Plaza, 20th Floor, New York, NY 10006, USA

477 Williamstown Road, Port Melbourne, VIC 3207, Australia

4843/24, 2nd Floor, Ansari Road, Daryaganj, Delhi - 110002, India

79 Anson Road, #06-04/06, Singapore 079906

Cambridge University Press is part of the University of Cambridge.

It furthers the University's mission by disseminating knowledge in the pursuit of education, learning and research at the highest international levels of excellence.

www.cambridge.org
Information on this title: www.cambridge.org/9781107165427

© German Historical Institute 2017

First published 2017

Printed in the United Kingdom by Clays, St Ives plc

A catalog record for this publication is available from the British Library.

ISBN 978-1-107-16542-7 Hardback

Contents

Contributors

Lawrence Black, Department of History, University of York

Frank Bösch, Center for Contemporary History, Potsdam

Donald T. Critchlow, Department of History, Arizona State University

John Davis, Faculty of History, University of Oxford

Marjet Derks, Department of History, Radboud University

Joshua D. Farrington, African and African-American Studies, Eastern Kentucky University

Martin H. Geyer, Historical Seminar, LMU Munich

Anna von der Goltz, Edmund A. Walsh School of Foreign Service and Department of History, Georgetown University

Thomas Großbölting, Department of History, University of Münster (WWU)

Michael Kazin, Department of History, Georgetown University

Bernard Lachaise, Center for the Study of the Modern and Contemporary Worlds (CEMMC), University of Bordeaux

Mark J. Rozell, School of Policy, Government, and International Affairs, George Mason University

Bill Schwarz, The School of English and Drama, Queen Mary, University of London

Martina Steber, Department of History and Sociology, University of Konstanz

Daniel Stedman Jones, Barrister, 39 Essex Chambers, London

Whitney Strub, Department of History, Newark College of Arts and Sciences University College, Rutgers University

Stacie Taranto, Department of History, Ramapo College

Britta Waldschmidt-Nelson, Department of History, University of Augsburg

Julian E. Zelizer, Department of History and Woodrow Wilson School of Public and International Affairs, Princeton University

Acknowledgments

Most of the chapters in this collection were originally presented as papers at the conference "Inventing the Silent Majority: Conservative Mobilization in Western Europe and the United States in the 1960s and 1970s," which was held at the German Historical Institute (GHI) in Washington, DC, in April 2013. The editors would like to thank the BMW Center for German and European Studies at Georgetown University, the GHI, the German Academic Exchange Service (DAAD), and the French Embassy in Washington, DC, for their generous financial and organizational support of the conference. We are grateful to the GHI and its former director, Hartmut Berghoff, for agreeing to include this volume in the Publications of the German Historical Institute Series. Moreover, we would like to thank all of our contributors for their essays and their patience throughout the revision stages. We are also obliged to the anonymous reviewers, who made important suggestions for improving the manuscript, and to David Lazar, who edited the whole text meticulously. Finally, we would like to thank Deborah Gerschenowitz at Cambridge University Press for her support of this project.

Anna von der Goltz and Britta Waldschmidt-Nelson

Introduction

Silent Majorities and Conservative Mobilization in the 1960s and 1970s in Transatlantic Perspective

Anna von der Goltz and Britta Waldschmidt-Nelson

With "Address to the Nation on the War in Vietnam" on November 3, 1969, asking "the great silent majority of . . . [his] fellow Americans" for their support, President Richard Nixon popularized a label that would help to reshape American politics in powerful ways in the years to come. The voices of ordinary Americans, Nixon warned, had been drowned out by a vocal, antiwar minority responsible for "mounting demonstration in the street" that sought to impose its view on the majority and threatened the future of the nation.[1]

Although such an appeal to the "forgotten" "real Americans" was not new – it had long been a staple of populist politics in the United States[2] – there was something about the notion of belonging to the silent majority that seemed to capture the imagination of vast swathes of the American public at that time of political and cultural upheaval. An estimated seventy million television viewers watched the carefully crafted speech, and tens of thousands of letters from self-declared members of the silent majority poured into the White House in the weeks that followed. Even the president's opponents conceded that the phrase had been "one of the most brilliant political inventions of recent years," and it entered common political discourse with astonishing speed.[3]

[handwritten marginalia: The term is still in the use in the (far) right]

---

[1] "Address to the Nation on the War in Vietnam," November 3, 1969: http://www
.nixonlibrary.gov/forkids/speechesforkids/silentmajority/silentmajority_transcript.pdf
(accessed February 2, 2016).
[2] Michael Kazin, "Democracy Betrayed and Redeemed: Populist Traditions in the United
States," *Constellations* 5, 1 (1998): 75–84; idem, *The Populist Persuasion: An American
History* (Ithaca, NY, 1998).
[3] Bill Schwarz, "The Silent Majority: How the Private Becomes Political," chapter 7 in this
volume; Matthew Lassiter, "Who Speaks for the Silent Majority?" *The New York Times*,

The idea of a silent majority did not just strike a chord with U.S. citizens who felt alienated by antiwar protesters and urban rioters or were unnerved by the acceleration of cultural change. The term was quickly taken up on the other side of the Atlantic to describe political realignments then underway in several Western European countries. Soon after the European press had covered Nixon's speech, an array of groups in Western Europe claimed to speak on behalf of this evocatively named group, often appropriating the label in an explicit attempt to mobilize forces on the center-right and to counter a resurgent and highly visible left.[4] In France, President Georges Pompidou appealed to the silent majority in speeches after the Gaullist Comités de Défense de la République had rallied in May 1968 to defend the republic against a left-wing insurgency.[5] In the United Kingdom, the self-styled housewife and Christian moralist Mary Whitehouse campaigned against sex, violence, and blasphemy on British television through her National Viewers' and Listeners' Association, and evangelicals sought to mobilize the silent majority of British Christians at the Nationwide Festival of Light.[6] In West Germany, center-right students deployed the label in their university election campaigns, calling on their peers to raise their voices against "small group[s] of revolutionary idiots" whose protests had deeply alienated much of the public.[7] The remarkable traction of the silent majority label on both sides of the Atlantic in the late 1960s and 1970s suggests that it managed to give shape to and to crystallize common perceptions of marginalization in the

November 2, 2011; Milton J. Rosenberg, Sidney Verba, and Philip E. Converse, *Vietnam and the Silent Majority: The Dove's Guide* (New York, 1970), 19. For an example of how the label was appropriated by U.S. college students on the right, see Mark Evans, *Will the Real Young Americans Please Stand Up? The Until-Now Silent, Youthful Majority's Call For a Return to the Traditional Principles That Made This Country Great* (Harrisburg, PA, 1973).

[4] On the press coverage of Nixon's "silent majority" in a European context, see Martin H. Geyer's contribution to this volume (chapter 12).

[5] Frédéric Bas, "'La majorité silencieuse' ou la bataille de l'opinion en mai–juin 1968," in Philippe Artières and Michelle Zancarini-Fournel, eds., *68. Une histoire collective (1962–1981)* (Paris, 2008), 359–366; François Audigier, "Le Gaullisme d'ordre des années 68," *Vingtième Siècle. Revue d'histoire* 116 (2012): 53–68; see also Bernard Lachaise's chapter in this volume (chapter 5).

[6] See essays by Bill Schwarz (chapter 7) and Lawrence Black (chapter 17) in this volume; Amy Whipple, "Speaking for Whom? The 1971 Festival of Light and the Search for the 'Silent Majority,'" *Contemporary British History* 24:3 (2010): 319–339.

[7] See Anna von der Goltz's essay in this volume (chapter 4); on the similar rhetorical strategies of right-wing students in France and Italy, see Andrea Mammone, "The Transnational Reaction to 1968: Neo-Fascist Fronts and Political Cultures in France and Italy," *Contemporary European History* 17:2 (2008): 220 and 223.

public realm. Those it spoke to in both Western Europe and the United States felt that significant political, social, and cultural shifts were underway in their societies that had given "noisy minorities" the chance to set the agenda and thereby hasten the pace of change.

Like most successful political concepts and labels, the silent majority was anything but clearly defined. It was first and foremost a rhetorical and political construct that captured genuinely felt anxieties and produced new political allegiances. At the same time, it was amorphous and open enough to appeal to a diverse set of actors, not all of whom, as Matthew D. Lassiter shows in his study of politics in the American sunbelt, were committed political activists or identified as conservative.[8] As a rhetorical weapon and symbolic home, however, the label was particularly attractive to a wide array of conservative and center-right groups, policymakers, pollsters, and activists – the actors who are the focus of this volume. Taking the remarkable transatlantic career of the silent majority as their point of departure, the contributors seek to shed light on the reasons for its strong international appeal and ask what this phenomenon tells us more generally about the 1960s and 1970s, a pivotal period in the histories of both the United States and Western Europe. In doing so, we seek to make a contribution to the broader historiography of these transformative decades and to foster the comparative and transnational study of conservative and center-right mobilization.

Historiography

The scholarship on conservative movements has grown exponentially in recent years. In the time since Alan Brinkley described conservatism as an "orphan" in the study of twentieth-century U.S. history in 1994, the topic has become a lively and widely researched subfield.[9] Many of the pioneering studies of conservative mobilization took the 1960s as their starting point and explained the ascendancy of the New Right from the 1970s onward as the result of a backlash against the radicalism of the civil rights movement, New Left protesters, feminists, and Democratic

---

[8] Lassiter demonstrates that the "Silent Majority" overlapped with Republican conservatism but extended beyond the right-wing base, representing the "vitality and volatility" of the political center. See his *The Silent Majority: Suburban Politics in the Sunbelt South* (Princeton, 2007), 8.

[9] Alan Brinkley, "The Problem of American Conservatism," *The American Historical Review* 99 (1994): 409; cf. Kim Phillips-Fein, "Conservatism: A State of the Field," *Journal of American History* 98:3 (2011): 723.

social policies stretching from the New Deal to the Great Society.[10] More recent research, by contrast, has not only expanded the chronological frame to include the entire postwar period; it has also highlighted the extent to which the movements of the left and right developed in tandem. Moreover, the right, often dismissed as hopelessly old-fashioned or out of step with the times, could in fact be strikingly modern when it came to political organization, showing considerable initiative and imagination in mobilizing working-class, female, and non-white activists.[11] What has emerged from this scholarship is an image of conservative movements that is less reactionary and more hybrid and diverse than the "backlash" school originally suggested, and many of the essays gathered here build on these more recent findings. Although the 1960s and 1970s are thus no longer seen as the cradle of conservative mobilization, these two decades remain pivotal in that the political and cultural crises that accompanied them did much to coalesce conservative forces into clearly recognizable movements and to shape their future trajectories.[12]

While the strong polarization of the political landscape in the United States in recent years and the concurrent vitality of grassroots groups on the right, such as the Tea Party, have arguably lent greater intellectual urgency to historical investigations of the phenomenon in the United States, research on the mobilization of conservative and center-right movements has also flourished in European scholarship. Attention has been devoted not least to conservatives' responses to and

[10] See Michael Kimmage, "The Historiography of Twentieth-Century American Conservatism," in *Oxford Bibliographies Online: Political Science*, http://www.oxfordbibliographies.com/view/document/obo-9780199756223/obo-9780199756223-0080.xml (accessed April 4, 2014). Examples of the "backlash" school include Thomas Byrne Edsall and Mary Edsall, *Chain Reaction: The Impact of Race, Rights, and Taxes on American Politics* (New York, 1991); Ronald P. Formisano, *Boston against Busing: Race, Class, and Ethnicity in the 1960s and 1970s* (Chapel Hill, 1991); Dan T. Carter, *The Politics of Rage: George Wallace, the Origins of the New Conservatism, and the Transformation of American Politics* (New York, 1995); Steve Fraser and Gary Gerstle, eds., *The Rise and Fall of the New Deal Order, 1930–1980* (Princeton, 1989).

[11] The literature on this is vast. Important examples include: Rebecca E. Klatch, *A Generation Divided: The New Left, the New Right, and the 1960s* (Berkeley, 1997); Lisa McGirr, *Suburban Warriors: The Origins of the New American Right* (Princeton, 2001); Angela Dillard, *Guess Who's Coming to Dinner Now? Multicultural Conservatism in America* (New York, 2001); Donald T. Critchlow, *Phyllis Schlafly and Grassroots Conservatism: A Woman's Crusade* (Princeton, 2005); Bethany Moreton, *To Serve God and Wal-Mart: The Making of Christian Free Enterprise* (Cambridge, MA, 2009).

[12] Bruce J. Schulman and Julian E. Zelizer, eds., *Rightward Bound: Making America Conservative in the 1970s* (Cambridge, MA, 2008); see also Zelizer's contribution to this volume (chapter 1).

involvement in the political and cultural upheaval associated with the symbolic shorthand "1968." As is increasingly clear from a growing body of scholarship, the political and cultural shifts that fostered the rise of the New Left also spurred the reorientation and revitalization of the center-right in many Western European countries.[13]

Even though U.S. scholarship may be ahead in terms of the sheer number of histories of conservative movements produced in recent years, European and American historians of conservatism alike have tended to focus on individual national case studies. Michael Kazin called for internationalist perspectives on the study of conservatism as early as 1992, and more recently Kim Phillips-Fein identified transnational investigations as a persistent gap in the scholarship.[14] Despite such calls to greater scholarly internationalism, however, relatively few historians have tried to place either American or European conservatism into an international context or trace the movement of ideas and actors across national borders.[15] This dearth is particularly surprising given the embrace of the transnational turn by historians of the New Left and associated movements of

[13] Jerry Z. Muller, "German Neoconservatism and the History of the Bonn Republic, 1968 to 1985," *German Politics & Society* 18:1 (2000): 1–32; Axel Schildt, "'Die Kräfte der Gegenreform sind auf breiter Front angetreten.' Zur konservativen Tendenzwende in den siebziger Jahren," *Archiv für Sozialgeschichte* 44 (2004): 449–478; Damir Skenderovic and Christina Späti, eds., *1968 – Revolution und Gegenrevolution. Neue Linke und Neue Rechte in Frankreich, der BRD und der Schweiz* (Basel, 2008); Marcus Collins, ed., *The Permissive Society and its Enemies* (London, 2007); Frank Bösch, "Die Krise als Chance: Die Neuformierung der Christdemokraten im siebziger Jahren," in Konrad Jarausch, ed., *Das Ende der Zuversicht? Die Strukturkrise der 1970er Jahre als zeithistorische Zäsur* (Göttingen, 2008), 288–301; Massimiliano Livi, Daniel Schmidt, and Michael Sturm, eds., *Die 70er Jahre als schwarzes Jahrzehnt: Politisierungs- und Mobilisierungsprozesse zwischen rechter Mitte und extremer Rechter in Italien und der Bundesrepublik 1967–1982* (Bielefeld, 2010); Lawrence Black, *Redefining British Politics: Consumerism, Culture and Participation, 1954–70* (London, 2010); Audigier, "Le Gaullisme d'ordre des années 68."

[14] Michael Kazin, "The Grass-Roots Right: New Histories of U.S. Conservatism in the Twentieth Century," *The American Historical Review* 97 (1992): 136–155; Phillips-Fein, "Conservatism," 742–743.

[15] Most existing studies with a transnational or comparative framework focus on economic thought and trace the rise of neoliberalism and the economic counterrevolution that spelt the end of the Keynesian consensus in the 1970s: Richard Cockett, *Thinking the Unthinkable: Think-Tanks and the Economic Counter-Revolution, 1931–83* (London, 1995); Juan Gabriel Valdes, *Pinochet's Economists: The Chicago School of Economics in Chile* (Cambridge, 1995); Philip Mirowksi and Dieter Plehwe, eds., *The Road from Mont Pèlerin: The Making of a Neoliberal Thought Collective* (Cambridge, MA, 2009); Daniel Stedman Jones, *Masters of the Universe: Hayek, Friedman, and the Birth of Neoliberal Politics* (Princeton, 2012); Angus Burgin, *The Great Persuasion: Reinventing Free Markets since the Great Depression* (Cambridge, MA, 2012).

the 1960s and 1970s. Studies of the "global 1960s" abound, but conservative and center-right movements are rarely made part of the story.[16] As Martin Durham and Margaret Power pointed out in a recent volume, it is the very interconnectedness of transnationalism with the study of social movements such as feminism or environmentalism, along with the assumption that the right is by definition nationalistic, that has stunted transnational research on conservatism.[17] By placing scholarly investigations of conservative and center-right mobilization in a variety of social settings in Western Europe and the United States side by side and by tracing some of the transnational links that did exist, this volume seeks to offer new perspectives and to contribute to the closing of this historiographical gap.

Divergent Traditions and Common Challenges in the 1960s and 1970s

In emphasizing comparative and transnational perspectives, we do not seek to gloss over the palpable philosophical and political differences that existed — and continue to exist — between conservative thought and movements in the different countries of Western Europe and across the Atlantic. Continental Christian Democrats and France's Gaullists both wedded a social and cultural conservatism with support for state intervention in the economy and a strong welfare state. The latter also championed a populist politics that was largely discredited in postwar Germany as a result of the Nazi dictatorship. In contrast to their French and West German peers, who often felt uneasy with the term, British Conservatives

---

[16] See, e.g., the special issue on "The International 1960s," *The American Historical Review* 114:1 & 2 (2009); Gerd Rainer Horn, *The Spirit of '68: Rebellion in Western Europe and North America, 1956–1976* (Oxford, 2007); Jeremi Suri, *Power and Protest: Global Revolution and the Rise of Détente* (Cambridge, MA, 2003), which includes great power diplomacy and responses to global protest but sees protest as an exclusively left-wing affair. The newer studies that place a specific national case in a global context also tend to exclude activists of the right, e.g.: Martin Klimke, *The Other Alliance: Student Protest in West Germany and the United States in the Global Sixties* (Princeton, 2010); Grzegorz Kosc, Clara Juncker, Sharon Monteith, and Britta Waldschmidt-Nelson, eds., *The Transatlantic Sixties: Europe and the United States in the Counterculture Decade* (Bielefeld, 2013); Timothy Scott Brown, *West Germany and the Global Sixties* (Cambridge, 2013). Thomas Borstelmann's U.S.-centric global history of the 1970s, by contrast, pays close attention to the conservative ascendancy. See his *The 1970s: A New Global History From Civil Rights to Economic Inequality* (Princeton, 2012).

[17] Martin Durham and Margaret Power, "Introduction," in idem, eds., *New Perspectives on the Transnational Right* (London, 2010); 1–10, here 1; see also Jerry Z. Muller, ed., *Conservatism: An Anthology of Social and Political Thought from David Hume to the Present* (Princeton, 1997), 23.

embraced the "conservative" label readily and explicitly. Although still pro-European in the 1960s and 1970s, they also became more receptive to libertarian and Eurosceptic ideas that eventually began to influence policy in the era of Margaret Thatcher. U.S. conservatism has also always been made up of highly divergent strands, including anticommunism, libertarianism, and traditionalism.[18] As this collection illustrates, in the 1960s and 1970s the ideological differences between the different national conservative movements were particularly palpable when it came to the salience of social morality in the political debate, attitudes toward the welfare state and enthusiasm for small government, and the public role of religion, which became a much more formidable political force in the United States than it ever did in Western Europe.

Though the real Eurosceptic turn in the party only came in the late 80s

Conservative and center-right parties enjoyed varying electoral fortunes in this period. In 1969, the West German Christian Democrats *— Until 1982* found themselves in opposition for the very first time since the founding of the Federal Republic – just shortly after the Republican Richard Nixon won the American presidency and was reaping the benefits of the dismantling of the New Deal coalition. While the 1980s saw the ascendancy of *(1981-89) Chirac (1977-85)* Ronald Reagan, Margaret Thatcher, and Helmut Kohl – developments *(1979-90) (1982-98)* that were closely connected to, if by no means overdetermined by, the mobilization of conservative forces in the preceding decades – French *(1981-95)* citizens elected François Mitterrand the Fifth Republic's first Socialist president in 1981. Without simply reading the success of some of the major conservative parties in the 1980s backward, the aim of this collection is to tease out not just what was similar but also what was nationally specific about conservatism and conservative movements in the 1960s and 1970s.

The different political trajectories and ideological characters of conservative and center-right parties and groups notwithstanding, the broader historical context in which they operated and mobilized adherents was remarkably similar on the two sides of the Atlantic. The 1960s and 1970s were decades of significant upheaval and transformation in both Western Europe and the United States; they were marked by far-reaching political, social, and cultural change, and, in the 1970s, by varying degrees of political and economic crisis. The 1960s gave rise to significant popular

---

[18] First described in the classic study by George Nash, *The Conservative Intellectual Movement in America since 1945* (New York, 1976; 3rd ed. 2006). On the intellectual varieties of European and American conservatism, see Muller, *Conservatism*; and the essay by Martina Steber in this volume (chapter 14). On Christian Democracy, see Michael Gehler and Wolfram Kaiser, *Christian Democracy in Europe since 1945* (London, 2004).

insurgencies ("1968") by youth movements, students, workers, and feminists who challenged traditional notions of deference, authority, and patriarchy.[19] Their quest to broaden the definition of the "political" changed the ground on which politics was conducted fundamentally and dislodged longstanding social foundations, which proved deeply unsettling to many conservatives and even some older liberals. As a result, gender roles, the family, and sexuality became sites of heavy political contestation.[20]

The ground of politics shifted in other ways, too. The questioning of traditional social norms did not just touch gender and generational relations but extended to racial hierarchies as well. The civil rights movement is a well-established part of the storyline of these years in the United States, but even in the absence of officially sanctioned racial segregation, race also surfaced in Western European discourses in powerful new ways in the 1960s and 1970s. Mass migration in the wake of the breakup of European colonial empires left a deep mark on European societies, and the presence of extra-European "others" became a source of recurring controversy.[21]

Moreover, the U.S.-led war in Vietnam, which seemed to signify the hypocrisy and imperialist character of liberal democracy at a time when it was pitted against Soviet-style communism in the confrontation of the Cold War, became the focal point uniting disparate protest movements. It had a significant impact on both sides of the Atlantic (and indeed globally), lasting well into the 1970s.[22] All these conflicts played out on television, a still relatively young medium. The extensive television coverage of the most tumultuous events of these years fueled conservative perceptions of crisis and political marginalization by the allegedly

---

[19] Maurice Isserman and Michael Kazin, *America Divided: The Civil War of the 1960s* (Oxford, 2000); Norbert Frei, *1968: Jugendrevolte und Globaler Protest* (Berlin, 2008).

[20] Janice Irvine, *Talk About Sex: The Battles Over Sex Education in the United States* (Berkeley, 2002). See also the contributions by Lawrence Black (chapter 17), Whitney Strub (chapter 16), and Stacie Taranto (chapter 15) to this volume.

[21] See Geoff Eley's round table contribution, Philippe Chassaigne, Geoff Eley, Hartmut Kaelble, Göran Therborn, and Andreas Wirsching, "The 1970s and 1980s as a Turning Point in European History?" *Journal of Modern European History* 9:1 (2011): 8–26; Camilla Schofield, *Enoch Powell and the Making of Postcolonial Britain* (Cambridge, 2013); see also Bill Schwarz's essay in this volume (chapter 7).

[22] Lien-Hang T. Nguyen, "The Vietnam Decade: The Global Shock of the War," in Niall Ferguson, ed., *The Shock of the Global: The 1970s in Perspective* (Cambridge, MA, 2010), 159–172; Wilfried Mausbach, Andreas W. Daum, and Lloyd C. Gardner, eds., *America, the Vietnam War, and the World: Comparative and International Perspectives* (Cambridge, 2003).

Which often camouflaged a deficit in the disenfranchisement? their opponents (w/ dox reax)

"liberal" media. This turned the silent majority into a particularly attractive symbolic home and lent special urgency to media strategies aimed at overcoming conservatives' alleged silence and lack of public visibility.[23]

The same people attend?!! (w/) endlessly about what

On both sides of the Atlantic, some of the most palpable shifts were economic. The seemingly endless boom of the postwar "golden years" — the *trente glorieuses* — came to an end in the 1970s, triggering widespread perceptions of economic "malaise," an "end of optimism," and the breakup of the Keynesian consensus on interventionist economic policies. The economic slowdown and discontent it provoked opened a window of opportunity for advocates of the free market and a turn toward a radical neoliberal austerity politics.[24] The 1970s are associated in popular memory in some countries first and foremost with mounting economic crisis. In Britain, especially hard hit, the crisis reached its apex during the fabled "Winter of Discontent" of 1978–1979, the backdrop to the electoral victory of Margaret Thatcher and the Conservatives the following spring.[25] *b May* The 1970s witnessed significant economic turmoil in the United States as well (as evidenced, for instance, by New York City's near-bankruptcy in 1975), while the Watergate scandal and Nixon's resignation provoked a deep sense of political crisis. *"Ford to City: Drop Dead"*

This period thus saw the unraveling of the postwar economic and social settlement, and the conservative and center-right movements investigated here gained their vibrancy at least in part from the powerful sense of disorientation and uncertainty engendered by these manifold shifts.[26] In

---

[23] David Greenberg, "The Idea of 'the Liberal Media' and Its Roots in the Civil Rights Movement," *The Sixties: A Journal of History, Politics and Culture* 1:2 (2008): 167–186; Christina von Hodenberg, "Mass Media and the Generation of Conflict: West Germany's Long Sixties and the Formation of a Critical Public Sphere," *Contemporary European History* 1 (2006): 367–395. See also the essays by Frank Bösch (chapter 13) and Martin H. Geyer (chapter 12) in this volume.

[24] Eric Hobsbawm, *The Age of Extremes: A History of the World, 1914–1991* (London, 1994), 257–286; Jarausch, *Das Ende der Zuversicht?*; Charles S. Maier, "'Malaise': The Crisis of Capitalism in the 1970s," in Ferguson, *The Shock of the Global*, 25–48; Chassaigne et al., "The 1970s and 1980s as a Turning Point in European History?"; and the essay by Daniel Stedman Jones in this volume (chapter 2).

[25] See Lawrence Black, "An Enlightening Decade? New Histories of 1970s' Britain," *International Labor and Working-Class History* 82 (2012): 174–186; Ben Jackson and Robert Saunders, eds., *Making Thatcher's Britain* (Cambridge, 2012); Niall Ferguson provides some useful figures to put the notion of the 1970s as especially crisis-prone into perspective, showing that this decade seemed particularly disastrous only in comparison with what came before, not after. He notes that there was nevertheless a strong *perception* of crisis in the 1970s. See his "Introduction: Crisis, What Crisis? The 1970s and the Shock of the Global," in Ferguson, *The Shock of the Global*, 1–23, here 14.

[26] See Borstelmann, *The 1970s*, 3.

fact, as several authors in this collection show, the commonality of the challenges they faced could strengthen the ties between otherwise ideologically dissimilar conservative and center-right movements and diminish the temptations of sectarianism.[27]

The Structure of this Collection

The thematic structure of this collection pays tribute to some of the larger historical shifts outlined above and illustrates the various ways in which conservative and center-right movements dealt with these mounting challenges on both sides of the Atlantic. The six parts of the book are organized in a way that intends to foster discussion of differences, similarities, and linkages across the transatlantic divide and to provide an impetus for future research.

Part I, *Origins and Ideas*, looks at the development and substance of conservatism and neoliberalism in the postwar period. Julian E. Zelizer's chapter challenges the widely accepted notion that twentieth-century liberalism was deeply rooted and stable in the American polity while conservatism was a relatively insignificant force before the 1970s. Instead, he argues, there were strong conservative political, economic, and social forces within American society throughout the twentieth century and he attributes much of the fragility of the New Deal coalition to the fact that a key constituency, Southern Democrats, were deeply conservative and put a brake on liberal initiatives.

Daniel Stedman Jones traces the transformation of neoliberalism from a Depression-era critique of Keynesianism into a defense of market mechanisms that, when taken up by conservative activists and politicians, had profound political and social implications. By the 1970s, neoliberal radicals had prepared the ground for a new era of belief in the free market, deregulation, and limited government that was to climax in the Reagan and Thatcher years. As Zelizer and Stedman Jones demonstrate, the era between the 1930s and 1970s was less a period dominated by the New Deal order than a time when conservatism, liberalism, and neoliberalism were all vibrant forces in American and Western European life, contributing to a new political, economic, and cultural infrastructure that would last for generations to come.

Part II of the book, *Political Mobilization and Responses to Left-wing Protest*, looks at some of the ways in which conservative and

---

[27]   See the contributions by John Davis (chapter 3), Martina Steber (chapter 14), and Anna von der Goltz (chapter 4) to this volume.

center-right groups responded to the challenge posed by the manifold protest movements associated with the New Left. John Davis's chapter takes an in-depth look at how conservative students began to organize at universities across the United Kingdom. He shows that the young Tories active in campus politics in the late 1960s were often quite liberal on social issues and distinctly Europhile. In sharp contrast to the Conservative Party's subsequent Eurosceptic turn under Thatcher, the young British conservatives of the 1960s eagerly sought to make common cause with their counterparts in Western Europe, especially in Scandinavia and West Germany.

Picking up on the theme of student mobilization, Anna von der Goltz's chapter shows that center-right students in the Federal Republic of Germany in the 1960s overlapped with their counterparts on the left when it came to identifying political, economic, and social problems. Both sides, for example, called for educational reform and criticized the authoritarianism of German political culture. However, the political landscape became more polarized in the 1970s. Left-wing and center-right students lost much of their common ground and began to view each other as intolerable extremists.

Bernard Lachaise examines the context of conservative mobilization in the nation to Germany's west. As his chapter demonstrates, despite the impressive Gaullist victory in the elections of June 1968, the massive protest wave of May 1968 had frightened French conservatives and motivated them to mobilize the *majorité silencieuse* in the early 1970s. By increasing media attention to the "left-wing threat" and mobilizing public support – especially by using martial rhetoric that drew on past moments of national danger and invoked memories of wartime resistance – the right wing's "Gaullism of Order" was quite successful and established a new conservative discourse that is still present in France today.

Donald T. Critchlow's chapter hones in on how similar concerns for "law and order" played out on the other side of the Atlantic in the 1960s and early 1970s. While many scholars have identified race as the most important issue to undermine the New Deal coalition, Critchlow maintains that it was left-wing politics – in its various forms from Great Society liberalism to New Left radicalism – that set off a chain reaction within the American polity and led to the conservative ascendancy of the 1970s and 1980s. The civil rights movement, student protests, urban riots, rising crime rates, and other social disturbances conflated in the perceptions of many concerned voters, who became convinced that the world was coming apart and blamed Democrats for the social disequilibrium. Without dismissing the importance of race entirely, Critchlow contends that voter anxieties about "law and order" were key to explaining the Republicans' electoral victories. The chapters in Part II show that, despite much animosity between the right and left, the 1960s and 1970s were decades in which these two forces often developed and mobilized in tandem, challenging, reinforcing, and transforming each other in the process.

The opening chapter of Part III, *Conservatism and the Issue of Race*, departs from Critchlow's emphasis on conservatives' desire for social discipline and throws the deep racial anxieties that fueled conservative mobilization on the two sides of the Atlantic into sharp relief. Focusing on one American and two British conservative icons, Bill Schwarz teases out the similarities that existed between conservative discourses on race in Britain and the United States despite the two countries' divergent histories of colonialism and segregation. He contends that Governor George Wallace's open support for white supremacy in the U.S. South was key to his success among Southern white voters during the 1960s and 1970s. Racial tension also surfaced in Western Europe during this period, not least in Britain, a country that had recently lost its empire and witnessed the mass immigration of people of color for the first time. As Schwarz shows, British conservatives such as Enoch Powell and Mary Whitehouse were motivated by and used racial (and sexual) fears to their advantage.

The following chapter focuses more closely on the role of the black freedom struggle in conservative mobilization and party politics in the United States. As Joshua D. Farrington demonstrates, some conservative African Americans enthusiastically embraced the concept of black capitalism. Although Nixon had opposed the civil rights legislation of the 1960s and continued to express his sympathy with white opponents of integration as president, his administration was keen to cooperate with black conservatives, for example by giving financial aid to black-owned businesses and black colleges. While most African Americans remained distrustful of Nixon, his racial policies, Farrington argues, were much more multifaceted and diverse than generally depicted. The chapters in Part III thus provide important new perspectives on the complex and substantial role that the issue of race played in conservative mobilization.

Part IV of our volume, *Religious Mobilization*, examines the role of religion in public life and within conservative party politics in the United States and in Western Europe. After giving a brief survey of the different histories and public roles of religion and religious institutions in Europe and the United States, Mark J. Rozell and Britta Waldschmidt-Nelson's chapter illustrates that the origins of the present-day American Christian right movement can be found in the reaction of social conservatives to the legalization of abortion, other liberal social policies, and the counterculture. Previously, most Christian conservatives had kept a strict separation between their faith and political activity, but discontent with what they perceived as an indulgence of sexual promiscuity and a rejection of traditional values brought Christian and secular conservatives together in a powerful alliance. As the authors show, the success of this self-proclaimed "Moral Majority" in mobilizing voters was an important factor in Reagan's victory at the polls in 1980.

The influence of Christian conservatives on politics in West Germany, in contrast, has remained rather insignificant. Thomas Großbölting argues that while the two major German churches sometimes participated in public debate, Christian fundamentalists were never able to obtain broad popular support. Internal efforts at conservative "revitalization" within the churches largely failed, and most Germans regard religious convictions as a private matter to this day. Compared to American Christian conservatives, Großbölting notes, even the center-right Christian Democratic Party is rather moderate when it comes to issues of social morality, such as abortion.

Conservative Christians in the Netherlands faced similar challenges, as Marjet Derks emphasizes in her chapter. By criticizing the progressive liturgical interpretations of the Second Vatican Council and proclaiming themselves the defenders of the true faith, conservative Dutch Catholics tried to stem the tide of secular liberalism in their society. Pointing out the important role of gender and generation in this dispute, Derks observes that the Christian right's failure to gain any real political influence can be attributed at least in part to the tendency of the Dutch press to focus on young, media-savvy progressive clergymen and theologians. As these chapters illustrate, the difference in the scope of the Christian right's social and political influence continues to be one of the most striking divergences between American and Western European conservatism, and the 1960s and 1970s are crucial for understanding this discrepancy.

Part V, *Languages and Media Strategies of Conservatism*, is most directly connected to our book's title and the notion of "silence." Rallying the silent majority meant making an allegedly "silenced" group more visible and vocal. Martin H. Geyer's chapter demonstrates the close proximity of social theory and media strategies. The idea of a "spiral of silence" put forward by the conservative German pollster Elisabeth Noelle-Neumann was remarkably close to Nixon's concept of the silent majority. Both were based on the conviction that people were unwilling to state their views openly for fear of appearing at odds with the majority view. As Geyer shows, Noelle-Neumann and her theories played an important role in new West German conservative strategies to "occupy terms" and thus regain control over language and public opinion.

Conservatives in America as well as Europe tend to believe that the public media favor the left. Frank Bösch examines why and how West German conservatives championed the introduction of private commercial broadcasting. Remarkably, in doing so, they drew on themes traditionally advocated by the political left, such as the promotion of diversity, while the Social Democrats used arguments more commonly associated with the right, for example the potential threat unregulated broadcasting allegedly posed to traditional family values. In the end, Bösch argues, conservatives won this battle, but the rise of private broadcasting led not to an increase of conservative votes but rather to a depoliticization of the television audience.

Martina Steber sheds light on the difficulties conservative parties encountered when they tried to form transnational alliances within Western Europe. Her research suggests that the problems were often more a matter of terminology than of substance because the diversity of national traditions and multilingualism made finding a common political language difficult. While British and German conservatives cooperated rather well in this regard, other center-right national parties did not. The ensuing linguistic battle about the core concept of "conservatism" in Western Europe, Steber concludes, was an integral part of the complicated and not always linear process of European integration. The use of language and control of the media proved to be significant tools inside and across national lines for the effort to raise the voice of the silent majority.

Finally, Part VI, *Cultures of Conservatism*, looks at the various ways in which conservatives dealt with social and cultural change, including shifting gender and sexual norms, and the wider challenges of modernity in the 1960s and 1970s. Stacie Taranto's chapter examines the Republican Party's stance on women's issues. After the more liberal "Rockefeller Republicans" had long supported feminist reforms such as New York's abortion reform law of 1970, hundreds of previously apolitical women, mostly from the suburbs of New York City, rose up in protest. They organized a viable political base to protect "traditional family values" and heteronormative gender roles. With the help of other anti-abortion groups, Taranto contends, these conservative female Republicans were able to triumph over the party's liberal wing and significantly change state politics in New York, foreshadowing some of the powerful ways in which female activists and the issue of gender would shape Republican politics in the years to come.

Tracing conservative discourse on pornography and obscenity from the 1960s through the 1980s, Whitney Strub shows that the Republican Party was much more reactionary when it came to gay rights. When many of the once-useful tropes of the right fell into disrepute as a result of the civil rights revolution and the rise of feminism, anti-gay moralism provided an effective new rallying ground for conservatives. Using legislative and judiciary venues, Strub argues, conservatives thus succeeded in establishing procreative heterosexuality as the norm of "sexual citizenship" until the beginning of the twenty-first century.

Focusing on the Conservative Party's youth organization, on activist Mary Whitehouse and party leader Margaret Thatcher, Lawrence Black examines the transformation of Britain's broader conservative culture in the late 1960s and 1970s. By taking a close look at particular aspects of the new British conservatism, such as its members' rather modern disposition and lifestyle, Black shows the complexity of political culture and stresses that Thatcherism altered conservative culture in Britain less than is generally assumed. In contrast to their American counterparts, British and other Western European conservatives seem to have gained less ground in the moral and cultural arena than in the economic one. As this part as well as others in this volume show, conservative mobilization in the 1960s and 1970s, on the two sides of the Atlantic, was not always a clear-cut "backlash" story, but rather a hybrid undertaking with many different goals and strategies, often relying on left-wing methods and grassroots participation to give the so-called silent majority a voice.

While some of the chapters gathered here will no doubt be of particular value to area specialists, we hope that the collection in its entirety will make its readers think further about comparisons and connections between different parts of Europe and the United States. In an effort to foster further comparative and transnational research on conservative mobilization, Michael Kazin's concluding afterword teases out some of the common threads of the collection and examines some of conservatism's major victories and failures since the 1960s.

PART I

ORIGINS AND IDEAS

American Conservatism from Roosevelt to Johnson

Julian E. Zelizer

The backlash against liberalism in the late 1960s has been one of the central storylines in most of our narratives about the United States in the *white* contemporary era. The argument goes that there was a revolt of working- class Democrats in the wake of the urban riots and the mobilization of right-wing conservatives against Lyndon Johnson's *(1963-69)* Great Society. By the end of the decade, conservatives had also joined the opposition to the Vietnam War, albeit on the grounds that Johnson had not been tough enough in fighting communism. As a result, the conservative movement flourished in the 1970s, remaking politics for decades to come.

The premise of this conventional narrative is that the period between the 1930s and 1960s was marked by the dominance of liberalism – of the ideas, interests, and policies set into motion by Franklin Roosevelt and the Democratic coalition during the Great Depression.[1] From the classic accounts by Richard Hofstadter and Arthur M. Schlesinger, Jr., to the pathbreaking collection on the "New Deal Order" edited by Gary Gerstle and Steven Fraser, these decades were characterized as a period when a coalition formed that explicitly championed government interven- tion to ameliorate social inequality and to help marginalized populations organize politically.[2] The coalition found a home within the Democratic

---

[1] For the best example of this narrative, see Allen J. Matusow, *The Unraveling of America: A History of Liberalism in the 1960s* (New York, 1984). See also Terry Anderson, *The Movement and the Sixties: Protest in America from Greensboro to Wounded Knee* (New York, 1996); John Morton Blum, *Years of Discord: American Politics and Society, 1961–1974* (New York, 1991).

[2] Arthur Schlesinger, Jr., *The Coming of the New Deal, 1933–1935* (Boston, 1960); Richard Hofstadter, *The American Political Tradition and the Men Who Made It* (New

Party. It included white industrial workers, farmers, immigrants, and African Americans as well as some progressive business leaders.

According to most interpretations of the New Deal, the Roosevelt administration forged a durable bond with these constituencies through the passage of public policies like the Wagner Act of 1935, which legitimated and protected industrial unions, as well as Social Security, which offered retirement benefits to the elderly. Workers overcame ethnic fragmentation to join forces along shared economic interests.[3] The coalition expanded in strength as the federal government tackled new issues, including civil rights after World War II and the promotion of liberal internationalism during the Cold War.

Even the election of President Dwight Eisenhower did not significantly weaken this coalition, according to previous analyses.[4] Indeed, historians have stressed how Eisenhower remained squarely in the liberal center, accepting most New Deal programs and urging the GOP against taking a reactionary stand on the grounds that doing so would be politically suicidal. "Should any political party attempt to abolish Social Security, unemployment insurance and eliminate labor laws and farm programs, you would not hear of that party again in our political history," Eisenhower wrote to his brother.[5] Conservatives were usually depicted by historians as a marginal or irrelevant force in public life, a "radical right" that lived on the fringes of the nation without having much power.

In almost all of these accounts, the New Deal coalition began to fracture in the mid-1960s as a result of bitter conflicts over race, culture, and Vietnam. The radicalization of civil rights activism with the onset of the Black Power movement alienated white working-class voters who had been supporters of the Democratic Party. Conservatism had a relatively minor role in this story, emerging out of the wreckage of

York, 1948); Gary Gerstle and Steven Fraser, *The Rise and Fall of the New Deal Order, 1930–1980* (Princeton, 1989).

[3] Lizabeth Cohen, *Making a New Deal: Industrial Workers in Chicago, 1919–1939* (New York, 1990).

[4] Stephen E. Ambrose, *Eisenhower: Soldier and President* (New York, 1991); David Blumenthal and James A. Morone, *The Heart of Power: Health and Politics in the Oval Office* (Berkeley, 2010); William M. McClenahan, Jr. and William Becker, *Eisenhower and the Cold War Economy* (Baltimore, 2011); Michael S. Mayer, *The Eisenhower Years* (New York, 2010); Ross Douthat and Reihan Salam, *Grand New Party: How Republicans Can Win the Working Class and Save the American Dream* (New York, 2008); Kim Phillips-Fein, *Invisible Hands: The Businessmen's Crusade Against the New Deal* (New York, 2009).

[5] Robert C. Lieberman, *Shifting the Color Line: Race and the American Welfare State* (Cambridge, MA, 1998), 115.

liberalism rather than constituting a defining force. ~~White~~ Working- and middle-class Americans, according to the traditional account, started to perceive that they were being "double-taxed," essentially forced to pay for their union dues as well as for government taxes that financed programs benefiting "other" constituencies.[6] The antiwar movement created an irreparable rift between the New Left and mainstream Democrats who were committed to an aggressive military stance against communism.

The image of a long era of liberal dominance from the 1930s to the 1960s in the United States stands in sharp contrast to historians' understanding of Western politics in this period. Acknowledging the "social democratic moment" of the late 1940s, most scholars have stressed the conservatism of Western European politics during the 1950s and 1960s. They explain the events of 1968 less as an implosion of liberalism – the common interpretation of the American case – than as a backlash against the conservative predominance of the preceding decades. Conservatives in Western Europe reinvented their brand name in the 1970s and reemerged as a powerful force by the 1980s.

[margin: To a great extent, Christian democrats dominated the entire glorieuses]

This interpretation of liberalism in the twentieth-century United States rests on the assumptions that liberalism was deeply and stably rooted in the American polity and that conservatism was a relatively insignificant force before the 1970s. Both assumptions are mistaken and obscure the intense interplay – more a dialectical than a cyclical alteration of dominant forces – between these two ideological impulses from the 1930s through the 1960s, a period that was more tense and fraught than previously thought.

The conservative backlash narrative overstates the newness of the right in the 1960s and undermines the deep history of conservative politics that was well in place long before the 1970s began. The so-called silent majority that President Richard Nixon appealed to in 1969 was built on the institutional, ideological, and electoral foundation that conservatives had been gradually building since the New Deal. The impact of conservatism was so intense after the 1960s not because the backlash against the Great Society was so fierce but because the foundation for this rightward shift in national politics was so strong.

[margin: not best from the perturnd anti-communism of this comp]

The forces opposing government intervention were powerful in the formative years of twentieth-century liberalism, as Doug Rossinow has

---

[6] Nelson Lichtenstein, "From Corporatism to Collective Bargaining: Organized Labor and the Eclipse of Social Democracy in the Postwar Era," in Gerstle and Fraser, *The Rise and Fall of the New Deal Order*, 144–145.

argued. Rather than a vital center that did not challenge the basic structure of the capitalist economy, contemporary liberalism grew out of a
tradition closely associated with left-wing reformist elements that profoundly challenged the contours of the political economy.[7] At a moment
when liberal democracy faced a huge international threat from fascism
and communism, FDR and the Democratic Congress moved forward with
a set of ambitious domestic policies that would be politically viable within
the United States to alleviate economic hardship.

Roosevelt was always keenly aware of the limitations of his coalition
as it challenged the status quo in the 1930s. During one Fireside Chat
in 1938, the president reminded his followers that "We all remember
well known examples of what an ill-advised shift from liberal to conservative leadership can do to an incomplete liberal program. Theodore
Roosevelt, for example, started a march of progress during his seven years
in the Presidency, but after 4 years of President Taft, little was left of the
progress that had been made. Think of the great liberal achievements
of Woodrow Wilson's New Freedom and how quickly they were liqui-
dated under President Harding. We have to have reasonable continuity
of liberal government in order to get permanent results."[8]

A crucial source of opposition to New Deal liberalism emanated from
Congress. When historians turn their attention toward Congress rather
than the White House or the shop floor, the power of conservative forces
becomes much clearer. In Congress, a coalition of Republicans and Southern Democrats emerged in 1937 and 1938 following FDR's attempt to
pack the Supreme Court and to strengthen the executive branch as well
as the initial efforts of Northern Democrats to deal with racial discrimination through anti-lynching legislation. The coalition worked through
congressional committees, many of which Southern Democrats chaired
because of their seniority, and as a voting bloc on the House and Senate floor to stifle legislation that was favorable to African Americans
and unions. The coalition possessed significant power as a result of the
committee process that left chairmen relatively autonomous from the
president and the party leadership. In the Senate, the coalition could rely
on the filibuster, which enabled a minority to hold up legislation unless
two-thirds of the chamber, sixty-seven members, voted for cloture.[9] The

[7] Doug Rossinow, *Visions of Progress: The Left-Liberal Tradition in America* (Philadelphia, 2008).

[8] Cited David M. Kennedy, *Freedom From Fear: The American People in Depression and
War, 1939–1945* (New York, 1999), 348.

[9] Julian E. Zelizer, *On Capitol Hill: The Struggle to Reform Congress and Its Consequences, 1948–2000* (New York, 2000), 22–32.

political scientist Ira Katznelson has shown how the huge domestic gains *(1933-45)* for liberalism in the 1930s and 1940s were made only after the Roosevelt and Truman *(1945-53)* administrations agreed to protect the non-unionized, racial order of the South.[10] Liberal policies were constructed through a constant negotiation with a powerful set of conservative actors on Capitol Hill who, when they wanted, had the ability to bury domestic initiatives for years at a time.

Conservatives did not have to rely only on political institutions in the 1930s, however. New Deal leaders were often ahead of public opinion when it came to domestic issues. Research by the political scientist Eric Schickler has found that public anti-labor sentiment was also extremely strong between 1936 and 1945.[11] The conservative coalition in Congress, according to this work, was not as out of step with the public as liberal commentators thought. According to Kathryn Newman and Elisabeth Jacobs's analysis of public opinion data from the 1930s – social scientists tend to agree that public opinion in any period does not tend to shift dramatically at any given time – Americans were very divided over the New Deal and "much popular opinion held that the unemployed were the authors of their own misfortune, that recipients of government benefits were cheaters and loafers who would have little trouble finding work if they really wanted it."[12] They argue that this pattern was replicated in the 1960s. *– and the 1990s. and ad nauseam until the Sun dies*

Congress and public opinion were not the only obstacles that the New Deal coalition confronted. Business leaders were another. Although there were a handful of business executives who threw their support behind New Deal initiatives – in large part as an effort to stave off more radical alternatives from the left – a majority of business leaders were not on board with Roosevelt's agenda. The backlash against the New Deal started as early as 1934. Kimberly Phillips-Fein has traced the history of an influential group of anti-New Deal businessmen who first joined forces in the American Liberty League just one year after Roosevelt started his presidency to oppose federal interventions into the economy.[13] In response to the Wagner Act, which these businessmen saw as a grave

The ALL allegedly was involved in a coup plot

[10] Ira Katznelson, *Fear Itself: The New Deal and the Origins of Our Time* (New York, 2013).

[11] Eric Shickler and Devin Caughy, *Racial Realignment: The Transformation of American Liberalism, 1932–1965* (Princeton, 1965)

[12] Kathryn Newman and Elisabeth Jacobs, *Who Cares? Public Ambivalence and Government Activism from the New Deal to the Second Gilded Age* (Princeton, 2010).

[13] Phillips-Fein, *Invisible Hands.*

danger to the stability of capitalist markets, the American Liberty League, which would claim over 100,000 members by 1936, released to the press a document, signed by more than fifty lawyers, declaring that the legislation was unconstitutional. These businessmen, known in the 1930s by New Dealers as the "Millionaires' Club," started a network that expanded over the years. The network financed conservative candidates, publications, and organizations. These were the forces whom FDR defiantly railed against in his acceptance speech at the 1936 Democratic Convention in New York City, when he said that "We now know that Government by organized money is just as dangerous as Government by organized mob. Never before in all our history have these forces been so united against one candidate as they stand today. They are unanimous in their hate for me – and I welcome their hatred."[14]

The mobilization against New Deal liberalism continued after the 1930s. Lemuel Boulware, William Baroody, and others provided the cash for operations like Leonard Read's Foundation for Economic Education that promoted laissez-faire economics. The president of Sun Oil, J. Howard Pew, was determined to combat the influence of liberal ministers in the Protestant churches. He helped create an organization called the Spiritual Mobilization that paid to send conservative books to ministers and to solicit money for this cause. Businessmen would continue to work with religious leaders to forge an alliance, using spiritual ideals to combat New Deal liberalism, throughout the 1950s. Los Angeles Reverend James Fifield championed "freedom under God" as a mantra for free and unregulated markets.[15]

During World War II and the early Cold War era, a number of outlets were created that offered an intellectual forum for conservative ideas, such as the journal *Human Events*, founded by Felix Morley, Frank Hanighen, and Henry Regenry in 1944, and the *National Review*, founded by William Buckley in 1955. Business leaders offered financial support to these initiatives. Roger Milliken, a wealthy textile manufacturer who had been tough with unions in his South Carolina plant, purchased *National Review* subscriptions for over a thousand of his friends and bought advertising space.[16]

[14] Franklin D. Roosevelt, Acceptance Speech at Democratic National Convention, 1936, University of California, Santa Barbara Presidency Project.
[15] Kevin Kruse, *One Nation Under God: How Corporate America Invented Christian America* (New York, 2015).
[16] Phillips-Fein, *Invisible Hands*.

When these conservative forces came together in specific campaigns, they could be enormously effective at shaping public policy. Following his dramatic upset reelection victory in 1948 against Thomas Dewey, President Harry Truman proposed national health care for all Americans. The American Medical Association undertook the most expensive lobbying and public relations campaign until that time to block the plan, which it saw as a threat to the power of the medical profession. It blasted the proposal as "socialized medicine" and warned that the government would deprive doctors and patients of the power to make medical decisions. It received strong support from the conservative coalition in Congress as well as from conservative intellectuals, who pointed to Truman's plan as the epitome of creeping statism fostered by liberal Democrats. The measure never even came up for a vote, as conservatives had killed it by late 1950. Indeed, many of Truman's domestic proposals suffered the same fate as he watched the forces of conservatism sweep away his efforts to extend the New Deal.

As did its UK counterparts — an argument rehearsed again and again

In addition to domestic policy and political economy, conservatives also opposed liberal internationalism during the 1940s and 1950s. Although this period is often remembered as a time of consensus on foreign policy – symbolized by the partnership between Michigan Senator Arthur Vandenberg and President Truman – foreign policy was in fact fiercely contested. The Republican right gained influence within the GOP in the late 1940s and through a network of organizations that challenged Democrats and their Republican allies on a series of national security issues. The Republican right focused on what it saw as the failure of Democrats to prevent the expansion of communism in Asia, blaming Truman for allowing China to fall to communism in 1949, for the stalemate in Korea, and for not doing enough to hunt down alleged communist spies who were operating within the United States. Senator Joseph McCarthy of Wisconsin was an outlier because of his tactics, not his general arguments.[17]

Key to the Marshall Plan

The Republican right had a powerful effect on national security debates. Its efforts helped to defeat Democrats in the 1952 elections when Republicans won control of the White House and both chambers of Congress. The politicization of national security created an intense battle between the parties over anticommunism, leading some Democrats to respond by attacking Eisenhower in his second term for not being tough

To last time they would do so before 1994

[17] Robert Griffith, *The Politics of Fear: Joseph R. McCarthy and the Senate* (Amherst, MA, 1970).

enough on issues like the construction of intermediate-range missiles. At
other times, political battles were not fought on party lines. Southern
Democrats teamed up with the Republicans, for example, to attack the
Democratic leadership for not being sufficiently aggressive in pursuing the
communist threat in the United States. This was the heated atmosphere
that shaped the early 1960s, when Presidents Kennedy *c(1961-63)* and Johnson *(1963-69)* felt
intense political pressure to avoid withdrawing from Vietnam because
they feared a repeat of 1952.[18]

Although he governed as a moderate when dealing with domestic policy, accepting much of the New Deal state on pragmatic grounds, President Eisenhower was still a Republican. And he was a Republican who
enjoyed a landslide reelection victory in 1956 and finished his term with
strong approval ratings. Although many historians have explained this
by pointing to Eisenhower's acceptance of much of the New Deal, the
president still was not a member of the party of FDR, and his success
suggests the limits of Democratic strength. "I think," Eisenhower said
after his reelection, "that Modern Republicanism has now proved itself.
And America has approved of Modern Republicanism."[19] Eisenhower
spent much of his second term fighting for a balanced budget and squar-
ing off against the Democratic Congress in an effort to reduce federal
spending. Eisenhower, unlike many other Republicans of his time and
later, was an equal opportunity economizer. He was as frustrated with
defense spending as he was with domestic programs, and he was willing
to burn up much of his political capital on the drive to reduce the size of
the government through spending cuts.

Conservatism was not simply an elite phenomenon that eventually
caught up at the grassroots level. A nascent conservative movement was
taking form at the grass roots during the 1950s. For instance, California-
based businessman Robert Welch, who had started out as a candy manufacturer in Massachusetts, founded the John Birch Society in 1958; by
1960, the organization claimed almost 60,000 members.[20] Welch was a
charismatic figure who argued that a group of bankers, business leaders,
and politicians were conspiring to promote communism in the United
States. Welch attacked Republicans, not just Democrats, as he accused

---

[18] Julian E. Zelizer, *Arsenal of Democracy: The Politics of National Security: From World War II to the War on Terrorism* (New York, 2010).

[19] David L. Stebenne, *Modern Republican: Arthur Larson and the Eisenhower Years* (Bloomington, 2006), 175.

[20] Rick Perlstein, *Before the Storm: Barry Goldwater and the Unmaking of the American Consensus* (New York, 2002), 118.

Dwight Eisenhower of being a "stooge" of communist forces. That statement was too much for most Republicans to take, but Welch's basic accusations against Democrats and liberalism did fit into a broader narrative about the recent past and the direction the country was heading. One of the most colorful organizations to attract a huge following in this period was the Christian Anti-Communist Crusade led by Fred Schwartz, an Australian who converted to Christianity from Judaism. In 1961, the organization conducted a rally in the Los Angeles Memorial Arena that drew more than 16,000 people. His newsletter and his books enjoyed a large and very loyal following. One book sold more than a million copies. "Even acute observers," he wrote, "noting the numerical weakness of the Communists, have taken false hope from this fact. Such people fail to understand that the Communists are able to rally into their service multitudes who are completely unaware that they are serving the Communist Cause."[21] The Americans for Constitutional Action, founded in 1958, published annual ratings of legislators.[22] The Young Americans for Freedom claimed a paid membership of 30,000 young conservatives and chapters on almost 200 colleges.[23]

Conservative radio talk show hosts like Clarence Manion and Dan Smoot railed against the Kennedy administration for its failure to stand up to the Soviet Union and for pushing the government to take too strong a role in domestic life. Manion, who resided in South Bend, Indiana, captivated listeners with his rousing voice and fiery rhetoric. *The Manion Forum of Opinion* aired on Sunday nights and attracted large audiences.[24] Although the Fairness Doctrine, a Federal Communications Commission rule instituted in 1949 that required all radio hosts to present both sides of a political issue, hampered the ability of hosts to talk about issues with a point of view, there was a group of conservatives, many of whom had been inspired by the radio broadcasts of Father Charles Coughlin in the 1930s, who tested the regulation during the 1950s and 1960s to see how far they could go. These conservative broadcasters far outpaced liberals

[21] See, for example, Fred Schwartz, *You Can Trust the Communists (to be Communists)* (New York, 1960).

[22] Warren Weaver, Jr., "Congress Cordial But Not Swayed," *The New York Times*, August 29, 1963.

[23] Myer Feldman to the President, August 15, 1963, John F. Kennedy Presidential Library, Boston, MA (JFKL), POF, Box 63, File: Harris, Louis; "Financial Scope of the American Right-Wing," August 1963, JFKL, POF, Box 106, File: Right Wing Movement Part I.

[24] Perlstein, *Before the Storm*; Jonathan Schoenwald, *A Time for Choosing: The Rise of Modern Conservatism* (New York, 2001).

in using the medium to promote their message, in part because liberals felt that the major organs of the news, such as the big city newspapers, were hospitable to their ideas. Conservatives also enjoyed a vibrant period of book publishing with companies like Regnery, founded in 1947 by conservatives in Chicago. There were also numerous religious leaders who blended the messages of conservative religious theology with the gospel of the free market.[25] With figures like this, the sociologist Daniel Bell observed, "the 'radical right' had emerged into prominence on the American political scene."[26] When President Kennedy instructed his advisor Myer Feldman to conduct a secret study on conservative organizations, he found that the radical right, which Feldman distinguished from the "conservative right," spent almost $425 million a year and produced broadcasts on thousands of radio stations. The support for these organizations was substantial, emanating from major foundations and corporations as well as wealthy individuals. Both men were shocked by the size of these groups and the close connections they had forged with mainstream Republicans. The outlook of radicals and conservatives varied "in degree and intensity, but not in kind," Feldman concluded. "The radical right-wing," Feldman said to the president, "constitutes a formidable force in American life today." It was a force that was more "successful, politically, than is generally realized." Kennedy subsequently authorized the creation of a special unit within the IRS that would investigate the proliferation of conservative organizations that were claiming tax-exempt status even though they were clearly engaged in political activities.[27]

Ronald Reagan was a product of the various networks that developed during this period in the history of conservatism. Reagan had begun his career as a Hollywood actor in the 1940s. Originally a New Deal Democrat, he began dabbling with conservative ideas when, as president of the actors' union, he cooperated with investigations into alleged left-wing forces in Hollywood. Reagan continued to shore up his conservative credentials as a spokesperson for General Electric (GE). The company sent

[25] Darren Dochuck, *From Bible Belt to Sun Belt: Plain-Folk Religion, Grassroots Politics, and the Rise of Evangelical Conservatism* (New York, 2011).

[26] Lisa McGirr, *Suburban Warriors: The Origins of the New American Right* (Princeton, 2001), 35–36; Schoenwald, *A Time For Choosing*, 45, 9; Daniel Bell, "The Dispossessed – 1962," in idem, ed., *The Radical Right: The New American Right*, revised edition (New York, 1979), 1.

[27] Myer Feldman, August 15, 1963, JFKL, POF, Box 63, File: Harris, Louis; "Financial Scope of the American Right-Wing," August 1963, JFKL, POF, Box 106, File: Right Wing Movement Part I.

him around the country to make speeches about the virtues of the free market as part of its effort to stave off pressure from unions to allow its workforce to organize. Reagan was a passionate reader of magazines like *Human Events*, which he said helped him "stop being a liberal Democrat," and interacted frequently with many of the organizations in the conservative movement of that time.[28] Through his speeches for GE, Reagan refined his ideas. He became increasingly vocal in his criticism of liberal domestic policies such as progressive taxation, and he developed a series of arguments challenging the policy of containment, which he said accepted the permanence of communism in certain parts of the world. A record of one of his speeches, in which he warned that Kennedy's proposed Medicare program to provide health care to senior citizens would open the door to socialism, proved extremely popular in conservative circles and was frequently played at gatherings to build opposition to the plan.

Human Events is still a going concern

The Truman Doctrine

Reagan did not repeal Medicare

Reagan made his first major national appearance in the 1964 presidential campaign of Barry Goldwater. The Arizona Republican attempted to push his party to the right. A coalition of supporters, largely from Arizona (and thus dubbed the Arizona Mafia) was responsible for winning over support at the convention over more moderate candidates such as Governor Nelson Rockefeller of New York. But Goldwater did not come out of nowhere. His candidacy was rooted in the ideas, policies, and political forces that had been shaping conservatism ever since Roosevelt took office. Though a candidate who stood for the purist conservative principles did not yet have the kind of national support that was needed to win a presidential campaign, the ideas that drove Goldwater had already gained deep-rooted support in a large range of political, private, and non-profit institutions that influenced the political arena.

(1959-74)

Goldwater lost in a landslide C61.1%. - 38.5%, 486 EV .52 EV

Not only were the forces confronting liberalism in the 1940s and 1950s much stronger than scholars long believed, the New Deal coalition was also much more fragile. Like the conservative movement in the 1970s, the New Deal coalition consisted of numerous factions who often had trouble working together. These internal tensions were already at the forefront of national politics during the 1930s. Even when Southern Democrats were fully on board with the New Deal before 1938, the administration and its allies in Congress were constantly forced to make concessions to them to ensure the success of administration-backed legislation. Roosevelt rejected many legislative proposals from the left or watered them down,

---

[28] "Reagan's Newspaper," *Human Events*, February 5, 2011.

partially in response to his strong sense of the limitations imposed by these coalitional challenges. On matters like the creation of Social Security in 1935 and the federal minimum wage in 1938, Roosevelt agreed to legislation that excluded agricultural and domestic workers, both of whom worked in low-wage sectors crucial to the Southern economy, so that Southern Democrats who controlled the committees would agree to pass the bill.[29]

And thus protect Jim Crow

The tensions in the coalition could best be seen at the local level. Racial backlash really was part of politics, in the South and the North, all along. White working-class Americans were never fully comfortable in the New Deal alliance when it touched on issues pertaining to race relations. In his seminal study of Detroit in the 1940s and 1950s, Thomas Sugrue argues that racial tensions ran high when the city tried to deal with issues like employment practices and residential zoning. Deindustrialization started to impact cities like Detroit in the immediate post-World War II period as a result of automation and the relocation of plants outside the cities: "The rusting of the Rust Belt began neither with the much-touted stagflation and oil crisis of the 1970s, nor with the rise of global competition and the influx of car or steel imports. It began, unheralded, in the 1950s."[30] Jobs moved, but African Americans could not. Public policy, racial tensions in communities, and business practices stood in their way.

The irony, writes Sugrue, was that New Deal programs had lifted the social and economic status of white working-class Detroiters, thereby allowing them to earn the money that they needed to move into better neighborhoods and to enjoy senior positions in unionized jobs. However, these workers then started to protect their gains from African Americans, whom they perceived as a threat. Many whites formed white citizens' organizations that mobilized politically and used outright intimidation to block African Americans' demand for their civil rights. They relied on public policies that made it difficult for African Americans to purchase

---

[29] Linda Gordon, *Pitied But Not Entitled: Single Mothers and the History of Welfare, 1890–1935* (New York, 1994); Robert Lieberman, *Shifting the Color Line: Race and the American Welfare State* (Cambridge, MA, 1998); Ira Katznelson, Kim Geiger, and Daniel Kryder, "Limiting Liberalism: The Southern Veto in Congress, 1933–1950," *Political Science Quarterly* 108 (1993): 283–302. These were not the only reasons exclusions were made. Martha Derthick and Robert Lieberman, taking issue with some of this literature, offer alternative causes that were also at work. See Gareth Davies and Martha Derthick, "Race and Social Welfare," *Political Science Quarterly* 112 (1997): 217–236.

[30] Thomas J. Sugrue, *The Origins of the Urban Crisis: Race and Inequality in Postwar Detroit* (Princeton, 1996), 6.

[handwritten: White people support white welfare for white people]

homes outside of the cities. Public housing facilities were also built in communities that maintained racial segregation. The kinds of tensions within the New Deal coalition normally thought of as being a reaction to the 1960s, Sugrue shows, had already been in play for decades.

Sugrue's work complements the research of Southern historians such as Matthew Lassiter, Kevin Kruse, and Joseph Crespino, who have objected to claims about Southern exceptionalism while agreeing on the centrality of a racial backlash to the New Deal coalition. Turning away from an emphasis on racial extremists in the South and looking instead at moderate suburban voters in the region, this group of Southern historians has found that conservatives in states like Mississippi and Georgia *[handwritten: Also]* abandoned explicit racial appeals and refocused their attention on issues *[handwritten: transport]* such as suburban rights, local taxation, neighborhood schooling, and *[handwritten: infrastructure]* residential zoning. By protecting the structure of suburbs, moderates in fact defended racial stratification because of the multiple barriers that *[handwritten: which]* hampered African American mobility. Rejecting the concept of a differ- *[handwritten: still]* ence between de facto and de jure segregation, these historians contend *[handwritten: exist]* that the same issues that drove conservative mobilization in the South spurred conservatives to action in the North, Midwest, and West as well.[31]

There were other obstacles that the New Deal coalition faced besides its own internal coalition and the power of conservative organizations. Institutions mattered very much as well. Even with the long history of government intervention in the United States, there were still formidable barriers to expanding government that continued to pose challenges to state-building. If conservatism was defined as resistance to the expansion of government, there was a certain amount of conservatism built in to the very structure of the American government.

The fragmented structure of America's political institutions made it extraordinarily difficult to achieve centralized decision-making and efficient public planning. The United States did not possess the kind of insulated government bureaucracy that existed in Western European nations. As a result, every act to expand government required extraordinary effort and the creation of new institutions over the ones beyond those already in existence. There was also a deep-rooted cultural resistance to the

---

[31] Kevin M. Kruse, *White Flight: Atlanta and the Making of Modern Conservatism* (Princeton, 2005); Matthew D. Lassiter, *The Silent Majority: Suburban Politics in the Sunbelt South* (Princeton, 2005); and Joseph Crespino, *In Search of Another Country: Mississippi and the Conservative Counterrevolution* (Princeton, 2007).

[handwritten marginalia: Partly bk of you pressed it racism]

exercise of federal power – even if that had not prevented the growth of government.

The most visible manifestation of this anti-statism was the strong opposition to direct taxation that remained prevalent throughout these decades. Another challenge was the continued power of localism, which pressured policymakers to jerry-build programs that respected local and state government. With all the growth of government that occurred, Sugrue argues, "rarely did federal initiatives dismantle local institutions and wholly undermine jurisdictional autonomy. Federal assistance and federal social programs did not flow smoothly to localities; instead local jurisdictional boundaries directed the stream of governmental assistance, channeling it to some places and away from others. Although late-twentieth-century America scarcely resembled the bygone world of 'island communities' memorably described by historian Robert Wiebe, the persistence of fragmented and autonomous local governments and authorities preserved a fair degree of local insularity – particularly with regard to race, education, land use, and social welfare."[32]

None of this – neither external challenges nor internal divisions – prevented liberalism from becoming the basis of a strong political coalition or from leaving behind a significant policy legacy. The evidence points to just the opposite. By the 1970s, the United States had a formidable state that maintained welfare policies for the disadvantaged. Liberal political organizations and the Democratic Party retained considerable strength.

[handwritten marginalia: Medicare, medicaid, Social Security, all active. The NDRB remains for us. dorse for Development, Education]

But the particular configuration of liberal policies makes more sense once we see the power of conservatism in this period. While earlier generations of historians often dismissed New Deal and Great Society programs as half-hearted and watered down, a sign that U.S. liberalism was an inherent laggard to European social democracy, many liberal strategies from this period were designed with the hope of overcoming and surviving conservative forces that were not on board with their agenda. Indeed, one of the reasons Great Society programs like Medicare have proved to be so durable since the 1960s is that they were designed with a keen understanding of the criticism of conservatives and the ways in which conservatives would try to weaken them. The liberal era in American politics was forged in a dialectic with conservatism. One of the most

---

[32] Julian E. Zelizer, "The Uneasy Relationship: Democracy, Taxation, and State Building Since the New Deal," and Thomas J. Sugrue, "All Politics is Local: The Persistence of Localism in Twentieth-Century America," in Meg Jacobs, William J. Novick, and Julian E. Zelizer, eds., *The Democratic Experiment: New Directions in American Political History* (Princeton, 2003), 276–326.

important strategies was to design programs that built on the tradition of the nineteenth century, when most government intervention was indirect and relied on third parties to implement programs. The political scientist Christopher Howard has offered compelling evidence that when one includes the cost of hidden tax subsidies, regulations, loan guarantees, and tort law, the role of government in the United States is comparable to most other Western industrialized democracies. Responding to the familiar question of whether the American welfare state is unusually small, Howard argues that the American welfare state "compares favorably with some of the largest welfare states in the world. Its size has been measured incorrectly by many people and many organizations for a long time... What seems clear is that its size is not now exceptional."[33]

[margin handwriting: Hence the bee stik management of unemployment insurance and Medicaid]

Historians have uncovered how the government played a huge role in subsidizing a private welfare state by providing favorable tax treatment of health care insurance and retirement pensions offered through the corporation. The result was that when organized labor pushed for collective bargaining agreements in the late 1940s and the 1950s, employers were more willing to agree to these kinds of benefits.[34] The federal government also provided tax breaks to encourage other kinds of activities, including home ownership. *[margin handwriting: For whites]*

[margin handwriting: which also favored whites]

In addition to tax breaks, policymakers used fiscal mechanisms such as earmarked taxation and budgetary trust funds to protect programs from retrenchment and to pressure politicians into dealing with the long-term costs of programs.[35] As in the nineteenth century, they also relied on third parties to administer programs. In 1965, for example, Congress decided to make Blue Cross/Blue Shield responsible for the administration of Medicare benefits.

Liberals counted on the political mobilization of those who benefited from federal programs to strengthen their coalition. From the time of

---

[33] Christopher Howard, *The Welfare State Nobody Knows: Debunking Myths About U.S. Social Policy* (Princeton, 2007), 25.

[34] Jacob S. Hacker, *Divided Welfare State: The Battle over Public and Private Social Benefits in the United States* (New York, 2002) and Jennifer Klein, *For All These Rights: Business, Labor and the Shaping of America's Public–Private Welfare State* (Princeton, 2003); Christopher Howard, *Tax Expenditures and Social Policy in the United States* (Princeton, 1997).

[35] Julian E. Zelizer, *Taxing America: Wilbur D. Mills, Congress, and the State, 1945–1975* (New York, 1998); Eric M. Patashnik, *Putting Trust in the U.S. Budget: Federal Trust Funds and the Politics of Commitment* (New York, 2000); Eric Patashnik and Julian E. Zelizer, "Paying for Medicare: Benefits, Budgets, and Wilbur Mills's Policy Legacy," *Journal of Health Policy, Politics, and Law* 26 (2001): 7–36.

the New Deal, liberals had been very cognizant that building a political base through public policy was an effective way to sustain their
coalition. New Deal public works jobs were often distributed through
the party machine so that Democrats developed political strength from
the expenditures.[36] The Wagner Act created the policy foundation for a
vibrant union movement that, until the 1970s, remained the lifeblood of
the New Deal coalition. New Deal farm programs, which offered price
supports and subsidies to the agricultural sector, solidified the farm bloc
within the Democratic Party. There were also policies, such as Social
Security and the GI Bill of Rights, that gradually created constituencies
for the party as citizens came to expect benefits as a right. Recent public
opinion research has shown how these programs, through a process that
social scientists have called policy feedback, stimulated beneficiaries to
become more politically active and organized.[37]

Finally, liberals were able to find ideological points of commonality
in the conservative era. Just as anticommunism would help unite the
various factions of post-World War II conservatism, the language of consumerism was essential to keeping the many factions of New Deal liberalism together and to dampening, as much as possible, the divisions that
existed. Meg Jacobs has explained how the New Deal agenda centered
on the idea of under-consumption. Liberals packaged programs – most
notably progressive labor and fiscal policies – through the argument that
they would help boost consumer demand and stimulate economic growth.
Policies aimed to dampen prices and increase the purchasing power of
working- and middle-class Americans. The Office of Price Administration, created during World War II and staffed by progressive Democrats,
was one of FDR's boldest attempts to create a government agency that
would pursue these objectives. The agency, Jacobs writes, was a "radical
model of statement management; a popular government agency working
in alliance with a coalition of labor, consumers, and social liberals that
challenged the right of private industries to set their own prices and sell
their items freely."[38]

---

[36] Jason Scott Smith, *Building New Deal Liberalism: The Political Economy of Public Works, 1933–1956* (New York, 2006).

[37] Andrea Louise Campbell, *How Policies Make Citizens: Senior Political Activism and the American Welfare State* (Princeton, 2003); Suzanne Mettler, *Soldiers to Citizens: The G.I. Bill and the Making of the Greatest Generation* (New York, 2005).

[38] Meg Jacobs, *Pocketbook Politics: Economic Citizenship in Twentieth Century America* (Princeton, 2005), 180.

As the 1960s unfolded, liberalism was forced to deal with the challenges that had existed for decades. It was not that the problems from that decade created a conservative movement, but rather they opened a window for the right to expand its power as the opposition crumbled. The reaction to the civil rights movement emanated from the deep-seated opposition to civil rights that had been seen in the 1940s and 1950s when African Americans and liberal activists started to push for new laws in the South and the North. The turmoil over Vietnam simply brought existing tensions to the forefront of national politics and energized conservatives, who sensed an opportunity to build on their strengths. Dramatic court decisions outlawing school prayer and liberalizing abortion rights antagonized the conservative values held by many Americans on social and cultural issues. In this light, the political turmoil that liberalism encountered in the 1960s, as well as the success of conservatism at chipping away at the New Deal coalition, is easier to understand. The 1960s was more of what political scientists call a focusing event, a window of opportunity, for various political forces that had been growing for several decades to finally take hold.[39]

Richard Nixon used the term "the Silent Majority" to describe the portion of the electorate that was craving for conservative politics and unhappy with the liberal direction that politics took in the mid-1960s – particularly those Democrats who had become disaffected from their party. The concept was extraordinarily useful in characterizing the voters who would support Republican policies in the decades that followed, and invoking it was an effective move on Nixon's part. Although Nixon depicted that majority as a new phenomenon born in response to the Great Society and the breakdown of law and order, it was in fact part of the electorate throughout the twentieth century. And it had often been neither silent nor firmly Democratic.

The decade of the 1960s, as the historians Michael Kazin and Maurice Isserman argue, was much more of a civil war between the right and left than an era when liberalism simply imploded to make room for conservatism.[40] The new histories of the decade also help explain more clearly why conservatives would not be able to wholly remake the political world. After all, liberals had been fighting against difficult challenges

---

39 The concept of focusing events comes from John W. Kingdon, *Agendas, Alternatives, and Public Policies* (Glenview, IL, 1984), 99–100.
40 Maurice Isserman and Michael Kazin, *America Divided: The Civil War of the 1960s* (New York, 1999).

for decades, and they had crafted strategies and policies that drew on successful traditions and that resulted in the establishment of institutions, policies, and organizations that were not easily dismantled.

The power of conservatism after the 1970s can only be understood after its origins are recovered. In recent years, historians have made great progress in recovering the longstanding roots of the right. The era between the 1930s and 1960s was less a period dominated by the New Deal order than decades when conservatism and liberalism were both vibrant forces in American life, producing an interwoven set of policies and leaving behind infrastructure that shaped the next century. The story in Britain was similar, as Daniel Stedman Jones shows in the next chapter.

Conservatism would continue to evolve in the next four decades as the movement grew in scale and scope, winning over a larger part of the electorate and continually shifting public debate further to the right. Conservatism in the United States would remain a distinct blend of religious activism, free market ideology, and grassroots mobilization facilitated by corporate funding, as well as a product of the ongoing tensions that grew out of the racial conflicts of the nineteenth century. Conservative leaders would thicken and expand the organizational structure of the movement in the 1970s and 1980s with the creation of think tanks, fund-raising operations, and new media outlets. Religious conservatives would also become ever more visible as growing numbers of spiritual organizations became less reluctant to enter into the political realm. They also had much more success at shaping presidential elections and the congressional leadership. As a result of the fallout from the 1960s, conservatives also faced a weakened opposition. After several decades since the New Deal, when liberalism enjoyed a robust set of interest group organizations, movement actors, and politicians, conservatives would have more of an opportunity to shift public policy and political debate in their favor.

But with the success of the post-1960s period came new challenges. As conservatism gained in strength, more divisions would start to emerge, such as the tensions between hawkish conservatives who were determined to build a massive defense system and use force liberally and those who were more restrained, especially after Vietnam, in search of a balance of power that upheld the primacy of the United States. Many conservatives would feel deflated as government continued to grow – even when Republicans were in control of both the legislative and executive branches. Members of the right lost some of the benefit that came from a vibrant liberal opposition because they felt less pushback against their positions.

With greater incentive to see how far they could move Republicans to the right and avoid the kinds of compromises that had previously been essential, conservatives lurched toward ideas that were increasingly off-center from the mainstream of the polity, even in an age when the electorate was ideologically more to the right than ever before.

The GOP's economic policies became by the 21st century increasingly extreme — forcing op making on authoritarian radical right platform more appealing

Which conservatives never dismantled — Social Security, Medicare, Medicaid, the NLRB

The Republicans could reduce government to serve the wealthy, but never really reduce it, or cut off redistributive spending

2

The Radicalization of Neoliberalism

Daniel Stedman Jones

The idea of the free market was transformed in the postwar United States. By 1971, a comprehensive and novel intellectual framework had been developed by a group of American economists associated with the Mont Pèlerin Society (MPS). The MPS, founded by Friedrich Hayek in 1947 at a meeting he organized in Vevey, Switzerland, represented the flowering of a predominantly European movement to reshape liberalism that had emerged in the 1930s and 1940s.[1] This earlier intellectual movement, given the name neoliberalism by Alexander Rüstow at the Colloque Lippmann convened in 1937 to discuss Walter Lippmann's book *The Good Society*, was an attempt to theorize anew a liberalism that was based on individual liberty, limited government, and a competitive market order but one that was not subject to the perceived errors of laissez-faire. The movement came most obviously to political fruition in Germany in the 1950s under the economic stewardship of Ludwig Erhard, first Chancellor Konrad Adenauer's finance minister (1949–1963) and then chancellor (1963–1966).

Building upon early neoliberalism, a deeper and broader idea of the free market was engendered in the postwar United States by Milton Friedman, George Stigler, James Buchanan, Gordon Tullock, and Gary Becker.

There were important American contributors to the development of early neoliberalism. The discussion of the American journalist Walter Lippmann's *The Good Society* (1937) in 1938 in Paris, for example, famously has been heralded as the moment when Hayek's idea of a neoliberal international crystallized. Equally, the economist Henry Simons, a friend of Hayek's who tragically died in 1946, and Frank Knight, another early member of the MPS, formed a contingent of American fellow travelers with the European neoliberals from Austria, Germany, Britain, and France.

From these thinkers arose the central ideas of monetarism, deregulation of industry and finance, privatization, and the introduction of market-based social policy in areas such as health, education, welfare, and public administration. All were associated with the MPS, which, as recent scholarship has shown, became more influenced by its American members during the 1950s and 1960s.[2] More profoundly, the Chicago School of Economics, led by Friedman and Stigler, and the Virginia School of Political Economy, founded by Buchanan and Tullock, transformed neoliberal thought. Their vision was an overarching commitment to markets as the self-correcting embodiment of economic freedom, without which other freedoms were impossible. That core belief has defined transatlantic, and global, politics after the 1970s.[3]

The new worldview built upon but significantly departed from early neoliberalism. Early neoliberals, especially in Germany, Austria, France, and Britain, responded primarily to the collapse of European liberalism, the onset of totalitarian dictatorships, and the Great Depression. The postwar American economists, by contrast, worked in an atmosphere of reconstruction and with a conviction in the superiority of American free enterprise. Rising economic prosperity, reaction against the New Deal, and the battle with the Soviet Union strengthened this belief. American liberalism was consciously reconstructed, to form what social scientist Sonja Amadae has termed "rational choice liberalism," in order to defend American capitalism in the Cold War.[4] This chapter describes the emergence of this radical market-centered *Weltanschauung* and highlights its difference from early neoliberalism. This difference is at its heart a story of the transatlantic movement of ideas between Europe and America in the twentieth century.[5]

* * *

In 1950, the Austrian émigré economist Friedrich von Hayek embarked on a journey from London to the United States. He had been to

---

[2] See, for example, Angus Burgin's *The Great Persuasion* (Cambridge, MA, 2012).

[3] Some of these developments, especially the political breakthroughs of neoliberal ideas, are discussed in detail in my book *Masters of the Universe: Hayek, Friedman and the Birth of Neoliberal Politics* (Princeton, 2012).

[4] See S. M. Amadae, *Rationalizing Capitalist Democracy: The Cold War Origins of Rational Choice Liberalism* (Chicago, 2003).

[5] Important economic methodological context rather than a political point of view is to be found in Marion Fourcade's *Economists and Societies: Discipline and Profession in the United States, Britain and France, 1890s–1990s* (Princeton, 2009). Daniel Rodgers has examined the wider effects of the attack posed by individualism and free markets on the central cultural assumptions of late twentieth-century America in *The Age of Fracture* (Cambridge, MA, 2011).

America before, spending a year at New York University in 1923–1924 as an assistant to economist Jeremiah Jenks and five weeks on the road during the spring of 1945, and then again in 1946, to promote *The Road to Serfdom* (1944), the polemic that made him famous.[6] He returned the following year as he organized the MPS. But his 1950 journey was different, both for Hayek himself and for what it symbolized in the transatlantic history of ideas. Hayek was leaving the London School of Economics (LSE), where he had been Tooke Professor of Economic Science since 1931. His destination was the Committee of Social Thought (CST) at the University of Chicago, a special multidisciplinary doctoral program. His move to Chicago was a turning point in the development of neoliberalism. Paradoxically, just at the moment that the founder of European neoliberalism crossed the Atlantic to work in the United States, the baton of the intellectual leadership passed from the European scholars who had been brought together by Hayek to form the MPS to a younger generation of American economists. These American thinkers largely rejected the qualified endorsement of the welfare state characteristic of early Hayekian neoliberalism.[7]

Hayek's journey to the "Windy City" resulted from a combination of personal and political factors. He had already received tentative offers from a few American universities after the war about a move to the United States. During his tours of 1945 and 1946, he had been introduced to several anti-New Deal activists, including Harold Luhnow, president of the Kansas City-based William Volker Fund (WVF), and Leonard Read, director of the WVF-funded Foundation for Economic Education (FEE), one of the earliest American libertarian think tanks sympathetic to Hayek's ideas. This connection prompted discussions about Hayek's possible move to supervise projects to promote the free market. Luhnow, supported by Chicago economist and member of the Law School, Henry

[handwritten margin note: Which Keynes penned]

---

[6] On Hayek's trip, see, for example, the introduction to the Institute of Economic Affairs' edition of the condensed Reader's Digest version of *Road to Serfdom* and the introduction by John Blundell (London, 2005). See also Alan Ebenstein's *Friedrich Hayek: A Biography* (New York, 2001).

[7] I am not suggesting that Hayek's work from this point was not influential or important: it clearly was. *The Constitution of Liberty* (1960) and *Law, Legislation and Liberty* (1973, 1976, 1979), as well as *The Road to Serfdom*, are central texts in the history of political thought. However, in terms of his influence on the economics profession, Hayek's eclipse by Keynes by the 1940s was mirrored on the right by the rise of his fellow MPS members in the Chicago and Virginia Schools. His political influence returned later, especially and famously in Britain after Thatcher's election in 1979.

Simons, wanted Hayek to write the American *Road to Serfdom*.[8] Hayek did not take the idea seriously. He had a scathing view of the intellectual content of the FEE's work, an organization that he called a "propaganda setup." Having written the original version, perhaps Hayek did not fully see the need for an American version.[9] In any event, he suggested his friend at Princeton, Friedrich Lutz, for the task. Shortly afterwards, Simons died tragically and prematurely.[10] Luhnow enlisted the support of the university's president, Robert Hutchins, in 1948 to propose that Hayek join the Chicago Economics Department. As will be discussed below, it was an idea flatly rejected by the department itself when put to a vote.[11] The plan to bring him to Chicago was seemingly stillborn.

By the late 1940s, however, Hayek was actively keen on a move to the United States because of a mixture of personal and professional considerations. His private circumstances contributed to his desire to move. In the midst of a painful and personally damaging divorce from his first wife, Hella, he needed money. Personal travails aside, Hayek's intellectual priorities had also begun to change. His research had begun to move away from economics.[12] With the controversies of the 1930s and his battle with John Maynard Keynes over monetary policy and the proper limits of economic planning behind him, he had begun to rethink liberalism and strategize for a change in the climate of political opinion. Hayek had been stung by the public acceptance of Keynes's ideas as well as his friend's perceived victory over the question of the utility of state intervention and the appropriate balance of economic policy. He became increasingly convinced that for his own economic ideas to succeed, it was necessary to

[handwritten margin note: Keynes died in April 1946, aged 62.]

---

8   On the history of the American *Road to Serfdom*, see the illuminating article, "The Rise of the Chicago School of Economics and the Birth of Neoliberalism," by Rob Van Horn and Philip Mirowski in P. Mirowski and D. Plehwe, eds., *The Road from Mont Pelerin: The Making of the Neoliberal Thought Collective* (Cambridge, MA, 2009). Mirowski and Van Horn show how Hayek was able to help place Aaron Director in a position at the University of Chicago funded by the Volker Fund to oversee the Free Market Study group.

9   Arthur Selden to Hayek, August 28, 1975, Hayek Papers, Box 27, Folder 6, Hoover Institution, Stanford, California.

10   Mirowski and Van Horn suggest that Simons's death was suicide. However, this position is disputed by Bruce Caldwell in his contribution to Mirowski and Van Horn's (with Thomas Stapleford) *Building Chicago Economics* (Cambridge, 2011), chapter 11, "Hayek, Chicago and Neoliberalism."

11   Bruce Caldwell, *Hayek's Challenge: An Intellectual Biography of F. A. Hayek* (Chicago, 2004), 297.

12   For a quick summary of the progression of Hayek's career see also Andrew Gamble's *Hayek: The Iron Cage of Liberty* (London, 1996), especially 10–21.

influence policymakers and opinion-makers in the way that Keynes had done.

Hayek admired the influence of the Fabian socialists who had founded the first think tank in 1884, the Fabian Society, and helped to establish the LSE. The Fabians – Beatrice and Sidney Webb, H. G. Wells, George Bernard Shaw, and others – were social activists and reformers in Britain at the end of the nineteenth and early twentieth centuries who believed in the gradual advance of non-Marxist evolutionary socialism. Several second-generation Fabians such as the economist Harold Laski and economic historian R. H. Tawney were colleagues of Hayek's at the LSE in the 1930s and 1940s. Hayek appreciated the impact of the Fabians on two major reforming governments of the liberal left in Britain, those of Liberals Asquith (1908-16) and Lloyd George (1916-22), and of Labour Prime Minister Attlee (1945-51). He believed that his ideas would only succeed once a similar influence was brought to bear on intellectual opinion. His famous essay, "The Intellectuals and Socialism" (1949), illustrated the shift in Hayek's thinking. He saw in the strategic success of Fabian socialism during the previous half century a model for shaping the economic and political agenda in Britain and beyond.[13] *The Road to Serfdom* and the MPS were the most obvious fruits of Hayek's attempts to shape opinion.

Though Hayek continued scientific and philosophical work, particularly on epistemology, his main attention was now diverted to politics, both the theory and practice of liberalism, and also to activism, through the promotion of diverse think tanks on both sides of the Atlantic. As he put it in *The Constitution of Liberty* (1960), the book he worked on throughout his decade at Chicago:

[T]hough I still regard myself as mainly an economist, I have come to feel more and more that the answers to many of the pressing social questions of our time are to be found ultimately in the recognition of principles that lie outside the scope of technical economics or of any other single discipline. Though it was from an original concern with problems of economic policy that I started, I have been slowly led to the ambitious and perhaps presumptuous task of approaching them through a comprehensive restatement of the basic principles of a philosophy of freedom.[14]

Hayek had initially been interested in Princeton, supposedly as a result of the recruiting efforts of the advertising pioneer Claude Robinson, but

---

[13] F. A. Hayek, "The Intellectuals and Socialism," *University of Chicago Law Review* (Spring 1949): 417–433.

[14] F. A. Hayek, *The Constitution of Liberty* (Chicago, 1960), 3.

it was likely the low salary that eventually put him off. Instead, Luhnow engineered the move to Chicago by funding a position in the interdisciplinary CST partly because Hayek was rejected by the Chicago Economics Department once serious discussions began in 1949–1950. Associated with the theoretically driven Austrian School of Economics, Hayek advocated a distinct business cycle theory anathema to most Chicago economists, namely, that the market should be left alone to correct itself. The Chicago School instead tended to view the Great Depression as having been exacerbated by the failures of central bankers.[15] Chicago economists, unlike their Austrian counterparts, saw an active role for the state in the operation of a stable monetary policy. This Chicago view would be developed fully by Milton Friedman and Anna Jacobsen Schwartz in their *Monetary History of the United States* (1963).

There was a further important cultural difference between Chicago and Austria that might have unfairly affected attitudes within the Economics Department toward a post for Hayek. The Chicago approach was grounded in empirical research, a method given a theoretical underpinning in Friedman's essay "The Methodology of Positive Economics" (1953). Friedman and his Chicago colleagues insisted that research hypotheses could and should be tested empirically and then refined accordingly. Austrian economists like Ludwig von Mises, Hayek's teacher, believed, by contrast, that principles of economics could be derived theoretically, a priori. Hayek actually tended toward the former view, a view closer to that of his friend, Karl Popper, who argued in his *Logic of Scientific Discovery* that scientific knowledge should be reframed around "falsifiability" – the idea that while a positive hypothesis cannot be proved beyond doubt, it may be disproved by a single conflicting example. Hayek and Friedman were therefore closer than Mises and Hayek because Friedman too, in his "Methodology" essay, was indebted to Popper. But undoubtedly Hayek's business cycle view closely identified him with the Austrian tradition.

Economic historian John Nef, co-founder of the CST, suggested another possible reason for the *froideur* of the Economics Department toward Hayek: namely, that the econometricians in the department were suspicious of *The Road to Serfdom* and other department members thought it "too popular a work" for a serious economist.[16]

---

[15] See Stedman Jones, *Masters of the Universe*, especially chapter 3.
[16] J. Nef, *Search for Meaning: the Autobiography of a Non-Conformist* (Washington, DC, 1973), 37.

Friedman, however, disputed this view, pointing out that the majority of his colleagues shared Hayek's views in *The Road to Serfdom*. Friedman thought the refusal to appoint Hayek was straightforward. The department wanted to choose its own people, and most members disagreed with Hayek's monetary and capital theory as espoused in *Prices and Production* (1931).[17]

* * *

Hayek's move to Chicago is significant. His activism, the creation of the MPS, and the coming to power of the social market economy in postwar Germany marked the culmination of early neoliberal thought as a "middle way" between laissez-faire and socialism. After 1950, Hayek, the early pioneer of neoliberal politics, was now on the sidelines as his fellow MPS members in the United States developed a new economic agenda.[18] Friedman and his colleagues were developing a new set of theories within the macroeconomic framework set by Keynes. By the late 1950s, others like Stigler and Becker transformed microeconomics through the application of market-based analysis and methodological individualism to new spheres such as information, regulation, discrimination, crime, family, and other areas of non-market activity. Hayek arrived just as the nascent second Chicago School began a transformation of neoliberalism, in which the motivations of the key protagonists were no longer merely the rescue of the free enterprise system from the clutches of revolutionary alternatives but the expansion of the market mechanism, originally espoused by Austrian theorists but now developed by Chicago economics, into unploughed terrain.

Hayek and his fellow Austrian émigrés were shaped by fascism and communism, the Great Depression and mass unemployment. They had mostly fled Nazi rule and, in Hayek's case, found a home in a Britain whose democracy and economic system, though put under pressure by the General Strike of 1926 and the economic collapse of the 1930s, had survived. Economic devastation and war had combined with liberalism in Britain to produce a new form of social democracy. Neoliberalism was a response to the terrifying reality of fascist dictatorship and fear of the communist alternative, on the one hand, but also, on the other, to the

---

[17] Ebenstein, *Biography*, 174.
[18] In making this point, I do not mean to suggest that Hayek's long-term significance was marginalized but, rather, that his specifically economic contribution lost its centrality in the development of neoliberal political argument.

development of the welfare state in Britain and the United States as an alternative to laissez-faire.

In place of dictatorship, depression, and reform, postwar American neoliberals experienced a new tension between rising economic prosperity and unparalleled wealth of the postwar boom, which consolidated the United States' position as a capitalist and liberal-democratic superpower, and the chilling effect of the Cold War. This new atmosphere incubated a radicalization of neoliberalism into a more virulently pro-market strain of political and economic thought that challenged the role of state action in the delivery of social justice or greater equality. Market incentives would better generate the social outcomes beloved of well-meaning liberals and leftists and at the same time would foster the individual initiative and responsibility central to conservative political aims. This version of primarily *American* neoliberalism has since become the cliché of the popular media and neo-Marxist left.[19]

To understand this decisive change in neoliberal economic thought after 1950, the moment of Hayek's transatlantic move, it is necessary to locate early neoliberalism more precisely. Neoliberalism first emerged in the interwar period in Austria, Germany, France, and the United Kingdom, among thinkers and economists who wanted to reform liberalism.[20] Hayek, along with German economists Walter Eucken and Wilhelm Röpke, sociologist Alexander Rüstow, and French philosopher Raymond Aron and economist Jacques Rueff, argued that the "night watchman state" of laissez-faire, exemplified by nineteenth-century Britain, had proved inadequate. The model failed, by strictly limiting state action, to address the problems of poverty and deprivation that the emerging welfare state was designed to solve. Laissez-faire also lacked a constructive response to the Great Depression. But Hayek and his fellow neoliberals also comprehended the grave threat to individual freedom posed by the defeat of liberal politics by more popular extremes during the 1930s.

Totalitarianism was not only to be seen in Hitler's Germany, Mussolini's Italy, or Stalin's Soviet Union. Its beginnings were also evident, according to Hayek's famous argument in *The Road to Serfdom*, in British "New Liberalism" and Franklin Delano Roosevelt's New Deal.

[19] Exemplified by David Harvey's *A Brief History of Neoliberalism* (Oxford, 2005) and Naomi Klein's *The Shock Doctrine* (London, 2006). The term is a commonplace in the media but is rarely specified or properly defined.

[20] The best accounts of the early neoliberals are provided by Angus Burgin's *The Great Persuasion* (Cambridge, MA, 2012) and Ben Jackson's article, "At the Origins of Neoliberalism: The Free Market and the Strong State," *Historical Journal* 53:1 (2010): 129–151.

Hayek argued that economic planning would suffocate other freedoms through a gradual encroachment of bureaucratic decision-making based on inadequate information. This was true for at least two major reasons. First, an exponential growth in economic decisions being taken by bureaucrats took choice away from individuals. Second, during the famous economic calculation debate of the 1920s and 1930s, first Mises and then Hayek argued that the price system was the only non-coercive information processor capable of effectively coordinating the economy. Therefore, planning did not work on a practical level. Economic planners could never hope to have the information necessary to make critical economic decisions – to invest, to sell, to spend, and so on. The price system automatically and impersonally adjusted market information to the basic laws of supply and demand resulting in the production of the goods and services that people want.

Although they considered socialism – or, as Hayek and his friend Popper called it, "collectivism" – theoretically flawed, early neoliberals took its appeal seriously.[21] It was impossible not to do so in the face of mass unemployment and, in Germany especially, inflation. The challenge posed by these economic catastrophes to the liberal parties of the European middle class was evident in their collapse in Germany and Italy and in the emergence during the 1920s and 1930s of new activist and interventionist policies of liberal politicians like David Lloyd George and Franklin Roosevelt. For neoliberals like Hayek, these new political manifestations distorted the strong focus of classical liberalism on individual freedom and limited government. But they were comprehensible amidst the failures of liberal parties to produce coherent responses to the crises of the 1930s. Instead, Hayek and the early neoliberals argued for a reformulated liberalism to address capitalist breakdown.

The defining features of early neoliberalism were, firstly, a focus on anti-trust (or anti-monopoly as it is known in Europe) and fostering the conditions for a competitive economy within a constitutional framework, and, secondly, more controversially and less universally, a concomitant acceptance of a basic welfare state.[22] Early neoliberalism is best

---

[21] Popper used the term in *The Open Society and Its Enemies* (London, 1945). Collectivism was a broad term intended to encompass all forms of politics based, as Hayek would have it, on the coercion of individuals against their will. It therefore included socialism, communism, fascism, and Nazism but also the "middle way" paternalism of Conservatives like Harold Macmillan. (95-63)

[22] Among the group around Hayek who formed the early MPS, there were those who, like Ludwig von Mises, objected strongly to the welfare state, although the majority of early participants accepted the need for a welfare state, of varying degrees, primarily to

exemplified by the explicitly neoliberal social market economy of postwar Germany. Eucken, Rüstow, and Röpke, along with fellow economists Alfred Müller-Armack and Franz Böhm, were the main theorists who began writing in the 1920s and early 1930s amid the wreckage of the German economy, seeking to counter socialism.[23] The German neoliberals of the "Freiburg School," where several of the leading theorists taught, argued, in the pages of *Ordnung der Wirtschaft* and, later, *Ordo* (founded in 1948 by Eucken and Böhm), that the capitalist system, together with a welfare state, properly regulated to produce and maintain a competitive free market, would achieve better the aims of the socialists than socialism itself. Socialism would not just be inefficient but also oppressive.[24]

For the Ordoliberals, as these theorists were also known, economic freedom was anchored to political freedom.[25] The living standards of the working poor must be sufficient to guarantee the conditions for the operation of the market, which would create the wealth. The emphasis on the market as the deliverer of social goods was very different from the motivation behind early twentieth-century "New Liberalism," which came to power in the context of the rise of universal suffrage. New Liberalism wanted to expand political and civil liberty in economic terms through the introduction of unemployment benefits and pensions, policies seen as essential for full and active participation in society. This belief in the importance of substantive economic rights was also a source of FDR's articulation of social citizenship in his State of the Union address of 1944.[26] Indeed, Roosevelt's administration and policies of 1933–1945, building on early twentieth-century Progressivism, marked the origins of

Though in the UK that actually followed the liberal victory 1906

---

protect the free enterprise system. In this respect, the influence of depression and war did loom large.

[23] On the ordoliberals, see especially R. Ptak, "Neoliberalism in Germany: Revisiting the Ordoliberal Foundations of the Social Market Economy," in Mirowski and Plehwe, *The Road from Mont Pelerin*, 98–138. See also Carl Friedrich, "The Political Thought of Neo-liberalism," *American Political Science Review* 49:2 (1955): 509–525; David Gerber, "Constitutionalizing the Economy: German Neoliberalism, Competition Law and the 'New Europe.'" *American Journal of Comparative Law* 42:1 (1994): 25–84, and, on Böhm, Knut Norr, "On the Concept of the 'Economic Constitution' and the Importance of Franz Böhm from the Viewpoint of Legal History," *European Journal of Law and Economics* 3:4: 345–356.

[24] Perhaps the most complete expression of the ideas of the German neoliberals was produced in Eucken's *The Foundations of Economics: History and Theory in the Analysis of Reality*, first published in Germany in 1940 when Eucken was Professor of Economics at Freiburg.

[25] See Anthony J. Nicholls, *Freedom with Responsibility: The Social Market Economy in Germany, 1918–1963* (Oxford, 1994), especially chapter 1.

[26] Edwardian "New Liberalism" and FDR's New Deal are the original social liberal political programs.

the term "liberal" to describe socially progressive politics in the United States.

German social market theorists had been strongly influenced by the depressing history of economic concentration, cartelization, and monopoly in Wilhelmine and Weimar Germany. German liberals were divided in the first decades of the twentieth century between those whose nationalism and reverence for the new German state saw them acquiesce in such abuses of the market system, and a small, impotent group of progressives in the German Democratic Party (Deutsche Demokratische Partei, or DDP) who had been unable, in the course of the 1920s and early 1930s, to carve out a popular program. Progressive liberals were unable to differentiate themselves clearly in the eyes of voters from the conservative and statist National Liberals or the socialist Social Democrats of the SPD. Eucken, Rüstow, and Röpke (all later members of the MPS) saw the urgent need to rescue liberalism from this crisis of legitimacy during the years leading up to, and following, Hitler's appointment as chancellor in 1933. In doing so, they placed the conditions of competition and the means by which to secure them at the heart of their economic agenda.

The Christian Democrats (CDU) adopted the main ideas of the German neoliberals in the immediate aftermath of World War II. Leading neoliberal politician Ludwig Erhard (also a member of the MPS) took advantage of his almost dictatorial powers as head of the Verwaltung für Wirtschaft, the agency in charge of the economy of the Western zones of occupied Germany before the currency reform of 1948. Erhard introduced sweeping currency reform and ended price controls. The CDU, driven by Erhard, adopted the so-called Düsseldorf Guidelines. According to these guidelines, the "social market economy" would be "socially anchored" in law. Individuals were seen as "integrated into a system that produced the highest level of economic benefit and social justice for all."[27] Freedom and responsibility were two core principles to help generate competition and challenge monopolies. The price system would "regulate the interaction between all market participants." Fundamentally, the economy of the new Federal Republic of Germany, as defined by neoliberal principles, would avoid the pitfalls of both "the command economy" and "free enterprise economy of liberal hue," otherwise known as

[27] *Düsseldorfer Leitsätze über Wirtschaftspolitik, Landwirtschaftspolitik, Sozialpolitik, Wohnungsbau* [Düsseldorf Guidelines for Economic Policy, Agricultural Policy, Social Policy, and Housing] (July 15, 1949); reprinted in Ossip Kurt Flechtheim, *Die Parteien der Bundesrepublik Deutschland* [The Parties of the Federal Republic of Germany] (Hamburg, 1973), 162–163.

laissez-faire. German neoliberalism would tread a "middle way" between planning and laissez-faire by supporting "planned efforts to influence the economy through the organic means of a comprehensive economic policy coupled with flexible adaptation to market studies." Finally, a welfare state was necessary "adequately to meet the needs of those parts of the population suffering hardship." By 1959, the SPD followed the CDU and committed itself to the principles of the social market economy in its "Godesberg Program."[28] Marxist socialism was thereby abandoned in West Germany as a mainstream political offering and the social market model became open to reform and adaptation from the left.

It abandoned key tenets of Marxism like a belief in class struggle & proletarian revolution and the abolition of capitalism

The architects of the West German social market economy were engaged, with Hayek and the other founders of the MPS, in what they perceived as the defense of the market economy. In the American postwar context, by contrast, the two most important drivers for a rethinking of liberalism were the New Deal and the Cold War.

L a much left alarming threat

* * *

By the late 1930s the New Deal had provoked a passionate response from many business leaders. Many business owners and corporate officials began to fund research and activism that would dent its political success. Jasper Crane, formerly of Du Pont, Lemuel Boulwere of General Electric (GE), and Harold Luhnow, for example, became leading organizers and fundraisers during the 1940s and 1950s in a war against New Deal policies. The Du Ponts funded the foundation of the American Liberty League to fight Roosevelt in 1934. General Electric was at the vanguard of corporate efforts to "reeducate" employees in the tenets of American capitalism. Luhnow transformed the WVF, previously a parochial Kansas fund founded by a wholesale furniture distributor, into a vehicle for the propagation of free market ideology through bankrolling research projects in Chicago, the MPS, and think tanks such as Read's FEE and the Intercollegiate Studies Institute after 1945.[29] Crane was an admirer of Hayek despite what he regarded as Hayek's concessions to state intervention. Boulwere, hired as marketing assistant by GE in 1946, was famous for his anti-labor stance, offering a model of how to break a union through his tough negotiating at GE. He ensured that pro-market

Hence its hiring of Ronald Reagan

The anti-union Taft-Hartley Act passed in 1947)

[28] See *Basic Program of the Social Democratic Party of Germany* (Bonn, 1959), 5–17, 20–22, reprinted in Jan Goldstein and John W. Boyer, eds., *Readings in Western Civilization*, vol. 9, *Twentieth-Century Europe* (Chicago and London, 1987), 419–425.

[29] See M. McVicar, "Aggressive Philanthropy: Progressivism, Conservatism and the William Volker Charities Fund," *Missouri Historical Review* 105:4 (2011): 191–212.

reading lists were distributed to managers, who could then promote the ideas to employees.[30] These anti-New Deal business activists were tireless in their efforts.[31] Alongside others such as the Relm Foundation, the Earhart Foundation, and the U.S. military-backed RAND Corporation, they funded and shaped research agendas in Chicago and elsewhere that radicalized neoliberalism after 1950.

The Cold War also shaped the development of neoliberalism after 1950. Firstly, the existential struggle with the Soviet Union colored the priorities of the United States federal government. Federal investment in the hi-tech industries and higher education research institutions and agglomerations that made up what historian Margaret Pugh O'Mara has called "Cities of Knowledge" transformed the urban and suburban landscape of the United States.[32] The deepening interrelation of defense and higher education was a cornerstone of what Eisenhower had termed the military-industrial complex of the 1950s and 1960s. Equally, private think tanks like the FEE and the American Enterprise Institute combined with publicly funded organizations like RAND to foster new modes of liberal thought. Rational choice liberalism, as Amadae's work has clearly illustrated, was developed in part as a result of experiments with game theory undertaken by the U.S. Department of Defense in order to respond to the new context of potential nuclear warfare.[33] The result was the development of a new theory of decision-making that placed the rational self-interested actor at the center of analysis in order to understand how individuals might operate in particular strategic contexts such as possible use of nuclear weapons.

The febrile atmosphere of the Cold War and the anti-communist crusade of the House Un-American Activities Committee and McCarthyism in the late 1940s and early 1950s also affected the motivations and attitudes of free market economists. Scholars like Milton Friedman and James Buchanan were, in keeping with their conception of economic freedom, deeply committed to the defense of the free enterprise system *from* government intervention.[34] Friedman in particular felt himself to be engaged

---

[30] Kim Phillips-Fein, *Invisible Hands: The Businessmen's Crusade Against the New Deal* (New York, 2009), 97–105.

[31] See also Elizabeth Foners-Wolf's *Selling Free Enterprise* (Chicago, 1995).

[32] Margaret Pugh O'Mara, *Cities of Knowledge: Cold War Science and the Search for the Next Silicon Valley* (Princeton, 2004). On the changing face of the postwar South, see also Bruce Schulman's *From Cotton Belt to Sunbelt* (Oxford, 1991).

[33] Amadae, *Rationalizing Capitalist Democracy*, Part I.

[34] This is to be contrasted with the sort of economic freedom, to engage meaningfully in economic and social life, through public provision of necessary basics such as benefits and pensions, which was the aim of New Liberalism.

in an ideological front of the Cold War in which part of his necessary task was to investigate the conditions that made the free enterprise system superior to its socialist rivals. And it did appear to be superior. GDP in the United States grew by 4 percent on average throughout the 1950s and 1960s.[35] Median household income steadily increased in a happy confluence with productivity until the early 1970s.[36] American capitalism seemed an unprecedented motor of prosperity. In *Capitalism and Freedom* (1962), Friedman argued that the free market was the key distinguishing feature of American liberal democracy when opposed to its mortal enemy of Soviet communism.[37] The book arose from Friedman's WVF-funded lecture series in the 1950s. It became the American *Road to Serfdom* that Luhnow had sought in his discussions with Hayek in 1946.

The distance from actual Communism and social democracy fostered an extremism

The economic confidence inspired by the boom years of the 1950s and 1960s fostered a subtle shift in the arguments made by American neoliberals. Friedman, Aaron Director, Buchanan, and Stigler had all attended the first MPS meeting in 1947. They had fraternized with their European colleagues, exchanged ideas, and participated in the discussions. In the late 1940s, the influence of the arguments made by European neoliberals combining a focus on competition and anti-monopoly with social welfare is clear. In 1951, Milton Friedman's article "Neoliberalism and its Discontents" in the Norwegian journal *Farmand* identified with the neoliberal cause and made the case for an alternative to both collectivism and laissez-faire. As with the social market, neoliberalism would:

Accept the nineteenth century emphasis in the fundamental importance of the individual, but it would substitute for the nineteenth century goal of laissez-faire as a means to this end, the goal of a competitive order. It would use competition among producers to protect the consumer from exploitation, competition among employers to protect workers and owners of property and competition among consumers to protect the enterprises themselves. The state would police the system, establish conditions favorable to competition and prevent monopoly, provide a stable monetary framework, and relieve acute misery and distress. The

---

[35] A useful chart of GDP annual growth since 1947 drawn from data from the U.S. Bureau of Economic Analysis is available at http://www.tradingeconomics.com/united-states/gdp-growth-annual.

[36] See "The State of Working America," a chart produced by the Economic Policy Institute (EPI) illustrating the twin paths of median household income and productivity, 1948–2013 – available at http://stateofworkingamerica.org/charts/productivity-and-real-median-family-income-growth-1947–2009/. The chart is drawn from the EPI's analysis of Current Population Survey Annual Social and Economic Supplement Historical Income Tables (Table F-5) and Bureau of Labor Statistics, Productivity – Major Sector Productivity and Costs database.

[37] See especially chapter 2 of Friedman's *Capitalism and Freedom* (Chicago, 1962).

citizens would be protected against the state by the existence of a private market; and against one another by the preservation of competition.[38]

These views, also expressed in his 1948 article "A Monetary and Fiscal Framework for Economic Stability," echo the themes of the social market theorists.[39] However, the Cold War and continuing reaction to Eisenhower's accommodation with much of the New Deal/Fair Deal policy settlement in 1950s America contributed to a change in the character of neoliberalism so that it became an unalloyed program of the deregulation, expansion, and liberalization of markets.

That is, one incorrectly white to "protection"

* * *

In the twenty years following 1950, the building blocks, both methodological and philosophical, of the new market-based perspective were put in place. Three developments paved the way.

First, the Free Market Study (FMS) group (1946–1952) and the Anti-Trust Project (1953–1957), located in the Law School at Chicago, funded by the WVF, and run by Aaron Director, progressively transformed the approach of Chicago economists to monopolies and anti-trust. Having taken no interest in pursuing the idea of the FMS personally, Hayek was instrumental, after much wrangling with the university administration, in the appointment of Director, Milton Friedman's brother-in-law, to lead it.[40] The idea almost collapsed when Luhnow's WVF tried to attach the string of tenure for Director to the money that would fund the project. The administration was understandably reluctant to go ahead with such a condition attached. A compromise was reached. Director was given a fixed five-year term funded by the WVF, which he accepted after persuasion from Hayek in 1946. The FMS was wound down in 1952, but it was the forerunner of another important project based at Chicago and funded by the WVF, the Anti-Trust Project. Director also led this project. It ran until 1957, producing a series of publications.

Both projects transformed what might be thought of as the Chicago position on monopoly and competition. Friedman, Director, and Edward Levi of Chicago's Law School took the lead in arguing for a departure

---

[38] Milton Friedman, "Neoliberalism and its Discontents," *Farmand* 17 (1951): 89–93.

[39] "A Monetary and Fiscal Framework for Economic Stability," *American Economic Review* 38:3 (1948): 245–264.

[40] I have relied in this paragraph on the account of the FMS provided by Van Horn and Mirowski in "The Rise of the Chicago School of Economics and the Birth of Neoliberalism," in Mirowski and Plehwe, *The Road from Mont Pelerin*, 139–180.

from the neoliberal position as exemplified by the German Ordoliberals. Whereas the Germans saw a role for government in regulating against monopoly to ensure competition, the Chicago theorists focused on the role of government in sustaining monopoly. They reversed the idea that competition is suppressed by monopoly, which in turn must be addressed by regulation to restore competition. Instead, the FMS focused on the role of government in sustaining monopoly. Monopoly without the assistance of government, the Chicago theorists maintained, could be defeated by competition. The conditions of competition, they argued, were replicable within the large corporation. As the historian Rob Van Horn has shown, "the triumvirate of Director, Friedman and Levi began to advocate the idea of monopoly, in all its forms, was almost always undone by the forces of competition; and consequently that a relatively sanguine attitude should be adopted toward both monopoly and large corporations. The corporations were said to have approximated the impersonal ideal of the market, even in what would appear, by conventional measures, to be fairly concentrated markets."[41]

The change in the approach to competition and anti-trust crucially shifted the neoliberal position away from state regulation, through an effective legal and constitutional order that preserved competition. It opened a path to deregulation. George Stigler, who left Columbia University in 1958 to join the Chicago faculty, further developed this idea in a series of papers beginning with "What Can Regulators Regulate? The Case of Electricity" (1962) and culminating in his essay "A Theory of Economic Regulation" (1971). In his case study of electricity, Stigler argued that the basic assumption of the efficacy of economic regulation should be challenged.[42] Regulation, he maintained, often had a negligible impact on the market activities, such as anti-competitive behavior or price-fixing, which regulators aimed to regulate. Consequently, regulation should be assessed according to its empirical effects before a proper theory of regulation could be developed.[43] His theory of regulation, which advanced

---

41 Van Horn, "Reinventing Monopoly," in Mirowski and Plehwe, *The Road from Mont Pelerin*, 207–208.

42 At the outset of his article, Stigler asks: "the most basic question one can ask about regulation: Does it make a difference in the behavior of an industry?" "What Can Regulators Regulate? The Case of Electricity?," *Law and Economics* 5 (1962): 1–16.

43 Stigler did this in a series of articles including "Public Regulation of the Securities Markets," *Journal of Business* 37:2 (1963): 117–142, "The Economic Effects of the Anti-Trust Laws," *Law and Economics* 9 (1966): 225–258, and, most famously, "The Theory of Economic Regulation," *Bell Journal of Economics and Management Science* 2:1 (1971): 3–21.

the impossibility of an objectively attainable public interest, became the starting point in analysis of regulation as a policy problem. It aimed to demolish the "idealistic view of public regulation" and provided one half of a two-pronged attack on the state.[44]

Economic deregulation advanced rapidly in the 1970s and 1980s in Britain and the United States. Interestingly, like Friedman's monetarism, it was picked up by administrations of the left before those on the right. For example, President Carter, with the support of Senator Teddy Kennedy, promoted deregulation of airlines, trains, and cars as well as beginning the long deregulation of the banking sector with the Depository Institutions Deregulation and Monetary Control Act 1980. President Reagan campaigned to strip away environmental and energy regulations in 1980 and continued the deregulation of the transportation sector. Bill Clinton's Democratic administrations pursued deregulation with gusto. In 1996, Treasury Secretary Robert Rubin supported the repeal of the Depression-era Glass-Steagall Act, which had kept the retail and merchant operations of the banks separate.

Margaret Thatcher's Conservative government promoted financial deregulation by lifting capital controls in 1979 and introducing the so-called "Big Bang," which stripped away many controls on the City of London, in 1987. New Labour under Tony Blair after 1997 made the Bank of England independent and took the financial and banking sectors out of either Bank of England or governmental oversight. Stigler's ideas had become a new received political wisdom. Regulatory barriers to the successful operation of markets, it was assumed among British and American policymakers, must be removed. Deregulation was blamed for the financial crisis of 2008. Supporters blamed instead the state support for subprime loans. Whatever the truth, deregulation profoundly influenced the policies of successive governments after 1970.

The second development that contributed to the emergence of a new market-based perspective was the rise of public choice economics, of which Stigler's ideas were a crucial part. The second prong of the neoliberal attack on the state, this theory revolutionized the idea of choice in the 1950s and 1960s. From the moment that economist Kenneth Arrow's RAND-funded doctoral thesis "Individualism and Social Values" (1951) appeared, doubt was cast upon the possibility of collectively rational outcomes.[45] Arrow's impossibility theorem built upon the Marquis de Condorcet's famous "voter paradox," which highlighted the problem

---

[44] Stigler, "Theory of Economic Regulation," 17.
[45] Kenneth Arrow, *Individualism and Social Values* (New York, 1951).

that majority voting preferences can sometimes produce no clear winner. Arrow attempted to show that it was impossible, in a stable choice
situation such as voting, for individual preferences to be respected in a
non-coerced way to produce an outcome that expressed at least a minimally desired rational preference for all participants. This idea seemed
to undermine democratic theories, like those of Rousseau and Marx,
based on notions of the collective will or the public interest because he
showed that it was impossible for such ideas to be the product of freely
chosen preferences. Hence, according to Arrow – and later, the public
choice theorists – there must be an element of coercion involved in the
implementation of policy based on such choices. This finding robustly
challenged the assumption, crucial to mid-twentieth-century liberal and
social democracy, that collectively rational outcomes are possible. If such
outcomes were not possible then should not such choices, such as those
made on our behalves by politicians and public servants, be minimized?

Building on the work of Arrow and other rational choice theorists,
James Buchanan and Gordon Tullock, the founders of the Virginia School
of Political Economy, combined public choice theory and constitutional
economics.[46] In *The Calculus of Consent* (1962), they argued that collective entities such as the state are merely the aggregation of individuals.
State action should reflect only policy choices that can be shown to be
in all individuals' interest. Public choice as elaborated by Buchanan and
Tullock challenged the idea of the public interest, arguing instead that
civil servants, public officials, and regulators were as self-interested as
anyone else. Enlightened objectivity on the part of elite and expert public
servants on the model that Keynes or William Beveridge, the British civil
servant and architect of social insurance, assumed was an illusion. Public
policy, Buchanan and Tullock concluded, should be shaped accordingly –
in other words, cynically.

"Rational choice" was a related field that shared public choice assumptions, and was promoted most prominently in the work of William
Riker and his followers at the University of Rochester.[47] Rational choice
accepted basic microeconomic utility maximization, which assumes that

46 James M. Buchanan and Gordon Tullock, *The Calculus of Consent* (Ann Arbor, MI,
    1962). See also the other key texts of the rational choice "canon," Duncan Black's
    work including his *Theory of Committees and Elections* (Cambridge, 1958), Anthony
    Downs's *Economic Theory of Democracy* (New York, 1957), William Riker's *Theory
    of Political Coalitions* (New Haven, 1962), and Mancur Olson's *The Logic of Collective
    Action* (Cambridge, 1965).
47 This group has sometimes been referred to as the Rochester School after the University
    of Rochester, where Riker and his students were based.

individuals will try to maximize their ends in a given stable environment. The unifying current with public choice was the application of rational self-interest to politics, elections, and state or local government activity. Both public choice and rational choice highlighted incentive structures according to which actors under consideration operated in order to predict how they would behave. Public choice in particular was central to deregulation, the introduction of market mechanisms to social policy and public services, and the reform of public administration and bureaucracy. A good example was the introduction of the internal market in Britain's National Health Service (NHS) and the reform of its bureaucratic administration after the 1980s under successive governments of both political hues.

A third innovation produced by the American neoliberals grew out of Milton Friedman's groundbreaking article "The Methodology of Positive Economics" (1953), which argued for empirical economics grounded in science and prediction. The essay founded much of the Chicago School's approach to economic research. In essence, Friedman argued that progress in scientific knowledge would occur through the testing of propositions for their predictive power. Friedman claimed that this sort of scientific work was independent from his ideological belief in a free market-based politics and society. Arguably, the acceptance of Friedman's claim about the absence of ideology accounts for the fact that policymakers have often seen Chicago findings as objectively neutral. (It may also be that this acceptance contributed to the elevation of economists above other social scientists as true "scientists," at least until the 2008 financial crisis.) According to Friedman, empirical research should be free of normative considerations. Upon the production of evidence, properly tested and shown to be applicable, economists of all political stripe should be able to agree about diagnosis and prescription. If on the evidence inflation was better controlled through the stable control of the monetary supply, Friedman argued, then public policy should be directed to that end.

Friedman's emphasis on empiricism and falsifiability was expanded and entrenched in the 1960s by a more ambitious Chicago-based project, one that became known, often pejoratively, as "economics imperialism," the colonization by methodological individualism and rational choice of new areas previously seen as immune to market-based analysis. Stigler's theory of regulatory capture was an early example, but possibly the most important example of "economics imperialism" was the work of Gary Becker. Beginning with his doctoral dissertation, which argued that competition could reduce discrimination, Becker was an intrepid methodological explorer.[48] He applied market logic to, for example, crime, the family, and drugs.[49] Other scholars have followed suit. Richard Posner, for example, introduced rational and self-interested models into the study of law.[50] This movement, together with social and public choice and methodological individualism, was responsible by the end of the twentieth century for a widespread belief that market analysis could and should be applied to virtually any social, economic, or political problem.

"Economics imperialism" has been just as significant for economic and social policy since 1980. Market mechanisms have been imported into health, education, housing, welfare, and urban regeneration policy. In Britain, for example, the Conservative governments of the 1980s and 1990s pursued a large-scale privatization program of housing, telecoms, airlines, gas, electricity, water, and rail. In the United States, the influence of "economics imperialism" was felt in the elaboration of policies such as school vouchers, enacted in several cities after 1990, and enterprise zones, which had been promoted by Reagan but were finally enacted in modified form under Clinton.

These shifts have necessarily only been sketched in this chapter. Hayek's move from the LSE to Chicago symbolized the gravitational pull in neoliberal thought away from Europe to the United States. All three intellectual developments took shape in the years that followed Hayek's move from London to Chicago and occurred without any significant input from him.[51] Yet they transformed understandings of the free market. To be sure, throughout the twenty-five-year period after 1950, Hayek, along with the public intellectual *extraordinaire* Milton Friedman, remained the glue that held together a transatlantic network of neoliberal political activists.[52] He worked on *The Constitution of Liberty* (1960) throughout the 1950s, a classic statement of a liberal legal, political, and

---

[48] Gary Becker, *The Economics of Discrimination* (Chicago, 1957).

[49] He did this in a series of important publications in the 1960s including his doctoral dissertation, "An Economic Analysis of Fertility" (in *Demographic and Economic Change in Developed Countries, a Conference of the Universities* – National Bureau Committee for Economic Research, Princeton, 1960) and "Crime and Punishment: An Economic Analysis," *Journal of Political Economy* 76 (1968): 169–217. These essays and others were collected in *The Economic Approach to Human Behavior* (Chicago, 1976).

[50] Famously articulated in his *An Economic Analysis of Law* (Chicago, 1973).

[51] Notwithstanding the argument made by Mirowski and Van Horn in *Road from Mont Pelerin*, which I accept, that Hayek may have been instrumental in the facilitation of the FMS.

[52] I discussed Hayek and Friedman's role in this development in detail in *Masters*, especially chapters 3 and 4.

constitutional order that was to become highly influential, at first among scholars and intellectuals and later, in the 1970s, among politicians and policymakers as well.

An important example was Sir Keith Joseph MP, a minister during Prime Minister Edward Heath's administration (1970–1974) who underwent a Damascene conversion to free markets after the government's fall. He became a convert to Friedman's monetarist arguments and began to develop a Hayekian critique of British trade unionism in a famous lecture entitled "Monetarism is Not Enough," which he delivered in Stockton on April 5, 1976. There is no doubt that *The Constitution of Liberty* and *The Road to Serfdom* exercised a powerful hold over a whole generation of British and American politicians who came to power in the late 1970s and early 1980s. The famous story of Prime Minister Margaret Thatcher throwing onto the table, around which a group of stunned civil servants sat, a copy of *The Constitution of Liberty* and exclaiming "this is what we believe" is probably apocryphal, but it does indicate the change in Hayek's position when compared to his defeat by Keynes in the 1930s. President George H. W. Bush crowned the transformation by awarding Hayek the Presidential Medal of Freedom in 1991, the year before he died.

That the radical neoliberal ideas promoted by Chicago and Virginia theorists dominated the economic programs of two self-proclaimed leaders of what President Richard Nixon had famously termed "the Silent Majority" is surprising. The supposedly neutral benefits of markets, competition, and efficiency were accompanied by a destructive potential most clearly described by another Austrian economist, Joseph Schumpeter. But it is not just new products and paradigms that are created by destruction. Markets disrupt and sometimes destroy traditional spheres of morality and culture that are often felt to be central to the social policy aims of the very conservative politicians who argued for markets and their benefits. Margaret Thatcher's and Ronald Reagan's electoral successes were partly the remarkable result of alchemy. They were able to mix a "traditional" morality with economic policies whose effects hastened the globalization of capital and labor flows and eroded the conditions that had supported the moral frameworks they valued. Early neoliberals such as Hayek recognized and worried deeply about the potential moral and cultural implications of the limitless extension of market principles. They consequently saw a role for state action to provide a basic safety net. Friedman, however, argued that the incentives and rewards of markets fostered the individual responsibility that he saw as essential to

[handwritten: That markets punish social conservatism]

true economic and political freedom. It is possible to see in the emergent American neoliberalism in the postwar period, then, the origins of a fundamental tension in conservative politics.

Yet these tensions came only later. In the 1950s and 1960s, neoliberalism as an intellectual force was changing. It was metamorphosing into a harder-edged creed that saw less and less role for state intervention of any kind and an almost universal need for the application of market-based models to public policy. Hayek's involvement in the cutting edge of neoliberal economic thought and policy subsided as he retreated into more philosophical and normative considerations.[53] Friedman, Stigler, Buchanan, Tullock, and Becker, on the other hand, forged ahead on a path that led to the radicalization of neoliberalism.

[53] Hayek continued to produce many more books and policy pamphlets. Of these, the most important was *Law, Legislation and Liberty* (1973, 1976, 1979), his three-volume exploration of alternatively produced, and understood, legal orders as the basis for liberty.

[handwritten: One reason the modern radical right is ambivalent towards markets, and frequently draws from places that do not prosper in contemporary markets]

PART II

POLITICAL MOBILIZATION AND RESPONSES TO LEFT-WING PROTEST

3

Silent Minority?

British Conservative Students in the Age of Campus Protest

John Davis

Higher education in Britain expanded rapidly in the 1960s. The implementation of the 1963 Robbins Report – prompting the conversion of ten colleges of advanced technology into universities and the expansion of student numbers across the higher education sector – created a new student "estate." The political potential of this student cohort was evident: policymakers expected them to become the opinion-formers of their generation. A Conservative government had accepted the Robbins Report's recommendations, and the Conservatives were, from the start, alert to its implications. As David Howell, then at the Conservative Research Department, noted in 1965, "as we move into an era in which it becomes the rule rather than the exception for young people to go on to higher education, effective organization of students in the Universities . . . is absolutely essential to our future electoral success."[1]

I am grateful to Jeremy McIlwaine for much help and advice on the contents of the Conservative Party Archive, to Martina Steber for sharing with me her research on the European Union of Christian Democrat and Conservative Students (ECCS), and, of course, to my seven interviewees. They were: Sir Tony Baldry (b. 1950, University of Sussex, 1969–1973, interviewed Bloxham, July 29, 2011); Stephen Kreppel (b. 1946, London School of Economics [LSE], 1965–1968, interviewed Ulaanbataar, by Skype, August 27 and 31, 2013); Roger Mountford (b. 1948, LSE 1967–1971, interviewed London, August 13, 2013); Anthony Speaight (b. 1948, University of Oxford, 1967–1970, interviewed London, September 18, 2012); Tom Spencer (b. 1948, University of Southampton, 1967–1970, interviewed Farnham, October 4, 2013); Ian Taylor (b. 1945, University of Keele, 1964–1967, LSE 1967–1970, interviewed London, October 16, 2012); Peter Watherston (b. 1942, LSE, 1965–1969, interviewed London, May 1, 2012). All interviews were conducted by the author. Unfootnoted quotations are taken from these interviews.

[1] David Howell, Memorandum "Conservative Party and the Universities," undated (January 1965), in the file "Links with Universities," Conservative Party Archives, Bodleian Library, Oxford [hereafter CPA], CRD 3/35/5.

Within a few years, this must have seemed a hollow aspiration, as many of Britain's universities became platforms for student Marxism. This raised problems not only for the Conservative high command but also for Conservative students on campus. It was, admittedly, always clear that the number of students identifying with the far left was more limited than many imagined. At the London School of Economics (LSE) and the University of Essex – arguably the two most radical campuses in the country – supporters of far left groups accounted for around 8 percent and 5 percent of the student body, respectively.[2] The problem was rather that students tended to be left-leaning even at the high point of national disenchantment with Harold Wilson's Labour government in 1967–1968. Avowed Conservatives accounted for only 18 percent of LSE students, against 45 percent supporting Labour and a further 16 percent the Liberals. In Essex, only 15 percent of the 1968 intake called themselves Conservatives. Tory support would doubtless have been higher on more conservative campuses like Bristol or Kent, and 28 percent of Liverpool students were said to support the Conservatives in October 1969,[3] but nowhere could Tory students be confident that they formed a majority. On most campuses outside Oxbridge, the "silent majority" was likely to belong to the soft left, to adhere to altruistic and internationalist political positions, and to sympathize with criticism of university authorities. The leaders of the national Federation of Conservative Students (FCS) accepted that the radical tone of student politics was inevitable: "the rejection of the old Oxbridge oriented view of the students' social position is geared to the increasing acceptance that higher education is a right for all those with good 'A' levels and not a privilege. It is only natural in this light that less is taken for granted, and students become more assertive. The outcome has been a revolt against old standards."[4] They feared that the "average" student, undoctrinaire but undeferential, would be susceptible to the arguments of militants,

[2] The LSE figure is calculated from Tables 3.1 and 3.15, combining home and overseas students' political allegiance, in Tessa Blackstone, Kathleen Gales, Roger Hadley, and Wyn Lewis, *Students in Conflict: LSE in 1967* (London, 1970), 36, 60–61; for Essex, see Ernest Rudd and Fiona Rudd, "The Political Positions of Students Entering the University of Essex in 1968," typescript in University of Essex Archives, Albert Sloman Library, University of Essex, Keith Ives collection, box 18(a), Table 2.

[3] Nick Thomas, "Challenging Myths of the 1960s: The Case of Student Protest in Britain," *Twentieth Century British History* 13 (2002): 283.

[4] Ian Taylor, "'Student Power': An Essay by the Chairman," May 21, 1968, CPA, CCO 60/2/2.

particularly over issues of university governance or facilities and particularly when university authorities proved irrationally intransigent.

The Essex survey of the 1968 intake found that Conservatives were significantly less interested in politics than other incoming students.[5] Conservatism being a difficult cause to promote on many campuses, there was a temptation to retreat into what might charitably be called "lifestyle Toryism" in the unpropitious circumstances of a provincial university. Tom Spencer, arriving at Southampton in 1967, found that the university Conservative Association "in those days was largely to do with drinking sherry." But the emergence of the student new left had turned the university into a political site – not only on those campuses where radical activists pursued ambitious "red base" strategies but wherever sit-ins, occupations, or the disruption of lectures disturbed university life. Beyond that, the student new left sought to exercise a kind of veto power over political discussion in the university – in the form of the heckling or barracking of opponents, attempts to deny a platform to visiting speakers, even occasional violence – that posed a real challenge to their adversaries and made political quiescence appear tantamount to surrender. The militant challenge was impossible to ignore.[6]

[handwritten margin note: Student activists still use all of these tactics]

The Marxist dominance of student debate induced many Conservative students to consider the basis of their opinions. It was no coincidence that this period of radical student protest saw the parallel development of a national student Conservative activism, not dominated by Oxbridge but drawn from across the tertiary sector. Their federation,[7] which had operated as "a debating society in effect" earlier in the decade,[8] now devoted itself to the mobilization of non-Marxist student opinion. This chapter looks at the evolution of university Conservatism during the peak period

---

[5] Nine percent of Conservatives claimed to be "very interested" in politics, against 20 percent of the total; 9 percent claimed to be "not interested at all," against 3 percent of the total: Rudd and Rudd, "Political Positions of Students," 5.

[6] This is not, of course, to challenge the central claim made by Nick Thomas, in his "Challenging Myths of the 1960s," that most British students did not belong to the militant left and held reformist rather than revolutionary views. For a more rounded recent study of the British student movement, see Caroline Hoefferle, *British Student Activism in the Long Sixties* (New York, 2013).

[7] The name Federation of Conservative Students was adopted only in 1968. Before then, the organization had operated under the cumbersome name of the Federation of University Conservative and Unionist Associations, and the inadvertently confrontational acronym FUCUA.

[8] Stephen Kreppel interview.

of student unrest in the late 1960s and early 1970s. It does so primarily through interviews with seven men[9] prominent in the Federation of Conservative Students and in Conservative politics on their own campuses. They included four FCS chairmen: Ian Taylor (1968–1969; Keele University and the London School of Economics), Stephen Kreppel (1969–1970, LSE), Roger Mountford (1970–1971, LSE), and Anthony Speaight (1972–1973, Oxford University), along with Sir Anthony (Tony) Baldry, an FCS vice chairman and the most prominent Conservative activist at Sussex University, Tom Spencer, chairman of the Southampton University Conservative Association and subsequently of the European Union of Christian Democrat and Conservative Students (ECCS), and Peter Watherston, chairman of the LSE students' union at the height of the disturbances there in 1967–1968.[10]

Watherston had joined the Bow Group before going to university and had worked for the Conservatives in Stratford-on-Avon in the 1964 general election. Kreppel, aged eighteen then, had also worked for the party in the Edinburgh Leith constituency. The others came from Conservative families with the exception of Speaight, whose father voted Liberal. At university, Speaight was "so horrified by the people on the left" that he abandoned Liberalism to join the Conservatives. All the others found their Conservative allegiance reinforced by the radical tone of campus politics and by the illiberal impulses which it appeared to engender. Spencer made himself "a marked man in the [Student] Union" by defending the right of Richard Beeching – deputy chairman of Imperial Chemical Industries and therefore a controversial figure to some students – to address a meeting at Southampton. Taylor, as an undergraduate at Keele, remembered the controversial Conservative front-bencher Enoch Powell being hurried out of the back door with police protection after a meeting, threatened not for his views on race – this was well before his 1968 "Rivers of Blood" speech on immigration – but for his free market economics. Taylor did not subscribe to Powell's economic prescriptions, but "I regarded them as views which you could hold." At Sussex, Baldry objected to the idea that "a commune of . . . the left decided who was and was not acceptable and

[9] British students were predominantly male in the 1960s, and this appears to have been still more true of the Federation of Conservative Students: Watherston counted six women and seventy men in a photograph of participants in an FCS residential conference in 1967 or 1968 (email to the author, February 20, 2014). The most prominent FCS woman to go on to a career in Conservative politics was Lynda Chalker, MP for Wallasey, 1974–1992, and a minister in the Thatcher and Major governments.

[10] "Unashamed Tory at the LSE," *The Times*, April 15, 1967.

on what basis they weren't all that acceptable to speak"; he mobilized a "free speech coalition" to challenge this censorship. He accepted the barracking of his own interventions in union debate as part of the lot of a Tory activist, and Taylor acknowledged that he found it "exhilarating" to defend a minority cause in an antagonistic meeting, but the "extraordinarily hostile atmosphere" that Speaight remembers hardly encouraged participation. The casual legitimization of political violence was disturbing. Mountford thought the "wish to resort to violence and even to suffer it" on the part of the LSE radicals rather self-indulgent. LSE students were prominent in the bloody anti-Vietnam War demonstration outside the U.S. embassy in March 1968, and Mountford found offensive the radicals' proposals "to set up the School as a 'field hospital' for the riots in Grosvenor Square." Kreppel's father had died from a heart attack, and Kreppel was concerned by the sight of a "thin line of elderly men trying to resist a direct attack by a mob of fit young students" during demonstrations at the LSE, where one porter would in fact later collapse and die during a demonstration. Speaight was "somewhat beaten up" touring campuses as an FCS officer; Taylor was physically assaulted at Newcastle in 1969.[11]

Violence was a menacing but infrequent symptom of what Taylor saw as "a much more threatening intolerance in political debate." More worrying, because more pervasive, was the development of a socialist intellectual monopoly at least in the new universities, where both students and the younger academic staff were likely to be left-leaning. Taylor remembered the publications of the free market think tank the Institute of Economic Affairs being banned in Keele university library. Spencer, during his first-year social science course at Southampton, took "a series of programs on Chinese agriculture taught by a young American [who] did not mention the millions of people who were killed during the [Great Leap Forward] – just didn't mention it. We were just taught the straight Maoist line." Like many Conservative activists of his generation, he felt impelled to immerse himself in the texts which inspired his opponents, taunting them with the claim that his Marxism was better than theirs. "You could not survive in British student politics of the late sixties and early seventies without understanding the language of the Left, and so you then invented your own – or developed your own – responses to it and they were not, they were not Thatcherite responses, but they tended

[handwritten margin notes: Joseph was associated w/ the IEA; actually tens of millions]

---

[11] Circular by Ian Taylor to Conservative Association chairmen, February 11, 1969, CPA, CCO 60/2/3.

to be on what we would now call the liberal wing of the party: they were internationalist, they were pro-development, they were pro-Europe."

As Spencer suggested, the Conservatism that emerged was generally not "Thatcherite," even in the economic sphere. To take one example, despite the salience nationally of the trade union issue in 1968–1969, neither in the interviews nor in the archival material does union power emerge as a pressing concern. "We would have been interested in that," Taylor explained, "but... I don't know that it was [our] essential focus. I think the real debate was more about the state." The state that worried them, though, was the interventionist state rather than the welfare state. Taylor felt that "Wilson was increasingly tending to put the emphasis on that the state was a virtuous being that could actually solve... problems." Mountford likewise "saw the Labour Party as a party of the state, that was interested in enlarging the state. I was firmly against nationalization of the utilities and so on." Even Kreppel, who of all the interviewees displayed the greatest commitment to economic liberalism, did not reject the welfare state. He had worked with Madsen Pirie, future founder of the free-market Adam Smith Institute, during the 1964 campaign and was attracted by the economic arguments of Enoch Powell, who, from the early 1950s, had advocated constraining the interventionist state and reducing the burden of personal taxation.[12] "I loved the beauty of [Powell's] logic," Kreppel recalled, "the radicalism of his thinking, and already by the age of sixteen in '64 I was hooked" – but he would not jettison the state's welfare role. He summarized his own position as "socially concerned and economically hard-headed." Taylor remembered defending the morality of taxation in a debate, arguing that "there was a moral purpose to taxation up to a certain point... because the state had a role to assist people who could not in various aspects of their lives, assist themselves." Mountford owed his survival from life-threatening illness in infancy to the National Health Service (NHS); his parents could not have afforded private medicine. This was a generation that had been nurtured by the welfare state.

Speaight took the existence of the welfare state "as read. I felt no sympathy with the libertarian right." In fact, the distinction between "wets" and "dries" over economic doctrine, which would become familiar during the years of Margaret Thatcher, does not adequately describe the contours of student Conservatism in the late 1960s. For much of the

[12] Simon Heffer, *Like The Roman: The Life of Enoch Powell* (London, 1998), 154–155, 191, etc.; Robert Shepherd, *Enoch Powell: A Biography* (London, 1996), 123, 375–376, etc.

The social market or moderate neoliberalism of the West Germans is not the virtually only...

statist
ucism
coalescic
in
the US

decade, the Conservative student right advocated Powell's economic liberalism. Powell enjoyed speaking to students, and the national party had been tacitly content for him to fly the flag on campus. Concerned that the party's backwoodsmen might suffer intellectual humiliation at the hands of a critical student audience, Conservative Central Office stressed that "speakers with a fairly high intellectual calibre are essential for University meetings. Not all M.P.s are suitable and many candidates are highly unsuitable."[13] Powell would fight his intellectual corner with anyone, of course, and according to his first biographer, he "won fervent admirers" among "the politically articulate young, particularly in the universities." The St. Andrews students who distributed car stickers claiming that "Enoch Talks Sense" did so on the strength of "his advocacy of laissez-faire principles and his fiercely ironic denunciations of bureaucracy" before Powell achieved fame as the advocate of immigration control.[14]

In his "Rivers of Blood" speech (April 1968), Powell warned that current levels of Commonwealth immigration would erode national identity and bring the kind of racial conflict already evident in the United States to the streets of Britain.[15] This one speech changed the tone of right-wing Conservative discourse in the universities as elsewhere. For Spencer, Powell was an "extraordinary man, but poisonous in terms of my own generation." His speech certainly had a polarizing effect. There was no necessary connection between the intellectual case for economic liberalism and the often emotive arguments for immigration restriction: many students who had been attracted by Powell's economic case were alienated by his arguments on race. Kreppel, previously an admirer, was shocked by the speech, which dispelled his earlier qualms about race relations legislation: "I formed the view then that sometimes legislation isn't there just to punish, it's there to make a declaration on the part of the state and make some things that should be unacceptable unacceptable." In 1969, he would write to *The Times* that "when Mr Powell makes speeches which he knows will be seized on by the prejudiced and intolerant... then he shows that it is he himself who is the 'threat to our national identity.'"[16] Mountford "just didn't care for the language" of the speech: "I thought it was painting an extreme case that was... likely

13 Maurice Chandler, "The Conservative Party and the Universities," undated (1966?), paper in the file "Links with the Universities," CPA, CRD 3/35/5.
14 T. E. Utley, *Enoch Powell: The Man and His Thinking* (London, 1968), 42.
15 Camilla Schofield, *Enoch Powell and the Making of Postcolonial Britain* (Cambridge, 2013), 208ff.
16 Stephen Kreppel et al., "Divisive Theme," *The Times*, June 12, 1969.

to bring about more tension . . . I certainly didn't think that it was the job
of senior politicians to make inflammatory speeches."

After April 1968, economic liberalism became more muted in Tory
student circles, and the nationalist right, emboldened by Powell's success
in reshaping the political agenda, became more confident. In that month,
a "small but vocal" group of Glasgow University students resolved to
affiliate to the far-right National Front, advocating a "ban on Afro-Asian
immigration, a resumption of trade with Rhodesia and South Africa,
the restoration of capital and corporal punishment, and a foreign policy
of opposition both to Communism and to US economic domination."[17]
Kreppel was disturbed by the emergence of National Front groups in
Kings College London, University College London, and the LSE, writing
in 1968 that: "we are now seeing the tactics of the left reproduced on the
right. This is worrying and it will get worse."[18] In reality, the nationalist
right remained a minority and the racist right a small minority in the
FCS, whose student electorate regularly reinforced liberal control of the
executive and of the principal federation offices, but the far right remained
vocal. Motions proposed for the federation's 1969 conference included
six calling for support for U.S. and South Vietnamese forces in Vietnam
(one of which proposed sending British troops there), four calling for
the recognition of Rhodesia, and two advocating the sale of arms to
apartheid South Africa.[19] Taylor felt it necessary to warn the FCS in his
1969 Annual Report of the dangers of "sinking into a non-intellectual
Right-wing extremism" in response to the dominance of the far left.[20]

"We were fighting that battle on the right as well as facing up to the
socialists," Mountford recalled. "That battle on the right" was, in the late
1960s, increasingly a contest between nationalism and internationalism,
and if any one feature defines the liberal Conservative students of this
period, it was their eagerness to look beyond Britain's shores to reinforce
democratic values in the Cold War world. The tensions that this caused
were doubtless heightened by the fact that they tended to look not to the
United States as a democratic role model but to Europe, already anathema
to the Tory right. Five years earlier, at the height of enthusiasm for the
Kennedy presidency, they might have become Atlanticists, but by 1968
it had become difficult to express unalloyed enthusiasm for the United

[17] Hoefferle, *British Student Activism*, 119.
[18] Stephen Kreppel, FCS S.E. Region Report, CPA, CCO 60/2/3.
[19] Program for the FCS Annual Conference, University of Surrey, March 23–26, 1969, in
    "FCS Conferences, 1966–70," CPA, Box 107.
[20] Ian Taylor, Chairman's Annual Report, 1969, CPA, Box 107.

States. In a youthful speech to the national party conference, Mountford said, "I'd visited America – I loved it, but I didn't want to be the fifty-first state." On the litmus issue of Vietnam, the impression given is one of agnosticism. There was no sympathy for the Hanoi regime and little sign of the outrage at American actions widely voiced on the left, but there was little confidence that the United States could win the war. A quarter of LSE Conservatives had opposed the U.S. involvement in Vietnam in 1967, a figure that is likely to have risen after the Tet offensive and the My Lai massacre in the early months of 1968 raised disconcerting questions about both American conduct and the prospect of victory.[21] Speaight thought it "a deeply misguided engagement." Mountford "thought that the Americans were making a mess of it, diplomatically as well as militarily," and considered carpet bombing and Agent Orange "horrible": "it didn't in itself worry me terribly if Vietnam was communist. I guess I thought that that wouldn't survive for ever anyway."

Rather than Vietnam, they saw Western Europe as the principal Cold War theater. Traveling in Cold War Europe was for the politically aware young Conservative the equivalent of the pilgrimage to Yugoslavia or Cuba for the left-wing teenager. European travel brought them physically closer to the Eastern bloc, instilling a greater awareness of Soviet power than was general in Britain. Baldry was in West Germany at the time of the Soviet invasion of Czechoslovakia in August 1968 and remembered being horrified by the West's inability to counter it. The more durable effect, though, was to promote contact with young conservatives on the Continent. Baldry describes center-right student politics at the time as being "quite well networked and established across Europe" as different national groups were drawn together by a shared antagonism to the radical left. All seven interviewees were active in the International Christian Democratic and Conservative Students' Union (rebranded as the European Union of Conservative and Christian Democrat Students – ECCS – in 1970), which aimed to create "a strong student grouping to promote university reforms and to counter revolutionary Left-Wing activities in European universities."[22] Taylor became its first British chairman in 1969, and Spencer would follow him in 1972. They became confrères of such rising young talents as Volker Rühe, the future German defense

[handwritten margin note: Note that Heath made no move to change Wilson's stance on Vietnam]

[21] Blackstone et al., *Students in Conflict*, 43.

[22] Ian Taylor, "Memorandum on the Organisation," undated (1969), in CPA, CCO 3/7/19. I am most grateful to Martina Steber for this reference and those that follow from this file.

(1992-99)　　　　　C2005-17)

minister, and Norbert Lammert, future president of the Bundestag, and, (1991-94) (2006-14) above all, of Carl Bildt, future prime minister and foreign minister of Sweden, who exercised a particular magnetism. Speaight similarly spent much time with young German conservatives whose experience of life in the shadow of Soviet power underpinned their views, and he traveled to Berlin to inspect the Wall. Spencer even accompanied Bildt on a risky trip to Budapest to distribute leaflets in the mid-1970s, driven by the feeling that "we wanted our Europe back."

Europe provided new horizons. As Taylor recalled, "you realize there are common threads and you . . . you have a sense of identification with other nations." Kreppel remembered discovering different speaking and debating cultures to those he had encountered in Britain, while Spencer found that he "developed a disdain, probably unjustified, for British politics: you know, the binary approach – left/right, black/white, government/opposition – didn't suit my particular cast of mind, whereas Europe was where you were building something new, where nobody had a majority." Of course, such open-mindedness might not obliterate policy differences within conservatism. Kreppel found on attending a conference in West Germany that he was "quite alienated from the Christian Democrats, who seemed to have unreconstructed left-wing views of economics and business which I thought were just nonsense." For Speaight, however, Christian Democracy

seemed to me to be a most admirable movement: they were the third thing. In countries like Italy, where there were Fascists and Communists, the Christian Democrats were the third thing, and clearly the decent thing, and the movement which Adenauer in Germany, De Gasperi in Italy were part of, together with people like Monnet and Robert Schumann – these people were all to a greater or a lesser extent influenced by the notion that a united Europe was a way of building a society that was decent but also was inspired by Christian values.

A practicing Catholic, Speaight identified more than the other interviewees with the religious dimension of European conservatism. Kreppel did not "think I ever really thought about this religion thing – it just didn't figure," which was probably more typical of British attitudes. Spencer acknowledged at the time that "the name 'Christian Democrat' suggests the involvement of religion in politics to an extent that causes unease to British and Scandinavian ears."[23] To generalize, the British Conservatives had least to do with Gaullists and other nationalist groups (who

[23] Tom Spencer, "Memorandum on the Name 'Conservative,'" December 26, 1971, CPA, CCO 3/7/19.

in any case often stood aside from pan-European movements) and were closest to the Scandinavians, and particularly to the Swedish Moderates (whom Speaight found "tremendously impressive"). Degrees of affinity varied, but the context has to be kept in view. Many of the continental students in ECCS had encountered variants of student Marxism more militant and aggressive than anything to be found in Britain. This enhanced the incentive to forge pan-European links between liberal conservatives and diminished the temptations of sectarianism. Spencer, as president of ECCS, pushed forward the creation of the European Democratic Party (EDP), which he envisaged as "one group [which] would reflect the convergence of the three lines of non-socialist thought in European politics, namely, Liberalism, Conservatism and Christian Democracy."[24] Kreppel enjoyed meeting "excellent people from all over Europe" in ECCS, drawn from, for example, the Austrian People's Party, the Young Giscardiens in France, the Scandinavian Moderates, and Christian Democrats from West Germany and even, clandestinely, from Franco's Spain. He is "still proud" of his own part in the creation of the EDP – "of the fact that I did manage to drive through . . . the first ever European political party, albeit a student one" when he helped persuade ECCS to adopt the objective of acting as a European party: "I proposed, quite simply, that it adopt a United Europe as its purpose."

In Baldry's view, "we on the center-right considered ourselves to be in a very exciting and interesting place, because here was the enlargement of Europe." Spencer described sitting down with Carl Bildt in 1974 and estimating on the back of an envelope when the countries of Eastern Europe would join the European Economic Community (EEC). As conscious as anyone of the opportunities opening up for those of his age in the late 1960s, Spencer saw "Europe" as part of that widening of horizons that his generation enjoyed: "we benefited from a high-quality free education, a breaking down of the social mores that would have formerly constrained our generation, a sexual liberation supported by a particular window of medications and a growing institution on our doorstep of the European Union [sic] that . . . so, you know, we are the lucky generation." He maintains that "my generation were ahead of the adult parties [on European integration] because we had been doing it at student level for two or three years." Enthusiasm for British membership of the EEC followed naturally. Taylor, Speaight, and Mountford had supported EEC

[24] Tom Spencer, "The Concept of a European Democratic Party – a Proposal for ECCS Action," May 26, 1972, CPA, CCO 3/7/19.

entry before university – in Mountford's case, from the time of Britain's first application for membership in 1961–1963. He was chiefly motivated by the freeing up of markets, but he was the only one of the interviewees to couch his Europhilia primarily in economic terms. Spencer, who became vice president of the Young European Federalists, advocated federalism (in the proper sense of the term) because "I am deeply suspicious of the concentration of power, whether that's fascist power or communist power, and that has remained with me." "As a democrat," Kreppel "hoped to see a European Parliament evolve, with European parties that straddled nations." Baldry believed that pan-European institutions would enable Europe's Conservatives to "face down the Warsaw Pact in a battle of ideas." Taylor "believed profoundly – and still do[es] – in the virtues of European union." He felt "huge frustration" at the small-mindedness of British attitudes, which he contrasted with the "generosity of political spirit" displayed by the architects of European integration: "bear in mind that I was born in 1945."

* * *

Speaight was struck by a poster issued by the Swedish Moderate Party that read: "There are really only two alternatives, and if you don't agree with Marx there's only one." On his prompting, the Federation of Conservative Students issued a poster with the same message. This approach echoed Taylor's tactics as FCS chairman in 1968–1969. As he put it to the parliamentary select committee investigating student unrest in 1969: "in student politics today, the traditional party labels are not entirely relevant. Simplifying matters, the division comes between Moderates (Tory and Labour supporters) and Extremists (Revolutionary Socialists). The distinction between these politically active groups lies in the desires of the former to improve the present system, and the determination of the latter to sweep it away."[25] In various memoranda that he penned as FCS chairman, he underlined the implications of the red base strategy adopted by some student militants: "the heroes of this organised few are Che Guevara and Stokely Carmichael, or more truthfully, Mao Tse Tung. The belief is in a continuous revolution against a system which is typified by consensus politics and an uncritical application of bureaucracy. There

[25] "Student Relationships in Universities and Colleges, Memorandum by the Federation of Conservative Students," House of Commons Papers, 1968–9 (449-ii), Report from the Select Committee on Education and Science, Session 1968–9, *Student Relations* (7 vols., 1969), 2:325.

can be no advance in university conditions without a change in society..."[26]

There was much that was tactical about this. With little chance that Conservatives could form an independent majority in radical student unions, mobilization depended upon compromise with other non-Marxist groups. Or as Taylor put it in 1969, "this is a political battle to ensure that weak liberals do not give misguided support to the Left. It is not one in which one can display pristine political virtues, which influence few but the converted."[27] He acknowledges having colluded with Geoff Martin, Labour president of the National Union of Students from 1966–1968, to marginalize the Marxist-dominated Radical Student Alliance, while Spencer cooperated with Martin's successor, the future Labour minister Jack Straw, (1969-71) in attempts to create a national Registrar of Student Unions to regulate student bodies receiving public funds.

That said, the heavy-handed response of most university authorities to almost any sign of student discontent did give cause for concern. Taylor lobbied Geoffrey Rippon, then shadow housing spokesman, on the paucity and squalid condition of much student housing, while Watherston promoted an organization – Student Co-operative Dwellings – designed to provide purpose-built student accommodation.[28] The FCS Memorandum for the parliamentary Select Committee on Education and Science's investigation into student relations in the spring of 1969 stressed the Federation's support for student participation in university governance: "if the University/College is to be a community, it is essential that students are involved in decisions."[29] Taylor's contempt for the arbitrary disciplinary action taken by university authorities, and for their underlying assumption that students should be seen but not heard, was evident in the interview: "This new body of students needed to have a sense of expression, and the old, patronizing university systems, which is 'you're very lucky to be here – shut up and go away and study' – that wasn't acceptable. We were the new generation, we were the leading lights of the sixties, and sod you – we were going to have our say."

What this meant, to the surprise of mainstream Conservative opinion, was that the FCS supported non-violent direct action where university authorities appeared intransigent in their response to student complaints

[margin annotations: "This is a muddled contrast from British party politics elsewhere" and "Straw went to Leeds"; "Rippon was environment secretary C1972-74 !"]

---

[26] Taylor, "Student Power."
[27] Taylor, Chairman's Annual Report, undated (1969), CPA, Box 107.
[28] Prospectus included with the letter from John Hands, Executive Director Student Co-operative Dwellings, to Geoffrey Johnson Smith, February 4, 1969, CPA, CCO 60/2/3.
[29] "Student Relationships in Universities and Colleges," 2:325.

or arbitrary in their treatment of dissidents – a response similar to that which Anna von der Goltz has described amongst West German Christian Democrat students.[30] Taylor joined in a sit-in at Birmingham demanding student representation on university committees, noting that the action had the support of the vast majority of the students: "unless we publicly made a stand to show that we mean what we say, there was a risk of becoming irrelevant within student politics." Watherston likewise actually proposed the motion in the LSE student union for the sit-in and lecture boycott of 1967, to protest against the disciplining of David Adelstein and Marshall Bloom, ringleaders of the 1967 disturbances at the School.[31] He sought to harness "a genuine feeling among the student body that this had been unfair and that they shouldn't have been penalized in the way they were... The Governors needed to take it on board." As Kreppel, also at the LSE, put it: "I think that what we were saying as our generation was: 'we don't reject the notion of authority – that would be fatuous – but we reject the notion of automatic authority. Authority must justify itself.'"

* * *

Such actions might have posed a problem for the party's top brass. Few grassroots Conservatives entertained any sympathy for student protest, whether violent or non-violent. The Birmingham sit-in had provoked a censorious editorial in *The Times* entitled "Time for Discipline,"[32] and Taylor's intervention in support of the protesting students was criticized by local Conservatives and, apparently, by the university's Conservative Association.[33] In the event, though, Geoffrey Johnson Smith, the party vice chairman dealing directly with the FCS, supported Taylor and his tactics. His stance reflected a change of approach in Central Office to the questions posed by the new universities.

The Conservative Party's immediate response to university expansion reflected a concern arising from its election defeats in 1964 and 1966 – that the party was perceived to be out of touch and, bluntly, unfashionable, and that there was an urgent "need, similar to that which

[30] Anna von der Goltz, "A Polarised Generation? Conservative Students and West Germany's '1968,'" in Anna von der Goltz, ed., *"Talkin' 'Bout My Generation": Conflicts of Generation Building and Europe's "1968"*(Göttingen, 2011), 207–208.

[31] Colin Crouch, *The Student Revolt* (London, 1970), 52; Hoefferle, *British Student Activism*, 48.

[32] *The Times*, December 3, 1968.

[33] Douglas Davis, chairman, Warwick and Leamington Spa Conservative Association, to Dudley Smith, MP, December 9, 1968, CPA, CCO 60/2/2.

existed in the late 1940s, for the Conservative Party to be made 'intellectually respectable.'"[34] This was taken to demand less a direct appeal to students than an effort to cultivate sympathetic academic opinion. If it was troubling that prominent members of the Labour government with [Foreign secretary (1976-77)] an academic past, like Richard Crossman, Anthony Crosland, and Wilson himself, felt comfortable in Oxbridge senior common rooms, it was far more alarming that the cohort of young lecturers recruited en masse into the new universities appeared overwhelmingly left wing. A scan of the new universities in November 1964 had revealed that "at Sussex all the academic staff are left-wing; at Lancaster they are reported to be on the Left; at York the lecturers are very Left and the head of the Political Department was a Labour candidate; at Essex most of the lecturers are left-wing."[35]

[chair of the 1922 Committee (2001-10)]

In 1965–1966, Michael Spicer, a recent Cambridge graduate working at Central Office, toured the expanded university sector to assess Conservative prospects. His findings suggested that the party's image problem on campus was unaffected by the election of the "modernizing" Edward Heath as leader in 1965, [(1965-75)] and that "the Socialists appear to have most academics on their side . . . largely because the Labour Party has systematically made it its business to get to know academics whereas the Conservative Party has not."[36] He advocated cultivating sympathetic academics in order to influence an electorate thought to be "increasingly motivated by a sense of 'deference' to expertise/intellectual accomplishment";[37] little attention was paid to the students themselves. Some feared that university Conservative associations were politically inert, primarily social organizations: Heath himself initially questioned student demands for participation in university governance on the grounds that "in his day [Heath never married] all students wanted to do was punt up the river with a girl."[38] With the growing evidence of student militancy from 1966 onwards, however, and in the light of the evidence from Paris in May 1968 that student activism could threaten public order and established authority, it became more difficult to speak over students' heads.

34 Michael Spicer, Memorandum, May 3, 1966, "Links with the Universities. Where now?" CPA, CRD 3/35/5.
35 Barbara Turner to Sir Michael Fraser, November 26, 1964, "Federation of University Conservative and Unionist Associations," CPA, CRD 3/35/5.
36 M. Spicer, Report no. 4, Edinburgh, Glasgow, Strathclyde, and Aberdeen, May 4, 1966, CPA, CRD 3/35/5. His informant was the economic historian A. J. Youngson.
37 Spicer, "Links with the Universities."
38 D. J. May, "Day out at the Albany," *Mercury: The Communications Letter of the Federation of Conservative Students*, undated (October 1968?), in CPA, CCO 60/2/2.

The academics who were lobbied in the hope of giving the party intellectual weight with the wider public, including such high Tories as Maurice Cowling, Robert Blake, and Hugh Trevor-Roper, would have been unlikely to appeal to any late 1960s student who was not already a committed Conservative. Most Conservative academics, in fact, were instinctively inclined to support university authorities in the face of student protest. Following the escalation of student militancy in 1967–1968, however, Johnson Smith and the shadow education secretary, Sir Edward Boyle, accepted in principle Taylor's argument that uncritical support of the authorities would drive an already left-leaning student population into the arms of the militants. The party leader Edward Heath, though often socially awkward, was, as Spencer recalled, "comfortable with bright young people." During his leadership, the FCS was cultivated in the hope of enhancing the party's appeal to the young. Its cordial relationship with the national party leadership contrasted, as Taylor pointed out, with "the distant relations of the Socialist and Liberal students with their parties."[39] Almost every debate at the annual party conference had an FCS speaker, and FCS and Young Conservative members were prominent on the conference platform. The FCS had its own office in the Conservative Central Office building. As chairman in 1970–1971, Mountford had easy access to the party's administration. "They saw us I suppose in two ways," he recalled, "firstly as a source of talent and, secondly, they wanted to be able to show the world the full involvement of young people."

Central Office was obviously aware during the late 1960s that the voting age would likely soon be lowered from twenty-one to eighteen (as indeed happened in 1969, enabling large numbers of students to register to vote in the 1970 general election). It probably also expected the expansion of higher education to allow the FCS to play the role previously played by the Oxbridge associations of nurturing the party's future leadership. As John Wilkinson, the organization's secretary, put it to Johnson Smith in March 1968, the federation looked to provide "help and guidance to those who should eventually occupy positions of authority and responsibility in society and it is to be hoped in the Conservative Party, to develop their political interests and talents to the full. This is a wise policy and the real *raison d'être* of F.C.S."[40]

This was a reasonable hope, but for this generation of Tory student leaders it proved to be misplaced. No Tory 68er would make the Cabinet.

[handwritten margin note:] William Hague made his political start in something like this manner.

---

[39] Taylor, "Student Power."
[40] John Wilkinson to Geoffrey Johnson Smith, March 28, 1968, CPA, CCO 60/2/2.

Of the interviewees, only Baldry and Taylor would get to Westminster –
and only in 1983 and 1987, respectively. Speaight felt that a lengthy
apprenticeship spent in voluntary political work and fighting "a hopeless
seat in Wales or something like that" would jeopardize his intended
legal career: he is now a distinguished barrister and Queen's Counsel.
Watherston's previously dormant allegiance to the Church of England
was activated by a "Christian conversion, if you like" in 1973. He stood
as a Tory candidate in February 1974, but "I just felt I . . . I don't want to
tell people to vote Conservative – I want to tell people to be compassionate
and take responsibility, and so I remember going to a selection board for
another seat in 1975, and, when I'd given my speech I realized it was
much more like a sermon than it was a political speech." He has been a
priest in a deprived area of East London for more than thirty-five years.
Spencer had campaigned in the early 1970s for a directly elected European
parliament; he would be elected to Strasbourg in the first direct elections
in 1979 and serve as an MEP for twenty years. Mountford, after working
for Heath in the 1970 general election, was invited to contest the safe Tory
seat of Bexleyheath in February 1974 but declined in order to pursue the
City career that he had envisaged for himself as a student. Kreppel worked
in the Conservative Research Department during his twenties, but he was
sufficiently self-aware to decide at the age of twenty-eight that a decade
in politics had made him "a very narrow person." At that point, in the
mid-1970s, "I felt that my main motivations had been satisfied. We were
in the European Union, things were going well, race relations was no
longer such an issue, everything was going smoothly."

Kreppel intended to return to politics after ten or fifteen years in the
outside world, but by then the Tory Party had changed radically. "Under
Thatcher there were times when I wanted to go back and I should have
gone back, and I just didn't." The abrasive tone of Thatcherite Conservatism after 1975 – its apparent contempt for the ethos of the welfare
state, its insular nationalism, its increasingly strident hostility toward
European institutions – would all prove uncongenial to the student leaders of the late 1960s. All seven interviewees defined themselves as liberal
Conservatives and none appeared anxious to repent. Taylor acknowledged that he was a Heathite in the 1960s "and I've remained so . . . I'm
still left wing – by modern Tory standards very left wing." Speaight
sees himself as "a sort of left-wing Conservative" and "to this day a
Christian Democrat." Their liberal views made them vulnerable to the
grassroots fundamentalism that welled up in the party in the mid-1970s.
Baldry remembers a difficult interview with a constituency party selection

committee at Willesden in 1974 that ended with him telling the assembled activists, "well, thank you very much for seeing me but, you know, either I am in the wrong party or... or you're in the wrong party – but we're certainly not in the same party." He did not gain the nomination.

In a sense, David Howell's 1965 assumption about the political influence of the enlarged university sector proved incorrect. The leaders of the Thatcher revolution had their own gurus in Friedrich Hayek and the monetarists, and they did not seek guidance from a young clerisy. The Heathite students of the late 1960s were perhaps also disadvantaged by their focus on what Taylor called "the student-type analytical issues," meaning large themes like the individual's relation to the state or Britain's place in a federal Europe. The domestic economic issues that would drive Thatcherism – inflation, taxation, the power of the unions – concerned them to varying degrees but were not normally uppermost in their minds. They ranged in attitude from Speaight, who believed that "Keynesian economic policies had been proved to work," to Kreppel, convinced by Powell's economic logic, but none welcomed the economistic emphasis within Thatcherism. Kreppel had indeed rejected the conservatism practiced by the Republican Party in the United States because it lacked a social dimension: "Republicanism seems to me to be about making business work and hoping that everything else will follow," while Speaight feared "a sort of Poujadiste, small business self-interest that was affecting the Conservatives" and "suspected the motives of those who wanted to move to a more free market approach." Spencer, with a Whiggish contempt for economic liberalism, was dismayed to encounter the first signs of the monetarist revolution when speaking to a university Conservative Association in 1972: "American money [had] moved in and said 'you remember all that Marxist rubbish? The real response to that is to be more ideological than the Left, and here is a whole new series of ideologies you can have – Austrian economists...'" He "hated" the party's change of direction "because I am a child of that postwar consensus, Butskellism, and so on." Still more tellingly, perhaps, Edward Heath's deposition in 1975 heralded the party's protracted self-detachment from Europe, nullifying what had previously appeared to be the seven interviewees' greatest asset – their familiarity with many of the rising stars of European conservatism.[41] Growing ideological discomfort was accentuated by unease at the tone of Thatcherite politics. Mountford had met Thatcher

----

[41] Baldry suggested plausibly that "we in student politics had better contacts, better connections [in Europe], than those in the senior Party."

[handwritten margin note, left side:] Or that those who offer will attract no sympathy

[handwritten margin note, lower left:] They represent a Heathite dead-ender — the mid 70s

(handwritten: C1970-74)

in 1970–1971, when she was Heath's education secretary and he was FCS chairman, but he "didn't actually like her very much . . . I didn't care for her style very much." Watherston had felt the doubts about politics as a vocation that would lead him to train for the ministry before Thatcher became leader in February 1975, but "I think the Thatcher revolution meant that the Conservatives went in a direction that I wouldn't have been very happy about." Clearly, Thatcher's Conservative Party would never be a comfortable home for liberal internationalist Europhiles. Kreppel feels that "the Conservative Party by the mid-seventies, certainly by the eighties, was becoming narrower and narrower . . . and it's just a trend that has continued." He would even vote Labour in 1997 in the belief that Tony Blair was more likely than John Major to place Britain at the heart of the European Union. *(handwritten: C1997-2009) (handwritten: C1990-97)*

* * *

The dominant narrative of Thatcherism has tended to treat Thatcher's opponents within the party as somewhat passé figures clinging to a tainted consensus politics – tainted because it presumed acceptance of a postwar settlement largely devised by their opponents. Their Europhilia was also depicted as generational, reflecting the wish of those who had served in 1939–1945 to prevent another European war – a noble sentiment, it was acknowledged, but also rather dated by the 1980s and insufficient to warrant the loss of sovereignty that EEC membership demanded. Regardless of whether this stereotype applied to the grandees slain by Thatcher in and after 1981, this chapter has argued that there was a younger generation of liberal Conservatives emerging in the universities in the late 1960s whose views were forged by the sharp-edged student politics of the time. Conflict with both the Marxist left and the nationalist right on campus instilled in them an internationalist liberal Conservatism, which evolved naturally into a conviction that European cooperation and integration could best protect democratic values in the Cold War world. They sought to further this belief by forging links with their equivalents on the Continent, which promised to place Britain, if not at the heart of Europe, at least at the heart of European Conservatism in years to come. If that initiative now looks as evanescent as the campus Marxism that they challenged – and a good deal less familiar – that is a measure of how comprehensively the party was Thatcherized after 1975.

(handwritten margin note: Heath served, Thatcher was of Oxford)

4

A Vocal Minority

Student Activism of the Center-Right and West Germany's 1968

Anna von der Goltz

The late 1960s saw the most significant expressions of political dissent by West Germany's young elites after 1945. Students demanded fundamental reforms in the higher education system, marched against the planned emergency legislation of the "Grand Coalition" of Christian Democrats and Social Democrats, fervently criticized the U.S.-led war in Vietnam, and attacked the remnants of Nazi authoritarianism in German political culture. Radical left-wing activists such as Rudi Dutschke were household names at the time.[1] According to one of the numerous opinion polls conducted to gauge the phenomenon of "student unrest," 98 percent of university students knew who Dutschke was in 1968.[2]

Student activists of the center-right were far less famous and rarely graced the covers of national news magazines, but they, too, mobilized in considerable numbers in this period. As in the United States, where conservative student groups such as the Young Americans for Freedom (YAF) successfully built "majority coalitions" of anti-radical students, a number of center-right student groups including the Christian Democratic student organization Ring Christlich Demokratischer Studenten (RCDS) and the newly created Deutsche Studentenunion (DSU) rallied to meet an

---

[1] Dutschke was a leading figure in the Socialist German Students League (Sozialistischer Deutscher Studentenbund, or SDS), which initiated many of the largest and most widely reported student protest actions in the Federal Republic. The group had close ties to the American group Students for a Democratic Society (SDS).

[2] See the report on a poll conducted by the EMNID institute compiled by the Federal Government's Press and Information Office, February 19, 1968, Bundesarchiv, Koblenz (hereafter BAK), N1229/213. The results were published in *Der Spiegel*, no. 8 (February 19, 1968).

increasingly vocal challenge from the left.[3] This chapter investigates West German student activism on the center-right at a time when the radical left began to question the very foundations of the Federal Republic and defied "the Establishment" in highly visible and provocative ways. It seeks to show that, much like in the United States where the mobilization of left-wing students in the 1960s went hand in hand with an increase in conservative campus activism at the grassroots, center-right students were an integral part of the broader political upheaval that characterized the 1960s and 1970s in West Germany.

Students who participated in political student groups constituted only about 5 percent of the West German student population. But many more were drawn into the protests: three quarters of students welcomed student demonstrations, and 36 percent had taken part in a political demonstration by 1968.[4] Although the revolutionary left never represented the majority of student opinion – only 27 percent reported that they agreed with Dutschke and 44 percent rejected his stance while 36 percent named former Christian Democratic Chancellor Konrad Adenauer as their greatest role model[5] – the student body was generally left-leaning. In 1967, 48 percent of all West German students said that they supported the Social Democrats (SPD) and only 26 percent the Christian Democrats (CDU/CSU). Student support for the Christian Democrats had dropped to 14 percent by 1973–1974 but then rose to 21 percent during the years that followed.[6] Taking their cue from U.S. President Richard Nixon, center-right students cast themselves as representatives of the silent majority marginalized by a sensation-seeking press. They saw it as their task to keep a "small group of revolutionary idiots from acting in … [their] name."[7] Their claim to speak for the majority, however, was true only insofar as most West German students did not support the revolutionary goals of the radical left.

---

[3] Gregory L. Schneider, *Cadres for Conservatism: Young Americans for Freedom and the Rise of the Contemporary Right* (New York, 1999), 113–121.

[4] See the analysis of a poll of more than 3,000 students conducted by Rudolf Wildenmann, April 26, 1968, BAK, B138/10262; and the report about the aforementioned EMNID poll (note 2).

[5] See the report on the EMNID poll cited in note 2.

[6] See the analysis of the Wildenmann poll cited in note 4; and the comparative analysis of eight different polls conducted by the Federal Ministry of Education and Scholarship, October 14, 1976, BAK, B138/33393.

[7] The RCDS's self-description in *Dialog*, no. 4, n.d., Archiv der Außerparlamentarischen Opposition, Berlin (hereafter ArchAPO), RCDS, file: RCDS-Brief; HDSU leaflet, July 1969, ArchAPO, SDS, file "Konter-Revolutionäre I."

Even if they could not count on their peers' whole-hearted backing, a vocal minority of center-right students formed umbrella organizations with a lively associational culture, contributed to the political debate in significant ways, and achieved considerable successes in student council elections from Kiel to Munich.[8] And yet, in contrast to their American counterparts, they have received little scholarly attention.[9] The few works that have paid attention to how West German conservatives responded to the challenges of 1968 typically focus on national party politics, debates between leading intellectuals, and broader ideological realignments on the right.[10] Such debates are useful windows onto the contested nature of democracy in West Germany – in a republic that had endured a series of fierce public debates as it worked to build a stable democratic order on the ashes of the Nazi regime.[11] This chapter builds on this research but shifts

[handwritten margin note: prior to which the CDU and CSU were utterly inaccessible]

In the winter semester of 1968/1969, for instance, the RCDS and/or DSU gained the largest number of seats in Cologne, Bonn, Frankfurt, Erlangen-Nürnberg, Giessen, Kiel, Mainz, and Regensburg. Westdeutsche Rektorenkonferenz, ed., *Übersicht über die Ergebnisse der Wahlen zu den Studentenvertretungen* (Bonn, 1968–1984). I am grateful to Jeffrey Herf for making this out-of-print source available to me.

9 Rebecca E. Klatch, *A Generation Divided: The New Left, the New Right, and the 1960s* (Berkeley, CA, 1997); John A. Andrew III, *The Other Side of the Sixties: Young Americans for Freedom and the Rise of Conservative Politics* (New Brunswick, NJ, 1997); Schneider, *Cadres for Conservatism*; an example of an otherwise exhaustive recent monograph on the Federal Republic that does not touch on center-right activists is Timothy Scott Brown, *West Germany and the Global Sixties* (Cambridge, 2013); exceptions are Massimiliano Livi, Daniel Schmidt, and Michael Sturm, eds., *Die 70er Jahre als schwarzes Jahrzehnt: Politisierungs- und Mobilisierungsprozesse zwischen rechter Mitte und extremer Rechter in Italien und der Bundesrepublik 1967–1982* (Bielefeld, 2010); Olaf Bartz, "Konservative Studenten und die Studentenbewegung: Die 'Kölner Studenten-Union,'" *Westfälische Forschung* 48 (1998): 241–256.

10 Axel Schildt, "Die Kräfte der Gegenreform sind auf breiter Front angetreten. Zur konservativen Tendenzwende in den Siebzigerjahren," *Archiv für Sozialgeschichte* 44 (2004): 449–479; Frank Bösch, "Die Krise als Chance. Die Neuformierung der Christdemokraten in den siebziger Jahren," in Konrad Jarausch, ed., *Das Ende der Zuversicht? Die siebziger Jahre als Geschichte* (Göttingen, 2008), 296–309; Jerry Z. Muller, "German Neoconservatism and the History of the Bonn Republic, 1968 to 1985," *German Politics and Society* 18 (2000): 1–32.

11 Dirk A. Moses, *German Intellectuals and the Nazi Past* (Cambridge, 2006); Jens Hacke, *Philosophie der Bürgerlichkeit: Die liberalkonservative Begründung der Bundesrepublik* (Göttingen, 2006); Dominik Geppert and Jens Hacke, eds., *Streit um den Staat: Intellektuelle Debatten in der Bundesrepublik 1960–1980* (Göttingen, 2008); Nikolai Wehrs, *Der Protest der Professoren: Der "Bund der Freiheit der Wissenschaft" in den 1970er Jahren* (Göttingen, 2014); Sean A. Forner, *German Intellectuals and the Challenge of Democratic Renewal: Culture and Politics after 1945* (Cambridge, 2014); Frank Biess, "Thinking after Hitler: The New Intellectual History of the Federal Republic of Germany," *History and Theory* 51 (2012): 221–245.

the focus from intellectual debates to student activism and mobilization at the grassroots level.

The student groups investigated here mostly shunned the label "conservative," which they considered tainted by its associations with Nazism. Instead, they saw themselves as reasonable "moderates" who defied traditional expectations of deference on the part of the young and believed in a reform of existing institutions but rejected their left-wing peers' calls for more radical change. Their reluctance to embrace conservatism as a political ideology distinguished them markedly from the YAF, who struggled with the radical left on U.S. campuses in the 1960s. Nonetheless, the situation in West Germany was in many respects similar to that in the United States, where "[c]ries for change sounded from both sides of the political spectrum."[12] West German activists of the center-right did not represent a straightforward countermovement to the student left; they did not oppose each and every change envisioned by the so-called extra-parliamentary opposition (Ausserparlamentarische Opposition, or APO), the wide-ranging protest moment that challenged the agenda of the Grand Coalition. Center-right activists were "part of the mix" associated with 1968, *reacting* to the left without necessarily championing a *reactionary* politics.[13] As we will see, only after 1969–1970, in the wake of the APO's disintegration and the turn of a small segment of its members to political violence, did the dividing lines sharpen markedly, pitting students firmly against each other and giving campus politics the feel of an existential struggle over the future of the liberal democratic order.[14]

A Partially Shared Critique and Joint Protests

In the 1960s, young activists of the center-right echoed significant elements of the critique of the postwar status quo – its political stagnation, bureaucratization, and disregard for human needs and individual happiness – that fueled the student protests across Western Europe and the United States. Western European politics of the 1950s and early 1960s were indeed relatively bland, with "gray men in suits" championing a conformist politics of the center ground and often displaying a lack of

---

[12] Andrew, *The Other Side of the Sixties*, 3.
[13] See Lawrence Black's contribution to this volume (chapter 17).
[14] Interestingly, this mirrors the trajectory of YAF's relationship to the radical left, which became much more fraught from 1968 onward. Schneider, *Cadres of Conservatism*, 110–111.

ideological imagination.[15] It was against this background that protests erupted across the Continent. According to a newspaper published by some of the Federal Republic's fraternities, it had been "highly intelligent" people who had "laid bare what is rotten in our social system. We should equally learn to listen to the ugly sounds. [Calling for] 'law and order' cannot be our response... Let us not forget that the radicals are always a mirror, a mirror of the times."[16] Christian Democratic students contended in a similar vein that the political unrest was not solely driven by neo-Marxist radicals but had its roots in the "immobility of state and society that they have uncovered." Repressive methods and a defensive attitude by the universities and other institutions would not calm the waters. "A debate about our future is indispensable," they argued.[17] Their critique of the existing state of affairs, in large part the result of twenty years of Christian Democratic governance, frequently brought Christian Democratic students into disagreement with their mother party. In a political climate ripe with generational conflict and anti-authoritarian sentiments, they charged their party elders with "authoritarian behavior" and declared that they no longer saw themselves as a natural extension of the CDU/CSU.[18]

In 1968, befitting an era that the historian Tony Judt termed "the great age of theory," the RCDS set up a political strategy unit designed to tackle some of the existential questions of modern society in a theoretically informed way.[19] Its members were convinced that the human desire for a meaningful life was at odds with advanced industrial society's quest for rationalization and that politics had failed to provide a "spiritual idea for the individual's role in modern civilization." In their view, the West German postwar status quo, with its short-termism and emphasis on material satisfaction, had neglected basic human desires.[20] Material

[Handwritten margin note: They also demanded more pluralism]

[Handwritten margin note: Attacking excessive materialism is hardly an un-Christian, un-conservative mode of thought]

[15] Martin Conway, "The Rise and Fall of Western Europe's Democratic Age, 1945–1973," *Contemporary European History* 13 (2004): 67–88.
[16] Carl-August Agena, "Bärte, Fahnen und Empörung – oder: Warum sind unsere Freunde so rot?" *Akademische Blätter* 10 (1969): 156.
[17] "Gesellschaftliche Immobilität in der Bundesrepublik," Beschlüsse der 18. Ord. Bundesversammlung 28.2.-3.3.1968, Archiv für christlich-demokratische Politik, Sankt Augustin (hereafter ACDP), 4/6/9.
[18] "Die jungen linken Christdemokraten," *Bonner Rundschau*, April 27, 1968; "Ein Hauch von APO in der CSU," *Münchner Merkur*, December 11, 1969.
[19] Tony Judt, *Postwar: A History of Europe since 1945* (London, 2005), 398; see also Lawrence Black's essay in this volume (chapter 17); "Bericht des Bundesvorstandes über seine Arbeit im SS 1968," ACDP, 4/6/13.
[20] Peter Radunski, "Zum Selbstverständnis des RCDS," Rednerdienst, no. 1 (September 1968), ACDP, 4/6/42/2.

wealth could at best be an interim goal; Western societies needed "real utopias" and fresh ideas.[21]   → *Liberal democracy does not yet end-goals, not collectively*

Center-right students did not, of course, buy entirely into Marxist-inspired critiques of the "affluent society."[22] The RCDS nevertheless ploughed through the theoretical tomes of the German émigré philosopher Herbert Marcuse – the Nestor of the transatlantic New Left – and found his analysis "sharp and in many ways extremely accurate."[23] But they were much less convinced by his proposals for transforming society. They feared that relying on an avant-garde of young intellectuals, who would supposedly help to cure people of their "false needs," would lead *Something that still reminds* to an "educational dictatorship." People could not be turned into "free, conscious, and democratic" citizens by force, they contended.[24]

Center-right students found a much more compelling vision of a more egalitarian and open society in Ralf Dahrendorf's influential *Society and Democracy in Germany*.[25] The liberal sociologist argued that the recent course of German history had been shaped by a structural deficit of democracy. Although political institutions had been formally democratized after 1945, West German culture and society had not yet caught up. Authoritarian tendencies prevailed, according to Dahrendorf, in the family and in most areas of public life, particularly educational institutions. The democratization of private and public institutions of socialization *The New Left demanded exactly this, although also advocated advocates of the abolition of capitalism* would therefore constitute the most important step toward liberalizing German society from below. There were more than traces of Dahrendorf's logic in the RCDS's contention that a discrepancy existed between the democratic model and the political realities of the Federal Republic and in their calls for a democratic restructuring of the education system.

Discontent with the postwar status quo also drew students of the center-right to some of the best-known protest events of the 1960s. A

---

[21] Helmut Pütz, "Ein Pladoyer für 'reale Utopien,'" ACDP, 4/6/16/1.

[22] Herbert Marcuse, *One-Dimensional Man: Studies in the Ideology of Advanced Industrial Society* (Boston, 1964).

[23] Philipp, "Herbert Marcuse: Zusammenfassung seiner gesellschaftskritischen Analyse"; *Runge Private Papers*, file "Politischer Beirat."

[24] Ibid.

[25] Martin Kempe, "Ralf Dahrendorf: Gesellschaft und Demokratie in Deutschland – Zusammenfassung. March 1968," Protokoll des Politischen Beirates des RCDS-Berlin, Arbeitspapier: Ausarbeitung von Kempe, March 17, 1968, in *Runge Private Papers*, file "Politischer Beirat"; Ralf Dahrendorf, *Gesellschaft und Demokratie in Deutschland* (Munich, 1965); on Dahrendorf in contemporary debates, see Ulrich Herbert, "Liberalisierung als Lernprozess. Die Bundesrepublik in der deutschen Geschichte – eine Skizze," in Ulricht Herbert, ed., *Wandlungsprozesse in Westdeutschland: Belastung, Integration, Liberalisierung 1945–1980* (Göttingen, 2002), 7–49, here 30.

famous spontaneous debate between Dutschke and Dahrendorf on top of a van in Freiburg on January 30, 1968 had been, befitting their reverence for the sociologist, initiated by RCDS activists who owned the vehicle. They persuaded Dahrendorf, who was in town to attend a convention of the liberal Free Democratic Party, to face the SDS icon in front of three thousand listeners.[26] Dutschke, wearing the revolutionaries' staple leather jacket, spoke of the "Establishment's corruption" and labeled party politicians "one-track specialists" (*Fachidioten*). The liberal professor, in turn, defended the parliamentary system and accused radical protesters of providing conservatives with ammunition to block necessary reforms.[27]

A few years earlier, a member of the Freiburg RCDS had organized a nationwide protest to call for reform of the education system. Inspired by the pedagogue Georg Picht's diagnosis of an "education catastrophe" in the Federal Republic, 40 percent of West German students heeded the call to march on July 1, 1965. The marches were the largest student demonstration the Federal Republic had witnessed up to that point.[28]

In October 1966, in the wake of youth riots against a significant increase in public transportation fares in Cologne – protests against fare increases were an important element of the upheaval in this period – Klaus Laepple, the twenty-six-year-old leader of the local student council and a member of the RCDS, gained national notoriety as the "'Provo' of the CDU," a label derived from the famous Dutch countercultural movement.[29] On October 24, secondary school and university students staged a sit-in on the tram tracks to block traffic in central Cologne, which led to the biggest clashes between protesters and the police that the city had seen since the founding of the Federal Republic.[30] The police were pelted with eggs and tomatoes, and "rioting youths smash[ed] in the windows of the blockaded trams, turning over public benches, and

[26] "6. Beschluss der 18. Ord. DV" and "Beschluss der 18. Ord. DV (60. Antrag)," ArchAPO, RCDS, 18. Ord. Bundesdelegierten-Versammlung, file 1968; author's interview with Ignaz Bender, Trier, May 27, 2014; author's interview with Meinhard Ade, Bonn, June 3, 2014.

[27] Rolf Zundel, "Liberale Blume im Knopfloch," *Die Zeit*, no. 5 (February 2, 1968), 3.

[28] Georg Picht, *Die deutsche Bildungskatastrophe: Analyse und Dokumentation* (Freiburg im Breisgau, 1964); "Heißer Sommer," *Der Spiegel*, no. 21 (1965), 77; also "Deutsche Studenten demonstrieren," *Die Zeit*, no. 28 (July 9, 1965), 9; Bender interview.

[29] Eva Schmidt-Häuer, "Der 'Provo' von der CDU," *Die Zeit*, no. 1 (January 6, 1967), 7.

[30] Kurt Holl and Claudia Glunz, eds., *1968 am Rhein: Satisfaction und ruhender Verkehr* (Cologne, 1998), 44.

setting fire to trash cans, boxes of grit, and ticket machines. Parts of the inner city were impassable for hours," *Der Spiegel* reported.[31] Laepple, who had made a name for himself locally as a spirited defender of student interests, had officially registered the protest and was later sued by the city-owned transport company for a whopping DM 89,292.45 in damages. Though initially acquitted by the state court, the Federal Court of Justice, Germany's highest court in criminal and civil matters, eventually came to the conclusion that the traffic blockade had put the tram drivers under "psychological duress" and ordered Laepple to pay. The so-called Laepple verdict became a precedent frequently used to criminalize demonstrators in the years that followed.[32] For his part, Laepple went on to become the leader of the DSU in 1968 and left his mark on West German student politics.[33]

Students of the center-right did not just participate in protests for educational reform or against fare increases; they also took part in numerous spontaneous debates and teach-ins with their left-wing peers.[34] There was still a relatively open, if often impassioned, dialogue between student activists from different political camps in the second half of the 1960s. RCDS leaders were invited to speak at the annual SDS convention, for instance, and SDS activists in turn explained their political outlook at gatherings of conservative fraternity students.[35] In her biography of her late activist husband, Dutschke's U.S.-born wife Gretchen remembers select Christian Democrat students with fondness. She identifies Jürgen-Bernd Runge, a leading member of the West Berlin RCDS chapter, as one of her husband's most effective opponents: "Runge countered Rudi at every event, and Rudi polemicized strongly but sincerely against him. In some ways it was admirable how Runge always fought against great

---

[31] "Mit faulem Obst," *Der Spiegel*, no. 52 (1966), 58–59.

[32] Alexander Sedlmaier, *Consumption and Violence: Radical Protest in Cold-War West Germany* (Ann Arbor, MI, 2014), 146–149, 291.

[33] Richard Schmid, "Was dürfen Demonstranten? Das Laepple-Urteil des Bundesgerichtshofs: ein Fehlurteil," *Die Zeit*, no. 38 (September 19, 1969), 11; Holl and Glunz, *1968 am Rhein*, 72–73.

[34] "RCDS – SDS. Evolution – Revolution," Hoover Institution Archives, Stanford, CA (hereafter HIA), German Subject Collection (GSC), box 87.

[35] Horst Teltschik, "Rudi Dutschke: Zusammenfassung seiner politischen Theorien" (September 1967), *Runge Private Papers*, file "Politischer Beirat"; "Rede des RCDS-Bundesvorsitzenden Wulf Schönbohm auf der Delegiertenkonferenz des SDS am 4. September 1967 in Frankfurt/M," ArchAPO, RCDS, file "BRD"; "Zur Ideologie des SDS: Ein Nachtrag zur Dreikönigstagung 1968," *Akademische Blätter*, no. 4 (1968), 69–70.

disapproval and never gave up. His appearances stimulated the discussion," she wrote.[36]

Given the frequency of such encounters, it is hardly surprising that the key incident in the development and radicalization of the left-wing protest movement also touched student activists of the center-right. On June 2, 1967, West Berlin policemen and Iranian secret service agents battered student demonstrators protesting against the visiting Shah of Iran. As the security forces violently dispersed the students, a West Berlin policeman shot and killed an unarmed student, Benno Ohnesorg. This event altered the trajectory of the student movement fundamentally: "the system" seemed to have revealed its brutally repressive side, and roughly a quarter of all students took to the streets in protest.[37] One of the emerging left-wing terrorist groups would later call itself the "June 2nd Movement" to illustrate that its own turn toward political violence had been caused by the police brutality of that day.[38]

Ignoring the mayor of West Berlin's initial attempt to blame the violence on the demonstrators, many center-right students expressed their "shock and outrage" over the conduct of the police.[39] Several RCDS activists attended Ohnesorg's funeral in Hanover on June 9, and the Christian Democratic student paper *Civis* invoked memories of Nazism to criticize the coverage of Ohnesorg's death by the West Berlin press, which was dominated by the right-wing Springer publishing house:[40] "Overnight, this city, where the majority did not vote for the Nazi Party in 1933, where the most Jews were hidden from the SS, where Hitler was not liked and Stalin was opposed, has lost its greatest virtue."[41]

Just as left- and right-leaning students were critical of many of the same political developments, so too did their responses to the broader cultural upheaval of the 1960s overlap to a certain extent. Although

---

[36] Gretchen Dutschke-Klotz, *Wir hatten ein barbarisches, schönes Leben: Rudi Dutschke: Eine Biographie* (Cologne, 2007), 121.

[37] See the analysis of the Wildenmann poll cited in note 4.

[38] Bommi Baumann, *How It All Began: The Personal Account of a West German Urban Guerilla* (Vancouver, 2006).

[39] Ulrich Grasser, quoted in *RCDS Notizen* 2 (WS 67/68), Hamburger Institut für Sozialforschung, Hamburg, Studentenbewegung, studentische Verbände, RCDS; "Gegen die Polizeimaßnahmen beim Schah-Besuch in der Bundesrepublik," *RCDS-Brief*, no. 4 (June 5, 1967), 15.

[40] See the list of events attended by members of the RCDS federal leadership, ArchAPO, RCDS, file "18. Ord. Bundesdelegierten-Versammlung. Mappe 1968"; Dutschke-Klotz, *Rudi Dutschke*, 135.

[41] Claus Menzel, "Das Maul stopfen," *Civis*, no. 7 (1967), 14–15.

paling in comparison to developments in the United States that are discussed elsewhere in this volume, a conservative backlash against social and cultural change, particularly against the so-called sex wave – manifested above all in advertisements featuring undressed young women and the box office success of "sex education" films – did occur in West Germany in the 1960s. The Protestant Concern for Germany Campaign (Aktion Sorge um Deutschland), for instance, campaigned against "sexual propaganda in schools and universities," organized doctors' protests against the birth control pill, and warned against the encroaching "dictatorship of indecency."[42] In the 1970s, some West German religious groups also staged street protests against the legalization of abortion.[43]

Sexual mores and reproductive rights were not, by contrast, an important point of dispute between left- and right-leaning students. Christian Democratic students, for instance, organized a high-profile campaign to make the birth control pill available to unmarried students in 1967, at a time when most physicians were reluctant to provide single women with prescriptions for the pill.[44] Although students of the center-right rejected making "the personal political" in a radical sense – shunning, for example, the experiments in communal living that were increasingly popular on the left – they began to cautiously rethink and expand the realm of the political.[45] Moreover, center-right students by no means condemned the sex wave as an attack on Christian values. Much like their left-wing counterparts, center-right student publications were littered with images of unclad women in suggestive poses. Such images were often part of an explicit attempt to woo their political opponents: "Aren't you tempted by the other side(s)?" asked the Munich Student Union in 1968

---

[42] Evangelisches Zentralarchiv in Berlin, rep. 81/3, no. 213 and rep. 87, no. 1107; see also Dagmar Herzog, "Sexual Morality in 1960s West Germany," *German History* 233 (2005): 379–380.

[43] Jana Ebeling, "Religiöser Straßenprotest? Medien und Kirchen im Streit um den § 218 in den 1970er Jahren," in Frank Bösch and Lucian Hölscher, eds., *Jenseits der Kirche: Die Öffnung religiöser Räume seit 1945* (Göttingen, 2013), 253–284; see also Thomas Großbölting's contribution to this volume (chapter 10).

[44] "AStA sucht Anti-Baby-Pillen," *Frankfurter Rundschau*, October 13, 1967. This campaign was later replicated by the left-wing magazine *konkret*; see Anna von der Goltz, "Von alten Kämpfern, sexy Wahlgirls und zornigen jungen Frauen: Überlegungen zur Bedeutung von Generationalität, Geschlecht und Populärkultur im gemäßigt-rechten Lager um 1968," in Lu Seegers, ed., *Hot Stuff: Gender, Popkultur und Generationalität in West- und Osteuropa nach 1945* (Göttingen, 2015), 29–51.

[45] For a more extensive discussion of these issues, particularly the role of gender, see von der Goltz, "Von alten Kämpfern."

next to a photograph of a pigtailed, naked young woman shown from behind.[46]

Center-Right Internationalism during the Cold War

A number of recent studies have highlighted the extent to which West German students of the left looked beyond national borders and were inspired by activists and ideas from the so-called Third World and the United States.[47] While student activists of the center-right certainly did not buy into the radical left's revolutionary internationalism, they were by no means focused exclusively on domestic issues.

In contrast to their peers in SDS, who had strong links to the American SDS and took over much of their protest repertoire from North American activists, center-right students only rarely had personal contacts to students in the United States – even if their tactics were often strikingly similar to those employed by U.S. organizations like the YAF. A trip by a group of young Christian Democrats to New York City in the summer of 1969, where they quizzed Greenwich Village hippies about their "attitude about life, society, and its consequences," was something of an exception.[48] Nevertheless, much like the YAF, young West German Christian Democrats became increasingly preoccupied with the U.S.-led campaign in Vietnam and were vocal defenders of U.S. policy in the former French colony.[49] Some, seeing parallels between the situation in Vietnam and the division of Germany, were convinced that a U.S. victory was of particular importance for the Federal Republic. The island city of West Berlin would be threatened should Hanoi prevail, they warned.[50] One young Christian Democrat even went as far as embracing the left-wing slogan "Vietnam is the Spain of our time." But whereas the SDS saw the United States playing a role akin to Franco's in the Spanish Civil War and endorsed the international fight against this new form of "fascism,"

---

[46] P.S.: Presse der Studenten 1/2, May 8, 1969, HIA, GSC, box 85.

[47] Martin Klimke, *The Other Alliance: Student Protest in West Germany and the United States in the Global Sixties* (Princeton, 2010); Quinn Slobodian, *Foreign Front: Third World Politics in Sixties West Germany* (Durham, NC, 2012); Brown, *West Germany and the Global Sixties*.

[48] Junge Union Deutschland, Studienfahrt in die USA vom 17. Juli bis 1. August 1969, ACDP, 4/64/1481.

[49] Schneider, *Cadres for Conservatism*, 93–97.

[50] See Jürgen Wahl's report for the Christian Democratic youth organization Junge Union (1968), ACDP, 4/7/75/2; leaflet of the RCDS at the Technical University of Berlin, February 8, 1966, in ACDP, 1/700/8412.

[Handwritten marginal note, upper left:] FKK is a porn - German phenomenon. Thought it was more popular in the GDR for several reasons

[Handwritten marginal note, lower left:] Oh God - that would have been hilarious

he saw parallels between the communist quest for world revolution in Spain and Vietnam. Just as a Republican victory in the Spanish Civil War would have extended Moscow's influence further into Europe, he argued, so too would a North Vietnamese victory be yet one more step toward the worldwide victory of communism.

Even if this activist's alarmist tone and Francoist sympathies were something of a rarity, Christian Democratic students had already set up an "Action Committee on Peace and Freedom for South Vietnam" in January 1966 to "counter all efforts to defame U.S. policy in Vietnam."[51] Aided by funds from the local America Houses (U.S. cultural institutions in West Germany that were often the target of left-wing protest against the war in Southeast Asia), the Action Committee engaged in a wide range of activities, including staging pro-American demonstrations and soliciting donations for South Vietnamese orphans.[52] It also cooperated with the Union of Vietnamese Students in the Federal Republic and sought personal ties to student leaders in Saigon.[53] Its primary goal, however, was to highlight the reasons for U.S. involvement in Indochina and to help craft a counternarrative to the increasingly negative coverage of the war in the West German press. This coverage, the Action Committee argued, was completely distorting the nature of the war:

> The acts of terror by communist gangs against their own population, against innocent women and children, the support of the [South Vietnamese] underground movement by the communist regime in North Vietnam and the delivery of Soviet and red Chinese weapons are being kept completely quiet. Based on a total misjudgment of the historical truth and the real will of the South Vietnamese people, fanatical partisans are being portrayed as freedom fighters.[54]

In late 1966, in what was to be their most widely reported event in support of U.S. policy, Christian Democratic Students at the Free University of Berlin invited the South Vietnamese ambassador to participate in a debate on campus on December 6. Before an audience of approximately one hundred listeners, Nguyen Quy Anh likened the situation in his home country to that of divided Germany and invoked the Berlin blockade of 1948–1949. Just as with West Berlin, South Vietnam's freedom and independence could not be sustained without U.S. involvement, he

---

[51] Statute of the Action Committee, ACDP, 4/6/40/2.

[52] Werner Gries to Wolfgang Weltin, February 2, 1966, ACDP, 4/6/40/2.

[53] See the annual report of RCDS chairman Gert Hammer, n.d. [1966], ACDP, 4/6/7; and Wulf Schönbohm to Lutz Bähr, July 28, 1966; Bähr to Schönbohm, July 14, 1966, ACDP, 4/6/40/2; Vu Duy-Tu to Erich Röper, June 2, 1966, ACDP, 4/6/40/2.

[54] Declaration of the Baden-Württemberg chapter of the RCDS, ACDP, 4/6/40/2.

argued.[55] Soon afterwards, the ambassador was interrupted by several hundred supporters of the SDS, who had been in another auditorium. Amidst shouts of "Long live the National Liberation Front!" they entered the room and demanded an open debate. Tumult ensued, and the ambassador chose to end the discussion and exited the building through the back door.[56] The event received substantial coverage in the national press and was the focus of a university inquiry. And the RCDS was very pleased with its "major action" for having helped it hone its public profile.[57]

Although West German students supported the protests against the war in Vietnam in growing numbers, the issue still proved a suitable vehicle in 1966 for center-right students to mobilize those who did not for their own cause. "[T]he stance of the RCDS on the question of South Vietnam really secures new members for us, especially those who actually guarantee active involvement," reported the head of the Baden-Württemberg chapter.[58] In the coming years, however, the escalation of the war and growing criticism of U.S. conduct made it more difficult to use support for the war as a rallying cry. The RCDS therefore adopted a more ambiguous stance, criticizing both the North Vietnamese and the U.S.-backed government in the South. Some members also began to question the RCDS's unconditional support for the United States, but they were never able to win a majority within the organization to their position.[59] Only much later would former Christian Democratic student activists reflect back on their erstwhile stance and admit that the Federal Republic's – and their own – backing of the war in Vietnam had been a mistake.[60]

They would similarly come to regret not having capitalized more effectively on the Warsaw Pact's invasion of Czechoslovakia in August 1968

---

[55] "SDS-Studenten störten an der FU," *Tagesspiegel*, December 7, 1966, copy in Landesarchiv Berlin (hereafter LAB), B. Rep. 014, 3213.

[56] "Bericht des Rektors der FU fuer den 1. Untersuchungsausschuss des Abgeordnetenhauses von Berlin, V. Wahlperiode," LAB, B. Rep. 014, 843; the reports by RCDS member Othmar Nikola Haberl to the Free University's Chancellor, December 15, 1966 and the report by SDS member Klaus Gilgenmann, December 12, 1966, LAB, B. Rep. 014, 3213.

[57] See the various press clippings, LAB, B. Rep. 014, 3213; the report about the election campaign of 1966 by Haberl, ArchAPO, RCDS, file "LV Berlin FU."

[58] Werner Gries to Wolfgang Weltin, February 2, 1966, ACDP, 4/6/40/2.

[59] RCDS leaflet about the decision of the university convention regarding Vietnam, ArchAPO, RCDS, file "Berlin Flugblätter Juni-Juli 1967"; and the press release on Vietnam by RCDS delegates, among them Runge and Rosorius, ArchAPO, RCDS, file "18. Ord. Bundesdelegierten-Versammlung Mappe 1968."

[60] Kurt Faltlhauser, "Die 68er-Bewegung: Persönliche und gesellschaftliche Wirkungen," *Politische Studien* 59:422 (2008): 27–28.

to suppress the "Prague Spring."[61] Young Christian Democrats had followed Alexander Dubček's political and economic reforms closely and welcomed his efforts to create "socialism with a human face" as a first step toward Western-style democracy.[62] This led to a somewhat bizarre spectacle during the International Youth Festival in Sofia in the summer of 1968: West German Christian Democratic students who trumpeted their anti-socialist credentials at home applauded the Czechoslovak delegation when they came in carrying pictures of the Communist Party leader. Members of the anti-authoritarian wing of the West German SDS, on the other hand, displayed their preference for alternative revolutionary socialist models from the Third World when they greeted the Czechoslovak delegates with chants of "Castro-Mao-Guevara."[63] Some observers would later see the Prague Spring as a more meaningful aspect of the international "1968" than the French May, including some left-wing activists, like Dutschke, who came to regret his erstwhile indifference toward dissident movements in the Eastern bloc.[64] Although they were later able to claim that, at least on Czechoslovakia, they had been on the right side of history in 1968, young activists of the moderate right never invested their campaign against the crushing of the Prague Spring with the same moral outrage that the left brought to the issue of Vietnam. Instead, they often invoked events in the Eastern bloc primarily to discredit the domestic left in an effort to gain political capital at home.[65]

Despite their anti-Soviet stance, their support of oppositional movements to the east of the Iron Curtain, and their backing of the United States on Vietnam, most of the leading Christian Democratic student

61 Ibid.

62 Frank Breitsprecher, "Liberalisierungstendenzen in der tschechischen Wirtschaft," *Runge Private Papers*, file "Politischer Beirat."

63 Slobodian, *Foreign Front*, 195; on East–West relations among left-wing activists, see James Mark and Anna von der Goltz, "Encounters," in Robert Gildea, James Mark, and Anette Warring, eds., *Europe's 1968: Voices of Revolt* (Oxford, 2013), 131–163.

64 Jacques Rupnik's interview with Rudi Dutschke, "The Misunderstanding of 1968," *Transit* 35 (Summer 2008), http://www.eurozine.com/articles/2008-05-16-dutschke-en .html; on such left-wing regrets, see James Mark, Anna von der Goltz, and Anette Warring, "Reflections," in Gildea et al., *Europe's 1968*, 283–325.

65 RCDS Pressemitteilung, no. 41, August 22, 1969, ACDP, 4/6/44/3; Horst Teltschik, "Die Argumentation der Außerparlamentarischen Opposition (APO) zur Entwicklung in der CSSR," Rednerdienst no. 4 (November 1968), ACDP, 4/6/42/2. On the left's moral outrage: Wilfried Mausbach, "Auschwitz and Vietnam: West German Protest against America's War in the 1960s," in Wilfried Mausbach, Andreas W. Daum, and Lloyd C. Gardner, eds., *America, the Vietnam War, and the World: Comparative and International Perspectives* (New York, 2003), 279–298.

activists of this period were not ardent cold warriors. Not only did they reject "irrational anti-communism," they also supported the legalization of the West German Communist Party, which had been banned in 1956.[66] Moreover, even before the new government under the Social Democrat Willy Brandt began to implement its "Neue Ostpolitik" (New Eastern Policy), the RCDS favored rapprochement with the German Democratic Republic. It advocated contacts on all levels and signaled its openness to the possibility of relations with the East German Socialist youth organization[67] – much to the dismay of the Berlin CDU, which suspended its monthly subsidies to the students for their refusal to go along with the party's practice of referring to "the 'GDR'" in all written communications: the use of quotation marks was the CDU's preferred way to refer to a country the Federal Republic did not officially recognize.[68]

As John Davis argues in chapter 3 on British Conservative students in this volume, the experience of being put onto the defensive by the left-wing challenge of the 1960s strengthened the bonds between West German Christian Democratic students and their fellow young conservatives elsewhere in Western Europe. Whereas they might otherwise have had difficulties translating their different brands of conservatism and Christian Democracy for each other, this generation was keener than its predecessors to strengthen transnational ties.[69]

The RCDS was a founding member of the International Union of Christian Democrat and Conservative Students (ICCS), which had been set up in 1961 and held regular meetings for like-minded students from Scandinavia, the United Kingdom, Austria, Belgium, and the Netherlands.[70] "[I]n response to extreme left-wing disruptions in the universities of Europe," the ICCS expanded its activities markedly in the late 1960s.[71] The very fact that left-wing mobilization was an international affair strengthened cross-border contacts amongst students of the center-right.

---

[66] "RCDS-SDS," in *Akut: Nachrichtenblatt der Bonner Studentenschaft*, no. 40 (May/June 1968), HIA, BFW, box 84; "Nachtrag zu den Beschlüssen der 17. ord. Delegiertenversammlung vom 16.–20. März 1967 in Heidelberg," ACDP, 4/6/8.

[67] Wulf Schönbohm, "Innerdeutsche Politik im Wandel," ACDP, 4/6/1/2; Martin Kempe, "Protokoll des Außenpolitischen Arbeitskreises des Bundesverbandes des RCDS, 19.–21. Januar 1968," *Runge Private Papers*, file "Politischer Beirat."

[68] "Immer Ärger mit den Jungen," *Stuttgarter Zeitung*, July 5, 1968.

[69] On this issue of "translation" see Friedbert Pflüger's foreword in *Taurus*, no. 6 (1977), BAK, B138/33493; and Martina Steber's essay in this volume (chapter 14).

[70] It was renamed European Union of Christian Democrat and Conservative Students (ECCS) in 1970, and renamed European Democrat Students (EDS) in 1975. For an organizational overview: Holger Thuss and Bence Bauer, *Students on the Right Way: European Democrat Students 1961–2011* (Brussels, 2012).

[71] "What is ECCS?," *Taurus*, vol. 1, no. 1 (1974), ACDP, 4/6/13/2.

In all Western European countries, the "sensation-seeking means of communication ha[d] given a distorted picture of the conditions at the universities," the ICCS argued.[72] Stressing that "Conservative and Christian-democrat students can also take a radical view of society . . . [that] would not be purely destructive," they compared their experiences with "student unrest" and contemplated the creation of a moderate European Student International, which they envisaged as a counterweight to the left-leaning International Student Union in Prague.[73]

When the RCDS hosted three hundred international students at its largest event to that date in Bonn in February 1970, it identified the belief in a "permanent reform of society . . . by evolutionary means" as the conviction that united young conservatives across Europe. Participants called on European politicians to "make parties and institutions more transparent, to strengthen inner-party democracy, to communicate more with their citizens, and to increase the incentive to become politically active."[74] This emphasis on student power and participation from below united Western European activists of the center-right with their left-wing student peers, indeed making many of their meetings sound "remarkably like . . . reunion[s] of [the prominent British Pakistani New Leftist] Tariq Ali and his mates," as the London-based *Guardian* noted with astonishment.[75]

Hardening Fronts in the 1970s

As the political ground shifted during the 1970s, the dividing line between an increasingly radicalized and sectarian student left and the center-right solidified. "What happened to the chaotic, revolutionary, fun-loving Left we knew so well in 1968? . . . Why are we now faced by dry, dreary Stalinists with no political flair and ideas straight from the 1930s?" European center-right students now wondered.[76]

Except perhaps in Italy, this shift was nowhere more evident than on West German campuses. With the dissolution of the SDS and the subsequent emergence of increasingly radical and sectarian left-wing

[72] Poul Juelsbjerg, "The political situation of students in Denmark," ACDP, 9/3/61.
[73] FCS leaflet on "Student Unrest" [1968]; FOEST press release, July 9, 1970, ACDP 9/3/62; *Aktuell*, April 24, 1970; RCDS press release, August 26, 1969, ACDP, 4/6/43/1; "Europäische Allianz der gemäßigten Studenten," Beschlüsse der 19. Ordentlichen Delegierten-Versammlung 11.–15. März 1969 in Soest-Westfalen, ACDP, 4/6/10.
[74] *Aktuell*, April 24, 1970, ACDP, 4/6/43/1.
[75] "Student Power Takes a Swing to the Right," *Guardian*, July 9, 1968.
[76] "New Left – Old Left?," *Taurus*, vol. 1, no. 1 (1974), ACDP, 4/6/13/2.

groups, including a number of left-wing terrorist groups that engaged in a campaign of violence against the state, the struggle against the left took on a new quality for many campus activists of the center-right: it became an actual struggle and sometimes a physical clash over two contrasting visions of the Federal Republic's political future.[77] This change was partly the result of fragmentation and change on the left, but realignments on the right played a role as well, notably the emergence of prominent neoconservatives and the defection of more liberal RCDS members in the late 1960s.[78] Furthermore, the fact that the CDU/CSU found itself in opposition for the first time since 1949 with the end of the Christian Democratic–Social Democratic Grand Coalition in 1969 gave conservative politics a much harder and defensive edge: a muscular anti-socialism and a decidedly confrontational rhetorical style were defining features of Christian Democratic politics in the 1970s, as Martina Steber shows in chapter 14 in this volume.[79]

Rather than considering themselves the left's intellectual sparring partners, the remaining or newly active RCDS members began to see themselves as democracy's first line of defense, tasked with saving the country from a dictatorial threat. Unlike in the 1960s, when Christian Democratic students had been very concerned about the growth of the right-wing extremist National Democratic Party (NPD), they now saw the student left as the primary threat.[80] The RCDS thus turned its attention to the newly founded German Communist Party's student wing, the MSB Spartakus, which had close ties to the East German regime and

---

[77] For a comparative examination of left-wing terrorism in West Germany and the United States, see Jeremy Varon, *Bringing the War Home: The Weather Underground, the Red Army Faction, and Revolutionary Violence in the Sixties and Seventies* (Berkeley, CA, 2004). This is not to suggest that the West German left as a whole embraced political violence or became radicalized in the 1970s – the nascent environmental movement is just one example of a different kind of left-wing politics in the 1970s – but these developments were particularly pronounced among the *student* left.

[78] The aforementioned Runge, for one, publicly announced his exit in May 1968, alongside other activists from the Berlin chapter, who had been at the forefront of the group's theoretical efforts. "Zwei Stellungnahmen zum Austritt des linken RCDS-Flügels aus dem Verband am 15.5.1968," FU Spiegel, no. 65 (June/July 1968), copy in *Runge Private Papers*; cf. Manuel Seitenbecher, "'Revolution in verträglicher Dosis': Der Ring Christlich-Demokratischer Studenten (RCDS) während der 68er-Jahre an der FU Berlin," *Zeitschrift für Geschichtswissenschaft* 6 (2010): 505–526.

[79] See generally Geoffrey Pridham, *Christian Democracy in Western Germany: The CDU/CSU in Government and Opposition, 1945–1976* (New York, 1977), 188–206; Frank Bösch, *Die Adenauer-CDU: Gründung, Aufstieg und Krise einer Erfolgspartei 1945–1969* (Stuttgart, 2001).

[80] RCDS Circular on a planned "Anti-Radicalism Event," July 2, 1969, ACDP, 4/6/53/3.

now dominated the proceedings in many student councils.[81] Joint debates between the center-right and extreme left became a rarity at West German universities. Members of opposing political camps often shouted each other down with megaphones or engaged in fistfights or even attacked each other with butyric acid.[82] Accordingly, the recollections of Christian Democratic student activists of the 1970s emphasize the hostile tone of student politics in a period during which each side carefully documented the other's transgressions and issued endless sensational indictments.[83] While the left denounced center-right students as "police agents and collaborators of fascists," the right, in turn, became obsessed with the left's allegedly pervasive embrace of violence as a political strategy and its general hostility to the constitution.[84]

While the notion of the Federal Republic as "fascist" was based more on neo-Marxist analysis than on the political realities of the early 1970s, the image of Christian Democratic students as "police agents" was not entirely without foundation. Much like the American CIA, which had lent covert financial support to Cold War liberal organizations in Western Europe since the 1950s, the Federal Office for the Protection of the Constitution (Bundesamt für Verfassungsschutz) enlisted the help of young Christian Democratic activists after student protests had become a mass phenomenon during the Grand Coalition government.[85] The RCDS complied readily, supplying material and expertise to help the agency figure out how to deal with the SDS and related groups.[86] After the change of government in 1969, select RCDS leaders also received substantial cash payments from the agency's secret fund dedicated to the "proactive protection of the constitution" – a key component of the Brandt

---

[81] Jeffrey Herf, *War by Other Means: Soviet Power, West German Resistance, and the Battle of the Euromissiles* (New York, 1991).

[82] "Dokumentation: Gewaltsame Sprengungen von RCDS-Veranstaltungen im Zeichen der linksradikalen Presse" (March 1974), ACDP, 4/6/13/2; Bremen's Attorney General to the Senator of Art and Science, July 19, 1978, Staatsarchiv Bremen (StB), 4.111/7/161.

[83] Gerd Langguth, *Mythos '68: Die Gewaltphilosophie von Rudi Dutschke: Ursachen und Folgen der Studentenbewegung* (Munich, 2001), 10.

[84] "RCDS: Polizeiagenten und Faschisten-Kollaborateure," *Rote Blätter*, no. 18 (1974), 21–26.

[85] Michael Hochgeschwender, *Freiheit in der Offensive? Die Deutschen und der Kongreß für kulturelle Freiheit*(Munich, 1998); Frances Stonor Saunders, *Who Paid the Piper? The CIA and the Cultural Cold War* (London, 1999).

[86] Wulf Schönbohm to the Federal Office for the Protection of the Constitution, November 3, 1967, ACDP, 04/006/045/3; President of the Federal Office for the Protection of the Constitution to the State Secretary in the Federal Chancellor's Office, April 23, 1968, BAK, B136/5035.

government's quest to achieve greater internal security by nurturing active democrats.[87]

Not surprisingly, center-right students backed the government's attempts to keep those whose political loyalties were suspect from the levers of power. They were ardent campaigners for the 1972 Decree against Radicals banning so-called left-wing radicals from the civil service; the government introduced this measure after the CDU/CSU had raised the specter of radical infiltration of the civil service.[88] On January 26, 1972, two days before Chancellor Willy Brandt announced the controversial ban, West German television viewers witnessed rowdy scenes from a "Spartakus Tribunal" that the RCDS had staged at the University of Hamburg. The right-leaning television political program *ZDF Magazin* showed heavily edited scenes of Christian Democratic student speakers, among them their federal chairman Gerd Langguth, being drowned out by incessant shouting by the left-wing audience and pelted with wads of paper and eggs before left-wing students stormed the stage.[89] Over the next few days, Brandt and Minister of the Interior Hans-Dietrich Genscher were inundated with letters from viewers who were reminded of the last days of the Weimar Republic and the violent street battles of that time. This incident well illustrates what the government and much of the public thought was at stake in ensuring students' loyalty to the state.[90]

Throughout the 1970s, the RCDS monitored all signs of student support for left-wing terrorism – a phenomenon that gripped the attention of the West German public and made campus politics all the more fraught.

---

[87] A high-level interministerial working group had identified the need for "supporting positive student forces" in their fight against political extremism as an urgent political task in early 1969, but found that this would be difficult to do through existing public channels. Ten years later, the *Frankfurter Rundschau* revealed that the RCDS and other moderate student groups had received money from the Verfassungsschutz since 1969. "Maßnahmen zum Schutz der freiheitlichen Demokratie gegen den Terror radikaler Minderheiten," Report by the State Secretary of the Interior to the Head of the Federal Chancellory, January 17, 1969, BAK, B136/5036, 52 and 64. Gunter Hofmann, "Richter über Gut und Böse", *Die Zeit*, no. 3 (1979), 4; on the Social-Liberal coalition's broader campaign for the "positive protection of the constitution" see Karrin Hanshew, *Terror and Democracy in West Germany* (Cambridge, 2012), 124–133.

[88] Gerard Braunthal, *Political Loyalty and Public Service in West Germany: The 1972 Decree against Radicals and Its Consequences* (Amherst, MA, 1990); Dominik Rigoll, *Staatsschutz in Westdeutschland: Von der Entnazifizierung zur Extremistenabwehr* (Göttingen, 2013).

[89] "Selbstentlarvung des ZDF-Magazins," *Die Zeit*, no. 5 (1972), 20.

[90] See the letters in BAK, B138/14834.

The huge public uproar surrounding students' reactions to the murder of Federal Attorney General Siegfried Buback, a key figure in the government's fight against left-wing terrorists, in April 1977, for instance, cannot be fully understood without taking the role of Christian Democratic students into account. Buback's murder had been the opening salvo in a string of terrorist attacks – later termed the "German Autumn."[91] On April 25, 1977, an anonymous student writing under the pseudonym "Göttingen Mescalero" published an "obituary" of Buback in the student newspaper of the University of Göttingen. Although the author argued that leftists should not become "killers" and cautioned that "our way to socialism... cannot be paved with corpses," he confessed that the murder of the attorney general, who had been a member of the Nazi Party, had brought him a "clandestine joy."[92] This "obituary" provoked a huge public outcry with its suggestion that the student left broadly supported acts of terror, including political murder. The scandal had actually been set in motion by the local RCDS chapter, which had first alerted a wider public to this obscure article.[93] On April 28, a Christian Democratic student leader petitioned to have charges filed against the anonymous author for condoning the murder, and he also penned an open letter to the chancellor of the university.[94] These actions set off the so-called Mescalero Affair. After the conservative dailies *Die Welt* and *Frankfurter Allgemeine Zeitung* quoted only the most incendiary passages of the "obituary," the federal minister of justice filed charges against the author and the national press began to fan the flames of the nascent scandal.[95] The RCDS kept adding fuel to the fire, doing its utmost to keep the public abreast of

---

[91] The events culminated in the kidnapping and murder of a prominent business leader, ~~Hanns-Martin Schleyer~~ the hijacking of a Lufthansa jet in an attempt to secure the release of imprisoned leaders of the Red Army Faction (RAF), and the suicide of several of the RAF prisoners following the liberation of the hijacked jet. ~~Baader + Ensslin among them~~

[92] "Buback: Ein Nachruf," *Göttinger Nachrichten* (GN), April 25, 1977, 10–12; available at http://www.graswurzel.net/news/mescalero.shtml (accessed October 7, 2013). Two decades later, one Klaus Hülbrock revealed that he had been the author: "Ich bleibe ein Indianer," *Tageszeitung*, February 10, 2001.

[93] "Jagdszenen aus Niedersachsen. Dokumentation der Kampagne gegen den Göttinger AStA," GN, May 20, 1977; "Staatsfeind Nr. 2," *Spiegel*, no. 10 (1980), 63; Hanno Balz, *Von Terroristen, Sympathisanten und dem starken Staat: Die öffentliche Debatte über die RAF in den 70er Jahren* (Frankfurt/Main, 2008), 100–108.

[94] Michael Schulte to Professor Beug, April 28, 1977, printed in *Output*, no. 3 (May 6, 1977), ACDP, 4/6/142/1.

[95] "Göttinger AStA billigt den Mord an Buback," *Die Welt*, April 30, 1977; "Gewaltverherrlichung in Göttinger AStA-Zeitung," *Frankfurter Allgemeine Zeitung*, April 30, 1977; *Recht. Eine Information des Bundesministers der Justiz*, no. 22 (1977).

similarly worded leaflets that surfaced on other campuses.[96] Eventually,
more than one hundred individuals were charged with criminal offenses
for distributing the "obituary," and several academics were reproached
and disciplined by their universities for having reprinted it. Without such
an organized campaign of communal outrage, the wider German public
would almost certainly not have taken notice of opinions voiced by an
anonymous student. After the RCDS had set the ball rolling, however,
the controversial sections of the Buback "obituary" reached publication
figures bested only by the Bible and the phone book, as *Der Spiegel* later
commented sardonically.[97]

In their quest to highlight that campus politics were of national importance, center-right students frequently invoked the specter of Nazism to
paint their opponents in the worst possible light. They warned of a "radical left-wing seizure of power," called for "resistance" against the red
mob, and, taking their cues from a famous statement by the philosopher
Jürgen Habermas, proclaimed that they were engaged in an existential
struggle against "left fascism."[98] This rhetoric reached its height in October 1977 when the RAF murdered the prominent West German business
leader Hanns-Martin Schleyer, who had been an SS officer during the
Nazi years. Friedbert Pflüger, the federal chairman of the RCDS and
future head of the Berlin CDU, turned the RAF's contention that Schleyer
had been a living symbol of the continuities between the Nazi period and
the "fascist" Federal Republic on its head. It was not Schleyer's career
trajectory but rather his murder that brought the Third Reich to mind,
he argued. The events of 1977 were "reminiscent of the period around
1933 ... Red flags are flying today instead of the brown ones back then.
But one sees the same hateful eyes, the same fanatical types, the same
strained gaze. Once again no regard is shown for human life. We are
dealing with a left fascism."[99] Schleyer had sacrificed his life in the battle for the preservation of the Federal Republic, Pflüger maintained, and

---

[96] "Dokumentation des Linksfaschismus. Der Buback-Nachruf," *Demokratische Blätter*,
no. 15 (1977), 13–14; "Menschenverachtender, grausamer Zynismus," in *RCDS-
Magazin*, no. 2 (1977), 8–9; "Neue Beleidigungen gegen Buback – Vogel stellt
Strafanträge," *Deutsche Presseagentur*, May 11, 1977.

[97] "Staatsfeind Nr. 2," *Spiegel*, no. 10 (1980), 63.

[98] *Contra*, vol. 1, June 20, 1969, ACDP, 01/365/88; Jürgen Habermas, "Meine Damen und
Herren, ich hoffe, dass Herr Dutschke noch hier ist...," June 9, 1967, in: Wolfgang
Kraushaar, ed., *Frankfurter Schule und Studentenbewegung: Von der Flaschenpost bis
zum Molotowcocktail 1946 bis 1995*, vol. 2, *Dokumente* (Hamburg, 1998), 254–255.

[99] Friedbert Pflüger, "Kampf dem Linksfaschismus: 1933 darf sich nicht wiederholen,"
Demokratische Blätter, no. 15 (1977), 12–13.

student activists had to "defend our social order, for which he fought and for which he died, against all those who are attacking it out of blind hate and with criminal motives."[100] This discourse cast West German politics – and campus politics in particular – as a life-or-death matter on which which the very survival of West Germany as a democracy depended. By this point, the playfulness that had characterized student activism in the second half of the 1960s seemed at best a distant memory.

which crossed out the RAF's power and made renewed German riots

* * *

Center-right activism on West German campuses was a significant – and often overlooked – part of 1968 and its aftermath. Even if students on the left set the agenda of political debate, center-right students were initially moved to political engagement by some of the same issues that motivated the left: the challenges posed by advanced industrial society, the policies of the Grand Coalition government, and the remnants of Nazi-era authoritarianism in West Germany's recently established democracy. Conservative student activism was not simply a matter of "backlash" against left-wing protest and cultural change. Rather, center-right students engaged and interacted with the revolutionary left in myriad ways. This changed considerably during the course of the 1970s, when deepening entrenchment and greater polarization became defining features of campus politics. While the center-right had formerly warned against repressive measures by state institutions, they came to see themselves as resisters against a "left fascism" in the 1970s. Former left-wing 68ers would later claim to have democratized the Federal Republic by ridding the system of its authoritarian residues; former activists of the center-right, by contrast, were convinced that they had been engaged in a "resistance" struggle to defend democratic institutions against the onslaught of extremists.[101] These sharply contrasting readings of 1968 and its legacies, which were grounded in diverging experiences of student activism, have shaped the German memory wars over this period to the present day.

they enforced many similar causes

---

[100] "Wir trauern um Hanns-Martin Schleyer," *Demokratische Blätter*, no. 15 (1977), 8. The fraternities, which had long held fraternity member Schleyer in high regard, endorsed the notion that he had "sacrificed" himself to the nation even more explicitly; see Rolf Clauß, "Ein Opfer für Deutschland," *Akademische Blätter*, no. 2 (1978), 37–40; also Hanns Martin Schleyer, "Jugend und Staat," *Akademische Blätter*, no. 5 (1976), 158–164.

[101] Cf. Anna von der Goltz, "A Polarised Generation? Conservative Students and West Germany's '1968,'" in Anna von der Goltz, ed., *"Talkin' 'Bout My Generation": Conflicts of Generation Building and Europe's "1968"* (Göttingen, 2011), 195–215.

As this chapter has attempted to show, however, both sides supported rather illiberal projects at various points. A segment of the student left did embrace violence as a political strategy in the 1970s; and much like the state itself, which revealed its repressive side when faced with the specter of left-wing terrorism, center-right activists hardened in their approach to political opponents, supported draconian measures against their peers (such as the Decree against Radicals), and fanned the flames of public hysteria about student support for the terrorists. Despite the considerable common ground that had once existed, therefore, real political conflicts characterized student activism in the wake of West Germany's 1968, which tend to be overlooked in the more sanitized accounts that highlight cultural liberalization as the chief legacy of these years. West German student activists did not just struggle against the "Establishment"; they also engaged – and increasingly fought – each other.

5

Mobilizing the Silent Majority in France in the 1970s

Bernard Lachaise

In France, as in the United States and elsewhere in Western Europe, the expression "the silent majority" dates back to the late 1960s.[1] It was coined there in the wake of the events of May 1968 by the opponents of political protest and unrest. It never completely disappeared from the French political vocabulary but came back into fashion when the candidate of the conservative Union pour un Mouvement Populaire (Union for a Popular Movement, UMP), Nicolas Sarkozy, used it during the 2007 presidential campaign and then again during his reelection campaign in 2012.[2] It has always been used by the right and extreme right, by those agitating "against the spirit of 1968."[3]

Together with the fortieth anniversary of May 1968, Sarkozy's embrace of the term silent majority spurred French historians to reflect on the country's silent majority. The first scholarly study devoted to the silent majority was Frédéric Bas's contribution to an influential work about May 1968.[4] The historian François Audigier has

---

[1] Frédéric Bas, "'La majorité silencieuse' ou la bataille de l'opinion en mai–juin 1968," in Philippe Artières and Michelle Zancarini-Fournel, eds., *68. Une histoire collective (1962–1981)* (Paris, 2008), 359–366.

[2] In the archives of INA (Institut national de l'Audiovisuel) the expression "silent majority" is used in 115 programs between 1970 and 2012. Nicolas Sarkozy used it on March 28, 2007, on March 1, 2012, and on March 6, 2012.

[3] To give some examples: Jacques Toubon, the general secretary of the RPR (Rassemblement pour la République) – one of the major parties from the 1970s to 2002 – used it in the context of strikes (January 8, 1987), and it was used by the leader of the Front National – the extreme right party – on October 27, 1988, just before the referendum on New Caledonia.

[4] Bas, "'La majorité silencieuse.'"

contributed the most to the historiography of the mobilization of the
silent majority with his work on what he calls "the Gaullism of order,"
notably in his studies on two Gaullist associations, the Service d'Action
Civique (Civic Action Service, SAC) and the Comités de Défense de la
République (Defense Committees of the Republic, CDR).[5]

Before taking a closer look at the 1970s, it should be noted that the
first step toward the successful mobilization of the silent majority was
the Gaullist demonstration of May 30, 1968, on the Champs-Elysées.
General elections followed on June 23 and 30, and the result was a
landslide victory for de Gaulle, a wholly unexpected outcome only weeks
after the student protests. These Gaullist successes were later interpreted
as having contributed to preventing an all-out civil war in France. Such
is the opinion, for example, of the sociologist Mattei Dogan. In response
to the question "How was civil war avoided in 1968?" Dogan replied:
"by giving a voice to the silent majority through the ballot box." That
view is also put forward by one of the organizers of the Champs-Elysées
demonstration, Jacques Belle, in his book *Le 30 mai 1968. La guerre
civile n'aura pas lieu* ("May 30, 1968: Civil War Will Not Happen").[6]

This memory of the events of 1968 and their outcome was at the
heart of the mobilization of the silent majority in the 1970s. As President Georges Pompidou explained, "what we coined by the fashionable
expression of the silent majority was precisely not silent and expressed
itself and knew how to express itself and made itself heard as it finally
made itself heard in May and June 1968. And that is how we moved
beyond terrible events."[7]

This chapter investigates how the term silent majority spread during the 1970s, who used the expression, and what it meant in different
contexts. It also looks at those who, either outside or on the fringes of
the political parties, worked to mobilize the silent majority. Lastly, it

[5] François Audigier, "Le SAC: un groupe de pression du gaullisme conservateur dans les
années post 68," in D. Rolland, D. Georgakakis, and Y. Deloye, eds., *Les Républiques
en propagande. Pluralisme politique et propagande: entre déni et institutionnalisation
XIXe–XXIe siècles* (Paris, 2006), 349–365; Audigier, "Le gaullisme d'ordre des années
68," *Vingtième siècle. Revue d'histoire* 116 (2012): 53–68; Audigier, "Les CDR: un
modèle militant original pour le gaullisme des années 68," in F. Audigier, B. Lachaise,
and S. Laurent, eds., *Les gaullistes. Hommes et réseaux* (Paris, 2013), 37–60.
[6] Mattei Dogan, "La classe politique prise de panique en mai 1968. Comment la guerre
civile a-t-elle été évitée?" Speech during the conference "Mai 68 en quarantaine," Ecole
Normale Supérieure de Lyon, May 22–24, 2008. Electronic Library; Jacques Belle, *Le 30
mai 1968. La guerre civile n'aura pas lieu* (Paris, 2012).
[7] Georges Pompidou, speech in Murat (Cantal), May 16, 1970, INA Archives.

analyzes their objectives and methods, and assesses the results of this mobilization.

The Silent Majority: A "May 68" Expression

What was the silent majority for the French in the 1970s? The expression itself was not actually used in May and June 1968, but it became, in Pompidou's words, "a trendy expression" in the early 1970s.

It was first and foremost politicians who used the phrase "the silent majority." Pompidou spoke publicly of the silent majority in a speech he gave on May 16, 1970. The president was speaking in his home *département*, the Cantal, in France's rural heartland. He used words he knew would touch his listeners: "We have the right to demand order. It is unacceptable for some, in order to assert their ideas or because their ideas relate simply and purely to destruction, to attack people, to attack property .... Let us try to use common sense and since we ourselves have some, let us try to inspire common sense in all French people." Such was the appeal to the "reason" of rural France in the face of the "madness" of the Latin Quarter of Paris, the main site of student protest.

Other politicians had invoked the silent majority before Pompidou. At the height of the May 1968 crisis, Valéry Giscard d'Estaing of the liberal-right Républicains Indépendants (RI), then a parliamentary deputy from Puy-de-Dôme, gave a definition of the silent majority without exactly using the term, referring to "the great majority of French people who uphold order, liberty, and progress, and who accept neither arbitrariness nor anarchy, has remained silent."[8] On April 30, 1970, a deputy from the Loire, Eugène Claudius-Petit of the centrist Progrès et Démocratie Moderne (Progress and Modern Democracy, PDM), seems to have been the deputy to use the phrase in the National Assembly: "in our democracy, it is the responsibility of each of us to keep minorities from imposing their law on the silent majority of this country."[9]

The notion of a silent majority also caught the interest of sociologists and journalists, who analyzed it as events were unfolding. In 1970, for example, Mattei Dogan published the results of an opinion survey conducted by the Institut Français d'Opinion Publique (French Public Opinion Institute, IFOP) in May 1968. From an analysis of responses to questions intended to gauge the state of mind of different social groups, he

[8] Valéry Giscard d'Estaing, May 19, 1968, in *L'Aurore*, May 20, 1968.
[9] In Bas, "'La majorité silencieuse,'" 361.

observed that the majority of the French population clearly wished to keep out of the political fight. But, as he wrote, "a thousand demonstrators are more visible and more efficient than a hundred thousand citizens who stay at home." Alluding to the outcome of the June elections, he added that "millions of electors can stifle the clamoring of the minorities whose demands are not always illegitimate."[10] In 1977, Maurice Dalinval, a journalist and former advisor to President Giscard d'Estaing, published *Une autre idée des Français* ("Another Idea of the French"). Aiming to move beyond preconceived ideas of the French, Dalinval pointed to the "silent majority," the majority, he wrote, "that has only to be silent and to listen to the vocal minority spurt its platitudes." He wanted to make "the silent ones," those "who don't have access to the mass media because they only represent themselves," raise their voice.[11]

Embraced by the conservatives, the notion of a silent majority also inspired the Belgian comedian Raymond Devos's skit "Acting Minorities" and the more taunting jibes of Jean Manan, a columnist for the influential satirical weekly *Le Canard enchaîné.* His *Pinarque* narrates the fight between two politicians – Pinarque (Jacques Chirac) and Loubard de Mirobol (Valéry Giscard d'Estaing) – between 1976 and 1978. The story ends with the victory of the left – and a coup d'état by Pinarque on December 2. The silent majority, Pinarque's voters, are described by the novelist as "the broad mass of the people."[12]

The traction that the notion of a silent majority gained in public debate can be explained by the particular political context of France in the 1970s. The conservatives were afraid of leftism, which was still strong during the first half of the decade, and of the rise to power of a united left. If one does not take into consideration the political atmosphere of the 1970s, the appeal of the right to the silent majority is incomprehensible.

Indeed, in contrast to most of the Western democracies, France was governed by a conservative majority without interruption from 1958 to 1981. The Gaullist parties and their allies dominated the National Assembly and formed the governments. The only change – sometimes described as the "little change of government" – occurred in 1974 with the election of Valéry Giscard d'Estaing as president of the Republic: a liberal right-winger succeeded two Gaullist presidents, Charles de Gaulle

[*Handwritten margin notes:* This is a way to disguise the real power of the French middle classes / PM 1974-76, mayor of Paris 1977-95 / A reference to the 18th Brumaire of Louis-Napoleon / The Common Program 1972]

---

[10] Mattei Dogan, *La majorité passive et les minorités actives en mai 1968: opinion des masses populaires* (Paris, 1970).

[11] Maurice Dalinval, *Une autre idée des Français* (Paris, 1977), 11–12, 173, 178.

[12] Raymond Devos, *Sens dessus dessous. Les 75 plus grands sketches* (Paris, 1976); Jean Manan, *Pinarque* (Paris, 1977), 19, 43.

and Georges Pompidou. But it was only in 1981, with the victory of the Socialist François Mitterrand, the election of a left-wing majority, and the formation of a government composed of socialists and communists, that France experienced its first real change of government under the Fifth Republic.

This domination of right-wing political groups, of a conservative majority, was seriously threatened several times by the electorate, most notably when parties on the left gained ground in the elections of 1967 and 1978 and the right barely held on to its majority. Apart from left-wing gains in national elections, political protest reached its peak during this period, most notably in May 1968, when a crisis within the universities turned into a broader social and then full-blown political crisis. The June elections of that year were described, and rightly so, as the elections of fear. According to the aforementioned survey by Mattei Dogan, "political behavior in times of crisis expresses a hostility against a party, against an ideology, rather than a deliberate choice for a party, for a leading figure.... In the parliamentary elections of June 1968, most citizens did not vote for a party but rather against other parties."[13]

This fear persisted with the continuation of leftist activism during the first half of the 1970s. The sociologist Jean-Pierre Le Goff has analyzed the period following May 1968, when "a second life began for the extreme leftist groups, particularly the Communist League and the Workers' Left [la Gauche prolétarienne]." Such groups, according to Le Goff, accounted for "the constant agitation in many universities – above all the liberal arts faculties – and in many high schools."[14] The historian of student activism in France, Didier Fischer, has described this "shockwave," this "violence at the university" during the 1970s, and outlined its consequences: "the presence in the universities of these extreme leftist groups, their relentless propaganda, the fraught relations they maintained among themselves and the political context after May 1968 partly account for this atmosphere which prevailed until the mid-1970s."[15] Both authors concluded that the agitation of radical leftists within the universities declined around 1972–1973. As Le Goff demonstrates, the contestation moved beyond the realm of the universities, most notably during the battles at the LIP watch factory at Besançon, the protest against the extension of a military

[13] Dogan, *La majorité passive*.
[14] Jean-Pierre Le Goff, *Mai 68. L'héritage impossible* (Paris, 1998), 143.
[15] Didier Fischer, *L'histoire des étudiants en France de 1945 à nos jours* (Paris, 2000), 441, 453.

base on the Larzac plateau in the southwest of France, and the fight against nuclear power. He stresses, however, that "the second half of the 1970s witnessed the collapse of the revolutionary hopes carried by the extreme left."[16]

The general decline of leftism during the 1970s did not allay right-wing concerns because this period also saw socialist, communist, and other radical left parties join ranks in a common government program in 1972.[17] Even if this union was called into question in 1977, it did not stop the significant electoral advance of those groups opposed to Gaullist and, later, Giscardian power. The leftist groups garnered good results in the 1973 general elections as well as in the 1974 presidential election, when François Mitterrand did very well. They also fared extremely well in the municipal elections of 1977; a large number of cities, especially in the traditionally conservative western part of France, went for the left. Another strong showing in the general election of 1978 was followed by the Socialist victory of 1981. The march toward a Socialist victory was thus clearly underway during the 1970s.

The Actors in the Conservative Mobilization

Confronted with this post-1968 protest and agitation, France's governing conservative parties were clearly on the defensive against a perceived threat, be it from the center-left or the Marxists. A reorganization of the parties on the right resulted in the creation of two new parties in the mid-1970s, the Gaullist Rassemblement pour la République (Rally for the Republic, RPR) led by Jacques Chirac and the liberal-centrist confederation Union pour la Démocratie Française (Union for French Democracy, UDF) inspired by Valéry Giscard d'Estaing. Both parties sought to mobilize the silent majority without using that term. The main actors driving this mobilization were not, however, from the parties' ranks. Remarkably, it was individuals and groups on the fringes of the parties who organized the silent majority. The initiative came from within French civil society and relied upon it.

A number of different groups that were linked to the Gaullists in one way or another worked to mobilize the silent majority by giving speeches,

---

[16] Le Goff, *Mai 68*, 157.

[17] The old Radical Party (founded in 1901) had divided into two parties in 1972: the left wing, which accepted the alliance with socialist and communist parties, and the right wing, which refused and entered into a new federation of parties (Union pour la Démocratie Française [Union for French Democracy], UDF) in 1978.

[margin annotations:]

And the emergence of the sociological movement / ecologist left

1973 Right 310 Left 180

They merged with UMP in 2002, which part of the UDF splintering off that faction is in a sense an ancestor of Macron

The PRG, which is I think still around (and once included Bernard Tapie, of all people)

publishing papers and books, and organizing conferences. In his satirical novel *Pinarque*, Manan depicted these activists as the "assault and shock forces" of the title character, Pinarque/Chirac. This praetorian guard went about "without a uniform, wearing a mere armband marked with their acronym, CDR."[18]

The oldest of the groups involved in the mobilization of the silent majority was the Service d'Action Civique (Civic Action Service, SAC). Founded in 1959 as the security service of the Gaullist Party and sponsored by Jacques Foccart, a close collaborator of Presidents de Gaulle and Pompidou, the SAC was one of the organizers of the Gaullist counterdemonstrations of May 30, 1968. According to François Audigier, "in the 1970s, the SAC was a political lobby acting as a conservative pressure group."[19] It grew weaker toward the end of the decade and was dissolved by the governing left in 1982. The second association was created at the height of the May 1968 events and its name indicates its objective more clearly: the Comités de Défense de la République (Defense Committees of the Republic, CDR). Much like the SAC, it was created at the initiative of Gaullists such as Foccart, Pierre Lefranc, Jacques Belle, and Jacques Godfrain to "give a voice to the 'silent majority' and open the camp for the defense of the regime to non-Gaullists."[20] The committees were active until 1976, when they were integrated into the RPR. The third association targeted a more specific public, that of the universities: this was the Union nationale interuniversitaire (National Interuniversity Union, UNI) established in February 1969 by two academics at the Sorbonne, Frédéric Deloffre and Jacques Rougeot, and a student at the Sciences Po in Paris, Suzanne Marton. Once again, the Gaullist Jacques Foccart was its sponsor, but its links with Gaullism were not as strong as those of the SAC or the CDR. The UNI sought in particular to act as an anti-Marxist pressure group within the conservative majority and to resist the extreme leftist movement on university campuses. As Nassera Mohraz has shown, it maintained good relationships with all the right-wing parties and its discourse was "very close to that of the counterrevolutionary right" of René Rémond.[21] Unlike the SAC and the CDR, the UNI still exists.[22] The members of these associations were frequently involved in other political

---

[18] Manan, *Pinarque*, 131–132.   [19] Audigier, "Le SAC," 351.
[20] Audigier, "Les CDR," 37.
[21] Nassera Mohraz, in Audigier et al., *Les gaullistes*, 63, 68, 72.
[22] The CDR entered the new Gaullist party, the RPR, in 1976; the SAC was dissolved by the Socialist government in 1982 after the murder of one of its leaders in the south of France in 1981.

organizations as well. Many members of the CDR were members of the Union pour la Défense de la République (Union for the Defense of the Republic, UDR), as the Gaullist party renamed itself in 1968, the Association nationale (AN), founded by Gaullists outside of the party in 1958, or the SAC. It was not impossible to be a member of the UNI, the CDR, and the UDR simultaneously. These associations derived their strength from their large memberships. The SAC had about 10,000 members at the end of June 1968, and the CDR had roughly the same number in the early 1970s.

Supplementing the efforts of these groups to mobilize the silent majority were the initiatives of numerous individuals. Three figures played especially important roles: Raymond Marcellin, a well-known politician; Jacques Rougeot, the founder of the UNI; and General Paul Etcheverry, one of the most unusual figures who sought to give voice to France's silent majority.

Marcellin is an exceptionally interesting example. A long-serving politician – he had first been elected to the National Assembly in 1946 – he stood out because he was not a member of the Gaullist party. He belonged, rather, to Giscard d'Estaing's Party of Independent Republicans, representing, alongside men such as Michel Poniatowski, Alain Griotteray, and Philippe Malaud, the party's more authoritarian wing. As minister of the interior under de Gaulle and then Pompidou between May 1968 and February 1974, he was the main representative of the policy of restoring order after the events of May 1968 and became, in the eyes of the extreme left, the symbol of repression and the "fascist threat."[23] Marcellin published two books to explain himself and to mobilize the French. The first appeared in 1969, not long after he had taken up his duties at the Ministry of the Interior. The other was published in 1978, ten years after the events of May 1968.[24] In these books, Marcellin tried to demonstrate that revolutionary groups in France and elsewhere posed a serious threat and, in turn, to argue that all means possible should be used to fight them.

Rougeot published his book, *La contre-offensive* ("The Counterattack"), in 1974. An associate professor of French language and literature at the University of Limoges, he explained that he became involved in political action because "the events of May '68 and their outcome showed

---

[23] Le Goff, *Mai 68*, 189.
[24] Raymond Marcellin, *L'ordre public et les groupes révolutionnaires* (Paris, 1969) and *L'importune vérité* (Paris, 1978).

him both the seriousness of the subversive peril and the weakness, not to mention the inexistence, of an effective means of fighting against it."[25]

Etcheverry's revealingly titled *Lettre ouverte à tous ceux qui la ferment... ou le prix de la liberté* ("Open Letter to All Those Who Remain Silent... or The Price of Freedom") was published in 1976. Etcheverry explained that France was under threat and French patriotism was too weak to confront that threat, and he presented an apologia of the national defense. Addressing the silent majority alluded to in the title of his book, the general rather aggressively explained his intentions and affirmed his right to self-expression: "in all democratic countries in the world, you are called the silent majority... I think I have the right to speak to you quite frankly without hiding my thoughts. I am convinced I have done much more for freedom and democracy than the sermonizers and signatories of protests at Les Deux Magots [the Parisian café famous for being frequented by left-wing intellectuals such as Simone de Beauvoir, Jean-Paul Sartre, and Albert Camus]."[26] He concentrated his argument on France's armed forces because it was the best means to safeguard French freedom.

It thus appears that a diverse array of collective and individual initiatives emerged during the 1970s that sought to mobilize the silent majority. Political leaders, activists operating on the fringes of political parties, and authors of various backgrounds called on the silent majority to react. Their objectives and favored methods are analyzed below. It is worth noting that French conservatives did not seek contacts on the other side of the Atlantic. Although numerous political and grassroots organizations in the United States also sought to rally the silent majority in this period, French conservative mobilization remained a very nationalist affair. If French actors invoked the United States, they did so to criticize American political protest movements. There were no meaningful links between French conservatives and conservative groups in Western Europe or in the United States.

Subversion and the Counterattack

All those who addressed the silent majority defined this group in a similar manner and shared the wish to make its members aware of the seriousness of the threat summed up in the single word "subversion." Their goal was

[25] Jacques Rougeot, *La contre-offensive* (Paris, 1974), back cover.
[26] Jean-Paul Etcheverry, *Lettre ouverte à ceux qui la ferment... ou le prix de la liberté* (Paris, 1976), 18.

to point out the "emergency exits," the actions to be taken to mount the needed "counterattack." The actors based their arguments on the speech given by Charles de Gaulle at the right-wing counterdemonstration of May 30, 1968. The president had denounced

the intimidation, the intoxication and the tyranny exerted by old organized groups and by a party which is a totalitarian enterprise, even if it already has rivals in this respect... In any case, everywhere and immediately, civic action must be organized... preventing subversion at any time and in any place. France, indeed, is threatened by a dictatorship that wishes to constrain it to resign itself to a power which would impose itself in the state of national despair, and which power would then, obviously and essentially, be that of the victor, which is to say that of totalitarian communism.[27]

The first objective of such appeals to the silent majority was to create an awareness of the groups described as hostages of "violent elites" (communists, agitators and troublemakers, leftist intellectuals, and so on). These "hostages" included, according to the SAC, "the families left without electricity after wild strikes, travelers caught in stopped trains and buses on the order of the CGT [the largest confederation of French trade unions], wage-earners forced to stop work by authoritarian picket strikes, the high school and university students kept from studying by a tiny majority of agitators."[28] Such individuals represented the silent majority that had to be mobilized.

Etcheverry had a similar vision of the silent majority. "You have yielded all of the ground to professional protesters who take the lead in the press, on television, in the cinema, in literature, in the universities and in the street." Resorting to irony, he chided his intended audience, "majority, that is what is said... but silent, yes! That's for sure!" And "you, silent majority, I sometimes wonder if you exist." This despair at the majority's silence accounts for the urgency of his appeal to his readers and his use of shock tactics to achieve maximum impact. "Wake up!... You may one day face the wall: either you lay down or you fight. If you prefer to live lying down, this letter has no reason to be. Better to fight in Verdun than to die in Dachau."[29] Thus the general invoked two contrasting French memories of war: the endurance and heroism of World War I and French victimhood in World War II. Etcheverry could be certain that all French people knew what he was referring to. Marcellin

---

[27] Charles de Gaulle, *Discours et messages. Vers le terme janvier 1966–avril 1969* (Paris, 1970).
[28] Audigier, "Le SAC," 352.   [29] Etcheverry, *Lettre ouverte,* 18, 187.

targeted much the same readership with his book *L'ordre public et les groupes révolutionnaires*.[30] Rougeot was irritated by what he called, in the face of "the army of subversion," "the weak underbelly of resistance" among which he classified "the unwitting accomplices, the partisans of inaction, and the partisans of vain or dangerous solutions." Rougeot made a similar reference to World War II when he invoked the "resistance," and he wanted to awaken or even shock the French people with the association of "weak" and "resistance." For the French, the resistance was a glorious episode of French history.[31]

Many of those who sought to awaken France's silent majority argued that the country was threatened by subversion from within and from abroad. Rougeot devoted two-thirds of *La contre-offensive* to a very long analysis of this threat. After explaining that "the revolution is a new form of war," he insisted "France is, indeed, as many other countries, undermined by an endemic war of a particular type, in which the aggressor's aim is not only to seize a territory, but to destroy traditional human relations in order to impose by all means a new form of society." He saw the roots of this subversive movement in the Marxist-Leninist principles to which "all the movements that today truly represent a totalitarian threat" adhered. Rougeot reminded his readers that communists considered "psychological and moral subversion" as tactics to be employed in their revolutionary total war. He showed at length the mechanisms of subversion at work on "the structures [of society] and on men" before describing what he called the "true launching-pads for ideological revolutionaries: teaching and the mass media."[32]

As François Audigier has shown, the SAC moved from a Gaullist stance toward an obsessive anticommunist ideology in the wake of 1968. Describing its mission as "counterrevolutionary," the association declared that its purpose was "to recognize and to fight against this secret and constant work of subversion."[33] The UNI likewise saw itself as dedicated to the fight against "Marxist subversion." Stressing "the systematic character of our anticommunism," Rougeot explained that "communism in itself is a system which is incompatible with any other regime in its principle as well as in its applications... By force of circumstance, one has to accept or reject communism as a whole. It's this second attitude

[30] Marcellin, *L'ordre*, 7.   [31] Rougeot, *La contre-offensive*, 107, 120.

[32] Rougeot, *La contre-offensive*, 10–11, 57.

[33] François Audigier, *Histoire du S.A.C. Service d'Action Civique. La part d'ombre du gaullisme* (Paris, 2003), 427, 431.

which is called systematic anticommunism . . . Thus, to enforce systematic anticommunism means to adapt the retaliation to the very character of the aggression."[34]

One characteristic of the type of subversion the French center-right denounced after 1968 was its international revolutionary dimension. Marcellin was the fiercest proponent of the theory of an "international conspiracy," and he made the fight against international subversion his priority. His book *L'ordre public et les groupes révolutionnaires* focused in large part on identifying the "revolutionary movements that played an active role in the days of May and June 1968" and explaining "the objectives, methods, and international relations of the agitators." Marcellin relied on the quality of the information available to him as minister of the interior to give weight to his arguments and went as far as to justify the publication of his book by referring to the wish "of a great many embassies and foreign government agencies . . . to access the reports of the French minister of the interior." For Marcellin, the subversive agitation was driven by an international dynamic: "the study of movements triggered in the Federal Republic of Germany starting in the spring of 1967, in Italy in November 1967, in Great Britain in 1968, and attempts observed in Holland, from February 1968 on, all showed a troubling simultaneity and a complete resemblance of the methods of action and intervention of revolutionary activist communist groups." Moreover, he maintained, "there was an undeniable solidarity between the revolutionary groups that have developed over the past few years in all the countries of the world." He saw proof of this in the fact that "the leaders of these movements often meet, more particularly the leaders of the student revolutionary movements who hold frequent meetings in Brussels, Amsterdam, Turin, Berlin, and London, where they decide on a common action." He also pointed to "the conference of Havana, called the tricontinental conference," that took place from January 3 to 13, 1966, an event he described as being "of primary significance on the ideological and 'organizational' levels." It was the first meeting "of leaders of government organizations from so-called socialist countries with revolutionary leaders representing revolutionary movements from around the world."[35]

These denunciations were intended to inform the public and to dispel the complacency of the silent majority. Despite their fears of the revolutionary international, however, French conservative leaders did

---

[34] Rougeot, *La contre-offensive*, 148–149.   [35] Marcellin, *L'ordre*, 9, 40–43.

not attempt to forge transnational alliances because their ideology was impregnated by a strong nationalism of long-standing.

The tools for the campaign to awaken the silent majority were very diverse. Conservatives drew on the whole range of modern means of communication and copied the methods of their opponents without hesitation. The main platforms were classic vehicles such as the press. Each antisubversion association published its own newspaper at some point. The SAC, for example, published *Action Civique* (Civic Action) between 1969 and 1981 along with occasional publications such as *Information-Combat* (Combat Information), issued on the occasion of the general elections of 1973, and a regional bulletin. The CDR produced the magazine *Citoyen* (Citizen). Starting in 1970, the UNI published a monthly newspaper, *L'Action universitaire* (University Action). Books, as noted earlier, were another means to counter the revolutionaries. Besides Etcheverry, Marcellin, and Rougeot, activist authors on the right included figures such as Roger Mucchielli, a neuropsychiatrist, and UNI members who published *La Subversion* (Subversion) in 1972.

Other means were undeniably more modern. As François Audigier notes, "the CDR made the lines move in so far as communication was concerned by implementing a new and efficient 'right-wing agit-prop' that used innovative techniques such as the political sticker, the loudspeaker... radio programs using the live reactions of listeners who called in... posters... with powerful texts... [and] Manichean visuals." The CDR, Audigier contends, succeeded in its "astonishing attempt to subvert the enemy's visuals" by adopting that enemy's "graphic codes in terms of image composition, register of color and typographical choices."[36]

This information campaign was, however, only the first step toward a successful counterattack. Conservatives also sought to dismantle the mechanisms of subversive action, to engage in what might be called antisubversion. They made the opposition of the "silent ones" visible in public actions. The titles of the aforementioned publications often used the word "action" and sometimes also invoked a "fight." Yves Lancien, the secretary general of the CDR, did not hesitate to use martial rhetoric to mobilize his troops in 1972: "the UDR is the body of the battle, the CDR is the army of partisans."[37]

[36] Audigier, "Les CDR," 53–54.

[37] Jérôme Pozzi, *Les mouvements gaullistes. Partis, associations et réseaux 1958–1976* (Rennes, 2011), 241.

Action against subversion began at the top of the state, even if a number of the propagandists engaged in the fight considered it to be too weak. Rougeot blamed the "big-hearted moderates who believe that one day they will bring these lost sheep [or these] moderates so often paralyzed by their scruples back into the fold."[38] They denounced the liberal reforms undertaken by Edgar Faure, Jacques Chaban-Delmas, and, later, Giscard d'Estaing. The gap between the conservatives and the center-right widened when Prime Minister Chaban-Delmas exhorted the governing majority in the National Assembly not to "change into a force of conservatism and immobility in the name of order."[39] Nevertheless, dynamic conservative associations were able to pressure the parliamentary majority and the government into taking a more conservative stance. They had a number of allies in the government, parliament, and the president's entourage, including Jacques Foccart, Joseph Comiti, Charles Pasqua, and Jacques Chirac.

The conservatives' greatest supporter in the governments between 1968 and 1974 was the minister of the interior, Marcellin. In his writings, he set out the theory behind his policies. Insisting that he was "defending democracy and Republican legality against subversion," he constantly reminded the members of the silent majority that "power is in the ballot box, not in the street." In practice, the minister wanted to "hit the head of the revolutionary groups in order to disorganize them."[40] He also justified serious infringements of democratic rights: "during all the years when revolutionary minorities systematically intervened and were ready to commit all kinds of acts of violence against property and people, [telephone] tapping was very useful to maintain public order."[41] In addition to an often brutal policy of repression, Marcellin played an important role in initiating two laws that prompted considerable controversy: the law of June 8, 1970, "aimed at repressing certain forms of delinquency," also known as "the antidelinquency law," and the law of June 24, 1971, which allowed prefects to subject certain associations to an a priori control by judicial authorities.

Some of the actions proposed to mobilize civil society were extremely modest, even timid, and others more daring and innovative. The first category includes Etcheverry's call in his "Open Letter" for the silent majority

---

[38] Rougeot, *La contre-offensive*, 118.

[39] Jacques Chaban-Delmas to the French deputies, April 20, 1971. See Jean-Pierre Machelon "Chaban-Delmas et les libertés," in Bernard Lachaise, Gilles Le Béguec, and Jean-François Sirinelli, eds., *Jacques Chaban-Delmas en politique* (Paris, 2007), 232–233.

[40] Marcellin, *L'ordre*, 66, 76.   [41] Marcellin, *L'impossible*, 10, 217.

to take action: "in a democracy such as ours, there is no lack of means. Write to your newspapers to make your disagreement known if necessary. Unsubscribe if they continue. Talk to your elected representatives, mayors, municipal councillors, deputies."[42] The second category includes the "countersubversive" methods practiced by the CDR: "the CDR would establish contact with the adversary in factories, in the administration, in the university or in the high schools to better confront it on the field."[43] That approach was identical to that extolled by Rougeot and the UNI: "total war... has to be answered by total defense, led both upon firm principles and according to a strategic movement, in which each member feels mobilized to fulfill his mission in the sector where he can be most efficient."[44]

[handwritten margin notes: An totally legitimate. This sounds a lot like national security doctrine]

To what extent, then, did the mobilization of the silent majority succeed? That is the final question to address in this chapter.

It is undeniable that there were numerous initiatives taken on the fringes of political parties – especially but not solely the Gaullist parties – by associations seeking to mobilize the enemies of "havoc" who otherwise had little incentive to get involved and to put up resistance against all sorts of agitators. An early example of this was given at a meeting organized by the CDR in Paris very soon after the successful demonstration of May 30, 1968. Taking place the day before the first round of national elections, the gathering of June 20, 1968, attracted around 40,000 people.[45]

It is very likely that the mobilization of many of "the silent ones" hindered the initiatives of the leftists and slowed down the electoral progress of the united left in 1973 for certain, and possibly in 1978 as well. The effect of the right's ideological counteroffensive is more difficult to assess. Its ideas reached the public through tracts, posters, meetings, and so on. Given the lack of sources, it is difficult to judge the impact of books by the leaders of mobilization. Certainly, authors such as Marcellin and Etcheverry enjoyed considerable media attention when they were invited to participate in television programs. The energetic and often brutal policy to protect public order carried out under Minister of the Interior Marcellin unquestionably had a significant impact on the action of the leftists. But it would be inaccurate to suggest that the government alone put an end to leftist activism. As the philosopher Louis Althusser noted during the funeral of the Maoist activist Pierre Overney, who had been killed by a guard at a Renault factory on February 25, 1972: "today we are

[42] Etcheverry, *Lettre ouverte*, 182.   [43] Audigier, "Les CDR," 47.

[44] Rougeot, *La contre-offensive*, 12   [45] Pozzi, *Les mouvements gaullistes*, 237.

The PS was almost deliberately radical!

burying not Overney but leftism."[46] And indeed, militant leftist activism had all but ceased by the mid-1970s. Some former leftist militants engaged in new social movements, such as environmentalism, feminism, and the defense of Eastern European dissidents. Some joined new political groups, such as the new Socialist Party (PS) established in 1971.

But given that the decade ended with an electoral victory of the left, is it possible to characterize the mobilization of "the silent ones" during the 1970s as a success? For UNI, the presence of a socialist in the Elysée and of communists in the government following the May 1981 election represented "a victory of the 'Marxist subversion.'"[47] However, the power of the PCF (French Communist Party) at the polls was no longer what it had been: the party's share of the vote had declined from 22.5 percent in 1967 to 20.5 percent in 1978. Moreover, it saw itself overshadowed from 1973 on by the PS, which had increased its share of the vote from 19 to 24.7 percent during the same period. The revolutionary threat that the spokespersons of the silent majority saw on the left had been thwarted by the time of the 1973 election, and the small organizations of the extreme left – Lutte Ouvrière (Workers' Combat, LO) and the Ligue Révolutionnaire (Revolutionary League, LR; later Ligue Communiste Révolutionnaire, LCR) – chose the route of lawful activity. They began competing in the electoral arena with the presidential race of 1974 and the parliamentary elections of 1978.

The mobilization of the silent majority contributed to the rightward move of French political life. The center-right Gaullist and Giscardian parties that had governed France since 1958 had their progressive left wings and their more conservative right wings. The events of 1968 stoked conservative fears of revolution, increasing the influence of the right wing. For the French left, the conservatives' shift toward the right seemed to be a rerun of the 1930s, which saw the rise of extra-parliamentary political movements, and of the war years, with Marshal Pétain's "national movement." The left thus warned of a "French-style Salazarization," and the far left went so far as to denounce the threat posed by "fascism" from above.[48]

Leaving aside the question of success, it is clear that the mobilization of France's silent majority in the 1970s was the opening salvo in a continuing attack on 1968. "Hatred of May '68" has grown steadily over the years and accelerated noticeably during the opening decade of the

---

[46] Fischer, *L'histoire des étudiants*, 455–456.
[47] Mohraz, in Audigier et al., *Les gaullistes*, 62.   [48] Le Goff, *Mai 68*, 167, 189.

twenty-first century. As evidenced by the speeches of Nicolas Sarkozy, denunciation of 1968 has become an important element in conservative discourse.[49] In his 2007 campaign, for instance, Sarkozy often explained that he wanted to liquidate the spirit of May 1968. The victory of the Socialist François Hollande in 2012 did not signal the end of the shift to the right. Hollande's victory was more a result of French voters' rejection of Sarkozy's leadership style than of their support for the Socialists' program. The 2014 election proved once again that right-wing groups and the extreme right have a real place in French political life.

[handwritten note top right: The FN/RN also detests the '68 legacy (though Marine has rehabille and tacitally accepted some d it]

[handwritten note: C4₀ (2-7)]

[49] Serge Audier, *La pensée anti-68. Essai sur les origines d'une restauration intellectuelle* (Paris, 2008).

[handwritten note: — LO ran Arlette Laguillier in '81, '7urvle]

[handwritten note: — A fear shared by Beringuer]

6

The Silent Majority

A Humean Perspective

Donald T. Critchlow

In the late 1960s and 1970s, Republicans seized on the law and order issue to attack Democrats as the party of discord. Richard Nixon employed "law and order" as a major theme in his successful presidential campaign in 1968 and again in his bid for reelection to the White House in 1972.

Democratic opponents at the time, and later scholars, accused Republicans of using law and order as sheer opportunism meant to tap into voters' racial fears, which had been intensified by urban riots and rising crime rates. "Law and order," critics charged, were only code words for racial prejudices and fears.[1] To accuse politicians, right or left, of opportunism seems rather banal, but the charge of racism needs to be taken seriously. Clearly, racial tensions had increased in the late 1960s in the aftermath of urban riots across the nation, the rise of black nationalism, and rising crime rates. Racial code words should not be dismissed in the call for "law and order." What should be noted, though, is that in survey after survey blacks were as supportive of the call for "law and order" as whites even if they were more inclined than whites to attribute social disturbances and rising crime rates to the problems of poverty and social

They were right /

---

[1] There is a substantial secondary literature arguing that law and order were code words for racism. For example see Dan T. Carter, *From George Wallace to Newt Gingrich: Race in the Conservative Counterrevolution, 1963–1995* (Baton Rouge, 1999) and *The Politics of Rage: George Wallace, The Origins of the New Conservatism, and the Transformation of American Politics* (Baton Rouge, 2nd ed., 2000); Joseph Crispino, *In Search of Another Country: Mississippi and the Conservative Counterrevolution* (Princeton, 2009); Manning Marable, *Race, Reform, and Rebellion: The Second Reconstruction and Beyond in Black America, 1945–2006* (Oxford, MS, 2007); and Donald T. Critchlow and Nancy MacLean, *Debating the Conservative Movement, 1945 to the Present* (Lanham, MD, 2009), 123–176.

inequality. Nonetheless, in surveys the majority of blacks expressed little sympathy for black nationalism or revolutionary groups such as the Black Panthers.

The use of rhetoric in American politics has attracted increasing attention by scholars. In focusing on the rhetoric of politics, we need to keep in mind the context in which language is used by politicians in order to explore more deeply the interplay between principle and practice in political life. A tendency to view the rhetoric of principle as only ex post facto rationalizations in the pursuit of ambition is an assumption easily reached if one believes that politics is about the acquisition and exercise of power. Indeed, the great student of English politics Lewis Namier concluded over fifty years ago that "considerations of principle or even of policy had only limited relevance" in the study of politics.[2] From the Namierite perspective, professed principles provide only a facade for the otherwise naked desire for power. Such a perspective, however, does not explain why politicians decide to campaign on one set of issues and not another, or to employ a certain rhetoric and not another. Focusing on the example of Lord Bolingbroke, Quentin Skinner has argued that Namier assumes that the Tory politician's use of language reflects an opportunistic use of principles.[3] Skinner counters that articulated principles, however rhetorical, do express actual political motives. He insightfully and logically maintains that stated principles can reflect genuine beliefs that motivate a politician even if at the same time expressing self-interest and political opportunism. In this way, the profession of principle and political opportunism are not mutually exclusive. Principle and opportunism might both spur a politician to seize upon a particular issue in the pursuit of votes and power. Principle can motivate a politician, while at the same time such a politician might behave opportunistically by seizing upon an issue or issues that he or she believes will win political power.[4]

In the late 1960s and 1970s, the demand for order reflected a reaction against social disturbances of the period. During the social discord of the 1970s, Republican rhetoric of law and order struck a deep chord in many segments of the American electorate distressed by what they were

[2] L. B. Namier, *Personalities and Powers* (London, 1955), 3.

[3] Quentin Skinner, "The Principles and Practice of Opposition: The Case of Bolingbroke versus Walpole," in Neil McKendrick, ed., *Historical Perspectives: Studies in English Thought and Society* (London, 1974), 93–128.

[4] There is an extensive literature on Bolingbroke, ably explored by Isaac Kramnick, *Bolingbroke and His Circle: The Politics of Nostalgia in the Age of Walpole* (Cambridge, MA, 1968).

— Or about them via mass media

witnessing in their streets, neighborhoods, and cities. Liberal Democrats appeared to some to condone and even encourage these destructive activities. Law and order rhetoric appealed to the natural disposition of most citizens for social order. The first obligation of government, most believed, was to maintain order and protect the safety of its citizens. If law and order projected "otherness" on rioters, protesters, and revolutionaries, this rhetoric also signified to voters that liberalism and the revolutionary left were twin threats to American stability.

Which was also racial — order. and at times had little to with the rule of law / Creating the wildview of the SHL radical

The revival of the Republican Party in the late 1960s and early 1970s, as evidenced in Richard Nixon's election (1969-74) to the White House, occurred only because of disarray within the Democratic Party and a foreboding sense within the electorate that the world was coming apart and the Democrats were unable to hold it together – and, indeed, had contributed to social disequilibrium. Urban race riots, student protests, identity politics, the perceived loss of American power in the midst of the Vietnam War, adventurist Soviet foreign policy, and radical calls for revolution caused many voters, "the Silent Majority" (Nixon's phrase), to turn to Republicans in their call for "law and order," restoration of national power, and responsible government.

But not crushing the Black elements & their coalition

Many scholars have categorized the American right as reactionary, often putting into one category Nixon Republicans, conservatives, the religious right, white supremacists, and right-wing extremists. Often scholars have found race as the catalyst in right-wing reaction. In exploring the right in the 1970s, this chapter maintains that distinctions should be made in exactly what is meant by the right wing and offers a more nuanced examination of how left-wing politics – in its various forms from Great Society liberalism to New Left radicalism – set off a chain reaction within American politics in unforeseen ways, including a deepening ideological divide within the electorate combined with a growing distrust of government. The Watergate scandal in Nixon's unfinished second presidential term then added to this distrust.

This comes perilously close to blaming the (left) unrefor their advocacies' actions and wrongdoing

Leftist activism, campus and antiwar protest, black militancy, and ethnic identity politics set the stage for the conservative ascendancy in the 1970s, but these political trends also transformed the Democratic Party and liberalism in this same decade. Scholars have paid great attention to the rise of conservatism in the 1970s and afterwards but have given less attention to the transformation of the Democratic Party and the progressive tradition.

In examining the external factors that set the context for the conservative ascendancy, many historians have pointed to the white backlash to racial integration and affirmative action.[5] Racial politics without a doubt was an important element in reordering electoral alignments. Without dismissing the importance of race, this factor needs to be placed in a larger and more nuanced examination of how this issue played into larger voter concerns of law and order and how Republican politicians translated voters' concerns into electoral victories. Law and order was only one of many issues that set the context for a Republican revival. Equally important for explaining the rise of the right in the 1970s were religion and national defense.

Whatever the immediate internal and external conditions that set the context for a political campaign, the articulation of broad principles and specific issues needs to resonate within the electorate. Societies develop, as philosopher David Hume observed in the eighteenth century, agreed-upon conventions that maintain order among contentious interests and factions that naturally emerge with development. By conventions, Hume means institutions, rules, and regular order that a stable, successful political state must have in order to maintain itself. Political authority provides necessary stability to maintain conventions that provide ways for people to live together and distribute political and social goods. Political authority, embodied in government and jurisprudence, allows for resolution of claims and adjudication. In any governmental system, political authority ultimately rests on the consensus and obedience of its citizens to the regime. A challenge to society's fundamental conventions proposes, in effect, to tear the polity or society by its roots and to begin another. Revolutions and civil war occur when a large number of people challenge existing conventions and thereby refuse to accept standing authority. In such conditions, the people show a willingness to topple the equilibrium between authority and obedience in hopes of finding a new one.[6]

If Hume is correct in his assessment of the importance of fundamental convention and political authority, politics in the 1960s and 1970s can be framed as a radical challenge to dismantle the existing consensus and the conservative response to this contest. An ethos of anti-authoritarianism prevailed in the intellectual and revolutionary left during this period. In

---

[5] Matthew D. Lassiter, *The Silent Majority: Suburban Politics in the Sunbelt South* (Princeton, 2007) offers a more complex view of this backlash interpretation of conservatism. Also see note 1.

[6] Andrew Sabl, *Hume's Politics: Coordination and Crisis in the History of England* (Princeton, 2012), 7–9, 32, 37, and 189. There is a rich literature on Hume's political thought, including, more recently, Russell Hardin, *David Hume: Moral and Political Theorist* (New York, 2007). Sabl and Hardin inform especially this brief discussion of Hume.

the end, most voters perceived neither the liberal nor revolutionary left as offering a *viable* alternative to the existing order that had come under intense attack, socially and politically. At a fundamental level, liberals and radicals both failed to make a case for a fundamental reordering of American society. Liberal Democrats promised more spending through programs to address the conditions that they believed caused high crime rates, urban riots, and social discord, but many voters felt that Lyndon B. Johnson's Great Society had tried this already and conditions had only worsened, leading to more crime, more riots, and more radical demands. The revolutionary left offered vague concepts of "community control," "participatory democracy," and socialist utopia. Many on the revolutionary left, in both the United States and Europe, looked to what was then called the "Third World," specifically China and Cuba, as models for authentic egalitarianism.[7] To the average American, the idea of a modern, post-industrial nation like the United States copying these nations seemed crackpot. Many leftists attracted to revolutionary regimes in Cuba and China, on the other hand, viewed America as a land of racism, with a three hundred-year history of slavery, legal segregation, and economic exploitation.

Sectarian proclamations, revolutionary party platforms, and inflammatory statements by radical groups found little audience within the general public. The Students for a Democratic Society's Port Huron Statement (1962), later reprinted in dozens of anthologies, mostly circulated in New Left circles and was vague on specifics of what kind of new society was envisioned, other than calling for more participation, less alienation, and more equity. It is doubtful that many people, even on the left, read the Revolutionary Youth Movement II's "Weatherman" Statement ("You Don't Need a Weatherman ... ").

What Americans did read about proposed alternative visions was not reassuring, except for those given to utopian beliefs. Charles Reich, a Yale University law professor, articulated utopian sentiment in his best-selling *The Greening of America* (1970). Reich envisioned in his book a coming revolution that "promises a higher reason, a more human community, and a new and liberated individual. Its ultimate creation will be a new and enduring wholeness and beauty – a renewed relationship of man to

[7] Especially insightful commentary on the left's infatuation with the Third World is found in Quinn Slobodian's sympathetic look at the German revolutionary left, *Foreign Front: Third World Politics in Sixties West Germany* (Durham, NC, 2012). Similar expressions of Maoist and Fidelist sympathies were found on the revolutionary left in France, Great Britain, the United States, and Latin America in this period.

himself, to other men, to society, to nature, and to land."[8] Offering only vague consciousness-raising rhetoric, Reich did not spell out exactly how this "greening" was to come about. Nor did he detail exactly what this new society was to look like beyond telling readers it would be better than what existed today in America or other countries.

Average voters – the "Silent Majority" – might not have been content with politics-as-usual, but Reich's call for a countercultural transformation did not offer a viable alternative. The Vietnam War, rising inflation, high unemployment, corruption in government, self-serving politicians, and a general sense of national decline exacerbated widespread discontent within the electorate. This discontent would be captured by populist demagogues such as George Wallace, segregationist governor of Alabama, in his bid to win the Democratic presidential nomination and his third-party movement in 1968.[9] Within the electorate, there were fears of social disintegration, but there was *not* a crisis of political legitimacy. The revolutionary left in America, never sizable but a visible presence in the anti-Vietnam War and civil rights movements, failed to understand this point. Its objections to the status quo and its proposed political programs failed to tap into current discontent within the general electorate or to generate a realistic political alternative to the existing order.

The violence of the revolutionary left as it developed in the 1960s shocked mainstream America, Nixon's silent majority.[10] Trashing campus buildings and burning down the neighborhood mostly validated the belief that radicals and rioters, for all their anger, were devoid of serious political ideas or constructive policies for change. This violence expressed the alienation of student radicals and militant blacks who rejected traditional notions of authority and the moral legitimacy of institutions.[11] Rejecting traditional moral constraints as artificial and arbitrary reflections of white ruling-class rule, radicals became increasingly susceptible to the seductive appeal of violence. Civil rights leader Martin Luther King's

---

[8] Charles Reich, *The Greening of America* (New York, 1976), 468.

[9] Carter, *The Politics of Rage*; see also Christopher Crispino, *Strom Thurmond's America* (New York, 2011).

[10] There is a multitude of books on the 1960s, student protest, youth radicalism, black nationalism, and counterculture. This author found David Farber, *The Age of Great Dreams: America in the 1960s* (Boston, 1994) especially useful, although it has been supplemented by more recent scholarship.

[11] This anti-authoritarian ethos is explored in Alan Petigny's unpublished manuscript, "The Crisis of Authority and the Rise of Moral Relativism: America, 1945–1980," which was left uncompleted before his death in 2013. (Copy of draft in the author's possession, with due thanks to Alan's close friend, David Beito.)

strategy of creative non-violence was rejected by the new radicals as ineffective and based on the false assumption that civil rights protesters' display of love and humility was capable of touching the hearts and changing the attitudes of racist oppressors. By the late 1960s, peaceful protest had been replaced in many left circles by Mao's belief that power "flows through the barrel of a gun."

King's call for non-violence was rejected in favor of violent insurgency by militant groups such as the Black Panthers and Weatherman. Inspiration was drawn not from Gandhi but from Frantz Fanon's *The Wretched of the Earth*, published shortly before his death in 1961. Fanon became required reading for Black Panther recruits. This obsession with violence as a means of social change manifested itself in posters of Che Guevara and Black Panther Huey Newton found in dorm rooms and on apartment walls; sales of *The Anarchist Cookbook*; readings of Mao's "Little Red Book" at the start of Panther rallies and radical student meetings; and the radicalization of Students for a Democratic Society. Revolutionaries represented only a small segment in black communities or on college campuses, but they were vocal and visible in the news and made their presence felt on the left.

This romantic fascination with violence had been evident a decade earlier when Norman Mailer published his essay "The White Negro" in the small but influential democratic-socialist magazine *Dissent* in the fall of 1957. A leading novelist of the period, Mailer emerged as a cultural icon whose fascination with violence portended a cultural turn for young radicals in the late 1960s. His 1957 essay offered a defense of the "black hipster" who used violence to purge himself of self-loathing and to express a vital, authentic existence. The black hipster understood "in the cells of his existence that life was war, nothing but war," and defied rightly in Mailer's view the Judeo-Christian ethic. Mailer went on to praise the "nihilism" of hip, which, he explained, "proposes as its final tendency that every social restraint and category be removed."[12] Of course, many liberal critics rejected Mailer's espousal of violence, seen in his personal life and writing, but his apology for violence was only one manifestation among others reflecting an infatuation with violence.

Militant pacifism was a strong force in the anti-Vietnam War movement in the United States and the United Kingdom. Pacifism, rooted in

[12] Mailer's essay was republished by City Light Books: Norman Mailer, *The White Negro: Superficial Reflections of the Hipster* (San Francisco, 1957). See also Mary Dearborn, *Mailer: A Biography* (New York, 1999).

Protestant and Catholic thought, had long been a facet of the American radical tradition and remained a potent influence in the postwar period.[13] Pacifists such as David Dellinger, Bayard Rustin, and Joan Baez remained committed to non-violence throughout these years.[14] This pacifist tradition on the American left notwithstanding, the heat of the Vietnam War softened at times the lines between non-violent protest and violent action within the radical peace movement. The most notable shift from non-violence to violence occurred within the Student Non-Violent Coordinating Committee (SNCC), which had been founded in 1961 by Southern black college students who admired Martin Luther King, Jr. This organization's rejection of non-violence for self-defense at first, and then self-defense and subsequent turn to revolution, came in direct response to violent attacks, including murder by segregationist white supremacist groups and individuals, as well as state-sponsored violence.[15] Less well known is New Left activist Tom Hayden's rejection of non-violence for revolutionary action that came with his support for Weatherman and Maoism.[16]

Arguably most striking in this move from non-violence toward violence were two Catholic priest-activists, the Berrigan brothers, Daniel, a Jesuit, and Philip, a Josephite. They became national news when they led seven other Catholic antiwar activists into the draft board in Catonsville, Maryland, in 1968 to seize and burn 350 draft files before a bevy of news reporters.[17] This action inspired other Catholic activists to conduct similar raids on draft boards across the country. In Milwaukee, fourteen

[13] Marian Mollin, *Radical Pacifism in Modern America: Egalitarianism and Protest* (Philadelphia, 2006); Caroline Moorhead, *Troublesome People: The Warriors of Pacifism* (London, 1987); and for the Catholic tradition, Anne Klejmert, *American Catholic Pacifism: The Influence of Dorothy Day and the Catholic Worker Movement* (New York, 1996).

[14] Andrew E. Hunt, *David Dellinger: The Life and Times of a Nonviolent Revolutionary* (New York, 2006); and Dellinger's autobiography, *From Yale to Jail* (New York, 1993).

[15] Useful on the militant civil rights movement is Glenda Gilmor, *Defying Dixie: The Radical Roots of Civil Rights, 1917–1956* (New York, 2008). Howard Zinn, *SNCC: Student Nonviolent Coordinating Committee* (Boston, 1968) captures the mood of the period. Also, see Joseph E. Peniel, *Stokeley: A Life* (New York, 2014) and H. Rap Brown, *A Political Autobiography of Jamil Abdullah al Amin* (Chicago, 2002).

[16] A good biography of Tom Hayden needs to be written, but a good starting place is his own *Reunion: A Memoir* (New York, 1989); and, for the early years, James Miller, *Democracy in the Streets: From Port Huron to the Siege in Chicago* (Cambridge, MA, 1994); and Todd Gitlin, *The Sixties: Years of Hope, Days of Rage* (New York, 1997).

[17] Shawn Francis Peters, *The Catonsville Nine: The Story of Faith and Resistance in the Vietnam Era* (New York, 2012); and Charles A. Meconis, *With Clumsy Grace: The American Catholic Left* (New York, 1979).

Catholic activists were arrested when they burned 10,000 draft records; raids followed in Boston and Washington, DC. Following their convictions for the Catonsville action, the Berrigans became fugitives, making the FBI's Ten Most Wanted List. Daniel Berrigan became a national figure.

Meanwhile, Philip Berrigan appeared to flirt with violence with Sister Elizabeth McCallister when they began talking about the feasibility of kidnapping National Security Advisor Henry Kissinger and blowing up underground steam tunnels in the nation's capital to disrupt the heating of federal office buildings. Although the government was unsuccessful in its prosecution of Sister McCallister and others involved in this alleged conspiracy, letters between her and Philip Berrigan revealed an openness to violence as a means of resistance. In this correspondence with Sister McAllister, Berrigan acknowledged that the kidnapping of Kissinger could lead to murder.

In his memoirs, Philip Berrigan maintained that he had never planned kidnapping Kissinger, but evidence suggested that he, his brother, and others involved in the case had explored the idea of making a "citizen's arrest" of Kissinger. Although conspiracy was not proved in the federal case against Berrigan and others, even entertaining such a plan, even if just idle talk, reveals how fragile the doctrine of non-coercive resistance had become in certain radical circles.[18]

Average Americans – black and white – felt threatened by the radical rhetoric of violence and all the more so by actual incidents of radical violence. Revolutionary violence in its rhetoric and action challenged the established conventions of a representative democratic polity in which change was directed through the electoral process. The challenge presented by young and black revolutionaries occurred within a context of racial rioting and rising crime rates. Race riots caused by social frustration among inner-city blacks did irreparable political damage to liberals largely because liberals were often slow to condemn violence.

Surveys showed consistently improving attitudes among whites toward blacks in both the North and the South, including a growing acceptance of school integration. Pronounced differences in how school integration was to be achieved, however, revealed that racial tensions had not entirely

[18] Philip Berrigan, *Fighting the Lamb's War: Skirmishes with the American Empire* (Monroe, ME, 2011), 126–127; and Murray Polner and Jim O'Grady, *Disarmed and Dangerous: The Radical Lives and Times of Daniel and Philip Berrigan* (New York, 1997), 282.

abated. Racial riots did not detour improving racial attitudes but raised apprehension among whites about social order and weakened support for Johnson's Great Society programs. A Gallup poll taken in 1967 revealed that 45 percent of whites (10 percent of blacks) blamed racial riots on outside agitators, while 16 percent of whites (36 percent of blacks) believed that "prejudice, promises not kept, and bad treatment" explained riots. Only 14 percent of whites (28 percent of blacks) believed that poverty, slums, and ghetto conditions caused the riots. Attitudes toward law and order at the time were revealed in a Harris poll that asked people whether "people who throw fire bombs in riots should be shot." Among whites, 68 percent said "yes," 22 percent replied "no"; blacks were nearly evenly divided on the issue with 47 percent answering "yes," and 42 percent responding "no."[19]

Only five days after Johnson signed the Voting Rights Act of 1965, the Watts riot in Los Angeles shocked the nation. Although not linked to the legislation, the Watts riot suggested that progress on civil rights was not necessarily a remedy for social ills in America's inner cities. The following year, there were thirty-eight riots that killed seven people and injured 500. In the first nine months of 1967, there were 164 riots. Riots in Newark, New Jersey, and Detroit, Michigan, lasted for a week each and left a total of sixty-four people dead. In Detroit, federal troops were called out to suppress the rioting – the third time in American history that federal troops were sent to quell a local insurrection.[20] These riots undermined white blue-collar and middle-class support for the Great Society. As a leading historian of law and order in this period concludes, "In the eyes of critics on the left and the right, the riots had discredited the entire liberal enterprise."[21]

Republicans sought to capitalize on these fears of riots, student protest, revolutionary violence, and rising crime rates, especially of violent crimes such as murder, mugging, armed robbery, and rape. Conservatives blamed the rising crime rate on lenient courts and liberals "soft" on crime. Later studies showed that rising crime rates in this period had more to

[19] For an excellent discussion of racial attitudes on urban riots, see Rita James Simon, *Public Opinion in America, 1936–1970* (Chicago, 1974), 55–75, especially 71–72.

[20] Sidney Fine, *Violence in the Model City: The Cavanaugh Administration, Race Relations, and the Detroit Riot of 1967* (East Lansing, MI, 2007); and Jerry Cohen and William S. Murphy, *Burn Baby Burn: The Watts Riot* (New York, 1967).

[21] Michael W. Flamm, *Law and Order: Street Crime, Civil Unrest, and the Crisis of Liberalism in the 1960s* (New York, 2005), 83. Also, James T. Patterson, *Grand Expectations: The United States, 1945–1974* (New York, 1996), 662–663.

do with a higher proportion of young people in the population, but at the time, many Americans were less concerned about the causes of rising crime rates than the fact that crime rates were rising and were perceived to be rising.[22] The issue of race, no doubt, factored into this call for law and order. After all, much of American history can be encapsulated into three Rs – race, religion, and real estate – that have dictated the course of the nation. Race, though, was not the only issue that gave salience to the Republican call for law and order. The shift to the Republican Party in the South was already underway before the 1960s when law and order emerged as important; and in the North, student protest and a generalized repulsion against the counterculture – symbolized by drug use and hippies – was apparent in the politics of California in the mid-1960s.

The South's transformation into a Republican stronghold had already begun on the presidential level in the 1950s, followed by a shift on the district level in statewide races in the 1960s. This shift was gradual and began in the suburbs. These suburban voters were concerned with issues such as low taxes, anti-unionism, and family values, and they moved into the Republican Party. Many were business-oriented traditional Republicans who had migrated from Northern suburbs. As political scientists Byron Shafer and Richard Johnston demonstrate in *The End of Southern Exceptionalism*, it was economics, not race, that won the South for the Republicans.[23] The burgeoning suburban middle classes went Republican in 1980 and in the elections that followed because of promises of tax cuts and a smaller federal government. In this regard, it is interesting to compare voting patterns in the South in the presidential elections of 1968, 1976, and 1980. In 1976, when Carter first ran for president, he picked up majorities in 79 percent of the districts in the South that had voted for Wallace in 1968 but carried only 59 percent of the districts in the South that went for Nixon in 1968. In the 1980 election, when Ronald Reagan swept the South, the majority of those districts that voted for Carter were those that had voted for Wallace in 1968. This suggests that Wallace was not the bridge candidate at the time who brought traditionally Democratic white voters in the South into the Republican Party.

Race and law and order played out in peculiar ways outside the South. California presents an especially interesting example of how racial

[22] An extensive literature can be found on rising crime rates in the late 1960s and 1970s. An excellent beginning point into this topic is found in James Q. Wilson, *Thinking about Crime* (New York, 2013).

[23] Byron Shafer and Richard Johnston, *The End of Southern Exceptionalism* (Cambridge, MA, 2006).

politics enabled Republicans to win the governor's mansion and launched the political career of Ronald Reagan. Since the 1930s, California had been a Democratic stronghold in terms of voter registration. After Edmund "Pat" Brown defeated Richard Nixon to win reelection to the governorship in 1962, the state Democratic Party was confident that California's factionalized Republicans had been decisively rendered the minority party in the state.

Brown's triumph in 1962 over Nixon left Democrats euphoric. Brown called for a further expansion of a bold legislative program. Nothing, it seemed, stood in his way politically. Brown, however, decided to push fair housing legislation through the state legislature against the advice of his closest advisors. His executive secretary Richard Kline had warned him as early as 1960 that "Housing is such an explosive social subject . . . The question is not what has to be done in this field, but what can be done from a politically realistic standpoint."[24]

Under pressure from civil rights groups and other lobbies, Brown announced that he was proposing the Rumford Fair Housing Act, named in honor of an African American legislator who had long advocated such a measure. The act banned discrimination in the sale or rental of private dwellings with a few exceptions. The legislation had been floating around the state legislature for a while, bottled up in committee by a group of powerful conservative Democrats representing rural districts. Rallying liberal groups to his side, Brown pushed through the measure by a slim margin. Real estate interests in the state reacted immediately by placing Proposition 14 to repeal the Rumford Fair Housing Act on the 1964 ballot. Brown came out immediately against Proposition 14, attending rallies where he denounced right-wing extremism and racism in California. The anti-Prop 14 campaign labeled the proposition "the segregation amendment" and attacked their opponents as right-wing extremists. For political powerhouses such as Speaker of the Assembly Jesse Unruh, Proposition 14 was a powder keg to be avoided at all costs.

By the fall of 1964, polls showed overwhelming support for Proposition 14. For many Californians, it was a matter of property rights over civil rights. Television advertisements argued that "a man's home is his castle," and he has the right to sell it or not as he pleased. The advertisements were effective because they suggested that Brown was trying to destroy the middle class, which was defined by home ownership. Brown's

[24] Matthew Dallek, *The Right Moment: Ronald Reagan's First Victory and the Decisive Turning Point in American Politics* (New York, 2000), 45.

The greatest crime is to call a racist white person a racist [handwritten marginal note]

vituperative language alienated voters who did not like being accused of racism or of being pawns of extremist right-wing forces. In October, the *Los Angeles Times* admonished Brown for provoking racial violence. This was hyperbolic. A leading historian later declared that the Proposition 14 campaign was "steeped not in the dark world of rightwing racism but in the murkier realm of California real-estate."[25] Real estate interests spent a fortune on television ads promoting the protection of a man's castle. With housing portrayed that way, Proposition 14 could not lose. Brown placed himself on the line, against the better counsel of advisors and liberal politicians such as Unruh, and he was left mortally wounded.

Republican presidential candidate Barry Goldwater lost the state, but fellow Republican George Murphy won election to the U.S. Senate, and Proposition 14 won by a greater majority *(65.4%)* [handwritten] than any candidate on the ballot. The Goldwater–Miller campaign had decided to stay away from the issue. Lyndon Johnson, on the other hand, spoke out against the proposition. Proposition 14 carried by over 60 percent of the vote. Although Proposition 14 proved to be a futile exercise when the U.S. Supreme Court held it unconstitutional, later analysis of the election showed that Californians in both the northern and southern sections of the state voted overwhelmingly for the measure. The San Francisco Bay Area voted 58 percent "yes," whereas the Los Angeles area voted 68 percent "yes." The measure drew support from Democratic voters across the state. Income and education appear to have made little difference on how whites voted on the issue. The Catholic Church campaigned heavily against Proposition 14, but a majority of Catholics nonetheless voted for it. A later survey showed that only 42 percent of Catholics in Southern California supported the Rumford Act, while 49 percent of Catholics in Northern California supported Rumford. Overall, about 61 percent of whites were hostile to Rumford. If there was underlying racism on the part of voters supporting Proposition 14, it was not apparent in the surveys. What was most interesting in later analysis of the vote was that Californians were more liberal in their racial attitudes than the rest of Americans. Most California voters believed that blacks were not discriminated against in California employment or housing opportunities. As a consequence, the attack by Brown, Salinger, and other opponents of Proposition 14 as a "racist" measure proved ineffective.[26]

That means they are just willfully stupid, which is racism. racist [handwritten marginal note]

---

[25] Dallek, *The Right Moment*, 59.

[26] Raymond E. Wolfinger and Fred I. Greenstein, "The Repeal of Fair Housing in California: An Analysis of Referendum Voting," *American Political Science Review* 62:3 (September 1968): 753–769.

The political importance of Proposition 14 went beyond the issue of housing. The vote in favor of Proposition 14 showed that simply attacking opponents as extremists and racists did not assure victory. Further damage was inflicted on liberal policies when student protesters at the University of California, Berkeley, became national news in the fall of 1964 and the residents of Watts rioted in August 1965. These events gave Republicans an opportunity to frame the 1966 governor's election as a referendum on "law and order" versus weak-kneed liberalism. Ronald Reagan proved to be the beneficiary.

When the riot erupted in Watts in August 1965, Brown was on a family holiday abroad. The riot started with a minor incident: on Wednesday, August 11, a white patrolman stopped a black youth driving drunk through the streets of South Central Los Angeles. When a crowd from the neighborhood gathered, the patrolman asked for backup. A five-day riot ensued as things got out of hand. As rioting continued, Los Angeles Chief of Police William Parker called on Lieutenant Governor Glenn Anderson, acting on Brown's behalf while he was out of the state, to call out the National Guard. Anderson arrived in Los Angeles on the second day of rioting, only to conclude that the riot had been quelled. On Friday, a riot erupted that would become the largest domestic disturbance the United States experienced in the twentieth century. Snipers were shooting firefighters and police. A desperate Chief Parker pleaded with Anderson and Brown's executive secretary to call out the National Guard. Neither trusted Parker, known for his tough stance on law and order. They refused his request. Brown was finally reached and informed of the situation. He cut short his holiday to fly back to California, and ordered to call out the National Guard. By this time, the riot was out of control. The five-day riot resulted in thirty-four deaths, more than 1,000 injuries, 3,400-plus arrests, and $40 million in damage. Liberals blamed the riot on poverty and a history of racism in the Los Angeles police force. While not dismissing social conditions as the cause of the riot, California voters, white and black, supported police and National Guard intervention to restore order. For Brown, the political damage from the riot hung over him throughout his campaign for reelection.[27]

After winning the Republican nomination for governor in 1966, Reagan used the rhetoric of law and order to attack Brown, holding up racial rioting, campus protests, and high crime rates as evidence that the state was out of control. On the problems at Berkeley, he asserted that "a

[27] Curt Gentry, *The Last Days of the Late, Great State of California* (New York, 1968) and Dallek, *The Right Moment*, 129–149.

small minority of beatniks, radicals and filthy speech advocates" brought
"shame to a great university." These protesters were polluting higher education in the state, encouraged by a permissive leadership in Sacramento
and a university administration unwilling to expel misfits. Confronted
with the "neurotic vulgarities" of the campus radicals, university admin-
istrators responded with "vacillation and weakness," Reagan claimed.[28]
"Our city streets," he cried, "are jungle paths after dark, with more
crimes of violence than New York, Pennsylvania, and Massachusetts
combined." Leadership was needed in Sacramento, he continued, not
moral turpitude.[29]

On Election Day, Reagan polled almost a million more votes than
Brown. He took fifty-five of California's fifty-eight counties, losing only
in the Bay Area, in the largest turnout to that point in state history.
Reagan won nearly 60 percent of the vote.

Reagan's landslide election pointed the direction for the Nixon campaign's strategy to win the South and pick up working-class white voters
in the North. Violence haunted the 1968 presidential contest. Two days
after Democratic presidential hopeful Eugene McCarthy won the Wisconsin Democratic primary on April 2, civil rights leader Martin Luther
King, Jr. was assassinated in Memphis, Tennessee. Rioting broke out
throughout the United States. In Washington, DC, the night skies were
lit up by fires across the city. SNCC leader H. Rap Brown captured
the anger within urban black communities when he cried, "Burn, baby,
burn!" Student protesters also turned to direct action. At Columbia University, students went on strike to protest an alleged racist takeover of a
park adjoining its Morningside Heights campus to build a gymnasium.
They were only evicted from occupying the university president's office
by forceful police action. The working-class cops used night sticks to let
students know what they thought of uppity middle-class kids. "I bleed,
therefore I am," was the new radical mantra. Robert Kennedy's murder
following the California Democratic primary in June further heightened
fears of violent disorder.

Americans witnessed further violence at the Democratic National Convention held in Chicago in late August. Given wide coverage on television
and the print media, city police and the Illinois National Guard used brute
force to contain protesters who had gathered outside the convention hall
to protest the Vietnam War. Chicago Mayor Richard Daley, anxious to

[28] Quoted in Dallek, *The Right Moment*, 103–104.
[29] Quoted in Dallek, *The Right Moment*, 195.

showcase his city, issued orders to use force to contain the protesters. Many had come to Chicago to engage in civil disobedience, but a minority clearly had violent intentions. Police made little effort to distinguish between non-violent and violent protesters. It did not help when newsmen Mike Wallace and Dan Rather were roughed up inside the convention hall by the police. The riot at the Chicago National Democratic Convention presented another image to the larger American public of a nation in chaos.

Surveys conducted over the decade of the 1960s reveal changing attitudes toward law and order issues, civil rights, and race. Most striking in these surveys are three salient results: first, both whites and African Americans supported the use of police in suppressing rioters, whether urban racial riots or antiwar protests in Chicago in 1968. Second, surveys reveal that white respondents placed greater emphasis on "outside agitators" as the cause of urban riots, while African Americans generally blamed social conditions for racial rioting. Even as racial tensions became increasingly apparent after 1965, African Americans were as likely as whites to voice concern about law and order, and they remained steadfast in expressions of patriotism.

The assumption that most blacks did *not* support riots was widely shared by both whites and blacks. For example, a Harris poll conducted in 1963 asked whether the "race revolt" was supported by "rank-and-file" African Americans. Thirty-four percent of whites said "Yes" compared to 91 percent of blacks. When asked four years later in the summer of 1967, a time of severe racial riots, both whites and blacks, by a large majority of 80 percent, believed that most African Americans did *not* support the riots. Responses in the 1963 and 1967 polls were not inconsistent. The 1963 poll asked whether marches, peaceful civil disobedience, boycotts, and the nomination of black candidates for political office were supported by the African American community. Most black respondents said these activities were supported by average African Americans. In 1967, the question pertained to violent racial riots, and black respondents replied, "No," these riots were not supported by the African American community.[30]

Even more revealing was the response by blacks to the question in the 1967 Harris poll, "How would you say that the police treat Negroes – very well, fairly well, badly or very badly?" Whites answered by 68

---

[30] These polls are discussed in Simon, *Public Opinion in America*, 71–72, drawing from Gary Marx, *Protest and Prejudice* (New York, 1967), 20.

percent that it was "not true" that white policemen often engaged in brutality against blacks. A surprising 58 percent of blacks agreed that it was not true that white policemen were brutal in their treatment of blacks, stating that police treated them "very well" or "fairly well."[31] This is not to deny that there was actual police brutality toward blacks in many urban areas, but the poll shows that the majority of blacks did not perceive widespread police brutality.

Further evidence of a general conservatism – cultural if not necessarily political – is evident in other surveys following the assassination of Martin Luther King, Jr. and the Democratic National Convention riot in 1968. In analyzing poll data, Howard Schuman and Shirley Hatchett at the Institute for Social Research at the University of Michigan reported that "the immediate effect of the [King] assassination was *conservative* [original italics], as shown by the results of two questions" that were asked in a 1968 attitudinal survey conducted just after the assassination: "Since Dr. King's assassination, do you think there are more whites in favor of equal rights, fewer whites or isn't there much change?" and "Some people are saying that the assassination of Martin Luther King will drive (Negroes) and whites further apart. Others think that it will bring them closer together. Which do you think will probably happen?" In response to the first question, 59 percent of blacks surveyed reported that more whites would be in favor of equal rights, while only 4 percent thought fewer whites would, while 35 percent thought it would not make much of a difference, with 2 percent reporting they did not know. In response to the question as to whether the assassination would drive whites and blacks further apart, only 9 percent of blacks thought it would, while 68 percent answered that it would bring them "closer together," 20 percent said "No change," and 3 percent answered "Don't know." This survey indicated that most blacks felt that King's assassination had led whites to be more in favor of equal rights and the races had drawn closer together.[32]

While riots across the country in response to the King assassination were often portrayed by the media and government reports as a race war of sorts, the African American community, although shocked and angered by the assassination, appeared at the time to be optimistic about race relations in the United States. The black community on the whole opposed rioting as a form of protest and supported police intervention and tactics

---

[31] Simon, *Public Opinion in America*, 73.
[32] Howard Schuman and Shirley Hatchett, *Black Racial Attitudes: Trends and Complexities* (Ann Arbor, MI, 1974), 6–9 and 12.

in suppressing these riots. Moreover, the survey revealed high patriotic attitudes among African Americans. Given the growing disillusionment with the Vietnam War in both the white and African American communities, when asked about their willingness to fight for the United States in a major war, 85.8 percent of blacks responded "Yes" to the question, "If our country got into a big World War today, would you personally feel that the United States is worth fighting for?" Only 14.2 percent answered "No." This high level of patriotism perhaps is not notable in itself, but what is surprising is that when this same question was asked in April 1971, the favorable response among African Americans had risen to 90.9 percent, while those who answered unfavorably fell to 9.1 percent.[33]

This conservative sentiment toward rioters and police actions expressed by blacks in these surveys did not translate into votes for Richard Nixon in the general election. African American voters remained steadfast in their support of the Democratic Party: Hubert Humphrey received 85 percent of the black vote, while Nixon garnered only 12 percent. What is important, though, is that these surveys showed the attitude of the general public, including African Americans, was hostile toward rioters and that voters were concerned about the breakdown of law and order in their communities.

Attitudes toward police actions at the Chicago Democratic Convention also reveal a different picture from the one presented by the media at the time. A rising crime rate, urban riots, and violent antiwar and campus protests tended to merge in the public mind into a general problem of the breakdown of law and order in American society. In response, the general public came down on the side of law and order. In the aftermath of the events in Chicago, a Gallup poll reported that 56 percent approved of Daley's actions, and a subsequent Harris poll revealed that 66 percent of those surveyed supported Daley and the policy. Only 14 percent believed that demonstrators had been denied their lawful rights.[34]

Campus disturbances, urban riots, and rising crime rates forced politicians left and right, Democrats and Republicans, to respond to public sentiment that placed "law and order" as the greatest issue facing the nation.[35] In late February 1968, Gallup polling reported that "crime and lawlessness" was the most important domestic issue on the mind of the

[33] Schuman and Hatchett, *Black Racial Attitudes*, 9 and 18.
[34] Cited in Flamm, *Law and Order*, 159. Also, for the Chicago demonstration, David Farber, *Chicago, '68* (Chicago, 1988).
[35] The following discussion of the political response to the law and order issue follows and draws heavily on Flamm, *Law and Order*, 142–178.

American electorate.[36] Voters saw riots, violent demonstrations, juvenile delinquency, and street crime as a single problem of lawlessness in American society. Close to a third of Americans revealed they were afraid to walk their neighborhoods at night, with women and urban dwellers showing even greater fear. The Detroit racial riot in the summer of 1967 appeared to have intensified voters' anxiety about the law and order issue. Richard Scammon at the Elections Research Center informed the White House that voters were demanding protection and warned of the "politically disastrous" potential of this issue.[37] President Johnson threw his support behind the Safe Streets Act of 1968, claiming that the enactment of this law was his greatest achievement to control crime. No longer was Johnson simply touting Great Society social programs as the best measures to alleviate urban crime. Other Democrats responded as well, carefully balancing liberal social justice concerns with allaying citizens' concerns that they were living in a lawless jungle. Having declared his candidacy for the Democratic nomination in March, Robert Kennedy proclaimed that America was being degraded by violence at home and abroad. Following King's assassination, Kennedy asserted, "Yet we seemingly tolerate a rising level of violence that ignores our common humanity and our claims to civilization alike."[38] In his campaign for the Democratic nomination, Kennedy learned on the campaign trail that everyone, voters and local politicians alike, wanted to talk to him about law and order. Organized labor leaders told him privately that the rank-and-file was more worried about crime in the street and riots than they were about wages and hours.[39] His campaign thus called for social justice for African Americans and security for whites.

The antiwar demonstration at the Democratic National Convention, and the widely watched television coverage of Chicago police suppression of demonstrators, inflicted irreparable damage on the presidential campaign of Democratic nominee Hubert Humphrey. Humphrey was not helped by the accusation – put forward by political allies and opponents as well as the press – that the riot at the convention had been caused by an unrestrained police force that had been given free rein by Mayor Richard Daley. While the media expressed shock at the "police riot," the public believed that the radicals got what was coming to them, as outlined above.

---

[36] Cited in Flamm, *Law and Order*, 141.
[37] Quoted in Flamm, *Law and Order*, 144.   [38] Cited in Flamm, *Law and Order*, 143.
[39] Dan T. Carter, *The Politics of Rage: George Wallace, the Origins of the New Conservatism, and the Transformation of American Politics* (New York, 1995), 377; and Flamm, *Law and Order*, 149.

By October, as *Time Magazine* reported, the law and order issue appeared to have "virtually anesthetized the controversy over Vietnam."[40] Confronted by the law and order issue, the Humphrey campaign fumbled as to parse law and order with social justice. Within Humphrey's inner circle, the general feeling was that he had not articulated to the voters where he stood on the law and order issues. Realizing that they could not compete with either Nixon or third-party candidate George Wallace on the issue, Democratic strategists urged Humphrey to come out strongly for law and order by insisting on the end to riots. Humphrey's subsequent approach called for civil order and civil justice. It was an approach that was hardly convincing to voters who believed, however unfairly, that liberals just did not have much to offer other than more antipoverty programs and welfare handouts.

Running as a third-party candidate on the American Party ticket, George Wallace exploited white working-class resentment toward African Americans, rising crime rates, black militants, hippies, and "bearded anarchists" in his campaign. His attacks on intellectuals and government bureaucrats, whom he accused of being soft on crime, drew rollicking enthusiasm from the crowds who turned out to hear his demagogic attacks on the establishment. His support for law and order did not, of course, include enforcement of civil rights laws concerning voting rights and the integration of public places. Nonetheless, Wallace struck a chord among lower-income white voters. In campaign speeches and press interviews, he stressed that blacks wanted law and order and better police protection as much as whites. He told television news anchor Walter Cronkite, "It is a sad day in our country when you cannot speak out against the destruction of cities, burning, arson, looting, and murder, and I'm not talking about race because the overwhelming majority of people of all races in this country are against the breakdown of law and order."[41] In the end, Wallace's support among voters, which reached a peak of 21 percent in early October, eroded under attacks from Democrats and Republicans.

Richard Nixon also tapped into the general public anxiety about the breakdown of law and order that was occurring on college campuses and in American cities. He selected as his running mate Maryland governor Spiro Agnew, who had taken a strong stand against rioters in Baltimore

---

40 "The Fear Campaign," *Time* (October 4, 1968), 21, and cited in Flamm, *Law and Order*, 162. Also, see Lewis Chester, Godfrey Hodgson, and Bruce Page, *An American Melodrama: The Presidential Campaign of 1968* (New York, 1969); and Allen J. Matusow, *The Unraveling of America: The History of Liberalism in the 1960s* (New York, 1984).

41 Quoted in Flamm, *Law and Order*, 166.

following King's assassination. Agnew's strong rhetoric in favor of law and order drew the attention of conservatives at the Miami Republican Convention who were eager to have a conservative on the ticket – even though Agnew's shift to conservatism had come only recently. Prior to 1968, before he endorsed Nixon in the primaries, Agnew had been a rock-solid supporter of liberal Republican Nelson Rockefeller. *(1958-74)*

Nixon's campaign for law and order in 1968 specifically attacked anti-war and campus protesters much like Reagan's gubernatorial campaign had done in 1966. Urban riots and rising crime rates, however, set the context for his speeches. Throughout his campaign Nixon made clear that he believed there was a crime crisis and that violent demonstrators were out of control. He pinned these problems not on a "sick society," but on liberals such as Attorney General Ramsey Clark and a Supreme Court that seemed to favor the rights of defendants over victims. Nixon declared himself in favor of what he called commonsense crime-control proposals and the need to restore traditional morality and a respect for law and decency in America. Nixon's campaign courted Southern whites, working-class ethnics, and the suburban middle class. *[margin: Miranda v. Arizona; Gideon v. Wainwright]*

[left margin: Who wrote against his own directives drug laws not later serve as vice president (1974-77)]

On Election Day, Nixon squeaked past Humphrey, winning 43.5 percent of the vote to Humphrey's 42.7 percent and Wallace's surprising 13.5 percent. Confronting a demoralized and divided Democratic Party, he made heavy inroads into the white ethnic vote in the Northeast and Midwest. Those gains among traditionally Democratic voters were crucial to Nixon's victory. In the South, he won only North Carolina, South Carolina, Tennessee, Florida, Virginia, and Kentucky.

Republican use of law and order as a major theme in the midterm elections in 1970 failed in the midst of an economic downturn. In 1970, in a faltering economy, economic issues trumped law and order. In the presidential campaign of 1972, however, Democratic nominee George McGovern made an easy foil for Nixon in his reelection campaign. Nixon painted McGovern as a threat to conventional order in a campaign that targeted his opponent as a supporter of abortion on demand, amnesty for draft evaders, and legalized drugs. Nixon carried forty-nine states. Picking up the five Southern states Wallace had won in 1968, he won 60 percent of the popular vote nationwide and 520 of 538 votes in the Electoral College.[42]

[left margin: And later to Reagan]

---

[42] The failure of this Republican midterm strategy is discussed in Donald T. Critchlow, *The Conservative Ascendancy: How the Republican Right Rose to Power in Modern America* (Lawrence, KS, 2011, rev. ed.), 93–94.

One of the great ironies of the 1972 election is that Nixon resigned from office in 1974 because of his attempts to subvert the law and the legal investigation into the break-in of the Democratic Party national headquarters at the Watergate complex during the campaign. Nixon's own abuse of presidential power and his thwarting of the law presented a direct challenge to the conventions of a representative democracy. He broke standing convention embodied in a republican tradition fearful of the abuse of power in government, protective of its political institutions, and committed to the rule of law.

The challenge to established convention, in the Humean sense, by young radicals and black nationalists turned revolutionary failed in the late 1960s and 1970s. Americans accepted change within the confines of conventional political and legal order. This entailed – although not without acrimony, legal protest, and political contention – racial integration, voting rights for blacks, and legal protection to extend equal opportunity to racial minorities and women. In the aftermath of the Vietnam War and Watergate, presidential powers were restrained through legislation. An unpopular war in Vietnam was ended through diplomacy. The results left many dissatisfied on both sides of the political spectrum, but nonetheless conventional order prevailed. The revolutionary left had failed in its direct challenge to this order partly because of its tactics and partly because of its inability to offer a viable alternative to conventional order. Modern liberalism was by no means dead, but in the 1980s and 1990s the Democratic Party on the presidential level found success by shifting to the middle politically.

In 2008, Barack Obama, the first biracial candidate to receive the presidential nomination of a major political party, won election on the promise of "hope and change." His appeal was to change within the confines of established convention. Accusations that he was a subversive and at heart a revolutionary failed to convince the majority of voters, who believed that he was a progressive seeking to strengthen democratic institutions, restore trust in government, and bring peaceful and meaningful reform within the established political order. Although Obama got no more of the white vote than McGovern did in 1972, he won the youth vote and the black vote, and the Hispanic vote that compensated for lack of gains in the white vote. By 2008, the white silent majority was not enough to sustain the Republican Party in presidential elections.

Established convention within the American polity prevailed in the midst of social, political, and economic turmoil that has characterized the postwar period. Established convention, a social construction, as Hume pointed out two centuries earlier, imparts an enduring force in political societies. The threat of civil war, revolution, and tyranny present direct threats to this order during times of intensive religious, political, and social turmoil. Hume warned of religious sectarianism and political faction as the most serious threats to the republican order. He prescribed republican institutions, the rule of law, deference to legally established authority, and well-tempered reform as necessary to preserving liberty and a well-ordered society. Without having read Hume, or even hearing of him, the silent majority in the late 1960s and 1970s had instinctively heeded his advice, even as opportunistic and sincere politicians took advantage of these sentiments for their own political gain.

They accepted the constitutional settlement but not (fully) its extension to African Americans, and in the new century the increasingly reject the constitutional order

PART III

CONSERVATISM AND THE ISSUE OF RACE

7

The Silent Majority

How the Private Becomes Political

Bill Schwarz

In the late 1960s, the idea of the silent majority emerged as a point of collective political identification, carrying a deep emotional charge, for foes and allies alike. There can be little doubt that – as either cause or effect – the political landscapes in much of the Western world were profoundly transformed. One index of this transformation is the very symbol of '68, signifying the radical, libertarian hopes of a generation. Commensurately, the notion of the silent majority invokes the idea of the political enemy of this volcanic radicalism. The silent majority represented the deepest impulses of what has been called the "other '68": that is, of those forces that set out to unhinge and break the radical challenge of the *soixante-huitards* and – as many of its adherents imagined – to turn the historical clock back, such that the customs of earlier, more ordered times could once more prevail.[1] As Antonio Gramsci deduced from his reading of Machiavelli (by way of Georges Sorel), the dynamic of public life is underwritten by "political passions." Indeed, for Gramsci political ideologies are given form – becoming, in effect, determinate ideologies – "by a creation of concrete phantasy, which acts on a dispersed and shattered people to arouse and organize its collective will."[2] Here, I endeavor to approach the idea of the silent majority in these terms, as an exemplification of Gramsci's "concrete phantasy."

---

[1] For the "other '68," Kobena Mercer, "1968: Periodizing Postmodern Politics and Identity," in Lawrence Grossberg, Cary Nelson, and Paula Treichler, eds., *Cultural Studies* (New York, 1992), 424–450; and his "Powellism: Race, Politics and Discourse," PhD diss., Goldsmiths, University of London, 1990.

[2] Antonio Gramsci, *Selections from the Prison Notebooks* (London, 1971), 125–126.

I focus on three figures in the making of the politics of the self-styled silent majority, in its Anglophone manifestations, seeking to address those whom they imagined to be "dispersed and shattered peoples." I introduce George Wallace, the governor of Alabama and a powerful agent in the remaking of race politics in the United States in the 1960s and 1970s; the mutinous English Tory, Enoch Powell, who, in his manner, worked to fuse together electoral politics with the popular instincts of back-street racism; and the seemingly more tranquil Mary Whitehouse, who presented herself as the archetypical English housewife and for whom political ambition appeared to hold no charm. These three are strikingly different historical personalities. The strategies of Wallace and Powell were primarily located within political society, whereas Whitehouse was principally concerned with the institutions of civil society as a counter to the depredations of the state. While Wallace and Powell are remembered for their mobilizations of race, expressions of race barely passed the lips of Whitehouse. But in her own way, she proved adept at translating domestic, feminine, lived experience into a highly wrought moral authoritarianism. All, I argue, were significant in redefining in these years the relations between the state and the people.

My chosen emphasis here falls on the relations between private and public. Race – or the idea of blackness in the white imagination – may not appear to have been, initially, a "private" matter that, in the moment of the silent majority, crossed the threshold and came to be of general political, public concern. Yet both in North America and in the United Kingdom, as the old hierarchies of white and non-white underwent radical recomposition, racist fantasies first took hold in the realm of the intimate, the sexual, the everyday: in a word, in private life. To focus on the silent majority allows us to track the transformations in which such "private" sensibilities entered political life and, as they did so, reconstituted how politics itself was to be experienced. Critical, I suggest, is the transition from the inchoate *sensibilities* of private life to the makings of new public, political forces.

The militants of the silent majorities were not the only social figures intent on devising an agenda in which formal politics was challenged to take cognizance of the imperatives of private life. The sexual radicals in women's liberation and in gay liberation were doing much the same, although to contrary ends.

But an overriding paradox of this situation was that many cadres of the silent majorities had to renounce their commitments to the private and to the ordinary in order to embrace the public world of politics.

Their success depended, not on their silence but on the collective noise they could generate. To triumph, they had to abolish their own founding precepts.

Wallace, Powell, and Whitehouse each subscribed to the notion that they represented an oppressed but socially unrecognized section of the population – that is, a silent majority. All three were largely conservative in affiliation; all three garnered, at various times, profound social support; and all three proved themselves to be serious agents in the transformation and expansion of the political domain.

This chapter differs in tone from other contributions to this volume. Unlike many of my collaborators, I remain persuaded by the idea that the emergence of the silent majorities represented a backlash against 1960s radicalism. To suppose that this was not so is, to my mind, to obscure what is most crucial. Those who argue in this manner, in the name of modern scholarship, are prone to short-circuit arguments that need more conceptual precision.[3] But this also raises the matter of historical method. My concern in this chapter, following Gramsci, is not only how ideas cross from private to public, thereby *becoming* recognizable political ideologies, but also how those who champion such ideas seek a measure of moral and intellectual authority. An exclusive focus on the internal properties of political institutions, narrowly conceived, has much to teach us. But it will only take us so far.[4]

George Wallace

In the autumn of 1963, George Wallace toured the Ivy League universities, joking with his audiences while demagogically taunting them at the same time. He wove together his opposition to the black civil rights

[3] Important is Kim Phillips-Fein, "Conservatism: A State of the Field," *Journal of American History* 98:3 (2011): 723–743, which proposes that the conservative radicalisms of the late 1960s and early 1970s were constituted by a deep historical duration and, second, that they possessed their own, autonomous forms of political creativity. On both counts Phillips-Fein is surely right. But to follow these perspectives does nothing, in itself, to expunge the idea of a political backlash.

[4] While I am sympathetic to his rejection of Lewis Namier and his allegiance to Quentin Skinner, it is on these grounds that I finally part company from Donald T. Critchlow's chapter in this volume (chapter 6). As I see it, he conflates the rational core of law and order discourse (the wish not to be assaulted or robbed, for example) with the heavily ideological articulations supplied by Nixon and by radical conservatives of the period. How understandable everyday aspirations – the desire to be free from the threat of abuse – came to be translated into *a politics* offers important clues to the workings of the silent majority.

movement with a new emphasis on low taxes and on rolling back state expenditure. In the new year, he opened his presidential campaign in Wisconsin. The breakthrough occurred on April 1. Booked by an ex-marine and bar-owner, Bronko Gruber, to speak at the Serb Memorial Hall in Milwaukee, Wallace faced an audience of "ethnics," to employ the psephological jargon of the time, consisting of Serbs, Poles, and Hungarians. As he entered the hall, the audience, in an unanticipated moment of congregation, sang "Dixie" both in English and in their native tongues. Wallace's fierce defense of a God-fearing America, in conjunction with his equally frenzied condemnation of civil rights – meaning, in this instance, nothing other than black rights – proved an intoxicating success. The dominating principles of a Southern populism had been smuggled across the Mason-Dixon Line in a configuration that few could have predicted. White migrants in the North opted to articulate their feelings of oppression in the language of those Southern whites, who, in turn, believed that their racial authority was on the point of vanishing. Shortly after, in the Indiana and Maryland primaries, Wallace stormed ahead.[5]

This vignette shows the mobility of political allegiances in this emergent conjuncture and also that the imperatives of racial whiteness could exert a significant gravitational pull on the business of national politics. In the Serb Memorial Hall, the curious dispositions of the silent majority could, in 1963, be discerned.

Wallace was a true son of the remembered Confederate past, born and bred a regular white supremacist in the Alabama manner. But what he knew in his lived experience did not necessarily, or easily, translate into a formal politics. As a young adult, he had been instinctively a Roosevelt Southern Democrat, for since Reconstruction the Democrats had functioned as the hegemonic political party in the South. In the late 1940s, when he first became active in politics, he only hesitantly allied himself to a politics of white supremacy. Wallace discovered, however, that the backwoods world of the white Methodist South in which he had grown up was on the point of dramatic dislocation and that the indigenous white citizens of Alabama on whom he depended for political

---

[5] Dan T. Carter, *The Politics of Rage: George Wallace, the Origins of the New Conservatism, and the Transformation of American Politics* (New York, 1995), 375. I rely on this fine account, summarizing as well my own response to Carter, Bill Schwarz, "Segregation Tomorrow," *New Formations* 33 (1998). For the longer duration Dan T. Carter, *From George Wallace to Newt Gingrich: Race in the Conservative Counterrevolution* (Baton Rouge, 1999) and Thomas J. Sugrue, *Not Even Past: Barack Obama and the Burden of Race* (Princeton, 2010).

advancement were not at all inhibited by the idea of turning race into the axiomatic political issue of the day. Events, however, passed Wallace by. In the immediate postwar years, the Klan had already reemerged as a significant force in Alabama.[6] Wallace watched as the state legislature humiliated his mentor, Governor Big Jim Folsom, for being soft on race during Folsom's first term (1947–1951). In the immediate aftermath of *Brown v. Board of Education* (1954), the white backlash assumed an organized political form, spreading from Mississippi across the Southern states and cohering around a variety of well-funded White Citizens' Councils. Wallace listened to these shifts in the popular mood. After the *Brown* ruling, he drew away from Folsom. Yet even so, in his first gubernatorial campaign in 1958 he was defeated largely due to the perception that he too was insufficiently attuned to the imperatives of white supremacy. The 1958 campaign stiffened his resolve. Wallace had been born into a civic world in which the power of racial sensibilities was strong. But in 1958, as his populist sympathies took shape, he began to learn *a politics of race*.

The next election for governor he won. On January 14, 1963, on a freezing day in Montgomery, Wallace delivered his inaugural speech. He took the oath of office standing on the gold star marking the spot where, a century before, Jefferson Davis had been sworn in as provisional president of the Confederate States of America. Those listening donned white flowers to signify their allegiance to Anglo-Saxon supremacy. His speech had been drafted by the former Klansman Asa Carter.[7] It played on memories of the Civil War, not as some distant historic event but as an imaginative act of the present. For Wallace, a new politics was required – heroic but driven by the will of the poor and of the neglected – in order to repair the ills perpetrated by the Washington elite and to ensure that the world was turned the right side up again. In this historic task, Alabama could call upon a providential history, for in Montgomery was to be found "this very heart of the Great Anglo-Saxon Southland." And Wallace himself was to embody this intransigence: "I draw the line in the dust and toss the gauntlet before the feet of tyranny . . . and I say . . . segregation now . . . segregation tomorrow . . . segregation forever."[8]

6 Glenn Feldman, "Soft Opposition: Elite Acquiescence and Klan-sponsored Terrorism in Alabama, 1946–50," *Historical Journal* 40:3 (1997): 753–777.

7 Asa Carter's commitment to the defense of racial supremacy in these years was absolute, Dan T. Carter describing him as "a professional anti-Semite and hard-line racial terrorist," *From Wallace to Gingrich*, 2.

8 Cited in Carter, *Politics of Rage*, 11.

On four occasions, he mounted a campaign for the presidency: in 1964, 1968, 1972, and – even after he was crippled following Arthur Bremer's attempt on his life on May 15, 1972 – again in 1976. Despite his growing ideological convergence with the Republicans, he stood each time as a Democrat (or just about) – which was, up to the 1970s, still the only viable political establishment in Alabama. In 1964, he reserved his most corrosive onslaughts for Lyndon Johnson and the Democrat leadership, and in July tried to persuade Barry Goldwater to adopt him as his running mate on the Republican ticket. In 1968, he represented his own American Independent Party, signaling the weakening of Democrat-Republican hegemony. The common characteristic of each of his campaigns was his wildcat populism, which, on the one hand, kept him wedded to his jeremiads concerning the injustice of white victimization but, on the other, sent him spinning in relation to the established party institutions.[9] For good reason, he could never be sure where his party allegiance at the national level should rest. Especially after first Goldwater, and then Nixon, made the running, his populist aspirations took him ideologically to the Republicans. And desperation – combined with a measure of cool strategic calculation – had him drawn to third-party machinations attracting, as even he came to admit, the full gamut of kooks, cranks, and charlatans, including, in one venture, Colonel Sanders of Kentucky Fried Chicken fame. In terms of the given political landscape, one never knew where he would be next and neither, it seems, did he. Despite the fire and brimstone, each campaign burnt him up, as if each victory brought his own political destruction nearer.

Ultimately, however, politics in the larger sense is only minimally about elections. Although Wallace's great ambition serially self-destructed, he could take credit for the fact that the political imaginary that he had made his own found an institutional home in the Republican Party. In moving from his natal incarnation as a New Deal Democrat to his emergence as the "alchemist" of the new conservatism, as Dan Carter puts it, Wallace proved a powerful agent in the making of the militant, populist conservatism of the 1960s and 1970s.[10]

From the perspective of poor white Alabama, this was no transformation at all. The New Deal was framed in the language of the autonomy of the little man confronted, as Roosevelt put it in his second inaugural,

[9] Michael Kazin, "The Grass-Roots Right: New Histories of US Conservatism in the Twentieth Century," *American Historical Review* 77:1 (1992): 136–155.

[10] Carter, *Politics of Rage*, 12.

"by blind economic forces and blindly selfish men."[11] In the 1960s, Wallace spoke out against the tyranny of big government, against the vested interests of federal politicians, judges, and bureaucrats, against the media, and, most virulently of all, against those liberal whites wealthy enough to buy themselves out of the social consequences of desegregation – out of, as it were, race itself.   *which is racist*

This was a populism that turned on race but that was spoken in terms of an external enemy bent on the destruction of the South's historic "way of life." When Wallace ran for governor in 1962, he declared that he would defend the rights of Alabama as a "sovereign state" – "even to the point of standing at the schoolhouse door" to resist desegregation – while denouncing his opponents, looking to compromise or to capitulate on the issue of segregation, as "sissy britches."[12] In June 1963, as governor, he made his stand. In a carefully orchestrated media event, he barred the entry of federal officials to the University of Alabama who were accompanying black students intent on enrolling. At the end of his oration, he proclaimed his determination to preserve the integrity of the state and "the freedoms of the citizens thereof"; but when the newsmen began packing up their cameras, the students, who had earlier enrolled elsewhere on the campus, were quietly escorted to their dorms and the drama ended. Integration continued, while the principled intransigence of Governor Wallace appeared, to his loyalists, to remain unsullied. His status as self-invented, media-constituted folk hero was confirmed.[13]

Rhetorical sallies of this type required much subterfuge on the part of the perpetrator and did much to disguise the vacillations of day-to-day politics. Yet Wallace was not simply a vulgar, eccentric recidivist, as the *New York Times* believed for too long; rather, he was a figure with the capacity to transform a local mentality into the raw material of a national politics. The zigzags that followed the standoff at the University of Alabama represent not just indecisiveness but genuine strategic dilemmas. In order to become a credible national politician, he had to espouse a reading of race that made it seem as if his backyard antipathies were a thing of the past, even as they proved his richest electoral asset. And what made his entry onto the national stage possible was precisely the legislative victories of the civil rights movement engineered by Presidents John F. Kennedy and Lyndon B. Johnson.

Donald Trump was a teenager

---

[11] F. D. Roosevelt, "Second Inaugural," January 20, 1937.
[12] Carter, *Politics of Rage*, 105–106.   [13] Carter, *Politics of Rage*, 149.

The main beneficiary of Wallace's interventions in national politics was Richard Nixon. Republican strategists in 1968 fell upon the core idea of "who hates whom?" and organized an electoral politics accordingly. In North and South alike, fear of now assertive blacks had become a dominating force, and white Southern Democrats were, at least potentially, a determining constituency. The radicalism of this new conservatism derived from the fact that its high command not only understood that American society would polarize as a result of the measures they advocated but also that such polarization was actively to be sought, as a virtue in itself. In purely arithmetical terms John Mitchell – Nixon's campaign manager and, later, attorney general – was convinced that this presented a winning strategy for the Republican Party. It marked a political frontline that divided the economically independent from the economically hapless of the ghettos, a frontline charged by unadorned racial fear.

It is difficult, in retrospect, to grasp just how volcanic the United States was in 1968 as Nixon made his second bid for the presidency. His campaign played out against the background of the Tet Offensive in January and February; the assassination of Martin Luther King in April and the consequent insurrections that swept across urban America; the assassination of Robert Kennedy in June; and the dark, epic fiasco of the Democratic National Convention in Chicago in August.

It was out of these events that Nixon's November 3, 1969, address to the nation, in which he called on the "Silent Majority" to support him on Vietnam, took shape.[14] After Black Power, Vietnam (abroad) and race (at home) could no longer be perceived as separate domains of American life: the conjoining of the two attested, for a new generation of radicals, to the colonial dynamic which worked as the driving force of the American will for power, whether at home or overseas.[15] These were days

[14] Richard Nixon, "The Silent Majority," November 3, 1969; http://watergate.info/1969/11/03/nixons-silent-majority-speech.html (accessed October 26, 2016). The term itself was not original, although the turbulence of the moment of Nixon's speech probably accounts for its impact. A while before, the AFL-CIO president, George Meany, had claimed that pro-war labor spoke for "the vast, silent majority in the nation": cited in Rhodri Jeffreys-Jones, *Peace Now! American Society and the End of the Vietnam War* (New Haven, 1999), 181. And for a disorientating entry into this mental world, Spiro Agnew, *Where He Stands: The Life and Convictions of Spiro T. Agnew* (New York, 1968). As Charles Kaiser reads the Nixon–Agnew connection, "Choosing Agnew meant a Southern strategy," in *1968 in America: Music, Politics, Chaos, Counterculture, and the Shaping of a Generation* (New York, 1988), 229.

[15] *Inter alia*, Stokely Carmichael (Kwame Ture), *Stokely Speaks: From Black Power to Pan-Africanism* (Chicago, 2007); and his *Ready for Revolution: The Life and Struggles of Stokely Carmichael (Kwame Ture)* (New York, 2003).

of heightened antiwar mobilization. October 15, 1969, had witnessed demonstrations across the United States. In New York, the children of both John Ehrlichman and Bob Haldeman, key Nixon aides, joined the protests; Spiro Agnew ordered his fourteen-year-old daughter to stay at home.[16] William Watts, an assistant to National Security Advisor Henry Kissinger working on Nixon's "Silent Majority" speech, emerged from his office to be confronted by the sight of his wife and daughter protesting.[17] The lines of political rupture were running through every family and every social institution in the nation.

Nixon's invocation of the silent majority proved "the administration's masterstroke."[18] An estimated seventy million people watched him delivering the speech, broadcast live on all three TV networks. White House officials claimed that, in the aftermath of the address, 80,000 letters of support were received by the president: although a portion may well have been planted, the majority seem to have been genuine. The arrival of this cache of post to the White House was exploited as a mighty photo opportunity.[19] This attests to the degree to which the media institutions were riven by discord, creating active symbolic locations in which the wider politics were fought out.[20] At the very moment of its formal inception – indeed, a consequence of its very naming – the silent majority ceased to be silent. As Nixon, sensing that the political tide was turning,

---

[16] In a speech to the American Legion in Baltimore on July 19, 1967, Agnew asked his audience to reflect on their duties as "citizen-soldiers." In response to his own invitation he enumerated eight precepts, the second of which counseled the need "[t]o develop a reverence for the law and a respect for those that enforce it within your home," Agnew, *Where He Stands*, 52.

[17] Richard Reeves, *President Nixon: Alone in the White House* (New York, 2001), 137–138.

[18] Jeremy Varon, *Bringing the War Home: The Weather Underground, the Red Army Faction, and Revolutionary Violence in the Sixties and Seventies* (Berkeley, 2004), 134.

[19] See the photo in Reeves, *President Nixon*, 320–321. Within minutes of his finishing the speech Nixon instructed Haldeman to be sure that the *New York Times* and the *Washington Post* received significant amounts of mail – "dirty, vicious" – denouncing their coverage of the speech, coverage which of course did not yet exist: cited in Reeves, *President Nixon*, 144.

[20] The mediations, in other words, are decisive. Television is central here, although the literature on TV and civil rights is undeveloped. However, much can be gleaned by thinking of the role of the press: Library of America, *Reporting Civil Rights*, vol. 1, *American Journalism, 1941–1963* and vol. 2, *American Journalism, 1963–1973* (New York, 2003); Richard Lentz, *Symbols, the News Magazine and Martin Luther King* (Baton Rouge, 1990); and Gene Roberts and Hank Klibanoff, *The Race Beat: The Press, the Civil Rights Struggle and the Awakening of a Nation* (New York, 2007). On photography, Bill Schwarz, "'Our Unadmitted Sorrow': The Rhetorics of Civil Rights Photography," *History Workshop Journal* 72 (2011): 138-155.

⌐ Nixon would pursue these bastards to destruction (his) –

put it: "We got those liberal bastards on the run now!"[21] This "other '68" did much to disorganize the libertarian impulse of the *hoi polloi* '68.[22]

Shortly after his "Silent Majority" speech, Nixon, much as Wallace earlier, toyed with the idea of breaking out of the two-party system. In July 1970, he first considered the possibility of ditching the Republican label and launching a new "Conservative Party" composed of authentic Republicans and of dissident, Wallace-influenced, conservative Southern Democrats. These hopes of consolidating the emerging array of conservative forces into a new political coalition coincided with Nixon's determination to address "the forgotten minorities" of the United States. With clear echoes of Wallace's speech at the Serb Memorial Hall, he imagined an America polarized between "Italians, Poles, Elks and Rotarians," on the one hand, and "Jews, blacks, youth" on the other. This was but a step away – or in stricter chronology, a matter only of weeks – from Nixon's discovery of the silent majority.[23]

Critically, Nixon gave this a Southern spin, the legacy of Wallace indelibly present. His chief of staff, Bob Haldeman, recorded a classically crazed Nixonite nocturnal monologue, delivered in private on the eve of his second presidential election. The wayward syntax communicates the hallucinogenic quality of the original:

He then got into his feeling for the South... Makes the point that union leaders are like the South. They want to abide by the law and they respect the Presidency... Our New American Majority appeals across the board for the same reasons to people. The basic American values. A strong United States patriotism, strong moral and spiritual values. Anti-permissiveness. They are turned off on welfare because it's wrong and because they are anti-elitist, plus they have selfish motives. They are American to the core. The Southerners are more so than the rest of the United States, because they are not poisoned by the elite universities and the media, but we're also high in Polish, Italian, mountain areas, farm states. Weak in the suburbia/big cities because here people are soft... That square America is coming back and that we didn't just gather a bunch of haters. The real issue is patriotism, morality, religion.[24]

---

[21] Reeves, *President Nixon*, 145.

[22] For the United States, Sohnya Sayres et al., eds., *The Sixties: Without Apology* (Minneapolis, 1984). And – more distant, less trenchant, and better on the music than the politics, but always informative – Kaiser, *1968 in America*, which is driven by the supposition that "For a surprisingly large number of Americans... 1968 marked the end of hope," x.

[23] As recorded by H. R. Haldeman, *The Haldeman Diaries: Inside the Nixon White House* (New York, 1995), 212, 218, and 242.

[24] Haldeman, *The Haldeman Diaries*, 631–632.

In such feverish musings, the Southernization of U.S. politics received its presidential imprimatur.

In May 1972, Wallace was shot and seriously injured. Nixon and his special counsel, Chuck Colson, immediately tried to implicate the gunman as a Eugene McCarthy loyalist. This was but a prelude to Watergate – to John Dean, Gordon Liddy, Howard Hunt, Jeb Magruder, and to the long march, as Haldeman, for one, discovered, to Lampoc Federal Prison. Much derived from their omnipotent desire to neutralize the enemies of the silent majority and to be certain that all true patriots allied themselves with the newly Southernized president. When Nixon arrived to visit Wallace in hospital, he was already made up, waiting for the TV cameras to roll. The passing of the populist mantle was, predictably, to be a television event.

[handwritten margin note: Nixon not a pardon]

[handwritten note: Nixon sought something close to a competitive authoritarian regime]

Enoch Powell

Despite the different historical circumstances, the structural parallels between the American and British experiences are illuminating. In historical situations so *unlike*, a common process of conservative mobilization can still be identified.[25] While Wallace's political rhetoric embodied the sensibilities of a bare-knuckle Southern prize-fighter, Enoch Powell – when not dropping into Urdu – spoke in the idiom of the high Victorian politics, with a discernible Birmingham twang. The parallel is to be located, rather, in the populist dynamic of Wallace's and of Powell's respective politics, founded on the conviction that those who had command of the state had turned into dangerous foes, traitors to race and nation.[26]

[handwritten margin note: He represented a seat in nearby Wolverhampton]

[handwritten note: The populism, authoritarianism, nativism and rather anti-intellectualism]

On April 20, 1968, Enoch Powell, the Conservative MP for Wolverhampton South-West, addressed the West Midlands Area Political Centre at the Midland Hotel in Birmingham. On paper, the event could hardly have sounded more innocuous. But Powell had planned things otherwise. The TV cameras were there. He had confided to a friend that his speech would "go up like a rocket" and "it's going to stay up."[27] And

---

25 I thank Michael Kazin for showing me his unpublished paper, co-authored with Stéphane Porion, "George Wallace and Enoch Powell: Comparing the Politics of Populist Conservatism in the US and the UK."

26 On populism Ernesto Laclau, *Politics and Ideology in Marxist Theory: Capitalism, Fascism, Populism* (London, 1977).

27 Mike Phillips and Trevor Phillips, *Windrush: The Irresistible Rise of Multi-Racial Britain* (London, 1998), 245–253.

so it proved, for Powell took to heart the issue of non-white immigration and determined to speak the truth of race. In doing so, he endeavored to denounce Britain's political power-brokers, who, he believed, had sought systematically to evade publicly confronting the issue of race for fear that, on this matter, the sentiments of the nation's governors were far from those of the nation at large. Whereas Wallace was wont to embrace the folksy, homespun mentality of rural Alabama, Powell was content to express his darkest forebodings by drawing from the classics. "Like the Roman, I seem to see 'the river Tiber foaming with much blood.'"[28]

And at the same time, the United States appeared as a dark foreshadowing of what Britain might yet become. "That tragic and intractable phenomenon which we watch with horror on the other side of the Atlantic but which there is interwoven with the history and existence of the States itself, is coming upon us here by our own volition and our own neglect. Indeed, it has all but come. In numerical terms, it will be of American proportions long before the end of the century."[29]

Powell intertwined lines from Virgil with quotations from *those who knew*: that is, from those who lived in proximity to Britain's new black populations, in contrast to the political class who sequestered themselves in privileged locales. Powell was giving credence to those who, in an older colonial rhetoric, *knew the native*. In quoting these sentiments but not quite articulating them directly in his own voice, he could distance himself from the undertow of racial violence that such statements seemed designed to invite as he simultaneously insisted that it was his job to give voice to the concerns of his constituents, whose fears received no social recognition. As a local workman, Sidney Miller, shouted out to Powell on the day after he had delivered his speech – the first popular voice recorded in the ensuing controversy – "It needed to be said."[30] What publicly had been unspeakable had now crossed the line from private reverie to a matter of high state and could claim consequent political purchase.[31]

This one speech did much to trigger popular mobilization and to draw out into the open the growing fissures in the social consensus that had underlain Britain's social-democratic state. The media gave form to the popular feelings that had been unleashed. Political strikes in support of

[28] Bill Smithies and Peter Fiddick, eds., *Enoch Powell on Immigration* (London, 1963), 43.
[29] Smithies and Fiddick, *Enoch Powell*, 41.   [30] *Birmingham Post*, April 22, 1968.
[31] Bill Schwarz, *Memories of Empire*, vol. 1, *The White Man's World* (Oxford, 2011); I borrow some of the formulations which appear there; important is Camilla Schofield, *Enoch Powell and the Making of Postcolonial Britain* (Cambridge, 2013).

Powell followed. Powell himself, in the aftermath, came close to becoming a political party in his own right, and he played fast and loose with his own home party, the Conservatives – just as Wallace did in the United States with *his* own home party. What other prominent Conservative could have generated such collective shock when, on the eve of the 1970 general election, he urged the country to vote Conservative?[32] Powell's was the decisive influence of the Conservative victory in 1970, and he was a considerable force, too, in the Labour victory of February 1974.[33] Politically, these were Powell's years; they were his because of the sustained popular support he could summon; and the popular coalition he created was united on one thing only – race.

The greatest index of the eruption of popular feeling in the wake of the "Rivers of Blood," as the speech swiftly entered collective memory, lay in the humdrum activity of letter-writing. In the 1960s, letter-writing and all its attendant customs still composed the routines of domestic communications not yet dominated by the telephone. Even so, this was the television age, in which the temporal and spatial structures of political life were compressed. One incentive for writing a letter to Powell would have been the knowledge gleaned from the news bulletins that thousands of others, friends and neighbors, were doing the same.

Letters to public figures, from "ordinary" (private) men and women, constituted a significant reworking of the public sphere. This was particularly so in terms of two arenas, which were seen to impinge intensely on the practices of everyday life: the question of race and the question of morality, particularly of sexual morality. Letter-writing came to be an activity in which those who imagined themselves to be the victims of new and unseen forms of oppression learned a public language in which their anxieties could be made known and recognized.

The most daunting aspect of this was the volume of letters received by Powell. Current calculations suggest that the total number, in the days and weeks which followed, was anything between 50,000 and 100,000. Some came from households, signed by husbands on behalf of their families; some from factories and workplaces, carrying many signatures. Countless more letters about the racial scenario conjured up by Powell were received by many other public figures.[34]

[32] Enoch Powell, "Vote Tory," in John Wood, ed., *Powell and the 1970 Election* (Kingswood, 1970).

[33] Douglas Schoen, *Enoch Powell and the Powellites* (London, 1977).

[34] Schwarz, *White Man's World*; Diana Spearman, "Letters of Blood," *New Society*, May 9, 1968; and Amy Whipple, "Revisiting the 'Rivers of Blood' Controversy: Letters to

In these letters, one can hear the silent majority, in its predominantly English expression, taking form. Some little while later, Powell received the following, written by a conscious exponent of the silent majority:

I belong to that majority – the silent majority, hidden and forgotten, largely ignored – I mean the English, white, protestant. We have had no spokesman for decades, no organisation, no party, we do not organise, we have no popular folklore, and our sense of nationalism is muted to a degree that its voice can hardly be heard. But we are a vast majority and we have responded to your voice.[35]

[handwritten margin note, left: "It is still whining"]
[handwritten margin note: "Not the British"]
[handwritten margin notes: "an awful sign of prohibition of the breakup of British at identification and"]
[handwritten underline note: "Bc we don't like people harder"]

The letter-writers were instrumental in creating a public community that imagined a shared ethnic predicament. The fantasized, mythic Powell invoked in these letters is called upon to *do* something, just as King Richard had to return to scourge evil barons and St. George had dragons to slay. Accordingly, Powell was addressed in a spirit of breathless deference – "Well done, sir!"; "Thank you, sir!" – while those identified as his political antagonists received envelopes stuffed with shit. Deference to Powell (the respectable, public voice of the silent majority) and hatred of his opponents (the darker, more belligerent dimension of the silent majority) are part of the same reverie. They represent a splitting of a single psychic object: on the one hand, the guardian of all virtue; on the other, all that is base and vile. The interior psychic work of these letters is embodied in the endeavor to stake out the frontiers between the two, desperate in their attempts to segregate virtue from all that defiles.

[handwritten margin note: "St. George was not English and Richard was Norman French"]

During these years, Powell opened a file which he named "The Thing."[36] In it, he recorded examples of subversion that he encountered, prompted in the first instance by the vision of student unrest. The drama of the universities he believed to be part of a deeper disorder. What had panicked Powell was the amorphous nature of this subversion. These were acts that occurred within civil society more often than they did in political society, and they were generally cultural in form. In themselves, they were of minor significance: instances of disrespect, perhaps, or insolence, indicating that inherited social hierarchies had slipped out of place. Cumulatively, Powell believed, these everyday acts of insubordination threatened not only civilized life but the very existence of the nation. Yet he was disturbed by the fact that what he understood to be the unraveling

[handwritten margin note: "Also supporting authoritarianism"]

Enoch Powell," *Journal of British Studies* 48:3 (2009). A portion of these are archived in the Powell Papers at Churchill College, Cambridge (POLL 8/1/8), which are the ones I have used; the greater bulk of them are lodged at the Stafford Record Office.

[35] Cited in Diana Spearman, "Enoch Powell's Election Letters," in Wood, *Powell and the 1970 Election*, 32.

[36] Powell Papers, Stafford Record Office, D4490/48.

of England proved, in practice, to be a curiously low-key affair. The very ephemera of its dramas, Powell implied, produced a strange invisibility, such that the deepest consequences of each moment of subversion could not be divined for what it truly was. These perplexed musings took him back to Edmund Burke and to Burke's famous call for unceasing political vigilance. Enlisted by the ghost of Burke, Powell took upon himself to speak out during these years. The forces of subversion were gathering in close, multiplying at every turn.

The silent majority represented all that "The Thing" was not: upright, white, and with the determination to take on the forces of disorder wherever they were to be found. For Powell, however, "The Thing" symbolized not only the unruly multitude but the end of the very possibility of politics itself. It was as if reason were about to be engulfed by unreason, sanity by insanity, civilization by anarchy, unleashing *the other* in all its unrepentant chaos.

In a curious and unexpected convergence, Powell's fantasized conception of "The Thing" resembles closely Jean Baudrillard's reading of the silent majority. For Baudrillard, the silent majority was profoundly intangible – a "nebulous entity" – signaling the end of the political and the end of the social. The concept itself he sees as "a soft sticky lumpenanalytical notion." Yet it has to be thus (for Baudrillard) as the termination of the social stipulates that representation itself has been superseded: both political representation, on the social stage, and the representation of the signified by the signifier, on the symbolic stage. As Baudrillard sees things, the masses themselves – the very embodiment of the popular, of Spinoza's multitude – defy all attempts to represent them. In essence, they are unrepresentable.[37] This marks a mirroring of Powell's anxious interpretation of the late 1960s. In the one, we confront the fantasized apparition of "The Thing," dissolving the rational domain of the political and bringing doom ever closer; in the other, we confront the fantasies invested in the silent majority, whose mere existence spells the end of politics. It is not necessary to follow the apocalyptical consequences of either. But what each does is to reconceptualize the terrain of the political from a recognition of the primordial effectivity of the popular.

Mary Whitehouse

On January 27, 1964, Mary Whitehouse and Norah Buckland launched the Clean Up TV Campaign (CUTV), which the following year turned

[37] Jean Baudrillard, *In the Shadow of the Silent Majorities* (New York, 1983), 19 and 4–5.

into the National Viewers' and Listeners' Association (NVALA). They circulated a pamphlet in which they explained why they felt compelled to intervene in public life:

Nothing seemed left but for the ordinary women of Britain to take matters into their own hands and to make it quite clear to the B.B.C. that we were prepared to fight for the right to bring up our children in the truths of the Christian faith, and to protect our homes from exhibitions of violence.[38]

The event was reported in the *Birmingham Evening News*, and the story was picked up in turn by the national press. As a result, similar meetings spontaneously took place across the country. Within forty-eight hours, the mail began to arrive at the Whitehouse home. Over the next three years or so, her postbag amounted to some 35,000 items. As Whitehouse explained, although most of the letters originated from Britain, they also came from abroad, particularly from the lands of the old empire. Many of the correspondents described how they had served in World War II – as, in fact, did many of those Writing to Powell. *That* past and *this* present were in close imaginative proximity.[39]

The following May, a giant public meeting was organized at Birmingham Town Hall. Patricia Duce, introduced as a niece of the explorer Sir Ernest Shackleton and wife of a motor engineer, was charged with demonstrating how the CUTV was to operate. She opened by reminding her audience that her uncle had personified "a Britain that was worthwhile, clean and strong," but then quickly moved to the business in hand. Over the previous weeks, she had led a small group who set about monitoring the output of 217 BBC television programs in terms of "the overall impact on the viewer and whether this impact was in fact negative, destructive or offending against moral standards." Those the CUTV deemed objectionable were "marred by one or more of the following features":

> Sexy innuendoes, suggestive clothing and behaviour.
> Cruelty, sadism and unnecessary violence.
> No regret for wrong-doing.
> Blasphemy and the presentation of religion in a poor light.
> Excessive drinking and foul language.
> Undermining respect for law and order.
> Unduly harrowing and depressing themes.

[38] Ben Thompson, *Ban This Filth! Letters from the Mary Whitehouse Archive* (London, 2012), 34.

[39] Mary Whitehouse, *Cleaning Up TV: From Protest to Participation* (London, 1967), 25–26.

Certain programs which contained "good features" sadly had to be classi-fied as objectionable because they "included such items as a discussion on whether a relationship was homosexual or not; a review of a book which led to a discussion on abortion, sterilization, etc., excerpts from a play which ridiculed the armed forces as well as having much bad language, etc." As Duce insisted, these programs worked to validate "freedom from the restraining influence of any decent instinct."[40]

Mary Whitehouse, taking the larger view, dwelled on the role of the BBC as a governing – and grievously wanting – institution. "The imme-diate object of this campaign is to restore the BBC to its real position of respected leadership of this country. We are NOT against the BBC, we are FOR the BBC." Even so, the BBC's readiness to ally itself with the forces of moral disorder presented itself to her as symptomatic of a deeper crisis of the state. The Ministry of Health she condemned for its lack of vigilance over the rise of venereal disease; the Home Office – the govern-ment office charged with the policing of British domestic life – she found lacking moral energy; while the Ministry of Education, it seemed, refused to follow its own guidelines on inculcating the proper views on sexual matters in schoolchildren. Yet notwithstanding her roster of malefactors, it was the BBC that worked most to unnerve her. Whitehouse's emphasis on the BBC derived from the fact that she was militant in her conviction that the Corporation possessed the greater responsibility owing precisely to its proximity to the formal institutions of the state. "We find it difficult to understand that those who weald [sic] power at Broadcasting House do not take account of the lesson of history – that a nation going soft at the centre is ripe for fall and take over." But all was not lost. If the British people had "abdicated [their] wider responsibilities in the tired years after the war," the fight was now on. "It is to do what we may to right this wrong that we have thrown overboard our anonymity and come out to fight!"[41] As proceedings drew to a close, the meeting agreed unanimously to send a telegram to the Queen and Prince Philip, "as parents of young children," demanding "a radical change" in the BBC.[42]

This catalogue of condemnation derived from the conviction that tele-vision came to serve as a pretext for making speakable the wider ills of society, which were, it seems, everywhere – contagious, rampant, closing in – while the state appeared to have lost its authority.[43] The weakening

[40] Thompson, *Ban This Filth!*, 68–69.   [41] Thompson, *Ban This Filth!*, 69–71.
[42] Whitehouse, *Cleaning Up TV*, 38.
[43] A wider contextualization can be found in Marcus Collins, ed., *The Permissive Society and its Enemies* (London, 2007).

of Christianity, "drinking and foul language," the collapse of law and order, homosexuality, abortion, sterilization, ridiculing the armed forces: all fell within the remit of Whitehouse and of her campaigners.[44] Television was taken to be a privileged medium by which these social ills came to be communicated to the nation. But it was only ever weakly the real issue. It principally served to make tangible and nameable the anarchy that seemed so proximate – an early apprehension of "The Thing." Yet through the practice of vigilant monitoring, what otherwise was amorphous and threateningly out of reach could be *located*, and those responsible named and brought to account.[45]

At the time the CUTV was launched, Whitehouse was in her fifties, a mother of three, and senior mistress at a secondary school where her duties included minding the moral welfare of the girls. Early publicity stills identified her as Mrs. E. R. Whitehouse, adopting not only her husband's surname but his initials too. Her political base, like Powell's, was the West Midlands. Two years before serving as the location for Powell's political intervention of April 1968 with the "Rivers of Blood" speech, the Midland Hotel in Birmingham had been the site of the first convention of the NVALA. Indeed, for a time, Whitehouse and Powell had been neighbors – living next door but one to each other – in Merridale Road in Wolverhampton before Whitehouse moved to "Postman's Piece," The Wold, Claverley, a few miles outside the conurbation. She had had virtually no experience of either the media or of making contact with influential public figures. Indeed, it was exactly her very "ordinariness" that supplied her political cachet.

[44] This is a collective mentality which closely conforms to that which was drawn to "mugging" as a prism through which to read the collapse of the nation: Stuart Hall et al., *Policing the Crisis: Mugging, the State and Law and Order* (London, 1978). Ann Whitaker, a moral activist in Bodmin, campaigned in early 1973 for the local authorities to ban the showing of *A Clockwork Orange*, on the grounds that it "provides an education in the techniques of 'mugging,'" Thompson, *Ban This Filth!*, 226.

[45] Whitehouse herself compulsively narrated her own public role in the CUTV campaign and in its successor, the NVALA. In all she wrote six published memoirs, in which the same themes – darkness and light, in which Whitehouse herself becomes the agent of light – are rehearsed: *Cleaning Up TV; Who Does She Think She Is?* (London, 1971); *Whatever Happened to Sex?* (Hove, 1977); *A Most Dangerous Woman?* (Tring, 1982); *Mightier Than the Sword* (Eastbourne, 1985); *Quite Contrary: An Autobiography* (London, 1993). These can be supplemented with Michael Tracey and David Whitehouse, *Whitehouse* (London, 1974); Max Caulfield, *Mary Whitehouse* (London, 1975); and Lawrence Black, "There Was Something About Mary: The National Viewers' and Listeners' Association and Social Movement History," in Nick Crowson, Matthew Hilton, and James McKay, eds., *NGOs in Contemporary Britain: Non-State Actors in Society and Politics since 1945* (Houndmills, 2009).

Norah Buckland, too, represented a potent symbol of provincial, middle-class or lower-middle-class ordinariness. She also was a mother of three and represented Stoke-on-Trent on the Watch and Social Problems Committee of the Mothers' Union, an important instrument of the Church of England. Both Whitehouse and Buckland had been involved for some years with Moral Re-Armament, an evangelical grouping that later came to be perceived as too cozy with the politics of the fascist right. It was at a Moral Re-Armament meeting that Mary Hutcheson met her future husband, Ernest Whitehouse. But although her sympathies were undoubtedly to the right, her conception of the world was one that had little time for formal politics. Her utopian imaginary, a manic politics of radical sameness, was peopled by those who were just like her: ethically civic and feminine, normatively heterosexual and English, dutifully committed to an endless round of church sales and community raffles. Television could be part of this world, but only if it were programmed to looped showings of *Songs of Praise* and *The Black and White Minstrels* (showcasing minstrelsy as light entertainment for twentieth-century Britain), which stood out to the NVALA as "clean, wholesome and entertaining."[46] It was important to Whitehouse that she was seen to operate in a moral cosmos untouched by profane political interests. In 1970, she wrote to the Reverend Michael Seward, the information officer at the Church of England, to make clear that she was neither of the left nor the right, and that the struggle that exercised her was that "between right and wrong." "We live," she concluded, "in a fallen world."[47]

The mobilization of the feminine and the domestic inevitably required accommodation with the business of politics, in which the ethos of the feminine and the domestic was hardly at a premium.[48] That this was so was soon to be discovered by Mrs. Thatcher. Although Whitehouse never felt, as Thatcher did, that her femininity was an unwanted imposition, there was much ideologically that they held in common.[49] Even as Whitehouse espoused the chimera of non-politics, or antipolitics, she had

---

[46] Thompson, *Ban This Filth!*, 375, citing a NVALA verdict.

[47] Whitehouse cited in Thompson, *Ban This Filth!*, 327.

[48] Thatcher was closest to Whitehouse in her early incarnations; see particularly Margaret Thatcher, *What's Wrong with Politics?* (London, 1968); Bill Schwarz, "The Thatcher Years," in Ralph Miliband, Leo Panitch, and John Saville, eds., *Socialist Register 1987: Conservatism in Britain and America: Rhetoric and Reality* (London, 1987); and Beatrix Campbell, *The Iron Ladies: Why Do Women Vote Tory?* (London, 1987).

[49] Heather Nunn, *Thatcher, Politics and Fantasy: The Political Culture of Gender and Nation* (London, 2003); Jacqueline Rose, "Margaret Thatcher and Ruth Ellis," *New Formations* 6 (1988): 3–29.

within her – as did Thatcher too – a substratum of Jacobin intransigence. The force of her interventions in public life was driven by her certainty that it was the duty of the citizen to be eternally vigilant. She, for one, took her citizenly duties to be paramount, sure in her own mind that public institutions should be accountable to those who funded them and to those whom they served. Her succession of authored books functioned as handbooks for social activism, carrying the necessary telephone numbers and addresses which every fledgling moral agitator would require. In October 1964, she abandoned her career as a schoolteacher to become a full-time CUTV cadre, forsaking what she publicly held most dear: her ordinariness.[50] Whitehouse was becoming an exponent of what Michelle Nickerson has termed "housewife populism."[51] When she announced her new-found role as a professional activist, she expressed the hope that this might bring about the return of Britain to the nation it had once been, "strong and clean."[52] It was time for the privileges of anonymity to be "thrown overboard" and the struggle to be enjoined.[53]

For Whitehouse, 1963 was the year in which everything began to fall apart. That was the moment when "homosexuality, prostitution and sexual intercourse became the routine accompaniment of the evening meal."[54] In March 1963, following a Sunday BBC television program on love and marriage, Whitehouse found the girls in her school not only imbibing lax morals on such matters but claiming the authority of the BBC in justification. For Whitehouse, the BBC was to be judged guilty of peddling "a sub-Christian concept of living."[55] That summer, she organized her first round of meetings with figures who governed the media, with senior churchmen, and with Enoch Powell, as minister of health. In the new year, the CUTV was launched, picking up various affiliates, such as the Action for Biblical Witness to our Nation, the National Pure Water Association (Southern Counties Branch), and the Farmer's Christian Postal Service Fellowship for Farming Women.

---

[50] On January 17, 1980, the BBC secretary, J. F. Wilkinson, pointed out to Whitehouse that she could no longer represent herself as an ordinary member of the public as she now assumed that she spoke on behalf of the "silent majority": Thompson, *Ban This Filth!*, 264.

[51] Michelle Nickerson, *Mothers of Conservatism: Women and the Postwar Right* (Princeton, 2012).

[52] Thompson, *Ban This Filth!*, 73.

[53] In mobilizing in the public world the morals of domestic femininity, Whitehouse was recovering the social purity campaigns of an earlier generation: Lucy Bland, *Banishing the Beast: English Feminism and Sexual Morality, 1885–1914* (Harmondsworth, 1995).

[54] Whitehouse, *Quite Contrary*, 13.   [55] Whitehouse, *Cleaning Up TV*, 16.

Over the years, in a marathon sustained by an indefatigable communion of collective duty, the CUTV/NVALA set about its work. All that had made "the sixties" move – and all this gave birth to – was censured. There was predictable stuff: The Doors, Hendrix, Chuck Berry, The Sex Pistols, the "pornographic" sensibility of The Beatles.[56] Allen Ginsberg, Henry Miller, Dennis Potter. *Straw Dogs, Clockwork Orange, Last Tango in Paris, The Devils, Kes, Walkabout, The Exorcist, Midnight Cowboy,* and anything by Jean-Luc Godard. There were the celebrated private prosecutions, against the publication, in 1976, of James Kirkup's poem "The Love That Dares to Speak its Name" in *Gay News,* and against the production of Howard Brenton's *Romans in Britain* at the National Theatre in 1980. There were, too, less expected forays, against wrestling on TV, for example, or calling into doubt the rectitude of such impeccably mainstream television personalities as Richard Baker, Michael Barratt, and Michael Aspel, from whom one could never even imagine a whisper of subversion.

[handwritten margin note: Ken Loach has out lived Whitehouse]

Whitehouse herself was assiduous. One likes to think that her knowledge of the French New Wave, or of R&B, exceeded that of most of her neighbors. One can find her troubled by the latest issue of *Playboy*; sending a telegram to Harold Wilson, the prime minister, objecting to an episode of the television sitcom *Till Death Do Us Part*; complaining to the head of BBC light entertainment that on Alice Cooper's single "School's Out," she detected "anti-law and order" sentiments, and the next day sending a copy to the Director of Public Prosecutions; staying up late to catch Alan Clarke's *Scum*.[57] Innocuous mainstream programming, such as *EastEnders* and *French and Saunders*, entered her field of vision, ready for indictment; and she implored the archbishops of Canterbury and York to take action against the comedy sketch *Not The Nine O'Clock News*. By 1990, by then getting on a bit, she wrote to inform the chairman of the BBC that rapid camera-work on the watchably bland series *Bergerac* should be prohibited.[58]

Almost anything and everything was imbued with danger. In the incessant volleys she fired off, it did not seem to matter where the individual

---

[56] Thompson, *Ban This Filth!*, 87.   [57] Thompson, *Ban This Filth!*, 176.

[58] I do not chart here Whitehouse's involvement with the evangelical Festival of Light, from its founding in September 1971, which built on the influence (from 1954) of Billy Graham in the UK: this can be followed in Amy Whipple, "Speaking for Whom? The 1971 Festival of Light and the Search for the 'Silent Majority,'" *Contemporary British History* 24:3 (2010): 319–339; and in John Capon, . . . *And There Was Light: The Story of the Nationwide Festival of Light* (Woking, 1972).

pot-shot fell or whether it exploded. It was less the individual depredations she witnessed on television that moved her than the degraded moral
circumstance of the entire social system they represented. Whitehouse's
conception of the ethical universe was stamped by her Christianity and
by the values she associated with the "respectable" classes of the white
nation. When she and her campaigners called for a "strong and clean"
nation, or deemed certain TV programs to be "clean," or even when
they sought to "clean up" TV, they were drawing from an older imperial
and proconsular lexicon in which "cleanliness" signified an ethnic identification of absolute rectitude. Whitehouse herself was possessed by the
overpowering notion that she lived in corrupt times and that – at some
point, somewhere – there had once existed a more disciplined, more virtuous moral order. Mostly this was articulated in theological categories,
in which she fashioned herself as a resurrected Pilgrim. We live in a fallen
world. But fantasized perceptions of lost times never operate unilater-
ally or in transparent or uncoded form. Confronted in the present by
a corrosive anarchy that threatened to undo all the good work of past
generations, Whitehouse and her supporters sought refuge in the idea of
a nation which had once been great and in which order had prevailed. In
the 1950s, she observed, "we watched our empire slipping away."[59] The
consequences of this loss were too enormous to comprehend.

Despite her posture that neither left nor right held meaning for her,
to imagine the nation once, in the old days, to have been "strong and
clean" prescribed a politics of authoritarian temper, where older colonial
investments can be discerned. Indeed, if vigilance were relaxed, then even
good folk could be turned. In a draft article of the autumn of 1963, just
at the time when her public persona was first beginning to cohere, she
addressed "parents and teachers everywhere in the country":

How can we give [children] what it takes to face the onslaught of dirty, material-
istic atheism which attacks them on every side? [This is] part of a deliberate plan
to soften up the characters of men and women that they will become "useable"
and "traitors."[60]

On such grounds, she identified those Quislings in the state who were
selling ordinary folk down the river. And on such grounds, too, she
determined to arouse her "dispersed and shattered" constituencies.

---

[59] Whitehouse, *Whatever Happened to Sex?*, 8.

[60] Thompson, *Ban This Filth!*, 27. Or alternatively: before the Nazis took over Poland
they flooded the bookstalls with pornography – "This is a fact," Whitehouse, *Whatever
Happened to Sex?*, 176.

Conclusion

To close, I will reflect on the political reimagining of the domains of public and private.[61]

The private domain, only falteringly represented by the given structure of party politics, was mobilized by the tribunes of the silent majority as the necessary counter to the morally bankrupt domain of institutionalized politics. This accounts for the paradox of Whitehouse, for example, declaring that, in order to succeed in her endeavors, she was required to abandon her anonymity as an "ordinary housewife" – which was exactly what gave credence to her political values.

In this activation of the ethos of domesticity, in which the public was challenged in the name of the private, the decisive medium was provided by the letter. This became the means by which the voice of the silent majority could be heard and demand recognition. It became the route by which putatively private concerns could be mobilized and made public. To subscribe to this emergent sensibility, no-one was required to learn a catechism, or master the finer details of a constitutional rulebook or navigate their way around a political meeting: all one needed was paper, envelope, and a stamp. Letters as a form of social protest have a long history.[62] A rudimentary literacy is, of course, a precondition. But there may have been a more particular determination at work. In England, at any rate, in the postwar period there developed new ("progressive") pedagogies founded on the conviction that *everyone had a story to tell*. In a great collective outpouring, those who wrote Powell and Whitehouse told their stories – as they had been taught to do.[63]

If the letter provided one means by which *the private became public*, there also occurred – through the arrival of television – the transposition by which *the public became private*. The rearrangement of the public–private nexus allowed new forms of political discussion to occupy the home. Whitehouse's politics sought to salvage the sanctity of the domestic after the arrival of TV. The presence of TV also worked to underwrite the collectivity of letter-writing: learning that neighbors, or more

[61] Brian Harrison, "The Public and the Private in Modern Britain," in Peter Burke, Brian Harrison, and Paul Slack, eds., *Civil Histories: Essays Presented to Sir Keith Thomas* (Oxford, 2000), 337–358.

[62] E. P. Thompson, "The Crime of Anonymity," in Douglas Hay et al., *Albion's Fatal Tree: Crime and Society in Eighteenth-Century England* (Harmondsworth, 1977).

[63] Carolyn Steedman, "State-Sponsored Autobiography," in Becky Conekin, Frank Mort, and Chris Waters, eds., *Moments of Modernity: Reconstructing Britain, 1945–1964* (London, 1999), 41–54.

distant unknown folk, were busy sending letters to Wallace or Nixon, or to Powell or Whitehouse, provided the spur for others to mobilize themselves.

But this was not the only effect of the growing universalization of TV, for it also enabled an imagined community to represent itself as a *knowable* community. This carries another paradox. Reminiscing about watching television as he was growing up, Henry Louis Gates explains, "I first got to know white people as 'people' through their flickering images on television shows."[64] This underlies the syndrome which emerged in these years of TV viewers writing to fictional characters who appeared in soap operas, or even in TV advertisements.[65] Television made those who spoke for the silent majority knowable. Letters to Powell and Whitehouse played upon the intimacy the writer felt toward the recipient, with the letter-writers themselves confiding their secrets to one whom they trusted. In these moments, the silent majority assumed itself to be a community of intimates.

These mediations, however, were double-edged, for the organs of the mass media, television included, could work to generate not only "knowable" people but also fantasized types who carried within themselves the dispositions of the demonic: Nixon's "Jews, blacks, youth." There were many occasions in these years, as there still are, when we can witness the media manufacture of such figures. That this is so should not lead us to denounce "the media": whether representations are deemed intimate and kindly or demonic and dangerous depends as much on the given politics of the viewer as on the images created within the media as such. Even so, moral panics happen; through a complex chain of discursive intervention particular evils come to be condensed in the idea of particular human types.[66]

Underwriting the cathectic charge of these moral panics was the conviction that in the past all had been well and that modern times were characterized by a social collapse of biblical proportions. Wallace imagined that the historic South had embodied harmony; Powell, that the social hierarchies bequeathed by empire allowed for the full realization

---

[64] Henry Louis Gates, *Colored People* (Harmondsworth, 1995), 20.

[65] One of the most celebrated occasions in Britain in these years was the post sent to "Katie," who advertised Oxo: Sean Nixon, *Hard Sell: Advertising, Affluence and Trans-Atlantic Relations, circa 1951–69* (Manchester, 2013), 193–195.

[66] Stanley Cohen, *Folk Devils and Moral Panics: The Creation of the Mods and Rockers* (St. Albans, 1973).

of human endeavor, when white folk could go about their business unmolested; and Whitehouse, that, at some point before 1963, families could be families. These fantasized *lost times* gave to those who believed that they were the silent majority their militant, Manichean conception of politics.

Though in the end he rejected empire & imagine a mono-ethnic hierarchical community)

8

African American Republicans, "Black Capitalism," and the Nixon Administration

Joshua D. Farrington

The traditional narrative of Richard Nixon and the "Silent Majority" has focused almost exclusively on white conservatives. From suburbanites to Southerners to blue-collar workers, whites dominate our understanding of Nixon's coalition.[1] Studies of conservatism in Europe have similarly focused on white opposition to communism or fears about cultural and religious decay. When race is addressed, such as in discussions of Great Britain's archconservative Enoch Powell, the focus is on white opposition to immigration, antidiscrimination legislation, and decolonization.[2] Unlike the postwar African, Middle Eastern, and Asian immigrants to Europe, African Americans constituted a significant percentage of the United States' population since its inception. In their centuries-long struggle for freedom, African Americans developed political ideologies that were unique to their experiences in a country built on slavery. In this distinctly American context, black conservatism – from the self-help ideology of Booker T. Washington to the black separatism of Marcus Garvey – has long existed within the African American political spectrum.[3] This conservative strain of black political thought continued through Nixon's

[1] See, for example, Matthew Lassiter, *The Silent Majority: Suburban Politics in the Sunbelt South* (Princeton, 2007); Lisa McGirr, *Suburban Warriors: The Origins of the New American Right* (Princeton, 2002).

[2] Camilla Schofield, *Enoch Powell and the Making of Postcolonial Britain* (Cambridge, 2013); Bill Schwarz, *Memories of Empire*, vol. 1, *The White Man's World* (Oxford, 2011); Bill Smithies and Peter Fiddick, eds., *Enoch Powell on Immigration* (London, 1963); Douglas Schoen, *Enoch Powell and the Powellites* (London, 1977).

[3] Though this chapter looks primarily at the economic conservatism that inspired black Republicans in the 1960s, there have long existed strains of cultural and religious conservatism within African American communities. Fundamentalist Christians, the Nation

tenure in office. However, unlike their white counterparts, most black Republicans in the late 1960s and 1970s did not envision themselves as anticommunist Cold Warriors, as anti-civil rights backlashers, or as cultural warriors defending "traditional values." Instead, their brand of conservatism was anchored in longstanding African American ideas of self-help and self-determination.

Despite Franklin Roosevelt's New Deal coalition, which solidified the relationship of mainstream black leadership to the Democratic Party, a sizable minority of middle-class African Americans continued to ally with the Republican Party through the mid-twentieth century. Though the New Deal brought economic relief, the Democratic Party remained the party of Southern segregationists, and Republicans appealed to the black middle class largely on its heritage as "the Party of Lincoln." From the 1930s through 1960s, successful black businessmen, such as T. R. M. Howard, Asa Spaulding, Robert Church, Jr., and George W. Lee, remained tied to the Republican Party, where they held leadership positions, ran for public office, and lobbied for civil rights legislation. In the same vein as Booker T. Washington and Marcus Garvey, they believed a thriving network of black business was essential to the uplift of their communities. The importance of "black capitalism" was not lost to middle-class magazines like *Ebony* and *Jet*, whose pages throughout the 1960s and 1970s exalted businessmen as pillars of black America.[4] George W. Lee, a Republican leader and insurance company executive from Memphis, believed businessmen were just as important to the black freedom struggle as civil rights activists, arguing that "a race that is always in front of the counter and never behind the counter, that is always buying and never selling can't make itself felt in the American economy."

of Islam, and some Black Power organizations in the 1960s and 1970s held deeply conservative views of masculinity, openly espoused male chauvinism, and believed the place of women should be confined to their homes. Rarely, however, did these strains equate to support for the Republican Party. Hanes Walton, Jr., "Black and Conservative Political Movements in the U.S.A.," *Political Science Review* 10 (July–December 1971), 107; Louis Harlan, *Booker T. Washington: The Wizard of Tuskegee, 1901–1915* (New York, 1986); Theodore G. Vincent, *Black Power and the Garvey Movement* (Baltimore, 2006); Edward Curtis, *Black Muslim Religion in the Nation of Islam, 1960–1975* (Chapel Hill, 2006).

4 David Beito and Linda Royster Beito, "T. R. M. Howard: Pragmatism over Strict Integrationist Ideology in the Mississippi Delta, 1942–1954," in Glenn Feldman, ed., *Before Brown: Civil Rights and White Backlash in the Modern South* (Tuscaloosa, 2004), 70; "The World of the Wealthy Negro," *New York Times*, July 23, 1967; Thomas Sugrue, *Sweet Land of Liberty: The Forgotten Struggle of Civil Rights in the North* (New York, 2008), 429–430.

According to Lee, blacks should embrace "ethnic pride" in supporting businesses owned by members of their race, and work to obtain a "black monopoly" in their communities.[5]

Many black Republicans joined white conservatives in criticizing welfare for enabling dependency. "I believe very strongly in self-help," declared Edward W. Brooke, a black Republican from Massachusetts elected to the U.S. Senate in 1966, "otherwise you make parasites of people. Sometimes, if you have too many crutches, you will never learn to walk."[6] Clarence Townes, Jr., head of the Republican National Committee's Minorities Division in the late 1960s, similarly claimed that "the Chinese used opium to control their masses" while the modern-day Democratic Party "continue[s] to give us a steady diet of this frustrating, humiliating, degrading, deteriorating welfarism."[7] Unlike white conservatives, however, black Republicans refused to embrace popular notions of the "undeserving poor" or the belief that welfare "stole hard-earned money" from workers. It was not that blacks did not deserve financial assistance from the government, or were inherently lazy, but that accepting welfare was intrinsically demoralizing and fostered a pathology of inferiority.

There also existed a conservative strain of black nationalism within the Black Power movement of the 1960s, which ranged from the Nation of Islam to black Republicans, that emphasized black-owned businesses. As Thomas Sugrue and other historians have discussed, racial uplift, self-help, and black capitalism – the guiding principles of black conservatives since the turn of the century – gained new salience among black nationalists in the late 1960s who were discontented with the failures of liberalism to solve the economic woes that plagued black America. Indeed, by the time of Nixon's nomination in 1968, one of the leading civil rights organizations, the Congress of Racial Equality (CORE), had moved away from its founding doctrine of interracial cooperation to embrace a conservative strand of nationalism. Under the leadership of Floyd McKissick, CORE espoused new nationalist ideas that overlapped with those of Stokely Carmichael, the Black Panther Party, and others in

---

[5] David Tucker, *Lieutenant Lee of Beale Street* (Nashville, 1971), 208; "NIA Must Regain Its Identity Says Old Guard Orator," *The Pilot* 19:4 (August 1970), Folder 2, Box 1, George W. Lee Collection, Memphis/Shelby County Public Library.

[6] "A Negro Leader's Advice to Republicans," *U.S. News and World Report*, February 1, 1965.

[7] Clarence Townes, Jr., interview by Robert Wright, July 7, 1970, Moorland Spingarn Research Center, Howard University.

the emerging Black Power movement. However, his definition of Black Power rejected Carmichael's and the Panthers' embrace of Marxism.[8] "Black Capitalism is so long overdue and of such importance," McKissick asserted, "that it takes precedence" over all job training programs, education, and other objectives of the civil rights movement.[9]

McKissick left CORE in 1968 to found McKissick Enterprises, a corporate entity that promoted black entrepreneurship by funding the creation of Afro-centric restaurants, publishing and theater companies, a shopping center, and even a new town in North Carolina – Soul City – that he touted as a haven of black self-determination. According to its motto, McKissick Enterprises was "Dedicated to Building Black Economic Power," as it insisted that African Americans "must control and productively utilize capital" and join white businesses in "profit-making." Rejecting the integrationist goals of the mainstream civil rights movement, McKissick argued that desegregated theaters and lunch counters were not worthwhile "if a Black man has no bread in his pocket." Black-owned businesses offered African Americans economic control of their communities, and would foster self-respect.[10] Interconnected with McKissick's emphasis on self-help was a rejection of welfare "handouts" that "do violence to a man, strip him of dignity, and breed in him a hatred of the system."[11]

McKissick was not alone among black nationalists in embracing self-help over welfare. His successor at CORE, Roy Innis, directed that "the total thrust of CORE's endeavors" center on "self-help bootstrap efforts."[12] Similarly, Nathan Wright, the co-organizer of the 1967 Black

---

[8] Sugrue, *Sweet Land of Liberty*, 427; Thomas Brooks, *Walls Come Tumbling Down: A History of the Civil Rights Movement, 1940–1970* (Englewood Cliffs, NJ, 1974), 267; August Meier and Elliott Rudwick, *CORE: A Study in the Civil Rights Movement, 1942–1968* (New York, 1973).

[9] Robert Brisbane, *Black Activism: Racial Revolution in the United States, 1954–1970* (Valley Forge, PA, 1974), 265.

[10] Devin Fergus, "Black Power, Soft Power: Floyd McKissick, Soul City, and the Death of Moderate Black Republicanism," *Journal of Policy History* 22:2 (2010): 152; Timothy Minchin, "'A Brand New Shining City': Floyd B. McKissick Sr. and the Struggle to Build Soul City, North Carolina," *North Carolina Historical Review* 82:2 (April 2005): 130; "F. B. McKissick Enterprises, Inc. Purpose and Potential," n.d., Folder 6443, Floyd B. McKissick Papers #4930, Southern Historical Collection of the University of North Carolina at Chapel Hill and the African American Resources Collection of North Carolina Central University (hereafter McKissick Papers).

[11] McKissick, cited in Dean Kotlowski, *Nixon's Civil Rights: Politics, Principle, and Policy* (Cambridge, MA, 2001), 132.

[12] Roy Innis, "Truth, Lies, and Consequences," in Jeffrey M. Elliot, ed., *Black Voices in American Politics* (New York, 1986), 244.

Power Conference in Newark and the 1968 Black Power Conference in Philadelphia, urged black Democrats to shed their partisan affiliation and turn toward "self-determination, local control...independence and self-sufficiency" and to reject welfare. "All men should have some kind of responsibility," he preached, "earning for self spells dignity." While the Democratic Party sought to keep blacks "on the plantation" of government dependency, according to Wright, the true friends of African Americans were "conservative business-oriented Republicans [who] will support your demands for economic power."[13]

During the 1968 presidential election campaign, Richard Nixon actively courted white Southern delegates at the Republican National Convention, promising Strom Thurmond and other segregationists that he would not "ram anything down your throats" via civil rights. After nearly a decade of civil rights demonstrations, Nixon pledged to restore "law and order," proclaiming that he opposed any "breaches of the law, whether they take the form of wanton rioting [or] of civil disobedience in the cause of civil rights."[14] Many observers saw his emphasis on law and order and opposition to busing as a means to integrate schools as part of a "Southern Strategy" designed to woo disaffected Democrats aligned with the segregationist campaign of George Wallace.[15] However, as many recent scholars have argued, Nixon's strategy avoided not only Wallace's overt racism but also his open courtship of hardline segregationists. Indeed, Nixon willingly conceded five states in the Deep South to Wallace on election night. Rather, Nixon embraced a "Suburban Strategy" that appealed to center-right suburbanites from the expanding middle class in the Sunbelt of the upper South and West.[16]

[13] Nathan Wright, Jr., *Let's Work Together* (New York, 1968), 94–95, 217; Nathan Wright, Jr., "The Social Arena of Black Political Action," in Nathan Wright, Jr., ed., *What Black Politicians Are Saying* (New York, 1972), 202; Ashraf H. A. Rushdy, *Neo-slave Narratives: Studies in the Social Logic of a Literary Form* (New York, 1999), 52.

[14] "The Public Records of Richard M. Nixon and Spiro T. Agnew," *Congressional Quarterly Weekly Report*, August 16, 1968, 2146; Statement delivered by Richard Nixon in Boston, February 15, 1968, Folder: Nixon, Richard M., 1968 (1), Box 14, Special Names Series, DDE Post-Presidential Papers, Dwight D. Eisenhower Presidential Library, Abilene, Kansas (hereafter Eisenhower Library).

[15] Kevin Kruse, *White Flight: Atlanta and the Making of Modern Conservatism* (Princeton, 2007), 253.

[16] Lassiter, *The Silent Majority*, 6; Kruse, *White Flight*, 253; Timothy Thurber, "Goldwaterism Triumphant? Race and the Republican Party, 1965–1968," *Journal of the Historical Society* 7:3 (September 2007): 374.

Though Nixon did not court mainstream black leaders, he reached out to black businessmen and nationalists by openly endorsing black capitalism. Courting McKissick, Innis, and other bootstrap nationalists, he openly embraced the controversial term "Black Power," a phrase his Democratic opponent, Hubert Humphrey, equated with "black racism."[17] In speeches during the spring primaries, Nixon told audiences that "the answer to the militants is not to say 'never,'" but to instead "forge new alliances" with those who advocated black self-determination.[18] On April 25, he delivered a nationally broadcasted radio address in which he laid out his most extensive argument for the creation of a new alliance between Republicans and black nationalists. His plan centered on "the development of black capitalism," and he pledged financial incentives and other resources "to start new businesses in the ghetto and to expand existing ones." Despite his own law and order rhetoric, he criticized the press for focusing only on violent "black extremists," arguing instead that "we should listen to the militants – carefully, hearing not only the threats but also the programs and promises." He went on to suggest that "much of the black militant talk these days is actually in terms far closer to the doctrines of free enterprise than to those of the welfarist 30's – terms of 'pride,' 'ownership,' 'private enterprise,' 'capital,' 'self-assurance,' [and] 'self-respect.'" He then pledged that under his watch the federal government would direct institutional support to programs "oriented toward more black ownership," so that "from this can flow... black pride, black jobs, black opportunity and yes, black power."[19]

Following the two speeches, John McClaughry, Nixon's special assistant for community affairs, told black nationalists that "it is conservatives, businessmen and Republicans who have the greatest potential for bringing community self determination to reality."[20] McClaughry arranged for a private meeting in May with McKissick and Innis at Nixon's New York apartment, where the Republican candidate again

---

[17] Manning Marable, *Black Liberation in Conservative America* (Boston, 1997), 217; "Humphrey Backs NAACP in Fight on Black Racism," *New York Times*, July 7, 1966.

[18] Statement delivered by Richard M. Nixon in Boston, February 15, 1968, Folder: Nixon, Richard M., 1968 (1), Box 14, Special Names Series, DDE Post-Presidential Papers, Eisenhower Library.

[19] Nixon for President Committee, "Bridges to Human Dignity," April 25, 1968, Folder: Nixon, Richard M., 1968 (1), Box 14, Special Names Series, DDE Post-Presidential Papers, Eisenhower Library.

[20] John McClaughry to John Conyers, October 29, 1968, Folder 6199, McKissick Papers.

pledged to support black capitalism. McKissick subsequently predicted
to reporters, "Nixon may fool a lot of people and do one Hell of a job
as president of this country. Nixon is a first rate American and there's no
doubt about that." The black militant newspaper *Liberator* even went so
far as to claim, "the conservative is the natural ally of the moment for the
Black man. Today, as Roy Innis of CORE has attested to, only Richard
Nixon is . . . hospitable to Black Power."[21]

Throughout the fall campaign, Nixon continued to tout his black capitalism program, purchasing a two-page glossy advertisement in a November edition of *Jet* magazine. The ad featured a black college student named
Homer Pitts, who pondered his future after graduating. The ad responded
to his fears, proclaiming, "a vote for Richard Nixon for President is a vote
for a man who wants Homer to have the chance to own his own business. Richard Nixon believes strongly in black capitalism. Because black
capitalism is black power in the best sense of the word."[22] Nixon also
made a campaign stop at a black-owned shopping center in Philadelphia,
where he was greeted by Leon Sullivan, founder of the Opportunities
Industrialization Center and staunch supporter of economic self-help.[23]
At another stop in Buffalo, New York, over one thousand African Americans, including the president of the Buffalo Urban League, greeted Nixon,
who promised that his black capitalism programs would make blacks
"truly independent."[24]

Though Nixon only won approximately 15 percent of the black vote
on Election Day, this was a marked improvement from Barry Goldwater's 6 percent in 1964. Much of the subsequent historical literature on
his administration has emphasized his "zig-zag" approach to civil rights –
that is, that for every liberal policy the administration supported ("zig"), it
offered a counterbalancing conservative policy ("zag"). Nixon expanded
the federal government's civil rights enforcement budget by 800 percent,
and his secretary of housing and urban development, George Romney,
built more public housing units in three years than had been constructed in
all previous administrations combined. At the same time, Nixon refused
to support Romney's efforts to integrate all-white suburbs, opposed

---

[21] Robert Weems, Jr. with Lewis Randolph, *Business in Black and White: American Presidents and Black Entrepreneurs in the Twentieth Century* (New York, 2009), 118.

[22] "This Time, Vote Like Homer Pitts' Whole World Depended on It," *Jet*, November 7,
1968.

[23] Matthew J. Countryman, *Up South: Civil Rights and Black Power in Philadelphia*
(Philadelphia, 2006), 116.

[24] "Nixon Gets First Big Race Turnout," *Oakland Post*, October 23, 1968.

— He put Rehnquist in the court

busing, and nominated numerous justices to the Supreme Court who had a record of resisting civil rights. These "zigs" and "zags" were essential to his strategy of maintaining the support of middle-class Americans in the Sunbelt, many of whom did not want to roll back black civil rights but also did not want any new race-conscious solutions to inequality that threatened their new status in suburbia.[25]

Nixon did not vacillate, however, when it came to implementing his program of black capitalism. On March 5, 1969, he signed Executive Order 11458, creating the Office of Minority Business Enterprise (OMBE). He tasked the office with removing "obstacles such as unavailability of credit, insurance and technical assistance" to make it easier for African Americans to create new businesses. The office provided a range of services, from training seminars and workshops to multimillion-dollar guaranteed loans and grants. Nixon instructed the secretary of commerce to give the OMBE "high priority," because supporting black entrepreneurship "is something long overdue."[26] The OMBE's role in the black business sector grew annually during Nixon's tenure in the White House. In 1969, it doled out $200 million to minority-owned businesses, and $300 million the following year.[27]

The modern Minority Business Development Agency, now in the Commerce Department

In March 1970, Nixon issued another executive order that authorized the Small Business Administration (SBA) to "particularly consider the needs and interests of minority-owned small business" in the lucrative arena of government contracts. Through the SBA's section 8(a) set-aside program, the government contracted over $240 million in goods and services from black-owned companies by 1972 (compared to less than $9 million annually when Nixon first took office). Additionally, Nixon lifted chartering regulations for black-owned banks, and urged federal

[25] Herbert Parmet, *Richard Nixon and His America* (Boston, 1990), 600; Melvin Small, *The Presidency of Richard Nixon* (Lawrence, KS, 1999), 162; Allen Matusow, *The Unraveling of America: A History of Liberalism in the 1960s* (New York, 1984), 233; Kotlowski, *Nixon's Civil Rights*, 57.

[26] Maurice Stans, "A Balance Sheet," in Kenneth Thompson, ed., *The Nixon Presidency: Twenty-two Intimate Perspectives of Richard M. Nixon* (Lanham, MD, 1987), 38; "Nixon Creates New Office to Help Minority Business," *Afro-American*, March 15, 1969; Leah Michele Wright, "The Loneliness of the Black Conservative: Black Republicans and the Grand Old Party, 1964–1980," PhD diss., Princeton University, 2009, 185–186; Judson Jeffries, *Huey P. Newton: The Radical Theorist* (Jackson, MS, 2002), 70.

[27] Maurice Stans, "A Piece of the Action: Report to the President on Minority Business Enterprise," June 30, 1970, Folder: Commerce Dept. Minority Business Enterprise 1969–1971, Box 130, John Sherman Cooper Collection, Margaret I. King Library, University of Kentucky; Weems with Randolph, *Business in Black and White*, 227.

departments to deposit money in minority firms. By 1971, the federal government had deposited over $200 million in black-owned banks, and the number of black banks almost doubled between 1969 and 1971 (and then nearly doubled again by 1974). Indeed, two-thirds of the one hundred largest black-owned businesses in 1975 had been founded after 1969, and from 1968 to 1972 the revenue of black businesses grew from $4.5 to $7.2 billion.[28]

Robert J. Brown, special assistant to the president and the highest-ranking African American in the White House, convinced Nixon to also increase federal support of historically black colleges and universities. Bootstrap nationalists like Roy Innis saw black colleges as superior to their white counterparts in terms of bolstering the values of racial pride and self-help. In 1972, Nixon asked his Domestic Affairs Council to write a budget that "cut substantially the subsidies" for white institutions of higher education so that they could "put a little more money into some of the black colleges," an endeavor that was "infinitely more important and more needed" than continued federal funding of "an Ivy League college." In 1970, Brown arranged a series of meetings between Nixon and black college presidents that resulted in a $29 million grant to historically black colleges. Indeed, by the start of Nixon's second term, federal funding to black colleges had increased to $400 million annually. Tellingly, enrollment in historically black colleges grew by 50 percent from 1969 to 1977.[29]

By the end of Nixon's first term in office, a number of new black Republican organizations had been formed in response to his embrace of black businesses and colleges. The Republican Congressional Campaign Committee provided startup funds for the creation of the National Black Silent Majority Committee (NBSMC). Under the leadership of black Republican Clay Claiborne, the NBSMC conducted a national tour of

---

[28] Robert J. Brown, "Nixon," *American Visions* 10:1 (February/March 1995): 45; John D. Skrentny, *The Minority Rights Revolution* (Cambridge, MA, 2002), 148; Maurice Stans, "A Piece of the Action," Cooper Collection; Theodore Cross, *The Black Power Imperative: Racial Inequality and the Politics of Nonviolence* (New York, 1984), 171; Richard Nixon, *The Memoirs of Richard Nixon* (New York, 1978), 438; Kotlowski, *Nixon's Civil Rights*, 145.

[29] Brown, "Nixon," 46; Robert Brown to John Ehrlichman and Leonard Garment, July 2, 1970, Folder: Black College Presidents and Black Colleges [2 of 3], Box 49, White House Central Files, Staff Member and Office Files, Leonard Garment, Richard Nixon Presidential Library and Museum, Yorba Linda, California (hereafter Nixon Library); Parmet, *Richard Nixon and His America*, 546; Leah Wright, "The Black Cabinet: Economic Civil Rights in the Nixon Administration," in Glenn Feldman, ed., *Painting Dixie Red: When, Where, Why, and How the South Became Republican* (Gainesville, FL, 2011), 259–260; Kotlowski, *Nixon's Civil Rights*, 153–155.

seventy-eight major cities to publicize Nixon's record. Claiborne denounced the Democratic Party for its programs that "continue to condemn too many of my fellow Negroes to the old, hopeless cycle of poverty and welfare and despair." Though the NBSMC never gained a widespread grassroots following, its support of the Nixon administration won the approval of the president, who wrote a public letter lauding the organization's "constructive role . . . in furthering the work of true social justice."[30]

The NBSMC was unique among black Republican organizations in its emphasis on the social issues that drove Nixon's silent majority of white voters, such as patriotism, opposition to demonstrations, and support of "traditional" values. Ignoring issues of structural racism, Claiborne's group was "dedicated to preserving the American way of life" and sided squarely with the administration on issues ranging from busing to law and order. However, while the NBSMC published its own newsletter and conducted a nationwide tour, its ability to produce sleek pamphlets and garner media attention came from the funding it received from the Republican establishment, not grassroots black Republican support. At its inaugural press conference, the NBSMC boasted only thirty members, many of whom would later claim that they had never agreed to join. Claiborne, who had been indicted for election fraud in 1964, appears to have been a marginal figure within the ranks of black Republicans, and the NBSMC was a one-man show.[31]

Indeed, many black Republicans were indifferent, or adamantly opposed, to the social issues that galvanized the silent majority. Groups such as Michigan's Wolverine State Republican Organization and California's Third World Republicans deemphasized social issues and instead emphasized Nixon's policies of black capitalism.[32] To them and other

---

30 "'Silent Majority' of Blacks Formed," *New York Times*, July 12, 1970; "'Silent Majority' Promotes Nixon," *Sacramento Observer*, August 12, 1971; Black Silent Majority Committee, "What is the Black Silent Majority?," n.d., Folder: National Black Silent Majority Committee, Box 9, White House Central Files, Staff Member and Office Files, Robert H. Finch, Nixon Library; Richard Nixon to Clay Claiborne, October 7, 1970, Folder: Civil Rights/Minorities. Althouse-Lund, Box 219, Rogers C. B. Morton Papers, Margaret I. King Library, University of Kentucky (hereafter Morton Papers).

31 "Black Silent Majority Meet," *Sacramento Observer*, October 22, 1970; National Black Silent Majority Committee press release, July 6, 1970, Folder: National Black Silent Majority Committee, Box 88, White House Central Files, Staff Member and Office Files, Charles W. Colson, Nixon Library; "'Silent Majority' of Blacks Formed," *New York Times*, July 12, 1970.

32 Wolverine State Republican Organization Inc., "Black Republican State Conference and Dinner," April 26, 1969, Folder: Minorities, 1962–73, Box 46, Republican Party

black supporters of the president, hot-button social issues were secondary to black capitalism. The largest organization of black Republicans, the National Council of Concerned Afro-American Republicans, which had 10,000 members in 1968, centered much of its attention on challenging Southern Republicans who excluded African Americans from party leadership. When the organization did address social issues like busing, it lamented, "the ugly spectre of . . . Strom Thurmond still casts its shadow" upon the party.[33]

The largest organization to cater to black Republicans was the National Business League (NBL), which touted black capitalism to the exclusion of the rest of Nixon's domestic agenda. Throughout the 1960s and 1970s, the NBL was headed by Burkeley Burrell, who envisioned himself "an updated version" of the league's founder, Booker T. Washington, and who frequently preached the virtues of bootstrap self-help and free enterprise. Burrell was a Republican, claiming that he was drawn to the "hallmarks of the party," above all self-determination through business. In large part because of Burrell's connections with the Republican establishment, the NBL grew exponentially under his leadership. By 1975, the league boasted 113 chapters (up from thirty chapters in 1962 when he first became president) and had a total membership of over 10,000. During the Nixon years, Burrell secured millions of dollars in OMBE grants for the NBL, and as the eventual vice president of Nixon's Advisory Council for Minority Enterprise he was relentless in his advocacy of federal support of black-owned businesses.[34]

Burrell joined other black businessmen and bootstrap nationalists in the Black Vote Division of the Committee for the Re-Election of the President in 1972. Joining him in the division was Floyd McKissick, who had officially become a Republican after the Nixon administration provided him millions of dollars for Soul City. The division first received national

---

(Michigan State Central Committee Records), Bentley Historical Library, University of Michigan; Clarence Townes to Leonard Garment, October 21, 1968, Clarence L. Townes Jr. Papers, Special Collections and Archives, James Branch Cabell Library, Virginia Commonwealth University.

[33] "Negroes Appeal to Nixon to Act," *New York Times*, November 7, 1968; "Southern Blacks Fight All-White Delegations," *Miami News*, July 25, 1968; "Quo Vadis, Mr. President?," *The Afro-American Voter*, May–June 1969, Folder: Civil Rights/Minorities, Box 177, Morton Papers.

[34] "The National Business League," *Black Enterprise*, June 1972, 38, 41; "Black Publishers to Honor Berkeley Burrell at S.F. Confab," *Sun Reporter* (San Francisco), June 7, 1975; Jim Bean, *Big Government and Affirmative Action: The Scandalous History of the Small Business Administration* (Lexington, KY, 2001), 77.

attention with a "Kick-Off Campaign" on June 12, 1972, that attracted more than 2,500 guests to a $100 per-person banquet. Included among the attendants were a number of prominent black celebrities and nationalists, such as the widow of Malcolm X, Betty Shabazz; the president of Malcolm X College, Charles Hurst; football star and actor Jim Brown; and the musicians Lionel Hampton and Billy Eckstein. McKissick delivered the keynote address, which juxtaposed welfare to black capitalism. The former Freedom Rider harkened back to his boyhood on a farm, comparing welfare to a "sugar tit." If one was from the rural South, McKissick claimed, he would know "what a sugar tit really is – it ain't milk – it is a substitute for milk, and it's a pacifier." By voting Democratic and accepting government welfare, African Americans "continue sucking sugar tits not ever tasting milk." Through Richard Nixon's support of black capitalism, he claimed, black entrepreneurs had been offered authentic "cream."[35]

McKissick was moderately successful in attracting a number of high-profile African Americans, such as Sammy Davis, Jr., Johnny Mathis, and the "Godfather of Soul," James Brown. However, African American support for Nixon in the voting booth remained unchanged from four years prior. To many African Americans, Nixon's support of black businessmen and black colleges paled in comparison to his opposition to busing and open housing in suburbs, unpalatable Supreme Court nominations, and lack of forthright leadership in the field of civil rights. Though black Republicans occasionally acknowledged Nixon's poor record outside of funding black businesses and colleges – Edward Brooke, for instance, condemned Nixon's "cold, calculated, political decision" to ignore mainstream black leaders – most bootstrap nationalists and businessmen held onto their faith in black capitalism and self-help. These ideas were simply not popular among the majority of black workers and impoverished families.[36] Additionally, McKissick and other black Republicans could not overcome the glaring inconsistency in their denunciations of welfare but acceptance of government funding for businesses. While claiming that African Americans who accepted "handouts" did not have "respect in the

---

35 Frank Carpenter, "Minutes of Black Surrogate's Briefing Meeting," September 7, 1972, Folder 7553, McKissick Papers; "F. McKissick Lauds Nixon," *Tri-State Defender*, June 24, 1972; "McKissick: 'It's Time to Give Up the Sugar Tit,'" *The Black Advance*, August 1972, Folder: Blacks II (14 of 14), Box 23, Committee for the Re-Election of the President Collection: Frederic Malek Papers, Series II, Nixon Library.

36 Kotlowski, *Nixon's Civil Rights*, 184; "Brooke Calls Nixon Policy on Civil Rights Negative," *Observer-Reporter* (Washington, PA), March 17, 1970.

minds of those who pass out the doles," McKissick openly urged black entrepreneurs to tap "the many pockets of funds available in the various agencies in Washington."[37]

The recession of the mid-1970s combined with Nixon's resignation following the Watergate scandal severely hampered the black capitalism movement. Though the federal government continued to give black entrepreneurs financial support, Presidents Gerald Ford, Jimmy Carter, and Ronald Reagan had no personal interest in funding black businesses to the same extent Nixon had. Even at its height under Nixon, black capitalism was a mere band aid that failed to slow the economic hemorrhaging of black communities in the economic downturn of the 1970s. Throughout Nixon's tenure, black businesses contributed less than 1 percent to the total receipts of American businesses. In an era of globalization and the growing corporatization of American commerce, most minority-owned firms in the 1970s were small businesses with fewer than five employees. Moreover, by the mid- to late 1970s, black businesses, including those that received federal support through the OMBE, failed at a rate of over 13 percent, as many – though not all – had limited markets in impoverished inner cities with high unemployment.[38]

The limitations of black capitalism, however, do not mean it should be ignored in our discussions of modern conservatism. Although black conservatives never made up a majority of the black electorate, their influence was manifest in their ability to secure hundreds of millions of dollars in federal funding. They also point to alternatives along the conservative political spectrum and the need to expand parameters beyond the white silent majority.

---

37 "What the National Committee for a Two-Party System, Inc. Does Not Believe," May 16, 1973, Folder: Soul City [2 of 3], Box 64, White House Central Files, Staff Member and Office Files, Bradley H. Patterson, Nixon Library; "McKissick Tells Blacks Forget OEO Dismantling," *Jet*, May 31, 1973.

38 Ibram H. Rogers, "Acquiring 'A Piece of the Action': The Rise and Fall of the Black Capitalism Movement," in Michael Ezra, ed., *The Economic Civil Rights Movement: African Americans and the Struggle for Economic Power* (New York, 2012), 139–141; Devin Fergus, *Liberalism, Black Power, and the Making of American Politics, 1965–1980* (Athens, GA, 2009), 227; Peter Carroll, *It Seemed Like Nothing Happened: The Tragedy and Promise of America in the 1970s* (New York, 1982), 47.

PART IV

RELIGIOUS MOBILIZATION

9

Awakening the Sleeping Giant

The Rise and Political Role of the American Christian Right Since the 1960s

Mark J. Rozell and Britta Waldschmidt-Nelson

The U.S. Christian right movement of today traces its origins to the 1960s and 1970s, having emerged largely in reaction to the outlawing of school prayer (by the Supreme Court decisions *Engel v. Vitale*, 1962, and *Murry v. Curlett*, 1963), the legalization of abortion (by the Supreme Court's *Roe v. Wade* decision of 1973), as well as the general discontent among conservative Christians regarding liberal social policies and the youth counterculture. Prior to this period, the core of the movement, composed of fundamentalist and evangelical Protestants, had not been effectively mobilized or unified politically for any length of time. Although conservative Christians had been concerned about certain political issues earlier, such as liberal New Deal policies, there had never been any successful effort among them to become politically organized and impactful. Indeed, such prominent pastors as Reverend Jerry Falwell preached against direct political activism and urged their congregations to maintain a strict separation between faith and political activity.[1] As has long been custom

This sentiment by Falwell, which subsequent movement leaders shared, changed once they concluded that a promiscuous culture had begun to overtake the United States, prompting them to see it as the duty of the faithful to reverse this trend. Secular conservative leaders, too, saw

---

[1] For more background information on the history of Christian conservatism and fundamentalism in the United States, see, e.g., David Farber, *The Rise and Fall of Modern American Conservatism* (Princeton, 2010); Kevin M. Kruse, *One Nation under God: How Corporate America Invented Christian America* (New York, 2015); David S. New, *Christian Fundamentalism in America: A Cultural History* (Jefferson, NC, 2013); and Axel R. Schäfer, *Countercultural Conservatives: American Evangelicalism from the Postwar Revival to the New Christian Right* (Madison, 2011).

an opportunity to create a new conservative movement in the United States, anchored by an alliance of traditional conservative groups with conservative Catholics and evangelicals who shared a common disdain for abortion, gay rights, feminism, and the counterculture movement. This politically powerful religious alliance, with its willingness to become actively engaged in party politics, stands in stark contrast to the rather restrained political role of religion in most European countries, especially in Germany, where the two major established churches, the Roman Catholic Church and the German Lutheran Church, have close ties to the government and usually refrain from making any overt political statements.

For the purposes of this comparative volume, this chapter will begin with a brief survey of some of the major differences in the history and current role of religion and religiousness in Europe and the United States before addressing the special role of Christian conservatism in the United States. Its main focus is the rise of the Christian right movement in the postwar decades, especially in the 1970s, with an emphasis on state-level events in the movement's home in Virginia. In some respects, Virginia is the birthplace of the modern Christian right in the United States. It was the original home to the two most important organizations of the movement – Moral Majority and Christian Coalition – as well as of the late Reverend Jerry Falwell and Reverend Pat Robertson, the leading figures in mobilizing social conservatives into politics. Both Falwell and Robertson tested the political waters in Virginia before they went national. This chapter will examine the early strategies of the Christian right in its political activism and the process by which it became increasingly pragmatic and effective. It will also explore how the movement matured politically and eventually succeeded in gaining mainstream acceptance.

Religion in the United States and Europe

In the United States, religion has always played a pivotal cultural role as well as a political one. "In God We Trust" is printed on every dollar bill, and most Europeans would agree with Gilbert Chesterton's remark that the United States is a "nation with the soul of a church." Most Americans, on the other hand, perceive Europe as a rather secular continent where religion has no significant social or political influence. Some are of the opinion that secularization has gone too far in the "Old World" and share the late Supreme Court Justice Antonin Scalia's opinion that Europe has

— Scalia is dead [handwritten]

become a "post-Christian" continent.[2] According to most surveys, more than 90 percent of Americans believe in God and about 80 percent are registered members of organized religious groups (70 percent Christians). *This is silly* [handwritten] More than half of all Americans pray daily, and over 40 percent claim to attend church services every week. By contrast, only two-thirds of Europeans confess a belief in God, church membership is slightly lower than in the United States, and fewer than 15 percent of Europeans attend church services every week (in Scandinavia regular church attendance is as low as 4 percent). Whereas active church membership has steadily declined in Europe since the 1960s, some American churches, especially evangelical ones, have enjoyed impressive membership gains during the latest decades. Moreover, a majority of U.S. citizens believe their country is God's chosen nation. Most Europeans regard this claim as either arrogant or naïve. Many Americans, on the other hand, deplore what many call the "immoral relativism" of Europeans.[3]

This "transatlantic religious divide" has sometimes been overstated, and a more intensive, careful analysis of survey data and other evidence shows that, in general, Americans are not as fundamentalist or fanatically religious as Europeans tend to assume and, conversely, Europeans are not as indifferent or hostile to religion as many Americans suspect. For example, according to a Pew Research Center study, the number of U.S. citizens who self-identify as Christian dropped from 78.4 to 70.6 percent between 2007 and 2014, and there seems to be a trend toward less strict religious commitment as well as more religious and cultural tol- *Who include who projections of atheists & agnostic?* [handwritten] erance, especially among younger Americans. At the same time, church membership in some parts of Europe, such as Ireland, Poland, and southern Germany, has remained rather high (75–80 percent), and in many countries, everyday culture is still saturated with Christian traditions (e.g., stores being closed on Sundays, church holidays being recognized as

---

[2] See Gilbert Chesterton, "What I Saw in America," in *Collected Works of G. K. Chesterton*, vol. 21 (San Francisco, 1990), 41–45; Sean Wilentz, "From Justice Scalia, A Chilling Vision of Religion's Authority in America," *New York Times*, July 8, 2002; http://www.nytimes.com/2002/07/08/opinion/from-justice-scalia-a-chilling-vision-of-religion-s-authority-in-america.html (accessed June 30, 2015).

[3] See "America's Changing Religious Landscape, Survey of May 2015," http://religions.pewforum.org/reports (accessed June 30, 2015); George M. Marsden, *Religion and American Culture* (Fort Worth, 2001); Dale Hurd, "Europe: The New Dark Continent," *CWN News*, February 27, 2004; http://www.sermonindex.net/modules/newbb/viewtopic.php?topic_id=3773&forum=35&o (accessed June 30, 2015); and Mattei Dogan, "Accelerated Decline of Religious Beliefs in Europe," *Comparative Sociology* 1 (2002): 127–149.

public holidays, and fish being served on Fridays). Nevertheless, it is certainly true that Europe as a whole has become a more secular place than the United States, and because of specific historic developments, churches and church members have played very different roles with regard to politics on the two sides of the Atlantic.[4]

In Europe, the relationship between church and state was virtually symbiotic for centuries. Until the nineteenth century, practically all European states had a firmly established system of state churches, which meant that church leaders were also worldly leaders with judiciary and military authority. Thus, government authorities controlled religious life; religious dissenters were assimilated, killed, or driven out of the country – and most of those who left found new homes in America. With secularization, the church lost much of its public power and influence; however, its special connection to the government has continued in many European countries to this day. In only a few European countries are church and state as clearly separated as in the United States, notably France and the Netherlands. Moreover, there are a number of European countries that still have official state churches, with the head of state serving as the head of the national church as well, for example Britain, Norway, and Denmark. In other countries, such as Spain, Italy, and Germany, one can also find a very close relationship between church and state, based on mutual beneficiary contracts that guarantee a close cooperation of both institutions.[5]

In contrast to the Constitution of the United States, the West German Basic Law of 1949 (*Grundgesetz*), for instance, explicitly mentions God as the one to whom the German people are responsible. Moreover, Article 140 of the Basic Law provides the legal framework for a mutually supportive relationship between the government and the established Christian churches. This includes, for example, the collection of church taxes as part of the regular income tax (a system instituted in the early nineteenth century to compensate the churches for their property losses

---

4 See "America's Changing Religious Landscape, Survey of May 2015"; Karl-Fritz Daiber, *Religion unter den Bedingungen der Moderne: Die Situation in der Bundesrepublik Deutschland* (Marburg, 1995); Thomas Howard, *God and the Atlantic: America, Europe and the Religious Divide* (Oxford, 2011); and Britta Waldschmidt-Nelson, "Faith and the Transatlantic Divide: The Different Role of Religion in America and Europe," in Carlos C. Seidel, ed., *Geheimdienste, Diplomatie, Krieg: Das Räderwerk der Internationalen Beziehungen* (Münster, 2013), 319–336.

5 See Christoph Elsas, *Religionsgeschichte Europas: Religiöses Leben von der Vorgeschichte bis zur Gegenwart* (Darmstadt, 2002); and Andrew M. Greeley, *Religion in Europe at the End of the Second Millennium: A Sociological Profile* (New Brunswick, 2003).

during secularization), the protection of Sundays and many Christian holidays as public holidays, church-controlled religious education in public schools and, partially, at universities, as well as church-sponsored social services such as childcare centers, hospitals, retirement homes, and public welfare facilities. As part of this agreement, the church is officially bound to abstain from direct political involvement and remain neutral with regard to party politics. This also means that ministers and priests cannot hold political office or openly favor one political party or candidate over another. While the churches still have an indirect but significant public voice there, Christians in Germany – and more generally in Western Europe – tend not to mix religion and politics. They usually do not align themselves as a group with one party, and there is very little Christian fundamentalism, certainly none that has notable political influence. (A more detailed discussion of the relationship between church and state in West Germany as well as the development of the situation of conservative Christians is offered in the next chapter in this volume by Thomas Großbölting.)[6]

The situation in the United States, of course, is entirely different. Many European religious radicals escaped persecution at home by emigrating to America. Their religious passions and resolve to realize their utopian dreams contributed to what became America's founding myth. The Puritans of Massachusetts Bay believed they had a sacred covenant with God and that he had charged them with transforming the wilderness into a new Eden, a "City Upon a Hill," that would enlighten and ultimately transform the whole world as part of divine providence. This belief in America as God's chosen nation soon became a central part of America's national self-image and is still evident in the religious convictions of many Christians, and especially among fundamentalists, in the United States today. The enduring power of this founding myth, together with the American tradition of radical religious revivalism (such as the First and Second Great Awakening) and the strict separation of church and state established by the First Amendment of the U.S. Constitution, are the three essential traits of American religious exceptionalism. Together, they created the framework of the unique religious vitality and pluralism of the United States as well as setting the stage for the rise of a strong civil religion and, eventually, the active involvement of

---

[6] Also see Waldschmidt-Nelson, "Faith and the Transatlantic Divide," 322–326; Karl-Fritz Daiber, *Religion in Kirche und Gesellschaft* (Stuttgart, 1997); and Robert Scribner, *Religion und Kultur in Deutschland* (Göttingen, 2002).

religiously minded people, especially Christian conservatives, in party politics.[7]

While the process of modernization in most European societies led to a higher level of secularization, i.e., a decline in the public role and political power of religious institutions as well as the level of religious practices among most of the population, this was not the case on the other side of the Atlantic. Strong religious convictions and revivals of religious enthusiasm continued to be a central feature of American society. It is important to be aware of these historical differences when trying to understand why a politically organized Christian right emerged in the second half of the twentieth century in the United States while Christians in West Germany and other parts of Western Europe displayed a much lower level of political mobilization.[8]

[margin note: In the US and one might add "not us"]

Conservative Christian Activism in the United States before the 1960s

A first surge of conservative Christian activism in twentieth-century America centered on campaigns against alcohol, Catholicism, and the teaching of evolution in public schools. The 1925 Scopes Trial was a pivotal event in this context. It ended with a ruling in favor of the opponents of the theory of evolution, which turned out to be a public relations disaster for Christian fundamentalists and was one of the reasons the fundamentalist Christian right faded from the political scene in the following years.[9] It was not until the 1950s that the next significant conservative Christian movement was formed, which was characterized mainly by anti-Semitic and anticommunist and some pro-segregationist activism. However, this first phase of political conservative Christian mobilization deflated significantly with the 1964 election: many conservative

[margin note: Prohibition]
[margin note: H cho wilw — William Bryan — Jennings Bryan]

---

7 See Robert N. Bellah, *Religion in America* (Cambridge, MA, 1967); A. James Reichley, *Religion in American Public Life* (Washington, DC, 1985); George M. Marsden, *Religion and American Culture* (Fort Worth, 2001); Mark A. Noll, *America's God: From Jonathan Edwards to Abraham Lincoln* (New York, 2002); and Waldschmidt-Nelson, "Faith and the Transatlantic Divide," 326–336.

8 For a more in-depth analysis of the historic institutional impediments that kept Christians in West Germany and other parts of Western Europe from mobilizing politically in a way similar to Christians in the United States, even though they often shared many of the same concerns (e.g., regarding the abortion question), see chapter 10 in this volume by Thomas Großbölting.

9 See Clyde Wilcox, *God's Warriors: The Christian Right in Twentieth-Century America* (Baltimore, 1992), 20; and Edward J. Larson, *Summer for the Gods: The Scopes Trial and America's Continuing Debate over Science and Religion* (New York, 1997).

Christians had allied themselves with the candidacy of Senator Barry Goldwater for president, and he suffered a historic landslide defeat. Goldwater's sentiments always were more libertarian than those of religious conservatives, and he later came to symbolize all that the religious conservative movement thought was wrong with the Republican Party.[10] Nonetheless, the deep-seated discontentment of Christian conservatives with what they perceived as fundamental, morally unacceptable challenges to the God-given social order – such as the prohibition of school prayer, sexual promiscuity, racial integration, and feminism – kept growing throughout the 1960s and motivated an increasing number to seek new political allies. In the 1970s, the battle against the legalization of abortion was to become a major rallying point for them, which helped them to forge powerful political alliances.

The Christian Right in the 1970s and 1980s

By 1972, neither national party had ever mentioned abortion in its party platform. But the 1973 *Roe v. Wade* Supreme Court decision changed this landscape and gave a powerful impetus for social conservatives to become involved in politics. In the 1970s, social conservatives in a number of communities began to organize in local politics on a variety of issues. Most of this political activity centered on public school textbooks, including those that taught evolution as scientific fact, and efforts by some communities to adopt antidiscrimination laws to protect gays and lesbians. There was also some conservative religious mobilization in opposition to the enforcement of black civil rights, especially the so-called school busing as a way of integration, which right-leaning politicians, such as the Democrat George Wallace and the Republican Richard Nixon, opposed adamantly.[11]

As outlined above, Virginia played an important role in the evolution and rise of the New Christian right in the South during the 1970s and 1980s. Even though this group started off as a rather decentralized collection of social movement organizations and leaders, with little cooperation or coordination, it was to become a pivotal center of Christian

---

[10] See Wilcox, *God's Warriors*; Robert B. Horwitz, *America's Right: Anti-Establishment Conservatism from Goldwater to the Tea Party* (Cambridge, 2013); and Farber, *Rise and Fall*, 77–118.

[11] See Farber, *Rise and Fall*, 98–103; and Judith F. Buncher et al., eds., *The School Busing Controversy, 1970–75* (New York, 1975).

right activity later on.[12] Initially, it was not necessarily foreseeable that these Southern conservative Christians would align themselves with the Republican Party. On the contrary, just as on the national level with Jimmy Carter's presidential campaign, in the mid-1970s, many evangelical and fundamentalist Christians in Virginia were mobilizing in Democratic Party politics. Carter, who caused a stir at that time by openly professing to be a proud born-again Christian, had an enormous, even transformative, role in politically mobilizing many previously apolitical born-again and evangelical Christians. In Virginia in 1976, Reverend Pat Robertson encouraged G. Conolly Phillips to run for the Norfolk City Council. Phillips claimed that the Lord had also called on him to run, and he won the office. In January 1978, Phillips said he had heard the calling of the Lord again and he announced his candidacy for the Democratic Party nomination for the U.S. Senate. Phillips expressed some surprise that God had told him to seek the Democratic Party nomination, as he would have preferred to run as an independent.[13] An important context, though, was the dominance of the Democratic Party in the Southern states during this period; moreover, Robertson's father had been elected a U.S. senator from Virginia as a Democrat.

It was only after President Lyndon Johnson's embrace of civil rights and the passage of the Civil Rights Act of 1964 and the Voting Rights Act of 1965 – over the outraged opposition of Southern Democrats – that a major realignment of the parties took place in the South. Many white segregationists left the Democratic Party, and a new, almost entirely white and socially very conservative Republican Party emerged below the Mason-Dixon Line. This constituency eventually became an important partner for the Christian right. However, what was most important for Christian conservatives at that point in time was to get organized. Robertson worked with Phillips to create a network of ministers throughout the state of Virginia to help mobilize a large number of conservative Christian activists, many of whom had never participated in any political campaign. In a crowded field of candidates, Phillips achieved a third-place finish at the party caucuses in April with nearly 400 committed delegates for the nominating convention to be held in June of 1978. The connection between religious fervor and political activity was apparently very

[12] Mark J. Rozell and Clyde Wilcox, *Second Coming: The New Christian Right in Virginia Politics* (Baltimore, 1996).

[13] Wilford Kale, "Phillips Says Faith Not Shaken," *Richmond Times-Dispatch*, June 11, 1978; and Megan Rosenfeld, "Candidate Answered 'Call' in Va. Race," *Washington Post*, April 12, 1978.

important to this success, as some observers described that "the Phillips supporters held prayer meetings and sang hymns during the mass meetings in many localities."[14]

Phillips's campaign made no secret of his emphasis on religious matters. He called his campaign "a ministry unto the Lord" and admitted that he had not taken positions on a number of issues because he had "not had time to study" them.[15] Phillips referred to his campaign headquarters as a "prayer room" and said that his strategy sessions were "more like church meetings than political meeting... This office, this is run somewhat like any other political office, but it's first a ministry, what I'm doing is first a ministry and second a campaign."[16]

Robertson, then best known as the host of the Christian Broadcast Network's program "The 700 Club," led a convention nomination day prayer breakfast for Phillips in which he told the gathering that it was time for "honest, God-fearing men to take charge of our government... This is the place where our government started and this is the place where God wants to reclaim it."[17]

After the convention officially made its choice, with Phillips finishing in third place, reporters asked him what it meant to be called by God to run and then lose. Phillips replied that God had told him to run "as a call to the Christian community to get involved. He may have used me to send that call." Moreover, Phillips expressed his hope that his supporters would see future Democratic Party activity "as a Christian duty and calling."[18]

That same year the Republican Party held a Senate nominating convention that remained a very close contest down to the final vote. Evangelical and born-again activists constituted a small portion of the convention – most had gone instead to that of the Democratic Party. But as John Warner later recalled, with 9,000 delegates and a tight race, his campaign manager urged him to start a spontaneous demonstration on the floor to delay the final vote past midnight into Sunday. The manager was

[14] Alan Abramowitz, John McGlennon, and Ronald Rappoport, "The 1978 Virginia Senatorial Nominating Conventions," *University of Virginia Institute of Government Newsletter* 55:4 (December 1978): 1.

[15] Paul G. Edwards, "Democrats Pick Delegates Today for June Convention," *Washington Post*, April 15, 1978.

[16] Rosenfeld, "Candidate Answered."

[17] James Latimer, "Prayer Breakfast Began Day's Work," *Richmond Times-Dispatch*, June 11, 1978.

[18] Kale, "Phillips."

hoping this move would ensure that the fundamentalist delegates backing the more conservative candidate, Richard Obenshein, would leave
and hand Warner the victory. Warner said he refused to follow his manager's advice, even though he knew it would cost him the nomination.
Having been raised by his uncle, an Episcopal minister, he stressed that
he would have felt personal shame to further his career by means of such
a tactic.[19]

Warner did eventually receive the party's nomination when the convention's victor Obenshein died in an airplane crash. Soon afterwards, on
a Sunday two weeks before Election Day, the U.S. Senate nominees of the
two major parties – Warner and Democratic nominee Andrew Miller –
attended Thomas Road Baptist Church in Lynchburg together at the invitation of its pastor, Reverend Jerry Falwell. At the time, Falwell's popular
ministry television program, the "Old Time Gospel Hour," was broadcast nationally and had made him the best-known "televangelist" in the
country. Both candidates were therefore hoping Falwell would embrace
them politically; Falwell did ultimately do this for Warner. Never again
would a Democratic candidate for statewide elected office seek Falwell's
approval.[20]

Warner won the general election by fewer than 5,000 votes, his campaign aided indirectly by the active engagement of a number of church
leaders headed by Falwell, who during the same period had successfully
organized to block a state referendum to legalize pari-mutuel (horse track)
betting. Falwell and the other pastors mounted an expensive television
and print advertising campaign against the referendum, which religious
conservatives widely opposed. A large majority of religious conservatives mobilized by this activity also supported Warner against a more
liberal Democratic nominee. Thus, the successful campaign of the pastors to defeat the betting referendum without doubt contributed to the
Republican's small but sufficient margin of victory. Realizing the importance of this outcome, Falwell announced that his organizational effort to
mobilize religious leaders in politics was a portent of "future endeavors
together."[21]

These 1978 votes were an important turning point because previously
Falwell had taken the more traditionally separatist view that religion and
politics should not mix. He, like most conservative Protestant leaders at

---

[19] John Warner, interview with Mark J. Rozell, Washington, DC, July 22, 1994.
[20] Rozell and Wilcox, *Second Coming*, 42.
[21] Joseph Gatins and Ed Briggs, "Churchmen See Future Alliances," *Richmond Times-
Dispatch*, November 9, 1978.

that time, had warned parishioners against getting involved in "matters of this world" and to let God work his will on society. Other conservative clergy also publicly declared that Warner's victory and the defeat of pari-mutuel betting encouraged them to stay politically active. Just as Falwell had predicted, the pastor's coalition against the betting referendum and in support of Warner was the beginning of a whole new host of future political endeavors of conservative religious leaders on both the state and national level. The formation of the Moral Majority, Christian Voice, and other religious conservative organizations on the national level, along with state chapters of these organizations, gave these clergy an organizational matrix for structuring and coordinating their activities.

As the executive director of the organization that opposed the pari-mutuel betting referendum, Dennis Pederson stressed that this campaign gave religious leaders in Virginia "a taste of what they could do in politics – how influential they could be." He added that this initial effort also brought together a wide spectrum of religious leaders who "had never sat around a breakfast table before to discuss how they could organize to pursue a common goal."[22] A number of other religious conservative leaders also emphasized they had come to realize during that 1978 campaign that they were God's stewards in this world and that it was their duty to become politically active to try to stem the moral decline of the United States. Many of them said that their largest challenge was convincing parishioners to get out of the pews and into politics after having communicated a different message for so long. At first, it was thus not easy to mobilize the Christian right, but a combination of factors converged to make this change happen.[23]

Prior to this mobilization, the movement that later became known as the Christian right had been a significant core of what President Richard M. Nixon called the "Silent Majority" – that sizable group of Americans who opposed the liberal reforms of the 1960s and 1970s but supposedly did not have a loud voice in politics, the media, and academia. As many social conservatives decided to no longer be "silent," the rise of the Christian right in the 1970s served as a major impetus to the ascendancy of conservatism in the 1980s. By the end of the 1970s, it was clear that conservative Christian activism in Virginia would focus on the Republican Party.

[handwritten margin note: Note how referenda were to control Christian and mobilization]

---

[22] Dennis Pederson, telephone interview with Mark J. Rozell, May 10, 1995.
[23] The list of interviewees for the Virginia Christian Right movement research project is contained in the acknowledgments in Rozell and Wilcox, *Second Coming.*

Falwell's success brought him to the attention of prominent secular conservative leaders, such as Richard Viguerie, Howard Phillips, and Paul Weyrich, who turned to him to help mobilize religious conservatives into forming a broad, nationwide conservative Republican coalition. In Virginia, however, these new developments also caused a major split within the GOP, as some party leaders openly expressed alarm over the prospect of conservative Christians controlling local Republican committees, thus foreshadowing the rift that would further develop in the party in the 1980s.[24]

Ironically, perhaps, on the national level Democrat Jimmy Carter had energized this potential constituency when he campaigned openly as a born-again Christian in 1976, stressing that his faith had always guided him in his public life. Many previously apolitical Southern evangelicals rallied behind his candidacy, only to later reject Carter due to disappointment with his social policies and Ronald Reagan's embrace of evangelicals in the GOP.

Inspired by Carter's electoral success, the three prominent secular conservative leaders Viguerie, Phillips, and Weyrich also saw an opportunity to forge new alliances. Their goal was to build a powerful coalition of secular and religious conservative groups that would allow the Republican Party to dominate for years. Therefore, they reached out to Falwell and supported him in forming a new national organization called the Moral Majority in 1979 – a word play on Nixon's "Silent Majority." Apparently, the "triumvirate of professional right-wing organizers" not only served as an important catalyst for the new Christian right but also came up with this clever name.[25]

The triumvirate also convinced candidate Ronald Reagan to make direct appeals to conservative evangelicals, believing that, if successfully mobilized, this group could deliver millions of new votes to the GOP. Reagan did exactly that. For example, in a significant speech at a gathering of some 17,000 religious conservative activists in Dallas, he caused the crowd to burst into an enthusiastic frenzy of applause when he deliberately assured them, "I know you can't endorse me, but I want you to know that I endorse you and what you are doing."[26]

---

[24] Frank B. Atkinson, *The Dynamic Dominion: Realignment and the Rise of Virginia's Republican Party since 1945* (Fairfax, VA, 1992), 393.

[25] Steven Bruce, *The Rise and Fall of the New Christian Right* (New York, 1989), 56.

[26] Donald T. Critchlow, *The Conservative Ascendancy: How the GOP Right Made Political History* (Cambridge, MA, 2007), 176; also see William Martin, *With God on Our*

The 1980 GOP landslide that made Reagan president surprised most observers, and Falwell claimed that his Moral Majority had helped to mobilize as many as four million previously apolitical evangelical voters for the GOP. Although this estimate may have been exaggerated, the conservative success of 1980 instantly made Falwell a major player in U.S. politics and the Christian right the big story of the resurgent GOP.

As it turned out, Viguerie, Phillips, and Weyrich had made a wise choice in joining forces with Falwell. In 1978, they had promised to support him with direct-mail technology, organizational backing, and the training of state and regional leaders if he would head an organization that would mobilize fundamentalist Christians for Republican politics. Falwell agreed and began to build an organization relying on his connections with pastors in the Baptist Bible Fellowship. He was a formidable force, and the triumvirate kept up its part of the bargain. Thus, Falwell was able to build up the Thomas Road Baptist Church, and the televised version of his worship services reached millions of households. His Liberty Baptist College (now Liberty University) became one of the best-known independent Baptist Colleges.[27]

As the national media cast the spotlight on Falwell, other Baptist Bible Fellowship pastors were taking charge of state chapters of the Moral Majority. These pastors were religious entrepreneurs who knew how to build church institutions – skills that were potentially useful for developing a political organization.[28] Nonetheless, many of them were still political amateurs who were not open to working with religious leaders of other faiths or denominations. Moreover, structures, tactics, and agendas varied greatly among Moral Majority state organizations, and there was consequently little effective coordination of their efforts.[29]

The Virginia state Moral Majority was headed by a succession of Baptist Bible Fellowship pastors who created county organizations in many parts of the state, especially in the south-central region near Lynchburg.

Side: *The Rise of the Religious Right in America* (New York, 1996), 216; and Farber, *Rise and Fall*, 186–189.

[27] Robert C. Liebman, "Mobilizing the Moral Majority," in R. Liebman and R. Wuthnow, eds., *The New Christian Right: Mobilization and Legitimation* (New York, 1983), 50–74. For a more detailed description of Falwell's role, see also Matthew A. Sutton, *Jerry Falwell and the Rise of the Religious Right: A Brief History with Documents* (Boston, 2012).

[28] Clyde Wilcox, "Premillennialists at the Millennium: Some Reflections on the Christian Right in the 21st Century," *Sociology of Religion* 55 (1994): 243–261.

[29] James M. Perry, "The Moral Majority Finds that Its Own Units May Need Guidance," *Wall Street Journal*, February 12, 1981.

Yet Reverend Calvin Eaves, former vice president of the state chapter, noted that the Virginia Moral Majority could best be described as a loosely connected group of about 200–300 pastors involved to varying degrees. County and local chapters sprang up in some parts of the state, but no one in the state office maintained a list of these chapters or monitored their activities.[30] In focusing so heavily on its national media profile and on building its direct mailing operation, the Moral Majority made little effort to build a strong grassroots presence and therefore failed to make the transition from being a social movement organization to an institutionalized interest group. This failure provided important lessons for Christian right leaders of the 1990s. Moreover, the Moral Majority employed a range of tactics and strategies that became positive inspirations for later groups. Of great importance, for example, were the organization's statewide voter registration drives, especially in Baptist churches. They encouraged many church members to become active in party politics, enabling the Moral Majority to provide as many as 700 delegates to the 1981 Virginia GOP gubernatorial nominating convention. It is also noteworthy that the organization established phone-tree communication networks to alert the pastors who formed the core of the organization of pending legislation in the Virginia General Assembly. Many other political organizations later copied this innovative and very effective communication tool.[31]

Although Falwell had a powerful following of religious conservatives on the national level, he was generally rather unpopular in the state of Virginia, due not only to his controversial positions on social issues but also because he had a penchant for engaging in overheated and at times offensive rhetoric. As a result, Democratic candidates developed strategies that relied on associating Republican candidates with him. As one observer stated in 1992, "Within three years, Falwell would succeed [liberal populist] Henry Howell as the state's premier political whipping boy; moderate Virginia Democrats would discover that suburban disdain for much of the Moral Majority's conservative social agenda could be as politically powerful as suburban opposition to Howell-style liberalism on economic issues."[32]

---

[30] Reverend Calvin Eaves, telephone interview with Mark J. Rozell, May 12, 1995.
[31] See Mark J. Rozell and Clyde Wilcox, "Virginia: Birthplace of the Christian Right," in John C. Green, Mark J. Rozell, and Clyde Wilcox, eds., *The Christian Right in American Politics: Marching to the Millennium* (Washington, DC, 2003), 41–58; see also Martin, *With God on Our Side*; and Critchlow, *The Conservative Ascendancy*.
[32] Atkinson, *Dynamic Dominion*, 388.

Soon after the formation of the Moral Majority, another Christian right organization, the Christian Voice, established a Virginia chapter. In a few counties, Christian Voice chapters held occasional meetings, although they never matched the membership or activism of the Moral Majority. Indeed, the Christian Voice made no effort to build a mailing list or a grassroots base, focusing instead only on providing information to sympathetic local organizations. In Virginia as elsewhere, the organization instituted a system of distributing scorecards that ranked legislator's "moral votes." Vern Jordahl, the group's former state director, noted that these scorecards were the first example of a tactic that has become rather common among Christian right groups since then.[33] The Christian Voice also distributed "action alerts" to various organizations across the state on matters pending before the assembly. Like the Moral Majority, the Christian Voice formed as an officially non-partisan organization and engaged in "voter education" efforts – a legal distinction in the United States that provides for tax exemption – although they presented information that was clearly tilted in favor of the more socially conservative candidates and, in general elections, almost always in favor of those nominated by the Republican Party.

In the next generation of Christian right groups, many adopted key tactics pioneered by these first-generation organizations, especially action alerts, voter registration drives, and new voter mobilization. Perhaps more importantly, the first generation of the Christian right succeeded in getting previously apolitical Virginians into political activism. Although the number of the newly mobilized people was small, the new activists constituted a significant constituency for the Republican Party, able to influence party nominations on the local and state levels because of porous boundaries and open nomination rules. This core of activists and the host of smaller local groups they had formed provided an important resource upon which future Christian right organizations could build.[34]

Perceptions and Legacies of the First Christian Right Mobilization

Over the past three decades, popular accounts have tended to characterize the Christian right at various times either as "taking over" American

---

33 Vern Jordahl, telephone interview with Mark J. Rozell, May 15, 1995.
34 Mark J. Rozell, "The Christian Right and Contemporary U.S. Politics," in Gillian Peele and Joel Aberbach, eds., *The Crisis of Conservatism* (New York, 2011), 114–128.

politics or as being on the verge of extinction. But the real story of the movement is one of continuity, although – as is the case with all social movements, interest groups, and party factions – its fortunes rise or fall at any period in time depending on a variety of circumstances. The core constituency of the Christian right has remained fairly stable since the 1970s, even though conservative Christians have turned out to vote more heavily in some elections than in others.

Clearly, the key power of the Christian right lies within the Republican Party, where the movement has succeeded in helping to nominate socially conservative candidates for various offices, leading many platform and rules committees. In the early period of Christian right mobilization, there was a fierce battle for party control between social conservatives and party moderates. By now, it is generally acknowledged that the social conservatives did eventually win that battle. However, the story is far more complicated than one group ousting another. What actually happened is that the Christian right learned over time how to be smarter in playing the political game and thus became a strong force in the GOP and within U.S. politics in general.

The first wave of postwar Christian right mobilization, generally from the 1970s to the end of the 1980s, is regarded by most observers as a political failure. By the end of the 1980s, the movement had made few social policy gains, the Moral Majority disbanded, and most coverage of the evangelical movement focused on several high-profile televangelist scandals. Reverend Pat Robertson ran for president in 1988, only to be soundly defeated.

Yet the movement endured. In 1989, Robertson formed a new organization: the Christian Coalition. He chose as its political director Ralph E. Reed, a young political operative who could give the Christian right a fresh look. The dynamic, well-educated, and attractive Reed turned out to be a brilliant choice since, unlike Falwell and some of the other early leaders of the Christian conservative movement, Reed could speak the secular language of politics as well as he could communicate with fellow evangelicals.[35] Thus, the end of the 1980s saw the rise of a second wave

---

[35] For more information regarding Robertson, Reed, and the building of the Christian Coalition, see Ralph E. Reed/Christian Coalition, *Contract with the American Family: A Bold Plan* (Nashville, 1995); Justin Watson, *The Christian Coalition: Dreams of Restoration, Demands for Recognition* (New York, 1997); Nina Easton, *Gang of Five: Leaders at the Center of the Conservative Crusade* (New York, 2000); and David E. Harrel, *Pat Robertson: A Life and Legacy* (Grand Rapids, 2010).

of Christian right mobilization with a look and form very different from that of the first wave led by the Moral Majority.

The "Second Coming" of the Christian Right

Determined not to give up after his defeat in the 1988 GOP presidential contest, Robertson decided to convert his large list of campaign contributors into a national grassroots organization. He called his brainchild the Christian Coalition and established it as an officially non-partisan entity, which soon engaged in a major effort to build state, county, and local organizations around the country.

Its new political director, Ralph Reed, recruited state and local leaders with backgrounds not only in religious organizations but also in business, interest group politics, or civic activity, which was a major shift from the Moral Majority's strategy of focusing almost exclusively on recruiting local pastors. This new strategy enabled the Christian Coalition to build a broadly ecumenical organization. The national lobbying office at various times included traditional Protestants, Evangelicals, Catholics, and at one point even a legislative director who was Jewish. State and local chapters in many parts of the country were similarly diverse. The traditional Catholics and fundamentalist Baptists in the Christian Coalition may not have agreed on religious doctrine or who would get to Heaven, but they did agree to work together to support pro-life (i.e., anti-abortion) – and almost always Republican – candidates for public office.[36]

The Christian right in the 1990s displayed signs of being a politically maturing movement that had learned from the mistakes of the Moral Majority and its allies in the previous two decades. By 1992, Reed, who himself had once compared his political tactics to guerrilla warfare and boasted that he ambushed opponents and left them in body bags, recanted the use of such language and wrote to supporters that "phrases like 'religious war' and 'take over' play to a stereotype of evangelicals as intolerant." Urging his followers to avoid using threatening-sounding language, he stressed: "We must adopt strategies of persuasion, not domination."[37] Reed was not alone in this sentiment and apparently served as a role model to others within the Christian Coalition. Studies of the Christian

[36] Green, Rozell, and Wilcox, *The Christian Right.*
[37] Joe Taylor, "Christian Coalition Revamping Image," *Richmond Times-Dispatch,* December 7, 1992.

right in the 1990s found that the rhetorical appeals of leaders sounded noticeably more moderate and the issues to be more broad-based than before. Moreover, the organizations of the movement had built wider ecumenical bases and stronger grassroots networks than the first wave of the movement.[38]

A telling case was that of Anne Kincaid, who had been the leading pro-life organizer in Virginia for years and went through a transformation that is typical of the new approach of the second-wave Christian right. Kincaid began to be active in the 1980s, becoming a movement leader for the Family Foundation and also the state director for Pat Robertson's presidential campaign. In these efforts, she was known to use extreme-sounding issue appeals, carrying pictures of aborted fetuses to editorial offices and to political rallies. Kincaid had a special draw on group activists in large part due to her own charisma and a compelling personal story of having fallen from grace as a young adult and then changing her life after discovering her faith. But in terms of political impact outside the social movement, she was considered a fringe figure and not influential. By the early 1990s, Kincaid changed her language and tactics, and her political stature grew enormously. In 1993, many credited her with delivering critical support among religious conservatives for George Allen's successful GOP gubernatorial nomination in Virginia despite Allen's moderate stance on abortion. After winning the general election with a substantial margin, Allen appointed Kincaid his director of constituent services, and she later went on to run a number of GOP campaigns in the state. It was no exaggeration for opponents and political observers to refer to her as the most formidable political strategist of Virginia. In a 1993 interview, Kincaid made the following remarks regarding her transformation from fringe activist to influential leader in the Republican Party: "I can remember using rhetoric that I don't use anymore, that sounded inflammatory. 'Onward Christian Soldiers' scared people. So you don't talk that way. Some still talk about witchcraft and the feminist movement. Yes, the Bible says that 'rebellion against men is of witchcraft.' It's all Biblical tenets, but the layman doesn't understand that. So it makes you sound like you've lost your marbles. The point is that you have to know your audience. That's not deception ... Unless you're talking to a Christian audience,

[38] Matthew C. Moen, *The Transformation of the Christian Right* (Tuscaloosa, 1992); Rozell and Wilcox, *Second Coming*; and Mark J. Rozell, "Growing Up Politically: The New Politics of the New Christian Right," in Corwin E. Smidt and James M. Penning, eds., *Sojourners in the Wilderness: The Christian Right in Comparative Perspective* (Lanham, MD, 1997), 235–248.

you don't put all the rhetoric out there that others won't respond to. I learned this lesson the hard way."[39]

In the 1970s and 1980s, it would have been unthinkable for major Christian right figures to back a GOP candidate who professed to having a "reasonably moderate" view of abortion, favoring abortion rights in the first trimester and in cases of rape, incest, or endangering the woman's life. Yet that was Allen's public stand, and in the 1990s Kincaid and a number of other pro-life leaders in Virginia still supported him because they believed that he could win and achieve some secondary limitations on abortion such as parental consent and notification. The new generation of Christian conservatives had learned from their mistakes of the previous decades, when they had given their support in Virginia's statewide campaigns only to puristic socially conservative candidates, all of whom had lost and were thus in no position to reward the Christian right's efforts.[40]

The example of the evolution of the Christian right in Virginia is not unusual. Indeed, a series of studies on the electoral impact of the movement in federal elections demonstrated that many other states such as Michigan, Ohio, Iowa, and South Carolina saw similar developments.[41]

In order to appeal to a broader audience, many leaders of the Christian right adopted the rights-based language of liberalism to describe their aspirations. Thus, rather than denouncing "infanticide," "murder of the unborn," or comparing legalized abortions to the Holocaust, they framed the issue as defending the rights or equality of the unborn. Rather than espousing the desire to "take over" GOP party committees or policymaking institutions, Christian conservatives now expressed their desire not to be discriminated against in politics because of their status as Christians, or maintained that they were angling only for a "place at the table" in American politics. Consequently, one can observe how, from the early 1990s, the new leaders of the movement focused increasingly on asserting that the goals of the Christian right were really no different from those of

39 Anne Kincaid, interview with Mark J. Rozell in Richmond, VA, November 17, 1993.
40 Rozell and Wilcox, *Second Coming*.
41 See Mark J. Rozell and Clyde Wilcox, eds., *God at the Grass Roots: The Christian Right in the 1994 Elections* (Lanham, MD, 1995); Mark J. Rozell and Clyde Wilcox, eds., *God at the Grass Roots: The Christian Right in the 1996 Elections* (Lanham, MD, 1997); John C. Green, Mark J. Rozell, and Clyde Wilcox, *Prayers in the Precincts: The Christian Right in the 1998 Elections* (Washington, DC, 2000); John C. Green, Mark J. Rozell, and Clyde Wilcox, *The Christian Right*; and *The Values Campaign? The Christian Right and the 2004 Elections* (Washington, DC, 2006).

the 1960s Civil Rights Movement: that Christian pro-life activists should be treated fairly, with dignity, and not be discriminated against.[42]

Such language certainly has been chosen for broader public consumption; clearly Christian right leaders do not sound so mainstream when speaking among their own kind or directly to their own supporters. Also, of course, by making so many public pronouncements over the years, prominent figures such as Robertson have sometimes let loose some terribly impolitic statements that, to slightly paraphrase Kincaid, make them sound "like they've lost their marbles."[43]

One particularly interesting strategy of the Christian right in the 1990s was the attempt to get *Roe v. Wade* overturned on the grounds that legalizing abortion was bad constitutional law rather than on the grounds that abortion was immoral. Reed himself argued that the Christian Coalition merely wanted the issue of abortion remanded to the states in keeping with the constitutional framers' notion of federalism rather than having the Supreme Court mandate a one-size-fits-all approach. Other major movement figures such as Robertson made similar appeals as Reed.[44] Of course, Christian conservatives hoped that such a change would lead to abortion restrictions in many of the states; they clearly aimed to limit access to abortions, not to restore the constitutional framers' view of federalism. But the new generation of Christian right leaders had come to understand that being effective meant sometimes avoiding moralistic appeals and finding more subtle strategies.

The recognition by many in the movement that abortion rights could be more effectively reduced by focusing on secondary restrictions in the current political climate was another example of the Christian right's growing political adroitness. Therefore, they promoted parental notification, parental consent, no taxpayer funding, no late-term abortions, mandatory waiting periods and counseling for those seeking abortion, and restrictions on what healthcare professionals and educators can tell young women about abortion options.[45]

Robertson himself signaled to the movement that it was necessary to focus energy on the politically feasible when it came to abortion restrictions. In a November 4, 1993, appearance on ABC television's *Nightline*, Robertson explained: "I would urge people, as a matter of private choice,

---

[42] Rozell, "Growing Up Politically."   [43] Kincaid, interview with Rozell (1993).

[44] Ralph Reed, "What Do Christian Conservatives Really Want?" Paper presented at the Colloquium on the Religious New Right and the 1992 Campaign, Ethics and Public Policy Center, Washington, DC, 1993.

[45] Rozell, "Growing Up Politically," 240.

not to choose abortion, because I think it is wrong. It's something else, though, in the political arena to go out on a quixotic crusade when you know you'll be beaten continuously. So I say, let's do what is possible. What is possible is parental consent."[46] Pro-choice leaders have referred to this strategy as "death by a thousand little cuts," meaning that the movement aims for the many secondary abortion restrictions around the country to eventually add up to a serious withering away of abortion rights.

[handwritten margin note: They had quite a lot of success with this]

Of course, all of these signals from the Christian right leaders would be ineffective unless the grassroots activists of the movement agreed that it was important to focus on the politically feasible and not the ideal. For a substantial number of Christian conservatives, to compromise on abortion is to consent to the ultimate sin. Nevertheless, there is evidence that the signals from the leadership have indeed had a real impact on many grassroots activists.

In a 1993 interview, the Virginia journalist Ed Briggs, who specializes in reporting on religion and politics, suggested that the changing face of fundamentalism in the United States may have made the grassroots activists more open to focusing on the politically possible. That is, fundamentalism had developed something of a "soft-side, becoming mainstream." Thus, as fundamentalists increasingly accepted the proposition that it was fine to partake in "matters of this world," many became more receptive to appeals to be realistic about the political world.[47] Anne Kincaid agreed with this sentiment when she said that the biggest challenge for her and other movement leaders initially was "getting people out of the pews" once in a while to participate in politics.[48]

[handwritten margin note: Which is where your ideas are greatly rebbed?]

Over time, Christian right organizations largely succeeded at reaching their core constituency and convincing as many Christian conservatives as possible of the need to become involved in politics. As these new activists entered the political world and many participated in training sessions and local political organizations, they became more knowledgeable about how to mobilize and to be effective. Thus, while the early wave of evangelical mobilization had radicalized the anti-abortion movement, most of the activists had either become more moderate or abandoned political activity altogether by the mid-1990s.[49]

---

[46] American Broadcast Company, "God at the Grass Roots," *Nightline*, November 4, 1993.

[47] Ed Briggs, interview with Mark J. Rozell, Richmond, VA, December 9, 1993.

[48] Kincaid, interview with Rozell (1993).

[49] Jon A. Shields, *The Democratic Virtues of the Christian Right* (Princeton, 2009).

Another important shift for the second wave of Christian right organizing is that socially conservative activists have come into contact more
frequently with other, primarily GOP-based, constituencies. Studies of
Christian right activists in the Republican Party have shown that the
Christian Coalition has achieved its goals of bringing social conservatives
into the mainstream of the party and forging a broad-based coalition
of social and secular conservatives. Pro-gun rights and anti-tax activists,
for example, do not share the same commitment to social issues as the
religious conservatives in the party, but they and other groups have frequently been willing to come together to support each other's favored
candidates. In many cases, religious conservative leaders and activists
worked to get moderate GOP nominees elected, with the understanding
that such loyalty to the party despite policy differences would be rewarded
with support from the moderates for future socially conservative candidates and issues.[50]

Thus, the story of the "second coming" of the Christian right has been
that of a largely transformed movement. The first wave of the movement
in the 1970s and 1980s was characterized by extreme rhetoric, absolutist
positions on moral issues, a refusal to compromise on principles, and
a lack of effective coalition building. The new wave of Christian right
activism emerged with a much more sophisticated and effective approach
to politics. The leadership, and even many activists, understood the need
to build a broadly ecumenical movement, to adopt mainstream rhetoric,
to focus on incremental goals on some issues, to accept the necessity of
compromise, and to build coalitions with various groups.

Real payoffs for the movement occurred over time, with the elections of sympathetic Republicans throughout the country. Especially the
election of the conservative born-again Christian George W. Bush as
president in 2000 was celebrated by many as a great success for the
Christian right. However, even though Bush was the most sympathetic to
the movement of any president, changes on social issues came about only
very incrementally during his presidency, and some conservative Christians were disappointed that he failed to appoint one of their own to the
Supreme Court. On the other hand, the politics of the Bush administration
could also be seen as evidence of the extent to which the Christian right
has been brought into the norms of American politics and government.
While most agree that the era of Barack Obama constituted a setback for
the Christian conservative movement, even this socially liberal president

---

[50] Green, Rozell and Wilcox, *The Christian Right*; and Shields, *Democratic Virtues*.

reached out to religious conservatives and acknowledged their legitimacy as a force in U.S. politics.[51]

Thus, despite many predictions of its demise and various ups and downs regarding its successes in local, state, and national politics, the Christian right in the United States has not been silenced or become as powerless as Christian conservatives in Western Europe; rather, it appears to have become a part of America's political landscape that is here to stay.

[51] See Timothy S. Goeglein, *The Man in the Middle: An Inside Account of Faith and Politics in the George W. Bush Era* (Nashville, 2011); Stephen Mansfield, *The Faith of George W. Bush* (New York, 2003); and *The Faith of Barack Obama* (Nashville, 2008); also Julian Go, *Rethinking Obama* (Bingley, 2011).

[handwritten margin note: But it has lost its edict moderation in the Trump era, and anyway won sweeping Cond dlephinell change by controlling SCOTUS]

[handwritten note: He did give them Roberts and Alito, two of the six monsters that we face etc]

10

Why Is There No Christian Right in Germany?

German Conservative Christians and the Invention of a Silent Majority in the 1970s

Thomas Großbölting

When comparing the United States and Europe, the very different role of religion in public and political culture is striking. Religious America, secular Europe: that is the leitmotif of a growing number of scholarly studies and articles in the press.[1] According to this master narrative, the United States remains, in Chesterton's words, a "nation with the soul of a church."[2] Compared to Europe, it is commonly pointed out, America "has had less aristocracy, less socialism, more guns, more violence, more patriotism in its civic culture – and more faith."[3] This idea is in no way new; it goes back to such noted commentators as Alexis de Tocqueville and Werner Sombart.[4] The flip side of the coin is the idea of growing secularization in Europe. A "secular age," as the title of Charles Taylor's magnum opus puts it, has dawned and swept aside the last vestiges of an earlier Christian society.[5] The past decade has seen a substantial discussion of the changing role of religion in Europe. The irreconcilable differences among the participants notwithstanding, there is no doubt that several parameters of religious commitment have declined in most

---

[1] Peter Berger, Grace Davie, and Effie Fokas, eds., *Religious America, Secular Europe? A Theme and Variations* (Farnham, 2012).

[2] G. K. Chesterton, *What I Saw in America*, 1922, in *Collected Works*, vol. 21.

[3] Mark Edward Ruff, "Religious Transformation since 1945: Is There an American Religious Exceptionalism?" *Schweizerische Zeitschrift für Religions- und Kulturgeschichte* 107 (2013): 33–48; cf. Sidney E. Mead, "The 'Nation with the Soul of a Church,'" *Church History* 36 (1967): 262–283.

[4] Alexis de Tocqueville and Arthur Goldhammer, *Democracy in America* (New York, 2004); Werner Sombart, *Warum gibt es in den Vereinigten Staaten keinen Sozialismus* (Paderborn, 2011).

[5] Charles Taylor, *A Secular Age* (Cambridge, MA, 2007).

European countries since the 1960s and that the public importance of religion has dwindled as a result.[6]

Religious America, secular Europe: researchers have called this leitmotif into question in recent years by analyzing, on the one hand, regional and generational differences in the United States and, on the other, the new public role of religion in Europe.[7] But all in all, one point remains undisputed: many Europeans are highly skeptical of the different dimensions and manifestations of civil religion and the existence of a powerful and politically influential Christian right in the United States. Although there is a broad spectrum of Christian Democratic parties across Europe as well as a number of religiously driven splinter parties, none of the more important mainstream parties pursues religiously defined objectives or justifies its positions on explicitly religious grounds.[8]

The situation in the United States is radically different. The politically engaged Christian right of today traces its origins back to the 1940s but did not become an influential political player until the 1970s.[9] It was the youth counterculture and, later, the legalization of abortion that transformed a more or less apolitical conglomerate of pious organizations and initiatives into a powerful faction within the Republican Party.[10] Undoubtedly, Richard Nixon's call to the "silent majority" to raise its voice struck a chord among these groups and their supporters. When the evangelical Southern Baptist pastor, televangelist, and political commentator Jerry Falwell started promoting his organization Moral Majority in 1979, he largely echoed the former president.[11]

The aim of this chapter is to use the example of the conservative religious counterculture to shed light on one of the most striking differences between the religious landscapes of the United States and Europe, namely,

---

6 See, for example, Hugh McLeod, *The Religious Crisis of the 1960s* (Oxford, 2009); Detlef Pollack, *Säkularisierung – ein moderner Mythos? Studien zum religiösen Wandel in Deutschland* (Tübingen, 2003); Steve Bruce, *Secularization: In Defence of an Unfashionable Theory* (Oxford, 2011); Thomas Großbölting, *Der verlorene Himmel: Glaube in Deutschland seit 1945* (Göttingen, 2013).

7 Ruff, "Religious Transformation"; José Casanova, *Public Religions in the Modern World* (Chicago, 1994).

8 Wolfram Kaiser, *Christian Democracy and the Origins of European Union* (Cambridge, 2011).

9 Cf. chapter 9 by Mark J. Rozell and Britta Waldschmidt-Nelson in this volume.

10 Daniel K. Williams, *God's Own Party: The Making of the Christian Right* (Oxford, 2010); Eleonore Pieh, *"Fight like David, run like Lincoln": Die politischen Einwirkungen des protestantischen Fundamentalismus in den USA* (Münster, 1998); Manfred Brocker, *God Bless America: Politik und Religion in den USA* (Darmstadt, 2005).

11 Cf. chapter 9 by Rozell and Waldschmidt-Nelson.

the absence of a politically potent mainstream Christian right in Europe. By using the expression "counterculture," I do not mean to suggest a parallel between religious conservatives and the hippie movement or the various alternative religious groups of the 1960s and 1970s. Many adherents of the conservative counterculture were absolutely traditional in religious and political terms. The differences among them notwithstanding, these groupings and organizations all had one thing in common: they sought to radicalize what it meant to live a life of faith. Structurally, the aspirations of the conservative Christian counterculture were similar to those of its counterpart on the left.[12] "Radicalization" was the pattern they had in common. Literally, the term meant to bring Christian life and worship back to their roots in the Gospel. Conservatives took that to mean a return to tradition; Christians on the left, by contrast, were drawn to the proto-communist ideals of early Christianity.

From this lowest common denominator onward, the development of the Christian conservative counterculture took a fundamentally different course on both sides of the Atlantic. The Christian right in the United States became a political giant. The German religious conservative movement started as a dwarf and never really grew. Obviously, the call to the "silent majority" to mobilize politically had some resonance among some political movements and parties in Germany.[13] Within the spectrum of conservative religious groups, however, the impact was extremely limited. A first cursory glance at the religious field in Germany demonstrates how insignificant this movement is. There are few occasions today when conservative Christians – members of the major churches as well as of the smaller denominations – appear in public. Celebrating the traditional Tridentine liturgy, as some of these groups do, is a more or less clandestine affair, usually done early Sunday mornings so that no one takes notice. Similarly, the effort to mobilize Christian believers to protest against abortion and to demand the protection of "unborn children" has had little success in Germany. Organizing committees in the country's mid-sized towns are proud if they are able to mobilize a few dozen anti-abortion activists. Such occasions are impressive above all as manifestations of the very limited influence of right-wing religious groups.

---

[12] Doug Rossinow, *The Politics of Authenticity: Liberalism, Christianity, and the New Left in America* (New York, 1998).

[13] For a state-of-the-art review see the introduction by Anna von der Goltz and Britta Waldschmidt-Nelson in this volume; Massimiliano Livi, Daniel Schmidt, and Michael Sturm, eds., *Die 1970er Jahre als schwarzes Jahrzehnt: Politisierung und Mobilisierung zwischen christlicher Demokratie und extremer Rechter* (Frankfurt/Main, 2010).

Una voce, the Protestant group Bekenntnisbewegung Kein anderes Evanglium (No Other Gospel), the Internet platforms kath.net and kreuz.net, the German branch of Opus Dei – these splinter groups represent only a very small part of believing Christians and church members in Germany. Reliable information about organizational structures and the number of members is scarce. It is estimated, for example, that the Legion of Mary has about 2,000 members in Germany and Opus Dei around 600. These groups pursue a diverse array of activities and goals. Una voce is engaged in restoring the traditional Catholic liturgy. Kein anderes Evanglium defends the literal truth of the Bible and argues against liberal interpretations of scripture. The Partei Bibeltreuer Christen (Party of Bible-True Christians) is a conservative evangelical political party that has two main goals: to block the legalization of same-sex marriage (German law recognizes "civil unions" but not same-sex marriage) and the liberalization of the country's abortion regulations (abortion is formally illegal but not punishable provided a woman has received state-sanctioned counseling).

None of these conservative Christian groups has a home within the German party system. Not even the Christian Democratic Union (CDU), a classic catch-all party with a strong attachment to a religious worldview, provides a platform for their political agenda. Although there is a certain ideological affinity between conservative Christians and right-wing nationalists alarmed by the growing visibility of Germany's Muslim communities, they have not joined forces and have largely steered clear of one another. Whereas extremist nationalists invoke the idea of Western Christendom as a cultural and social entity, conservative German Christians have a more faith-centered conception of Christendom.[14] In some respects, their ideology is not too different from the worldview of some of the conservative Christian groups. And yet, this ideological proximity created neither strong bonds to conservative religious groups nor a boom for the conservative counterculture itself. Many Christian conservatives reject the idea of Christendom as a cultural formation of Western civilization and instead prefer a faith-based approach.[15] Looking back to the beginning of conservative religious mobilization in the 1970s can

14 Alexander Häusler, *Rechtspopulismus als „Bürgerbewegung": Kampagnen gegen Islam und Moscheebau und kommunale Gegenstrategien* (Wiesbaden, 2008).

15 See, for example, Dominik Clemens and Hendrik Puls, eds., *33 Fragen und Antworten zu Pro Köln/Pro NRW: Entwicklung, Ideologie und Strategien einer vermeintlichen Bürgerbewegung* (Cologne, 2014).

help to explain why this part of the silent majority never rose to greater prominence in Germany.

A Lack of Unity and a Common Enemy: The Unstable Foundation of Conservative Mobilization

Looking at the small field of religious conservative groups, there is one reason in particular why it is so difficult to identify a substantial and coherent counterculture in the Federal Republic of Germany. The many diverse splinter groups on the Christian right pursue divergent agendas. The few organizations and groups founded in the 1960s and 1970s that still exist today do not have a common understanding of political and religious action. They share a distinctive understanding of Christianity and what it means to be a Christian, but otherwise they have very different worldviews. The student movement of 1968 is only one item on the conservatives' long list of deplorable developments associated with that decade. For conservative Catholics, the 1960s were, of course, the decade of the Second Vatican Council and the introduction of new liturgical rites. Their Protestant counterparts criticized new approaches to understanding the Bible and the move toward the ordination of women. Conservative Catholics and Protestants alike condemned the established churches for their growing profaneness.

From the perspective of a conservative Christian in West Germany, there was already much at stake in the mid-1960s. It seemed as though God had disappeared. At the very least, there were serious doubts about the deity's existence. Theologians, clergymen, and churchgoing Protestant and Catholic laity were confronted by numerous innovations. Evening prayer sessions with strongly left-leaning messages; scholarly questioning of the Bible's status as the word of God; Christmas celebrations without the Christ child or the manger – the 1960s and 1970s were difficult times for German Christians attached to traditional forms of piety and worship.

An increasing chorus of Christian theologians argued that God should no longer be thought of as some kind of supernatural magician moving people around like chess pieces, permitting or averting plane crashes, and responding to pleading prayers by working miracles.[16] Progressive

---

[16] Cf. Dagmar Herzog, "The Death of God in West Germany: Between Secularization, Post-fascism, and the Rise of Liberation Theology," in Michael Geyer and Lucian Hölscher, eds., *The Presence of God in Modern Society: Transcendence and Religious Community in Germany* (Göttingen, 2006), 431–466.

German theologians of the 1960s and 1970s aimed at two points: to draw lessons from the Nazi past, when, according to critical theologians, the churches had been too close to the regime, and to undo the impact of the conservative, apologetic forms of Christianity that had predominated in the decades after 1945.[17] This development was part of a European trend. Numerous theologians in Britain, France, and Italy, Catholics and Protestants alike, were singing the same song. They too felt the impact of *nouvelle théologie*, personalism, the Second Vatican Council, the "Death of God" movement, political theology, and liberation theology.[18] Advocates of such trends argued that the churches should adapt their messages to the changing times and practical human needs, that older notions of God needed revision, and that solidarity with the oppressed and poor was the way to be properly faithful. All in all, the 1960s and 1970s were a time of heated debate – among theologians and lay people alike – about the lessons of the Gospels, about the relationship between faith and politics, and about the very nature of God.

While the majority of Christians in West Germany stuck to the old traditions and practices, small groups within the German churches were radicalized by the traumatic experience of "1968." In their eyes, 1968 signaled the end of the "re-Christianization" of German life that both Catholic and Protestant leaders had called for immediately after the end of World War II. German public life, clergy, theologians, and many conservative politicians agreed, could be successfully reestablished after the disaster of Nazism only with a reaffirmation of Christian values. According to advocates of re-Christianization, the barbarism of the National Socialist dictatorship was the result of a profound secularization of public life, which, in turn, had led to a moral vacuum and the rise of a totalitarian ideology. Reestablishing German society's moral compass would require reversing that process through re-Christianization. The concept was from the outset somewhat vague; what re-Christianization meant in practice or how it was actually to be achieved was never spelled out. But some core elements of the concept can be identified, most notably the notion of a "Christian occident" and a strong anticommunism. In practical political terms, this cultural product of the Cold War reached deeply into many aspects of daily life, such as sexuality, gender roles,

---

[17] Herzog, "The Death of God," 433.
[18] Cf. Gerd-Rainer Horn, *The Spirit of Vatican II: Western European Progressive Catholicism in the Long Sixties* (Oxford, 2015); Gerd-Rainer Horn, *Western European Liberation Theology, 1924–1959: The First Wave* (Oxford, 2008).

the family, and education. Belief systems and traditional forms of faith gained their strength and their importance for social life by defining this linkage between the sphere of private everyday life and wider public culture. In postwar Germany, Catholic and Protestant belief systems laid out the moral significance of different social institutions and institutional arrangements. They set forth the social and moral meaning of marriage and the family, the needs and objectives of education, the principles of law, and so on. In some respects, this cultural hegemony had been backed by the state: the Basic Law, the Federal Republic's constitution, does not mandate an absolute separation of church and state.

The constitution guarantees freedom of religion but also grants the status of public corporations to officially recognized religious communities. The Protestant and Catholic churches benefit from the system of state collection of church taxes, and they exercise considerable – and constitutionally secured – influence in cultural matters and in the public education sector. Organized Christianity was thus firmly enmeshed in social and political life of the Federal Republic from the outset.

Despite these favorable circumstances, re-Christianization seemed to many of its supporters to have failed by the 1960s. Indeed, the one thing that united the very disparate and generally small groups of conservative Christians in this period was the feeling of a very special loss. Many members of these groups shared the conviction that "1968" was the decisive starting point of ecclesiastical and political decline. Another unifying force was the identification of a shared enemy. From the perspective of conservative Christians, the student movement of the late 1960s in general and student parishes in particular were the most dangerous enemies. Catholics characterized these groups as the successors of the false prophets of the sixteenth century; Protestant conservatives accused the "new radicals" of exerting the same sort of influence on public life that the Nazi storm troopers had. Indeed, many student parishes became hot spots of neo-Marxist thinking in West Germany.[19] Interest in Karl Marx, especially his early writings, and a longing for church reforms often went hand in hand among religiously active students. Not "ortho-doxy" but "ortho-praxis," not teaching but action in the world were, young left-leaning Christians insisted, what made an individual a real Christian. At the beginning of the 1970s, the Kirchenvolksbewegung, a lay reform initiative, tellingly called for the church to adopt a *Frohbotschaft* (message

[19] Großbölting, *Der verlorene Himmel*, 137–148.

of joy) instead of a *Drohbotschaft* (warning).[20] From the perspective of conservative Christians, these developments threatened to obscure the true message of the Bible.

There are several reasons why these grievances did not lead to a broader protest movement among conservative Christians. The first and most important was that the two major Christian churches were – and still are – very closely linked to the state in the Federal Republic. As previously noted, the separation of church and state under the country's constitution does not preclude extensive cooperation between them and, indeed, allows religious bodies considerable influence in public life. Already in the early years of the Federal Republic, Rudolf Smend, an expert in canon law, characterized this system as a "limping separation" between state and churches. The most important church–state connection is the system of ecclesiastical finance: the government tax agency collects the so-called church tax from all taxpayers who are registered as Catholics or Protestants, regardless of whether they are regular churchgoers, and turns the revenues over to the churches. This system makes the German Catholic dioceses and the Protestant *Landeskirchen* (regional churches) the richest religious communities in the world today.

Just how extraordinary the German "limping separation" of church and state is becomes evident in looking at the other end of the church–state spectrum, namely, the example of the United States. The First Amendment of the U.S. Constitution does not allow close connections between governmental agencies and religious organizations. According to Thomas Jefferson, the Constitution erected a "wall of separation between church and State." The Establishment Clause forbids the United States Congress from passing legislation that would establish a state religion. The second half of the clause, known as the Free Exercise Clause, guarantees both individuals and collective bodies freedom from governmental interference in religious affairs. What the separation of church and state means in practice is the subject of ongoing, often heated debate. Concerning the field of financial assistance to ecclesiastical institutions as schools or hospitals, the lowest common denominator can be described by two principles: a strict distinction between the sacred and the secular and a prohibition on direct financial aid to religious institutions. Two decisions of the United States Supreme Court illustrate these dominant lines of reasoning dealing

---

[20] Marc Edward Ruff, "A Religious Vacuum? The Post-Catholic Milieu in the Federal Republic of Germany," in Geyer and Hölscher, *The Presence of God in Modern Society*, 351–379.

with public funds going to religious non-profit organizations: in 1947, *Everson v. Board of Education* set the standards for financial relations when declaring that "no tax in any amount, large or small, can be levied to support any religious activities or institutions, whatever they may be called, or whatever form they may adopt to teach or practice religion."[21] In *Lemon v. Kurtzman* from 1971, the Supreme Court ruled that government authorities may not "excessively entangle" with religion.[22] There is no doubt that the relations between the German state and churches in general and the system of church taxes in particular would not meet these U.S. legislative standards.

In the early decades of the Federal Republic, the "limping separation" was generally accepted as a given. For conservative Christians, this special arrangement was boon and bane at the same time. To stay under the umbrella of the official church meant a continuous and stable cash flow. To break away would certainly have helped with creating a significant public profile. At the same time, however, the founding of a separate and new church would have meant pulling the rug out from under the new religious community because of the loss of financial support.

A second reason why conservative mobilization among religious conservatives remained relatively limited can be found in the differing memory politics championed by the various activist groups. Within such a small movement, the confessional divide between Catholics and Protestants has had significant consequences. Conservative Protestants and Catholics share a common list of enemies they hold responsible for attacks on traditional worship and morality, but they take very different historically focused approaches to making sense of the developments they deplore. Each group stresses the historical significance of its own confession and distances itself from the other.

Missing the Authority of "Mother Church": The Memory Politics of Conservative Catholics

Conservative German Catholics who mobilized in the wake of 1968 sought intellectual legitimation for their position by invoking the work of the church historian and priest Hubert Jedin. He was – and remains – best

[21] https://supreme.justia.com/cases/federal/us/330/1/case.html, 330 U.S. 1, 15–16 (accessed June 21, 2015).

[22] https://supreme.justia.com/cases/federal/us/403/602/, 403 U.S. 602 (accessed June 21, 2015).

(1545-63) — *the launchpad for the Counter-Reformation*

known for his seminal history of the Council of Trent and his multivolume history of the church.[23] But it was not his scholarly work that drew conservative laypeople to rally around Jedin. In 1968, three years after the concluding session of Vatican II, Jedin wrote a "Letter to the German Bishops" and offered his scholarly advice. "To us historians, especially concerned with the history of the Reformation," Jedin wrote, "this crisis [i.e., the upheavals of the 1960s] suggests parallels to the events that led in the sixteenth century to the schism of the Church in the West. It compels us to draw inferences from the historical experience for the evaluation of the present moment in the Church."[24]

What were the "inferences" Jedin identified? Jedin first stressed a very Catholic concern: church authority. Like Martin Luther, the participants in the 1968 national Catholic assembly, the Katholikentag, at Essen, tried to destroy the influence of the hierarchy. In 1968, during one session of the Essen gathering, participants overwhelmingly rejected the papal encyclical *Humanae Vitae* and its prohibition on artificial contraception. Around 5,000 participants in another session publicly declared that they would not obey Rome. According to Jedin, this course of action was the basis of all the subsequent condemnable developments.

obedience to Rome is in many ways, Catholicism's distinct trait

Jedin's second "inference" was a slap in the face for the German conference of bishops. When confronting Luther and the Lutheran movement, one of the church's major mistakes had been a symptomatic indecisiveness and weakness. "Without wishing in the least to explain away the mistakes and oversights committed by the Roman Curia at that time and subsequently, the passivity of the German episcopate must be admitted. They were not sufficiently trained theologically, and with a few exceptions the prince took precedence over the bishop in leading the people." Both in the sixteenth century and in the 1960s, Jedin argued, the bishops underestimated the extent of the danger posed by ongoing developments. "The bishops considered the 'Luther conflict' as a quarrel among theologians and overlooked the fact that the foundations of the Catholic concept of the church were being not only shaken but destroyed."[25]

---

[23] See Hubert Jedin, *A History of the Council of Trent*, 4 vols. (Freiburg/Breisgau, 1976); Hubert Jedin and John Patrick Dolan, *History of the Church*, 10 vols. (London, 1980).

[24] Hubert Jedin's 1968 Memorandum to the West German Episcopal Conference, a translation of Hubert Jedin's Lebensbericht, Mainz 1984, 266–274. Translation by Reverend Joseph W. Koterski, S.J. Introduction and notes by Reverend Brian Van Hove, S.J. http://www.ignatiusinsight.com/features2009/bvanhove_jedinmemo_octo9.asp (accessed February 17, 2014).

[25] Hubert Jedin's 1968 Memorandum, 270.

From this process of erosion new uncertainties arose, according to
Jedin:

The Church's present crisis in Germany is in its innermost essence, as in the 16th
century, a matter of uncertainty and disorientation in the faith. Protestant biblical
criticism has broken into Catholic theology on a broad front... The question "Is
there anything still Catholic?" is not just something asked only by older and
so-called "traditional" Catholics, but comes from the very core of sincere and
genuine believers. This too was brought about not just by the constant change of
liturgical forms and the ever more encompassing capriciousness in liturgy, but is
the result of real uncertainty and the need for knowledge.[26]

Jedin's diagnosis was as clear as the therapy he proposed:

In the parallels pointed out above and the sample proposals derived from them, I
have taken into consideration that in present day Church developments there are
at work strong religious forces not unlike those in the sixteenth century movement
enkindled by Luther. The saying of St. Augustine applies to both of them: "There is
no false doctrine without some truth intermingled." ("Nulla porro falsa doctrina
est, quae non aliqua vera intermisceat." Quaest. ev. 11.40) I am convinced that
the true and the good which has emerged from the new awakening of the Church
at the Council and through the Council up to today can only be fruitful if it
is separated from error. The longer the painful operation is put off, the greater
will be the danger that valuable sources of strength are going to be lost because
they will be amalgamated with error. Then there will occur among us not only
a separation from the Church, but a defection from Christianity itself. The more
clearly the bishops speak and the more decisively they act, the greater the chance
to maintain the movement of awakening within the Church and thereby to uphold
the Church.[27]

Jedin and his followers had no doubt about who was to blame for this
negative development: the most passionate and most powerful champi-
ons of the Lutheran movement were the "intellectuals" of that time, the
humanists, in whose eyes the current theology, scholasticism, was a hin-
drance to progress. Also included were numerous priests and clerics who,
fascinated by the slogan of "evangelical freedom," cast off the vows they
had taken upon themselves. Finally there were some from the classes
threatened by social decline, such as the imperial knighthood and the
well-to-do farmers, throughout a great part of Germany.

Jedin's writings helped trigger a turn toward traditionalism among
German Catholics and the emergence of splinter groups that became
a small but distinctive feature of the German religious landscape.
Some commentators, such as Michael Ebertz, have labeled these groups

---

[26] Hubert Jedin's 1968 Memorandum, 270.
[27] Hubert Jedin's 1968 Memorandum, 271.

representatives of a "Catholic fundamentalism," a term as inexact as it is suggestive. The Catholic variant of conservative mobilization was characterized by the desire to return to traditional liturgical forms of the past or to give greater emphasis to Marian forms of piety. Some of the conservative groups, for example the Legio Mariae, had long existed on the fringes of the church. Others, such as Opus Dei, had enjoyed the support of the Catholic hierarchy.

Mark Ruff, one of the most important specialists on the history of the German Catholic Church, has offered critical insights into the conservative branch within German Catholicism. He insists that we must be careful not to place the church hierarchy solely within the camp of traditionalism. German bishops have been divided, for example, on questions of morals and sexual ethics. Since the 1980s, the conference of bishops has been hobbled by seemingly unbridgeable ideological differences and has not been able, as Jedin observed earlier, to act as a strong leading institution.[28] Many seminarians – young men who prepare themselves to become members of the clergy – now see themselves as a countercultural movement. The more liberal clergy who came of age in the late 1950s and 1960s are gradually retiring.

While tremendously fragmented, these different initiatives and splinter groups emphasizing tradition were variously a reaction against the reforms of the Second Vatican Council and those progressive Catholic institutions and movements that had adopted positions attacking the church hierarchy for its conservatism on questions of values and especially sexual ethics. Although divided among themselves, conservative and traditionalist Catholic groups in Germany were united in their opposition to the reforms of the Second Vatican Council and to progressive Catholic initiatives. The conservatives were particularly critical of the progressives' attacks on the church hierarchy and their stance on values and moral issues, especially questions of sexual ethics. Like the Catholic leadership of the nineteenth century, German conservative Catholics were consciously hostile to modernity. Those opposed to liturgical innovation even went so far as to refuse to use modern means to defend their position..

"The Church Struggle Never Stops": How Protestant Conservatives Made Sense of the 1970s

Protestant fundamentalism resembles the Catholic fundamentalism sketched above only loosely. Protestant conservatives often believe in the

[28] Ruff, "A Religious Vacuum?," 378.

It's not the Catholic. they don't take the Bible literally but they must also accept the Church's magisterium

literal truth of scripture, and the range of conservative movements among German Protestants is extremely diverse. The most traditional and distinctively German Protestant conservatives identify themselves with the Bekennende Kirche (Confessing Church), which had opposed the Nazi regime for its interference in church matters. "The Church struggle never ends," declared Rudolf Bäumer, one of the two founders of Kein anderes Evanglium.[29] This initiative, established on March 6, 1966, became the leading group within the umbrella organization Konferenz der Bekennenden Kirchen in Deutschland (Conference of the Confessing Churches in Germany).

The name Kein anderes Evanglium can be traced back to the Epistle of St. Paul to the Galatians: "I marvel that ye are so soon removed from him that called you into the grace of Christ unto another gospel: Which is not another; but there be some that trouble you, and would pervert the gospel of Christ. But though we, or an angel from heaven, preach any other gospel unto you than that which we have preached unto you, let him be accursed" (Galatians 1:6–8). In the second half of the 1960s, for the supporters of Kein anderes Evanglium, it was not Hitler and Nazis who had to be opposed but rather Rudolf Bultmann, who advocated the demystification of the Bible, and Dorothee Sölle, a proponent of the God-is-dead theology. In 1977, Bäumer, saying the situation was growing worse, declared that the "second church struggle" was more pressing than resisting the pressure of National Socialism had been.[30] Additionally, we can observe some new transitions and overlapping gray areas between these Protestant fundamentalist groups and new internationally organized evangelical movements coming up.

This denies the victimhood of the Nazism while upgrading Bäumer and his allies

To speak in terms borrowed from political science, we can say that left- and right-wing Protestants, individuals as well as groups, used the tool of memory politics to position themselves on the religious spectrum. The emergence of a conservative Christian counterculture was the result of efforts to break with the mainstream Protestant churches. One way conservatives could set themselves apart was to invoke the Nazi past, above all the struggle of the Confessing Church. They urgently needed to gain public attention to win recognition. Referring to the Nazi past was an extremely effective way for them to dramatize their disagreement with

---

[29] Friedhelm Jung, *Die deutsche evangelikale Bewegung: Grundlinien ihrer Geschichte und Theologie* (Bonn, 2001), 108.

[30] Rudolf Bäumer, "Dieser zweite Kirchenkampf ist viel ernster," *epd Zentralarchiv*, no. 76, April 20, 1977, 6.

the mainstream churches, to heighten the conflict, and to call attention to their positions.

Like students on the left, conservative Protestant activists did not hesitate to identify their opponents with the Nazis.[31] In 1969, for example, Helmut Thielicke, a professor of theology at the University of Hamburg, echoed a frequent conservative charge when he likened the student movement to the Nazis' storm troopers.[32] Hellmut Frey, a leading figure in Kein anderes Evanglium, argued along similar lines. From his perspective, the Protestant church assembly (Kirchentag) of 1965, where popular political theologians on the left were given an opportunity to speak, was the same kind of event as the famous rally Nazi Minister of Propaganda Joseph Goebbels had organized in Berlin's Sportpalast in 1943.[33]

It would be wrong to interpret these and many other similar statements as mere rhetorical exaggerations made for tactical purposes. Such comments derived, rather, from a very special interpretation of Germany's recent past. For the overwhelming majority of German Protestants, coming to terms with the Nazi past posed a great challenge. Recognizing their own complicity in the crimes of the Nazi regime was a very protracted and complicated process for most of them. There is no doubt that the Evangelical Church's Stuttgart Declaration of Guilt of October 1945 was a strong and thoughtful theological push to engage with the Nazi past. The famous pastor Martin Niemöller and his co-authors laid blame upon themselves "for not standing to our beliefs more courageously, for not praying more faithfully, for not believing more joyously, and for not loving more ardently."[34] The impact of the Stuttgart Declaration in the 1940s was, however, limited.[35] The majority of Germans were not yet willing to accept responsibility for Nazi rule.

31 Stephan Linck, "'Jetzt hilft nur noch eine Flugzeugentführung': Die Radikale Linke und die Evangelische Studierendengemeinde in Hamburg 1973 bis 1978," in Klaus Fitschen et al., eds., *Die Politisierung des Protestantismus: Entwicklungen in der Bundesrepublik Deutschland während der 1960er und 70er Jahre* (Göttingen, 2011), 77–89.

32 Hartmut Lehmann and Detlef Pollack, "Schlussdiskussion mit Tagungsberichten," in Siegfried Hermle, Claudia Lepp, and Harry Oelke, eds., *Umbrüche: Der deutsche Protestantismus und die sozialen Bewegungen in den 1960er und 70er Jahren* (Göttingen, 2007), 353–379.

33 Lehmann and Pollack, "Schlussdiskussion mit Tagungsberichten," 361.

34 For an English version of the declaration see http://www.history.ucsb.edu/faculty/marcuse/projects/niem/StuttgartDeclaration.htm (last accessed November 28, 2016).

35 Matthew D. Hockenos, *A Church Divided: German Protestants Confront the Nazi Past* (Bloomington, 2004); Victoria Barnett, *For the Soul of the People: Protestant Protest against Hitler* (New York, 1992).

As with the denazification of most aspects of West German life

In fact, the self-denazification of the church was largely a failure. Protestant bishops, pastors, and laypersons were unanimous in their rejection of the Allied accusation of collective German guilt for the acts of the Nazi regime. This is a thoroughly examined and well-known example of the way in which the churches handled the past. Some members of the *Bruderräte*, the informal groups that took the lead in organizing the Confessing Church, gained a strong symbolic and social position within the Evangelical Church in Germany (Evangelische Kirche in Deutschland, EKD) as the umbrella organization of the Protestant churches after the war. But their ideas on church reform and renewal were not put into practice. Leading figures from the *Bruderräte* recommended, for example, that the role of the parishes within the church be strengthened. In practice, however, ecclesiastical reorganization after 1945 left established hierarchies and structures largely intact. The theology of the *Bruderräte* did not become influential until the 1960s, when the Christian left counterculture invoked some of the traditions of the Confessing Church.

From the perspective of conservative Protestant activists, the ideas promoted by left-wing Protestants – their emphasis on the right to resist authority, for instance, and their advocacy of establishing structures independent of the church – were as threatening to the church and to the true faith as the Nazis had been decades earlier. Thus Joachim Beckmann, the longtime head of the Protestant Church in the Rhineland, drew parallels between the politically charged evening prayer meetings of the 1960s and the conventions of the so-called German Christians (*Deutsche Christen*) who had aligned themselves with the Nazi dictatorship.[36]

Though this really happened only

As she related in her autobiography, Sölle, one of the organizers of the evening prayer meetings, was deeply shocked when confronted with such accusations.[37] Fulbert Steffensky, her second husband, told friends that Sölle never got over them. Sölle saw herself as engaged in liberalizing West German society and helping to free the world from "fascist repression." Her adversaries, by contrast, cast her as a follower of the Nazis. As this episode suggests, it was not simply a difference of opinion that divided left- and right-leaning Protestants: the two opposing camps were separated by a wide, even insurmountable gap of perception.

And right-wing opportunism

These and other conflicts promoted significant changes within the Protestant churches. The term "evangelical" was for the first time used

---

[36] Cf. Lehmann and Pollack, "Schlussdiskussion mit Tagungsberichten," 368.

[37] See Peter Cornehl, "Dorothee Sölle, das 'politische Nachtgebet' und die Folgen," in Hermle, Lepp, and Oelke, *Umbrüche*, 265–284.

in 1966 and gained currency a number of years later.[38] In 1966, a group of Protestant ministers founded the Kein anderes Evanglium. The organization attracted 19,000 people at its first mass gathering in Dortmund. The complicated title of the group indicated both its roots in the Pietistic awakening movement and an attempt to tap into the symbolism of the anti-Nazi Bekennende Kirche of the Third Reich. This branch of Evangelicals thus understood itself as a victim of totalitarian aggression. In their eyes, the rise of a critical theology had diluted and falsified the sole truth of the gospel, because it applied the historical-critical method to biblical texts and followed the progressive *Zeitgeist* in the form of political theology. From the perspective of evangelical Christians, modern theologians and radical priests were the protagonists of the modern aberrances.

Beginning in 1969, they made several attempts to establish an alternative institutional presence on the West German religious scene, undertaking their own missionary programs, for example, and establishing their own press outlets.[39] With a few exceptions, such as the news agency IDEA, these initiatives failed.

Conclusion: The Silent Majority Versus God's Elect Minority

In Germany, neither the Protestant nor the Catholic conservative protest camp ever developed into anything more than a loose coalition of splinter groups. The relationship — the "limping separation" — between the established churches and the state acted as an institutional barrier to the rise of a conservative Christian counterculture. Additionally, the protest camps were divided by confessional bias: there was no way to overcome the religious and cultural gap between Protestants and Catholics and to build an interconfessional conservative coalition. Both sides were restricted to the small in-group of their confessional fellows.

"Church must remain Church" – *Kirche muss Kirche bleiben*: the battle cry of the Protestant countermovement never found much resonance.[40] There was no majority, silent or loud, on the West German religious landscape that mobilized in protest against left-leaning movements within the churches or in the political sphere. Indeed, the "silent majority" image gained no traction as a self-description among conservative

[38] See Rudolf Bäumer, Peter Beyerhaus, and Fritz Grünzweig, *Weg und Zeugnis: Bekennende Gemeinschaften im gegenwärtigen Kirchenkampf 1965–1980* (Bielefeld, 1981).

[39] Gisa Bauer, *Evangelikale Bewegung und evangelische Kirche in der Bundesrepublik Deutschland: Geschichte eines Grundsatzkonflikts, 1949 bis 1989* (Göttingen, 2012).

[40] Adalbert Hudak, ed., *Kirche muss Kirche bleiben* (Stuttgart, 1979).

German churchgoers. To the contrary: conservative German Christians were drawn to role models – the early Christian communities in the Roman empire, the Confessing Church of the Nazi era – that underscored their minority status. They saw themselves as the small flock remaining unwavering and firm in the face of dangerous trends and hostile political forces.

There is no doubt that, politically, this self-image pointed in the same direction as much of the conservative mobilization of the silent majority in the United States and in Europe. From a cultural perspective, however, their self-perception rested on a very different foundation than that of other conservative activists. Essentially elitist, this self-stylization characterizes the Christian counterculture not as a "Silent Majority," but as a small and steadfast group: God's elect minority.

[Handwritten margin notes:]

Albeit somewhat disingenuously

Like the alt right

A sect + not a counterculture, and counterculture, and one who the wider political interest to generate wider and less widespread activism

11

Modern Crusaders

The Conservative Catholic Politics of Resistance in Post-Conciliar Netherlands

Marjet Derks

In the spring of 1967, *Time Magazine* published an article on "the radical, revolutionary Church of the Netherlands." It depicted the Netherlands as the most progressive province in the Roman Catholic Church worldwide, where clerics and laypeople worked closely together to make renewal happen. A photograph of Cardinal Johannes Alfrink, the influential Dominican theologian Edward Schillebeeckx, and a laywoman, Tine Govaart-Halkes, carried a caption explaining that they were "questioning everything from original sin to celibacy." The article suggested that more than 60 percent of all Dutch Catholic women were on the pill. Govaart-Halkes, a mother of three, was introduced as an opinion leader who had been present at the first two sessions of the Second Vatican Council as a journalist. "I started taking the pill when I was attending the Council," she was quoted as saying. In her view, she explained, sex did not necessarily imply marriage. The American author of the article concluded in unconcealed amazement that despite Govaart-Halkes's liberal views, church leaders in the Netherlands did not censor her in any way and even allowed her an influential position in the upcoming Pastoral Council of the Dutch Church Province. Schillebeeckx, a professor at the prominent Catholic University of Nijmegen, was quoted saying: "What we discuss openly, is often discussed behind closed doors elsewhere."[1]

The *Time* article caused considerable furor, both in the Netherlands and abroad. The Dutch press jumped onto it, writing about the "theologian Provos" (referring to a contemporary protest group of

---

[1] "Roman Catholics: The Radical, Revolutionary Church of the Netherlands," *Time Magazine*, March 31, 1967, 63.

provocative Dutch youngsters) and reprinting the photograph of Alfrink, Schillebeeckx, and Govaart-Halkes.[2] Govaart-Halkes felt that she had been misinterpreted; the reporter had reduced a lengthy interview to a few catchy phrases. She did, however, state again that married people should be allowed to make their own decisions on the use of contraceptives. Moreover, she suggested, the real source of problems was the secrecy surrounding sex.[3] Cardinal Alfrink too was not happy about the *Time* article. He wrote to Govaart-Halkes that, once again, the foreign press was turning Dutch Catholics into a caricature and, by doing so, was damaging their reputation.[4] Alfrink was referring to the 1966 Christmas edition of the popular French magazine *Paris Match*, which had caused an international commotion by zooming in on several unauthorized liturgical experiments in the Netherlands. It had shown numerous photos of unprecedented modes of celebrating mass in Holland, including not only the use of rock music but also ecumenical celebrations and people and priests gathering in private homes to exchange bread and wine. Liturgical renewal in the Netherlands, *Paris Match* declared, was "spectacular."[5] As a result of this report, the Roman Congregation of the Rites and the Post-Conciliar Council for Liturgy officially condemned the Dutch liturgical experiments.[6]

The list of media "incidents" became longer and longer. Dutch Catholics had obviously become an item that sold copy. The *National Catholic Reporter* and the *New York Times* published articles about them in January and September 1967, and European newspapers and journals followed suit.[7] Two months after the *Time* article, a new Italian journal, *Panorama*, opened its first issue by referring to it. In an unabashedly

---

2 "Time over r.k. Holland," *Het vrije volk*, April 6, 1967; "Avant-garde," *De Tijd*, April 7, 1967.

3 "Onze 'theologische provo's," *De Stem*, April 1, 1967; Tine Govaart-Halkes, letter to *De Stem*, 1967, Govaart Family Archive, private collection.

4 Bernard Alfrink, letter to Tine Govaart-Halkes, April 7, 1967, Govaart Family Archive, private collection.

5 Robert Serrou, Noëlle Namia, and Michel Leclerq, "La Nouvelle Messe," *Paris Match*, no. 923, December 17, 1966.

6 "Liturgie-experimenten door Rome veroordeeld," *De Tijd*, January 5, 1967.

7 Clyde H. Farnsworth, "Dutch Catholics in Ferment of Change as Old Practices are Modernized," *New York Times*, January 17, 1967; Edward B. Fiske, "The Dutch as Catholic Avant Garde," *New York Times*, August 13, 1967; Farnsworth, "Dutch Are Trying New Supper Rite. Weekly Eucharistic Meals Held by Interfaith Groups," *New York Times*, September 9, 1967. For a survey of all articles see R. Huysmans and Y. Schnabel, "Buitenlandse literatuur over de katholieke kerk in Nederland, 1965–1970," *Jaarboek Katholiek Documentatie Centrum* (1970): 149–163.

disapproving tone, *Panorama* depicted Dutch Catholics as a rebellious, uninhibited avant-garde who had no fear of hell and who were prepared to put everything of value at risk.[8]

During the 1960s, in short, Dutch Catholics were almost always portrayed as progressive advocates of renewal who were at the forefront of avant-garde thinking within the church following the Second Vatican Council. Bishops from other countries – West Germany, Belgium, France, Switzerland, and Austria as well as the United States and Canada – had also been among the progressive forces during the council, but liturgical change and the attack on the church's traditional teaching on contraception and on clerical celibacy had progressed furthest in the Netherlands: hence the international attention. This was a remarkable development: the Dutch Church seemed to have been quickly transformed from one of the most loyal and obedient provinces of the church to one of the most rebellious. From the late sixteenth century until the nineteenth century, Catholicism had been suppressed in the Netherlands. Emancipation in the nineteenth century eventually led to the emergence of a growing and overly self-conscious, triumphalist Catholic minority in the twentieth century. In a 1960 census, more than 40 percent (4.6 million) of all Dutch declared themselves as Catholics, the highest proportion since the beginning of the nineteenth century.[9]

Dutch Catholics were purportedly putting their stodgy, conservative past behind them – and quickly – during the 1960s. Only when Rome responded to this challenge to accepted doctrine by appointing conservative bishops at the beginning of the 1970s did this short era of renewed church life ("called to freedom," as one historical account revealingly phrased it[10]) begin to erode. Eventually, this and an emerging secular drift led to numerous disappointed Catholics leaving the church, never to return.[11]

---

[8] "Nieuw Italiaans weekblad: Nederlanders niet bang voor de hel," *De Tijd*, May 18, 1967.

[9] The southern provinces of the country were predominantly Catholic. Self-described Protestants, divided among six denominations, made up 40.1 percent of the population and atheists 18.3 percent. Hans Knippenberg, *De religieuze kaart van Nederland* (Assen, 1992).

[10] Walter Goddijn, Jan Jacobs, and Gerard van Tillo, eds., *Tot vrijheid geroepen. Katholieken in Nederland 1945–2000* (Baarn, 1999).

[11] This is the main characterization in Dutch historiography. See Maarten van den Bos, *Verlangen naar vernieuwing Nederlands katholicisme 1953–2003* (Amsterdam, 2012); Peter van Rooden, "Oral history en het vreemde sterven van het Nederlands christendom," *BMGN* 119:3 (2004): 524–515; James Kennedy, *Nieuw Babylon in aanbouw.*

As will be argued in the first part of this chapter, historical accounts have echoed this dominant media portrayal of Dutch Catholicism in the long 1960s.[12] This is in large part a result of the fact that most of the authors who have written on the topic were either involved in the process of church renewal or based their work on studies by those who were. This has led to what Rick Perlstein termed the "generational gap," which characterizes many studies on the 1960s in general.[13] The actors of the 1960s were so self-conscious about their role as historical agents that they were inclined to experience "possessive memory." Certain recollections are inseparably tied to their identity. Recently, however, scholars have questioned the dominant view of religious life in the 1960s, arguing that it highlights one high-profile group while obscuring other actors and other currents of thought.[14] Among the groups long overlooked by historians are conservative Dutch Catholics, who thought they better represented the views of Dutch Catholics as a whole than the advocates of reform did.

The Netherlands was not alone in seeing the emergence of conservative Catholic groups during the 1960s. Opus Dei, for example, was one of several conservative organizations active in Belgium during this period.[15] Also, the traditionalist organization Society of Pius X founded by French bishop Marcel Lefebvre spread to more than thirty-two countries. The

Nederland in de jaren zestig(Amsterdam, 1995), 82 [translation of *Building New Babylon: Cultural Change in the Netherlands during the 1960s*]; Richard Auwerda, *De kromstaf als wapen. Bisschopsbenoemingen in Nederland* (Baarn, 1988); Ernst Kossmann, *De lage landen, 1780–1940. Anderhalve eeuw Nederland en België* (Amsterdam, 1976), 331. More critical is Erik Borgman, "Einen Weg gehen, den es nicht gibt: Vom Niederländischen Pastoralkonzil zum Ende der Acht Mei Beweging – und weiter?," *Wort und Antwort* 47:1 (2006): 12–18.

12 This term was coined by Arthur Marwick, *The Sixties: Cultural Revolution in Britain, France, Italy and the United States, c. 1958–1974* (Oxford, 1998), 7; also Hugh McLeod, *The Religious Crisis of the 1960s* (Oxford, 2007), 1.

13 Rick Perlstein, "Who Owns the Sixties? The Opening of a Scholarly Gap," *Lingua Franca* 6:4 (1996): 30–37.

14 Marjet Derks, "The Gospel of the Old: Media, Gender, and the Invisible Conservative Catholic in the Long 1960s," *Schweizerische Zeitschrift für Religions- und Kulturgeschichte* 104 (2010): 135–154; Jos Palm, *Moederkerk. De ondergang van rooms Nederland* (Amsterdam, 2012). For an international revision, e.g., Mark Massa S.J., *The American Catholic Revolution: How the '60s Changed the Church Forever* (Oxford, 2010). Massa states that throughout the United States traditionalist movements were established after the implementation of the new liturgy, its most famous protester being a Belgian priest from Baltimore, Gommar De Pauw.

15 Bart Latré, *Strijd en inkeer. De kerk- en maatschappijkritische beweging in Vlaanderen 1958–1990* (Leuven, 2011), 242–246.

United States saw the rise of the charismatic renewal movement. Heated debates on a number of divisive issues led to what sociologist of religion James Davison Hunter typified as the new culture war.[16]

Nevertheless, because of the international attention given to Dutch progressive renewal and reform, the existence of conservative Catholic groups in the Netherlands calls for more historical research. It is difficult to estimate the number of adherents they had. The only solid indicators are the subscription figures of several magazines (10,000), the number of petition signatories (up to 1,500), attendance figures of public gatherings (generally in the hundreds), and the votes that the conservative Roman Catholic Party of the Netherlands received in 1972 (35,000).[17] However, as will be argued in the second part of this chapter, the impact the conservative groups had was much larger than such figures might suggest. They actively tried to mobilize other Catholics to act as a counterforce to ongoing events and discourses that both the national and international media were focusing on.

Furthermore, I dispute the dominant image of the conservatives in historical studies as a monolithic movement that simply rallied against renewal. Although they often were portrayed this way, there was not just one but rather a multifaceted conservative mobilization in the Netherlands during the 1960s and 1970s. Considering their efforts to fight the spirit of the age by using military metaphors, portraying the 1960s as a time of war, while describing themselves as "soldiers" or "modern crusaders," they were a silenced group, not a silent one.

The "Media Lads"

Who were the Catholics who fed the progressive, even rebellious image of Dutch Catholicism? This image rested in large part on the appearances and performances of several relatively young and mediagenic priests, theologians, and social scientists. Most were men, aside from the occasional woman, and most were of middle-class background. They were pushing for change and welcomed and embodied an image of progressiveness,

16 James Davison Hunter, *Culture Wars: The Struggle to Define America* (New York, 1992); also Claire Wolfteich, *American Catholics through the Twentieth Century: Spirituality, Lay Experience and Public Life* (New York, 2001), 51–100.

17 Derks, "'Die treue Majorität'. Konservatieve Mobilisierung in den postkonziliaren katholischen Niederlanden, 1966–1985," in Peter van Dam and Friso Wielenga, eds., *Religion als Zündstoff. Gesellschaftliches und politisches Engagement in den Niederlanden seit 1945* (Münster, 2013), 117–138: 130–134.

modernity, youthful vigor, and masculine prowess. Their age is worth noting: in the early 1960s, they were not in their teens or twenties but in their early forties. By the standards of the church, however, they were young. Furthermore, they presented themselves, in the spirit of the 1960s, as young and rather rebellious.

From a sociocultural perspective, the architects and the advocates of renewal were much alike. They were all members of a generation that was liberating itself from old Catholic ties and networks – angry young Catholic men. They were able to come to the forefront of Catholic life in the Netherlands because of a structural transformation in Catholic publishing and broadcasting. Older church-abiding journalists were first overshadowed and then replaced by their younger and more critical colleagues. In other words, there was a change within the social arena in which the media operated, within what sociologist Pierre Bourdieu has designated "the media field." Consequently, the agents, positions, and rules of the field transformed as well.[18] Many of these new media actors were former seminarians or priests who had left the priesthood in order to marry. They were firm critics of church hierarchy, and they became more radical over time, often ending up working for leftist newspapers or magazines.

Furthermore, these journalists were members of a "secondary elite"; they were the products of the postwar expansion of the Dutch education system and were often the first members of their families to attend university or to earn a professional degree. The establishment, however, prevented their social ascent, thus frustrating their ambitions. This caused a sense of like-mindedness and fellowship among the secondary elite, along with the conviction that great things could lay ahead if only the right people were in charge.[19]

As a result of this generational change, the Dutch Catholic press and television in the 1960s had a strong preference for a particular set of protagonists, namely church renewers, who were quoted again and again and whose pictures could hardly be missed. Especially television, the new medium that had been introduced in the Netherlands in the early 1950s

[18] Pierre Bourdieu, *The Field of Cultural Production: Essays on Art and Literature* (New York, 1993).
[19] Jan Bank, "Televisie in de politieke cultuur van de jaren zestig," in J. Th. J. van den Berg, ed., *Tussen Nieuwspoort en Binnenhof: De jaren '60 als breuklijn in de naoorlogse ontwikkelingen in politiek en journalistiek* (The Hague, 1989), 34–46; J. E. Ellemers, "Nederland in de jaren zestig en zeventig," *Sociologische Gids* 26:6 (1979): 429–443.

and was on the verge of becoming a mass medium by the early 1960s, kept on showing the young and mediagenic progressives. Catholic modern mass media and consequently also other denominational media thus echoed and co-created the so-called narratives of the new and provided a platform for those who spoke of renewal.[20]

Because of the dominant culture of rebellious "laddism" in the media, certain actors, subjects, and trends tended to be neglected, especially if they were at the opposite end of the ideological spectrum. That included all who held conservative views on society and religion. The latter's complaints about the media's progressive preferences may have been overstretching the point on occasion, but Dutch media coverage on church renewal was indeed vast.

The Catholic pillar / holder had its own share of public broadcasting (and I think still does)

Historical Marginalization and Stereotyping

A similar frame can be identified in historical writing, both within and outside the Netherlands. Men who were actively involved in the renewal process set the tone for the first wave of scholarship. The starting point in the Netherlands was a couple of books by a Franciscan sociologist, Walter Goddijn – nicknamed "the Dutch Pope" – who had been the advisor of the Dutch episcopate from 1962 onward. His books were quoted over and over again.[21]

Internationally, the tone was set by a dissertation written by an American Jesuit, John Coleman. He had lived in a progressive Jesuit community in Amsterdam in the early 1970s and felt strongly connected to its members and their ideas. In *The Evolution of Dutch Catholicism*, Coleman portrayed a small group of progressive priests who sought to abolish clerical celibacy in positive terms as representatives of a broad current of opinion among Dutch Catholics. He characterized conservative counterforces, on the other hand, as a "sect" and a "minority."[22] Unsurprisingly,

[20] Frank Bösch and Lucian Hölscher, eds., *Kirchen, Medien, Öffentlichkeit. Transformationen kirchlicher Selbst- und Fremddeutungen seit 1945* (Göttingen, 2009); Nicolai Hannig and Benjamin Städter, "Die kommunizierte Krise. Kirche und Religion in der Medienöffentlichkeit der 1950er und 60er Jahre," *Schweizerische Zeitschrift für Religions- und Kulturgeschichte* 101 (2007): 151–184. Also Derks, "The Gospel of the Old."

[21] Walter Goddijn, *De beheerste kerk. Uitgestelde revolutie in R.K. Nederland* (Amsterdam and Brussels, 1973); Goddijn, *Roomsen, dat waren wij* (Hilversum, 1978).

[22] John Coleman, *The Evolution of Dutch Catholicism, 1954–1978* (Berkeley, Los Angeles, and London, 1978).

Goddijn wrote a very positive review of Coleman's book, as did other reformers.[23] Other scholars both in the Netherlands and abroad followed Coleman's line of reasoning.[24] In 2007, British historian Hugh McLeod still referred solely to Coleman in his depiction of radical Dutch Catholicism during the religious crisis of the 1960s.[25] Conservative Catholics were either non-existent or portrayed as the straggling remnants of elitist resistance to change.

Conservative Multiformity

Conservative Catholic movements in both Europe and the United States shared certain characteristics during the long 1960s. In their perception, post-conciliar church renewal signified an attack on the traditional church that had to be countered. They equated this renewal with liturgical "abuses," the rhetoric of choice, insufficient respect for papal authority, a failure to obey Catholic teachings on artificial birth control, abandonment of the traditional modes of devotion, and a disregard for the conclusions of scholastic theology. Adapting to contemporary society in this way, they maintained, would cut the church off from its sacred roots. First and foremost, conservatives feared the church would lose touch with the great voices of the past – from the early Christian era, from the Middle Ages, and, in the Dutch case, from the heyday of Dutch Catholicism in the 1920s and 1930s. Renewal thus meant a break with history, which had to be countered by means of an *expeditio sacra*, a holy crusade.

In this respect, they revealed a profoundly romantic disposition: the true church was at risk of being lost. Citing authoritative writings and arguing from history, they defended the unity of the church as they saw it and claimed that religious authenticity, rooted in early Christianity, was theirs alone. They thus saw themselves, as one conservative put it, as cleansers. They were "the loyal majority" fending off an attack upon the church.[26]

However, if conservatives invoked the early church to defend their position, so too did the progressives, who similarly invoked "the sources"

---

[23] Lambert van Gelder, "Toetssteen des aanstoots," *Het vrije volk*, July 11, 1974.

[24] Herman Bakvis, *Catholic Power in the Netherlands* (Montreal and Quebec, 1981), 113; Ernest Zahn, *Regenten, rebellen en reformatoren. Een visie op Nederland en de Nederlanden* (Amsterdam, 2005; original *Das unbekannte Holland*, 1989), 200–210.

[25] McLeod, *The Religious Crisis of the 1960s*, 153–154, nn. 31 and 32.

[26] Winand Kotte, letter to the faithful, September 29, 1969, inv. no. 6, Archive Confrontatie, Catholic Documentary Center (CDC), Nijmegen.

in their calls for change.[27] They claimed their vision of a small-scale, democratic church had its roots in early Christian practice. Conservatives and progressives used a similar politics of memory, grounding their diverging visions of the "beloved community" in the same historically remote era. The call for authenticity, an important identity marker for many movements of the 1960s, was clearly an ideologically contested territory.[28]

Looking more closely, however, we need to distinguish different types of Dutch Catholic conservatism. As in the United States, three main movements, with some overlap in membership, can be discerned.[29] By far the largest group consisted of mainstream conservatives who generally disliked the doctrinal interpretations of progressive Catholics and desired to restore the discipline of the so-called authentic church. They advocated obedience to papal authority and liturgical orthodoxy, and they rejected moral laxity, which they identified in particular with abortion and the use of contraceptives. A second movement can be characterized as separatist. Its sympathizers, often members of the clergy, rejected the Second Vatican Council and aimed at restoring pre-Vatican II priestly power. They tended to set up communities apart from existing church dioceses; the aforementioned Society of Pius X of Bishop Lefebvre is the best known example. A third, rather marginal, group consisted of devotees of private revelations, above all in connection with apparitions of the Virgin Mary. Expecting imminent disaster, they warned that the church renewal movement and cultural change would soon bring divine punishment down upon sinful humanity.

Another hitherto unmentioned aspect of Dutch religious conservatism of the 1960s and 1970s is the echo of World War II. After years of silence and postwar reconstruction, public debates on the war first began to emerge during these decades. This coincided with the rise of the conservative movements whose supporters belonged to a generation for whom the war had been a formative experience. A remarkable number of them had been active members of small resistance groups or prisoners in Dutch

---

[27] Frits van der Meer, *Open brief over geloof en eredienst* (Tielt and Utrecht, 1973).

[28] Doug Rossinow, *The Politics of Authenticity: Liberalism, Christianity and the New Left in America* (New York, 1998). For the Netherlands, Hans Righart, *De eindeloze jaren zestig. Geschiedenis van een generatieconflict* (Amsterdam, 1995).

[29] Michael W. Cuneo, *The Smoke of Satan: Conservative and Traditionalist Dissent in Contemporary American Catholicism* (New York, 1999), 4–6; also M. J. Weaver and R. Scott Appleby, eds., *Being Right: Conservative Catholics in America* (Bloomington, 1995), 1–16.

or German concentration camps or in Japanese prison camps in the Dutch East Indies. Others had at least held a firm anti-German position. Both implicitly and explicitly, views adopted during the war played a role during the religious conflict of the 1960s. The conservatives frequently cast their opposition to the progressives as resistance to a hostile force that was trying to take over the church. Consequently, they often accused progressive priests of "betrayal" and "atrocities" and used military terminology to describe their own actions. Furthermore, they tended to judge individuals on the basis of their wartime beliefs and actions. The religious culture war of the 1960s was therefore also shaped by the actual war of the 1940s.

Given the diversity and complexity of the opposition to the progressives, the monolithic term "conservatives" – or, as the well-known Dutch historian and critic of the Catholic past L. J. Rogier dubbed them, "renegades" – is inadequate.[30] In the following sections, I will elaborate on these movements within Catholic conservatism and analyze their social background, viewpoints, and action repertoires.

An Old Elite Speaks Out: Loners and Opportunity Formations

A high-profile group within the mainstream conservative movement was composed of intellectuals who were opposed to both ecclesiastical and social renewal as such. They were part of a close-knit network, often based on both family and collegial relationships. Some spoke out on their own behalf; others forged strategic alliances with kindred spirits. They sometimes dubbed themselves "conservative" but more often "orthodox" or simply "worried." One of them, the later Cardinal Ad Simonis, referred to himself as "strict," in contrast to the "moderate" reformers during the Pastoral Council.[31]

These intellectuals – doctors, professors, lawyers, and architects, both priests and laity, men and a distinct group of women – owed much of their professional and social career to Catholic emancipation and the Dutch system of organizing educational institutions and social services on confessional lines (known as "pillarization"). Others had converted to Catholicism precisely because of its tradition and liturgical richness, which they regarded as a source of "warmth" in the cold modern world. As said earlier, several had been active members of clerical resistance

---

[30] L. J. Rogier, *Vandaag en morgen* (Bilthoven, 1974), 50.
[31] "Preciezen tegen de rekkelijken," *De Tijd*, January 1, 1969.

groups during the war, and some had even been decorated by the Dutch government for their wartime service. All felt they had much to lose in societal breakdown of authority at large and the progressive renewal of the church in particular.[32]

Their main form of action was writing letters of protest against objectionable developments. The letter to the editor was one of the most important and frequently employed avenues of religious resistance, not least because conservatives felt that it was more or less the only remaining means to make their voices heard in public. One of their most frequent complaints was that the media ignored them and paid disproportionate attention to progressive forces. Whenever events triggered their indignation, conservative Dutch Catholics could be counted on to write the newspapers and broadcasting companies, particularly the Catholic Broadcasting Company. Conservatives in other countries similarly relied on letters of protest, which functioned, as British historian Bill Schwarz has written, as the "conservative voice in a progressive landscape."[33]

Liturgical renewal was a particularly sensitive subject, prompting conservatives by the score to take pen in hand. The large numbers of letters published in Catholic newspapers are striking for their militancy and emotional tone. Changes such as the abolition of Latin and Gregorian chant in the liturgy, critical Bible study, the stripping of opulent traditional church interiors, and the lack of respect for ecclesiastical authority were a "historical atrocity" that created confusion and brutally deprived worshippers of valuable, centuries-old traditions without giving anything in return.[34]

A letter that twenty "worried" Catholics sent to a great number of priests in the Netherlands in 1968 was the product of a joint conservative effort. It complained that the priests had betrayed their sacred task and blamed them for causing "the present divide in the church." The letter ended with a call to put an end to this disorder and return to the foundations of Catholicism: "back to asceticism, faith, truth, servitude, and allegiance to God, goodness and authority."[35] Less well known were the

[32] Paul Luykx, *"Daar heerst nog poëzie, nog kleur, nog warmte"*. *Katholieke bekeerlingen en moderniteit in Nederland, 1880–1960* (Hilversum, 2009).

[33] See Bill Schwarz, "The Silent Majority: How the Private Becomes Political," chapter 7 in this volume.

[34] Frans Raymakers, letter about confession, *De Tijd/De Maasbode*, March 28, 1964.

[35] Letter by some Catholics to all the priests of the Roman Catholic Church in the Dutch Church Province about the divide between the present and the past, December 1968, Archive of the Pastoral Council of the Dutch Church Province, no. 801, CDC, Nijmegen.

letters of similar content that thousands of Catholics sent between 1966 and 1968 to the so-called council mailboxes that church authorities had created in each diocese to gauge lay opinion in preparation for the Pastoral Council. Hundreds of those who wrote made clear that they were confused about the changes in the church and felt that they were under attack.[36]

The conservatives' most effective weapon was invisible to the public. They informed Rome of who in the Netherlands was not adhering to doctrine, hoping that the curia would intervene to set matters right. An important intermediary in Rome was Sebastiaan Tromp, a conservative Jesuit who lectured in Rome at the Pontifical Gregorian University. Shortly before the war, Tromp had published a translation and commentary on the papal letter *Mit brennender Sorge*, in which he condemned National Socialist thinking even more strongly than Pope Pius XI had.[37] During the 1950s, acting as an official visitor on behalf of the Vatican, Tromp reported on grievances within the church in the Netherlands. From that time on, he was an important intermediary between Dutch conservatives and the curia. Another go-between was Monsignor Karel Kasteel, a member of the curia whose diplomat father was a famed resistance hero well known for his strict Catholic beliefs. He frequently organized private audiences for Dutch conservatives with the pope.

It was to a large extent due to these connections that Edward Schillebeeckx was summoned to explain his theology to the Congregation for the Doctrine of the Faith. The curia's suspicions had been aroused in large part by letters from Cornelia de Vogel, a classicist by profession and a convert to Catholicism who was strongly opposed to Schillebeeckx's radical views about Jesus. The Dutch conservatives' contact with the curia was also responsible for the pope's instruction to Professor Christine Mohrmann, a famed Latin scholar known for her conservative views on religion, that she support the newly appointed conservative Bishop Jo Gijsen by lecturing at his seminary.[38]

A third Roman address for Dutch conservative Catholics was the married couple Mieczyslaw de Habicht and Charlotte van Berckel. De Habicht was a former Polish diplomat who had played an important role at the Second Vatican Council as a lay auditor. He was a personal

---

[36] Jan Zuiker and Jan Westerlaak, *Brieven aan het Pastoraal Concilie: analyse van 2000 brieven toegezonden aan de Concilie-postbussen* (Nijmegen, 1968).

[37] J. T. P. Barten, "Tromp, Sebastiaan Peter Cornelis (1889–1975)," http://resources .huygens.knaw.nl/bwn1880-2000/lemmata/bwn1/tromp.

[38] Derks, "The Gospel of the Old," 146–150.

[handwritten: —the archbishop of Krakow C(1978-2005)]

friend of his compatriot Karol Woytila, later Pope John Paul II. His
Dutch wife Charlotte van Berckel had fought in the resistance during
the war and spent several years in Ravensbrück concentration camp for
women. Both were clearly opposed to the ecclesiastical developments in
the Netherlands, which they perceived as a betrayal of hard-won values.
They received like-minded people in Rome and later in their hometown
of Fribourg, and they shared their concerns with high-placed members of
the curia.[39] *[handwritten: in Switzerland]*

Confrontation

A second form of religious protest within the mainstream conservative
opposition was driven by groups of priests and laypeople who united to
act together against the reforms. Because of their distrust of the existing
media, they organized their own means of communication. They held
public meetings, wrote articles and booklets, and founded magazines.
Within a short span of time, four such groups came into being.

The most influential of these groups was Confrontatie (Confrontation), named after a journal of the same name. Among the founders was
a former editor of the Catholic newspaper *de Volkskrant*, which had
undergone an ideological shift in the early 1960s. Confrontatie wanted
to serve "the universal church" even if that meant criticizing the Dutch *[handwritten: Vatican II]*
bishops. The group focused its activism in opposing liturgical renewal and *[handwritten: he had backed the first, but not the second]*
the call for abolishing clerical celibacy. Not a formal organization, Con-
frontatie consisted of a group of individuals associated with the journal
who undertook a number of collective actions. At its height, the group's
journal (subtitled "Journal of Catholic Faith Proclamation, Faith Defense
and Faith Experience") had 5,000 paying subscribers. This readership was
not limited to the elite, as some scholars and critics have suggested, but
ranged from priests and intellectuals to teachers, nurses, and social workers. The journal was also distributed among Dutch Catholics in Flanders,
Luxembourg, Italy, the Congo, the Philippines, and Indonesia. Financial
support came from generous conservatives in the Netherlands as well as
from Rome. Tromp collected funds for the journal in Rome and also
contributed. The pope was reportedly aware of Confrontatie's activities
and supported them.[40]

---

39 Charlotte van Berckel, *Je vis en espoir. Mémoires* (1991); Auwerda, *De kromstaf als
   wapen.*
40 Bongaarts, letters to Tromp, 1964–1970, Archive Confrontatie, no. 98, CDC, Nijmegen.

Confrontatie organized a number of protest actions. In 1966, it drafted an anonymous protest claiming that 80 percent of the radical *New Catechism* was false. It was sent to the pope by a nuncio, Giuseppe Beltrani.[41] The petition, particularly the fact that it was anonymous, was sharply criticized by people from progressive circles.[42] Another public petition was issued when the papal encyclical *Humanae Vitae* (which officially continued the Vatican anti-contraceptives policy) in 1968 was ill received in progressive Dutch circles and even the episcopate publicly expressed its disappointment. Confrontatie collected 12,000 signatures.

[handwritten margin note: Humanae Vitae remarks in face largely ignored]

A year later, Confrontatie sent a telegram to the pope to complain about the Pastoral Council of the Dutch Church Province. The council, it charged, did not represent the view of the majority of Dutch Catholics and was not adhering to papal policy. Confrontatie activists withdrew from the conciliar preparatory commission on contemporary perceptions of faith because they felt it was not in line with the decrees of the Second Vatican Council. Shortly before, a meeting between representatives of Confrontatie and several well-known progressive thinkers arranged by Cardinal Alfrink ended in angry outbursts and mutual reproaches. During the Pastoral Council, issues such as the disconnection between sacramental priesthood and the obligation to celibacy were included on the agenda and put up to vote. When a majority voted in favor of progressive positions, conservatives, including the Confrontatie group, were shocked to the core. Their anxiety was shared by like-minded people in Germany, including Dean Gerhard Fittkau from Essen. He had been appointed as an official observer at the Pastoral Council and felt that the council's chief organizer, the Franciscan sociologist Walter Goddijn, had used opinion polls to steer the process in a particular direction. Fittkau, a former anti-Nazi, accused Goddijn of "pastoral technocracy" and charged the Dutch episcopate with excessive leniency.[43]

Groups of "Discontented"

Confrontatie was by no means the only group of discontented Catholics. In fact, the conservative landscape was fairly crowded. In the predominantly Catholic southern province of Limburg, there were two groups

---

[41] Petition to the pope, November 24, 1966, Archive Confrontatie, no. 2.

[42] "Dr. P. den Ottolander is een der initiatiefnemers smeekschrift aan de paus," *De Tijd*, November 23, 1966.

[43] Fittkau, letter to Bongaarts, July 17, 1976, Archive Confrontatie, no. 47.

led by priests that opposed liturgical renewal and decried the general decay of morals: Katholiek Leven (Catholic Life) and Waarheid en Leven (Truth and Life). The latter published a journal of a similar name that sold 8,000 copies each month. These groups were worried about the decline of priestly vocations (between 1943 and 1947, 160 men were admitted to the priesthood for every 100,000 Catholics in the Netherlands; the figure fell to 100 vocations for every 100,000 Catholics between 1957 and 1962). Compared to the prewar generation, the number of seminary students that successfully completed their studies dropped by 40 to 50 percent. Furthermore, the conservative priests believed that the remaining seminaries were completely dominated by the spirit of progressiveness.[44]

Besides Katholiek Leven and Waarheid en Leven, there were a number of smaller, informal orthodox groups that met irregularly. So-called Faith Groups of priests – again, active above all in Limburg – held readings and liturgical celebrations. The Association for Latin Liturgy had local chapters all over the country. There were also other local groups. They did not have fixed memberships, and individual believers sometimes participated in multiple groups.[45]

One of the less well-known groups of discontented Catholics was the seemingly secretive "Reymersbeek Circle." It drew its members from the nobility, the ranks of local officials and regional leaders, the clergy, and the intelligentsia. They met at Castle Reymersbeek, which belonged to an old aristocratic family. Attendance was strictly by invitation only, and the proceedings were confidential. All those involved were concerned about the democratization of the church, which they felt had gone way too far. Believing that the incumbent bishops were too weak, they tried to devise strategies to turn the tide. Fittkau sometimes attended these meetings. The efforts of this group helped pave the way for the appointment of a conservative bishop, Jo Gijsen, in 1972.[46]

The most militant group was Michael's Legion. Its name referred to the Archangel Michael as well as to a fascist, strongly anti-Semitic Romanian organization of the prewar period. This was important: the legion's leader, Louis Knuvelder, had published a biography of Arnold Meijer,

---

44 Bakvis, *Catholic Power in the Netherlands*, 105.
45 Conference at Castle Reymersbeek ["strictly confidential"], CDC, July 11, 1967, Archive Confrontatie, no. 32.
46 Conference at Castle Reymersbeek; Gian Ackermans, Peer Boselie, and Jan van der Wal, *Wij hebben het woord gekregen: schertsen en portretten van de solidariteitsgroep Limburg (1972–1981) en de Vereniging van Pastoraal Werkenden Roermond (1981–2006)* (Roermond, 2006).

the leader of the Dutch fascist movement Black Front, and writings on Franco. After the war, he became mesmerized by an Amsterdam visionary who claimed to receive messages from Mary, Lady of All Nations. She prophesied punishment if the world continued its deviation from the correct ecclesiastical path and was supported by various wealthy, conservative Amsterdam Catholics.[47]

Adherents of Michael's Legion came from all social backgrounds. The legion held regular meetings that drew several hundred attendees. On one occasion, interested journalists were – quite rudely – thrown out. After this meeting, the majority of the initiators resigned, because they did not agree with Knuvelder's "battle plan." Other conservatives harbored mixed feelings about the legion. Members of Confrontatie opposed Knuvelder's movement, which they considered too extreme and too much of a one-man show. Their objections were reinforced when the Vatican announced it had found the claims of the apparition of the Virgin in Amsterdam to be unsubstantiated. Out of loyalty to papal power, the Confrontatie leadership therefore objected to Knuvelder, whom they also distrusted because of his earlier fascist sympathies.[48]

A Separatist Movement

The Community of Saint Willibrord of Father Winand Kotte, a classics scholar and member of the Order of the Assumption, went a step further than groups like Confrontatie and Michael's Legion. Kotte shared a similar academic background with other traditionalists, but his energy as a letter writer exceeded theirs. Claiming he was working directly under the supervision of the pope, he bypassed the Dutch episcopate and tried to establish a new branch of the church altogether. Its name captured the spirit of the movement. Willibrord was the Irish monk who had brought Christianity to the Netherlands and thus signified authenticity. In the community's neo-Gothic church in Utrecht, the center of the archdiocese, more than 1,500 Catholics – among them numerous members of the upper class and members of parliament – gathered every week to celebrate traditional Tridentine Mass delivered in Latin and accompanied by

---

[47] Peter-Jan Margry, "Marian Interventions in the Wars of Ideology: The Elastic Politics of the Roman Catholic Church," *History and Anthropology* 20:3 (2009): 245–265.

[48] Tromp and Thywissen, report of visit to Bongaarts, August 31, 1966, Archive Confrontatie, no. 98; Bongaarts, letters to Tromp, March 1 and October 3, 1968, Archive Confrontatie.

Gregorian chant. The church had officially been closed by the archdiocese but was "saved" from demolition by Kotte and his adherents, who were able to gather enough money to keep its doors open. This heroic intervention, as supporters described the initiative, and the fact that the church's old interior had been maintained enhanced its status as a "locus of liturgical resistance."[49]

Kotte had his own flock of believers. He preached and heard confession, creating thereby in effect his own parish. He even pleaded explicitly for the creation of a separate diocese for conservative believers. He often sought the public limelight and announced to anyone who would listen that it was not he but rather Cardinal Alfrink and his reform-minded colleagues who bore responsibility for the division within the Catholic Church in the Netherlands. When Cardinal Alfrink, in his capacity as archbishop of Utrecht, forbade him to say mass or perform other pastoral duties in 1975, Kotte simply ignored the directive. Ultimately, the Roman Congregation for the Clergy, the highest authority, acquitted him of all charges – as Kotte had expected all along.[50]

Kotte held a special position within the conservative countermovement. He was a separatist who was trying to start his own church in the Netherlands but never turned against Rome. Lefebvre was better known (and more influential). Some of Kotte's adherents were Lefebvrians, but others, loyal to Rome, refused to follow Lefebvre in breaking entirely with the church. Confrontatie members disliked Kotte's self-glorification and the way his followers worshipped him. Moreover, as faithful followers of Rome and the universal church, they were disturbed by the prospect of the emergence of so-called *petites églises*, small separatist churches, and by the threat of sectarianism posed by Kotte and Lefebvre.[51]

Political Resistance

A final group chose not the ecclesiastical but the political domain to fight its battles. Sharing many of the beliefs of the other movements described here, this group differed in laying blame on Catholic politicians as well as on the clergy for failing to uphold traditional Catholic values. The

[49] Palm, *Moederkerk*, 225–230; Ton H. M. van Schaik, *Alfrink: een biografie* (Amsterdam, 1997), 396.

[50] Frank Bosman, "De gewonnen strijd van pater Kotte," http://frankgbosman.wordpress .com/2011/03/15/de-gewonnen-strijd-van-pater-kotte/ (accessed November 15, 2013).

[51] Bongaarts, letter to Tromp, November 11, 1969, Archive Confrontatie, no. 98; report Reymersbeek meeting, June 21, 1969.

Katholieke Volkspartij (Catholic People's Party) was increasingly willing to compromise with other parties and was working toward a union with Protestant parties. Conservatives accused the party of supporting the widespread use of contraceptives and of not being strict enough on drugs and pornography. They also feared it might relax its stand on abortion.

A first conservative response came in January 1971 when Tine Cuijpers-Boumans, who repeatedly referred publicly to the fact that she had been imprisoned in a Japanese camp during the war, founded the Nieuwe Roomse Partij (New Catholic Party). It was intended to be a counterforce to progressive Catholicism and moral decline, especially the liberal policy on contraceptives. "Close the abortion clinics, reopen the confessionals," was Cuijpers-Boumans's motto.[52] The party's leadership sympathized with the Marian movement, thus aligning political and religious conservatism in a very specific way. The party participated in the elections of 1971 but was not able to win enough votes to enter parliament. Another orthodox party was successful, however, receiving 0.9 percent of the valid votes in November 1972 and thereby winning one seat. The party soon imploded as a result of internal tensions and found itself entangled in legal disputes.[53]

Cuijpers-Boumans's leadership of the Nieuwe Roomse Partij was a reflection of the prominent role of women in the conservative movement. The issues of abortion and contraception, over which Dutch women were deeply divided at the time, were particularly important in mobilizing conservative women. Women made up the majority in small but highly visible pro-life groups, and many women supported the orthodox Catholic political party because of its firm anti-abortion stance. A couple of dozen conservative women activists gathered once a month to protest on the doorsteps of the Dutch parliament and of abortion clinics. Because of the liberality of Dutch regulations on abortion, these clinics attracted thousands of pregnant women from outside the Netherlands. In 1970, several hundred middle-class women, dissatisfied with the progressive leanings of mainstream Catholic women's organizations, joined forces and established a movement of their own. Led by the fierce Jo van den Toorn-Jansen, the wife of a former prisoner of war, Women in the Roman Catholic Church declared themselves loyal daughters of the

---

52 http://www.rijckheyt.nl/sjablonen/rijckheyt/pagina.asp?subsite=100%26pagina=91 (accessed November 29, 2013).

53 Emmanuel Thomassen, "Beuker, Klaas (1924–2000)," *Biografisch Woordenboek van Nederland*, http://www.historici.nl/Onderzoek/Projecten/BWN/lemmata/bwn6/beuker (accessed November 29, 2013).

church who opposed abortion, the use of contraceptives, and the general laxity of morals. Recently appointed conservative bishops embraced the new group and showed it favor at the expense of more progressive women's organizations. The constant anti-abortion protests inspired Minister of Justice Dries van Agt, himself a Catholic, to attempt to close down Bloemenhove, the country's largest abortion clinic, in 1974 and in 1976. Fierce resistance from feminist women and opposition parties in parliament finally forced van Agt to withdraw his plan.[54] The willingness of conservative politicians and the episcopacy to support groups like Women in the Roman Catholic Church attests to the impact they had, despite their relatively small membership, and also served to magnify that impact.

Conclusion

Contrary to the major historical accounts, the transformation of religious life in the Netherlands during the long 1960s was not solely of an (ultra)progressive nature. This period can also be seen as a moment in the radicalization of conservative Catholics. This chapter has shown that the focus on progressives was partly the product of early accounts by journalists who actively engaged in church reform during the 1960s and 1970s. Furthermore, it argued that the most influential historical studies of this era were written by people who had either been directly involved in the reform movement or explicitly sympathized with it. The products of this first wave of historical writing served as the basis for subsequent studies. This has led not only to a historiography dominated by studies of reformism, but also to the marginalization and stereotyping of "conservatives" as a coherent, elitist male group from the southern part of the country.

As the sources demonstrate, however, "conservatives" were far more diverse and more deeply anchored in Dutch society than previously assumed. Conservatives were men and women – the latter frequently assuming leadership roles – of all ages. Some acted on their own, others participated in one or more of the numerous conservative groups and organizations. The diversity in the social makeup of the conservative movement went hand in hand with a diversity of outlook. Conservative groups often found themselves disagreeing with one another and, giving

54 http://observatrix.blogspot.nl/2012/10/in-memoriam-mevrouw-jjm-van-den-toorn .html (accessed November 30, 2013).

in to the narcissism of small differences, engaged in constant feuds and wars of words.

Nevertheless, they did share certain traits and characteristics that set them apart from the "culture of the new." To explain the decline in church membership, they did not point to larger social processes such as individualization or secularization. Rather, they saw the progressive forces that had allegedly appropriated the heritage of Vatican II and would not hesitate to revolt against Rome as the culprits. For many conservatives, the chaotic changes of the long 1960s felt "like a break with the old world." The debate on renewal of the church trigged memories of World War II in many conservatives, especially those for whom the fight against the German occupiers had been a formative experience. For them, the religious culture war of the 1960s resembled the actual war of the 1940s.

The intertwining of these experiences produced a melancholic yet militant discourse. Conservatives felt a "historic homesickness": they longed to go back to a time when the Catholic Church had allegedly been big and powerful.[55] Consequently, their counteractions were phrased in terms that expressed this underlying sentiment: restoration, a holy fight, a crusade. Both the conservative and the progressive movements claimed to represent true or authentic Catholicism and aimed at purifying the world, but whereas the latter willingly displayed a rebellious disposition, the former underlined its loyalty. "A loyal majority" was how the conservatives identified themselves.[56] This self-representation echoes Richard Nixon's trope of the "silent majority," which apparently had traction in the ecclesiastical realm too.

The focus on the progressive forces in the Dutch Catholic Church in accounts of the long 1960s obscures the more multifaceted character of the era. Despite the prevailing progressive atmosphere, conservative Catholics were successful in creating a countermovement. The conservative network proved adept at using international media attention toward the Dutch Provos, as conservatives dubbed progressives, to raise concern in the curia. Rome became sufficiently worried about developments in the Netherlands that it appointed conservative bishops and thereby brought about a turning of the tide. The role of conservative Dutch Catholics in this process should not be underestimated. Ultimately, however, secularization would prove to be a much more powerful force for

---

[55] Bosman, "De gewonnen strijd van pater Kotte."
[56] Report of Reymersbeek meeting, April 12, 1968, Archive Confrontatie, no. 32.

change within the church than Dutch conservatives and progressives had anticipated while battling one another. At the beginning of the twenty-first century, the Netherlands is one of Europe's most secularized countries and has seen religious revivals only in its Protestant Bible Belt and its Muslim and Hindu communities.[57] Ironically, these are the denominations the conservative Catholics least want to associate with.

[57] Tomáš Sobotka and Feray Adigüzel, *Religiosity and Spatial Demographic Differences in the Netherlands* (Groningen, 2002).

PART V

LANGUAGES AND MEDIA STRATEGIES OF CONSERVATISM

12

Elisabeth Noelle-Neumann's "Spiral of Silence," the Silent Majority, and the Conservative Moment of the 1970s

Martin H. Geyer

References by Richard Nixon and his vice president, Spiro Agnew, to the silent majority in 1969–1970 echo in the work of the West German public opinion pollster, writer, and scholar Elisabeth Noelle-Neumann. In 1973–1974, Noelle-Neumann put forward her theory of the "spiral of silence" to explain the dynamics of public opinion.[1] A reviewer of the English translation of her book *Die Schweigespirale* (*The Spiral of Silence*) noticed "shades of the 'silent majority' of the Nixon era."[2] Indeed, Noelle-Neumann not only raised the question why "majorities" might opt for silence and remain silent in various situations but also tried to develop a general theory of public opinion.

Although heavily criticized, even ridiculed, by some from the very beginning, *Die Schweigespirale* has been debated ever since its publication, perhaps even more intensely in other parts of the world than in Germany.[3] That, however, is not the topic of this chapter, which looks

---

[1] Elisabeth Noelle-Neumann, "The Spiral of Silence: A Theory of Public Opinion," *Journal of Communication* 24 (1974): 43–51; Elisabeth Noelle-Neumann, "Die Schweigespirale," in Ernst Forsthoff and Reinhard Hörstel, eds., *Standorte im Zeitstrom. Festschrift für Arnold Gehlen zum 70. Geburtstag am 29 Januar 1974* (Frankfurt am Main, 1974), 299–330, reprinted in Jürgen Wilke, ed., *Öffentlichkeit als Bedrohung. Beiträge zur empirischen Kommunikationsforschung* (Freiburg, 1977) (this German version is quoted in the following); Elisabeth Noelle-Neumann, *Die Schweigespirale: Öffentliche Meinung, unsere soziale Haut* (Munich, 1980); Elisabeth Noelle-Neumann, *The Spiral of Silence: Public Opinion – Our Social Skin* (1st ed. Chicago, 1984; all of the following quotes are from the 2nd ed., 1993).

[2] Myra Marx Ferree, "Zeitgeist as an Empirical Phenomenon," *Contemporary Sociology* 14 (1985): 434–436, quote on 436.

[3] For a good introduction to the contemporary debate, see the volume and particularly the essay by Wolfgang Donsbach, Charles T. Salmon, and Yariv Tsfati, "The Legacy of

instead at the specific time when the theory was formulated. *Die Schweige-spirale* was an exercise in scholarly theory-building – Noelle-Neumann had been a professor of communications studies (*Kommunikationswis-senschaft*) at the University of Mainz since 1965 – with a very pragmatic angle. The book must be seen in the context of the conservative polit-ical strategies put forth by Noelle-Neumann, who was also a pollster, advisor to the government, and the owner-director of the Institut für Demoskopie (IfD), an institute that she and her husband had founded after the war.[4] From early in the history of the Federal Republic, Noelle-Neumann had been involved in predicting and explaining election results, a task that made her as much of a media star as one could become in a country where all television was public. Although the IfD remained independent, Noelle-Neumann was on close terms with the Christian Democratic Union (CDU). She not only provided the party with gen-eral public opinion data on a wide variety of issues but also advised it on how to recover from its losses in the 1969 and 1972 parliamentary elections.

Theory and practice were thus closely intertwined for Noelle-Neumann. The silence of silent majorities was both a theoretical and a very practical issue. In fact, Noelle-Neumann's theory had been derived largely from practical experience – she would have called it "life" – not vice versa.[5] As this chapter will demonstrate, the second half of the 1960s and the 1970s – in particular the years between the elections of 1969 and 1976 – provided Noelle-Neumann with the opportunity to carry out the research and field work that provided the empirical foundation for her theory of the spiral of silence. One aim of this chapter is to frame this history of the spiral of silence in the context of similar contemporary efforts at recasting and giving a new voice to conservatism. Another goal is to address questions about the ways in which strategies to mobilize silent majorities or to facilitate their self-mobilization actually worked. Nixon's appeal to the silent majority, cast in anti-intellectual and anti-elitist terms, was a call for those dismayed by recent political and cultural

---

Spiral of Silence Theory: An Introduction," in Wolfgang Donsbach, Charles T. Salmon, and Yariv Tsfati, eds.,*The Spiral of Silence: New Perspectives on Communication and Public Opinion* (New York, 2014), 1–18; Hans Mathias Kepplinger, "Three Contexts of the Spiral of Silence Theory," in ibid., 44–53.

[4] For a survey, see Anja Kruke, *Demoskopie in der Bundesrepublik Deutschland: Mein-ungsforschung, Parteien und Medien 1949–1990* (Düsseldorf, 2007).

[5] See also Kepplinger, "Three Contexts," 50–51.

developments to take action, to mobilize and participate in the political process at the grassroots level.[6] Some of this could be observed in Germany as well. Noelle-Neumann and other observers assumed, however, that the German silent majority was passive. Due in no small measure to the political system itself, the task of recasting conservatism and broadening its appeal was envisioned as, and indeed became, primarily a party affair, an elitist project driven by conservative intellectuals.

The Echoes of Nixon's Silent Majority Speech in Germany

Richard Nixon's reference to the silent majority in his address to the nation on the war in Vietnam on November 3, 1969, was indeed noted in West Germany. However, it was the various utterances of Vice President Spiro Agnew that attracted more attention.[7] Speaking in the name of the silent majority was unusual enough; but Agnew's disparagement of anti-war activists, "snobs," changing sexual mores, drug use, and crime, and in particular his attacks on the news media, received extensive coverage in the German media, more so than Nixon's talk of a silent majority. Such massive criticism of the press by so high-ranking a public official was as unusual in Germany as it had been in the United States up to that point. At any rate, the English term "silent majority" instantly caught on. Just as Nixon had hoped, it was considered a trademark of his presidency – and not merely by chance. At the end of November 1969, it was widely reported that the United States Information Agency had distributed a 16-minute-long film entitled *The Silent Majority* to 104 countries in 18 languages. This film, which had been produced for political television shows abroad, tried to depict "the silent majority" in visual terms. Its underlying message was that, the constitutional right of American citizens to voice their dissatisfaction notwithstanding, "politics that were formulated on the street" would bring only misfortune. As depicted in the film, the silent majority was made up of working people – more often than not white males – and the elderly. James Gallup appeared in the film

---

[6] Bruce J. Schulman and Julian E. Zelizer, eds., *Rightward Bound: Making America Conservative in the 1970s* (Cambridge, MA, 2008).

[7] For a summary of the events on the American side, see Robert Mason, *Richard Nixon and the Quest of a New Majority* (Chapel Hill, 2004), 27–30, 61–66; Jules Witcover, *Very Strange Bedfellows: The Short and Unhappy Marriage of Richard Nixon and Spiro Agnew* (New York, 2007), 35–110; "Agnew, Nixons Nixon," *Der Spiegel*, no. 48, November 24, 1969.

to explain how this silent majority could be grasped by public opinion polls.[8]

The term "silent majority" was intriguing to those who saw a similar constellation in West Germany. Americans who stood for law and order were tired of "anarchistic festivals" and found themselves nodding in agreement with Agnew's often controversial statements. Time and again, the German press stressed that the clashes and shootings on university campuses did not reflect the general mood in the United States, which was altogether much more conservative.[9] At the same time, many German commentators were just as quick as their American colleagues to point out that the invocation of the silent majority created adversarial groups and pitted those groups against each other. Nixon and Agnew appeared to be splitting the country politically and culturally.[10] It remains contested whether these conflicts reflected real divisions within American society or whether they were the result of demagoguery, be it on the part of the radical left or of the administration. Following a logic reminiscent of Carl Schmitt's theories, the Nixon administration divided society into clear camps of "enemies" and "friends": proponents of "law and order" and defenders of the war in Vietnam on one side, activists responsible for protests, riots, and disorder verging on terrorism on the other.

Unlike the outspoken minority, which had a clear counterpart in the Federal Republic, the American silent majority remained a rather unknown entity in Germany and therefore a subject of speculation. The German media had difficulty not only in defining it in social, ethnic, or religious terms but also in finding the German vocabulary to discuss it. The terms *Kleinbürger* and *Spießbürger* – loosely, petty middle class – were sometimes used but had a peculiar ring.[11] Those terms called to mind the provincialism and political quietism attributed to an older

---

[8] "Washingtons Film über die 'schweigende Mehrheit,'" *Frankfurter Allgemeine Zeitung* (*FAZ*), November 29, 1969; USIA, *The Silent Majority: Description of the Attitudes of the "Silent Majority" towards the War in Vietnam and the Anti-War Demonstrations*, Nixon Presidental Library and Museum, Yorba Linda, CA.

[9] Hans A. Weseloh, "Agnew – stille Hoffnung der Konservativen," *FAZ*, November 19, 1969; Heinz Barth, "Nixon übersteht die Krise," *Die Welt*, June 24, 1970; "Die Meinungsmacher in Amerika," *Der Donauschwabe*, June 6, 1970.

[10] "Nixon kehrt die Probleme unter den Teppich," *FAZ*, January 26, 1970 with references to Arthur Schlesinger; "Agnew attackiert wieder Opposition," *Frankfurter Rundschau*, May 25, 1970; see also Milton J. Rosenberg, Sidney Verba, and Philip E. Converse, *Vietnam and the Silent Majority: The Dove's Guide* (New York, 1970).

[11] "USA. Vertrauenskrise. Bleibt friedlich," *Der Spiegel*, no. 21, May 18, 1970; Sabina Lietzmann, "Finster in die siebziger Jahre. Amerika am Ende einer liberalen Ära," *FAZ*, December 27, 1969.

[handwritten: — peht bourgeois's]

generation estranged from modern life. But *Kleinbürger* and *Spießbürger* were also associated with an alluring albeit subliminal radicalism akin to what Richard Hofstader identified in the 1950s as "irrational politics" in the United States – a concept he used in trying to explain the attraction of the middle class to fascism.[12]

The New York "hard hat riots" of May 1970 appeared to prove the point. In an article titled "The Silent Majority Marches," Sabina Lietzmann, the long-time New York correspondent of the center-right *Frankfurter Allgemeine Zeitung* (FAZ), described an atmosphere, she wrote, that reminded her of the Sportpalast in Berlin as Josef Goebbels's delivered his "total war speech" in 1943 and the Nazi Party rallies at the Maifeld in Nuremberg. Unsettling to Lietzmann were not just the anti-Semitic slogans directed against New York's Republican mayor, John Lindsay (who was not Jewish), and the invectives against the hippies and students ("Schlagt sie tot, die Taugenichtse": "Beat them to death, the good-for-nothings"), but also the apparent support the bystanders showed for the rioting construction workers. In tune with American commentators, the German correspondent depicted these events as a failure on the part of Nixon and his vice president and presented them as a reminder of the dangers of populist mobilization. Instead of uniting the country, the administration was dividing it.[13]

[handwritten margin note: 1965-73 — Abe Beame, his successor, was NYC's first Jewish mayor]

References to the silent majority raised the question of what the German equivalent was. Quite untypical was the call of the Christian Democratic politician Bernhard Vogel to include the "silent majority" of Catholics into the upcoming synod of the church, which could be understood as a call to increase democratic participation in the ongoing process of church reform.[14] However, the idea of "silence" was disconcerting to most observers, for it contradicted the idea of the politically sovereign citizen. In his speech on the occasion of the twenty-fifth anniversary of the German capitulation on May 8, 1945, the Social Democratic chancellor Willy Brandt stressed that the Federal Republic of Germany had neither a "schweigende Mehrheit" nor an anti-democratic minority of any consequence. Brandt's message was that, in light of the actions of Hitler, Germans, including the younger generation, had a particular

[handwritten: (1969-74)]

[handwritten margin note: it sure) well does now as of late was)]

[12] Richard Hofstadter, *The Paranoid Style in American Politics and Other Essays* (London, 1966).

[13] Sabina Lietzmann, "Nixon Fehleinschätzungen," FAZ, May 13, 1970; Sabina Lietzmann, "Die schweigende Mehrheit marschiert," FAZ, May 19, 1970; "Schweigende Mehrheit marschiert weiter," FAZ, May 22, 1970.

[14] Erik-Michael Bader, "Das Wagnis der deutschen Synode," FAZ, April 28, 1970.

responsibility and had to be politically aware.[15] There could be no doubt that the Social Democratic slogan *Mehr Demokratie wagen* – "Daring more democracy" – was incompatible with silence. This explains why the silent majority was often associated with anachronistic nostalgia. Journalist Johannes Gross identified West Germany's silent majority as "the large number of those among whom resentment against progress and its prophets is building" and noted that many politicians were taking the "discovery" of the silent majority as an opportunity "to start trading in political antiques." That approach, Gross suggested, would be fruitless. Because the silent majority is not politically engaged, he speculated, the CDU should instead try to capitalize on the silent majority's negative inclination – its tendency to vote against what it opposes rather than for the politicians and policies it supports.[16]

The Pervasive Feeling of Being Silenced

After their defeat in the general election of 1972, the CDU and its Bavarian sister party, the Christian Social Union (CSU), had good reason to be concerned about silent majorities within their own ranks. Since the late 1960s, Noelle-Neumann had been making disconcerting observations about silence, majorities, and political mobilization. On the basis of materials and information provided by Noelle-Neumann, Kurt Reumann, a journalist with the *FAZ* who had earlier been employed by IfD, described a curious phenomenon in a full-page article that ran in early 1973: adherents of the SPD demonstrated and expressed their convictions more openly than members of the CDU/ CSU. In fact, a considerable number of CDU/CSU supporters and party members denied having voted for the parties. This was most obvious in post-election polls. In 1970, 52 percent of voters polled said they had voted for the SPD in the 1969 Bundestag election; in a 1972 poll, the figure was 53 percent. According to the official election results, however, far fewer voters had in fact backed the SPD: only 42 percent. In 1972, when the Social Democrats gained in strength (as did their coalition partner, the small, liberal Free Democratic Party, FDP), this phenomenon could be observed again. Reumann also noted that CDU/CSU voters were apparently "insecure" and thus ready to join the majority opinion, which favored the Social Democrats

---

[15] "Unsere Wirklichkeit durch Hitlers Niederlage entstanden," *FAZ*, May 9, 1970.

[16] Johannes Gross, "Spiegel Essay: Konservativ auf deutsch," *Der Spiegel*, no. 12, March 15, 1971, 196–197.

and the FDP. Unlike the conservative clientele, Social Democrats openly professed their allegiance to their party, for example by wearing campaign buttons. More importantly, they were far more versed – in the words of Reumann, "downright discussion-addicted" – in abstract political and theoretical debates, which gave them an advantage in private conversations and public debates. According to Noelle-Neumann, this phenomenon was quite recent and had not appeared before 1969. It became challenging to predict elections accurately on the basis of the available polls because figures in pre-election polls had to be adjusted in a complicated process, which in turn raised some questions as to the political influence of pollsters.[17]

Reumann's article was based on a wealth of survey data as well as, most likely, the analysis of the 1972 elections that Noelle-Neumann's IfD had prepared for the CDU. In many respects, this report did not say anything that many observers inside and outside the party did not know already.[18] The CDU, it explained, had found it difficult to mobilize not only its traditional voters but also its card-carrying members; there existed a "resigned disinclination" (*resignierte Abneigung*) to take a prominent stance. The IfD report also pointed out, however, that many voters detected an "increasing interchangeability" of the two major parties and that voters' trust in the SPD and confidence in its competence on core policy issues had grown. Clearly, the SPD had been flourishing in a favorable "opinion climate."[19] That affected issues of the greatest importance to the CDU/CSU and conservatives generally, including abortion, the cohabitation of unmarried couples, the death penalty, the presence of foreign workers, and, not least, relations with the Soviet Union, Poland, and the German Democratic Republic.[20] Nothing better illustrates this experience of isolation than the oft-cited complaint that no one dared to call themselves a "conservative" any longer or to take a "conservative position," especially because the left conflated

---

[17] Kurt Reumann, "Schwierigkeiten beim Bekenntnis zur Union," *FAZ*, January 27, 1973.

[18] See the debate during a CDU party retreat that took place from January 27–29, 1973, with presentations by Noelle-Neumann, Werner Kaltefleiter, and the sociologists Max Kaase and Erwin K. Scheuch, Archiv für Christlich-Demokratische Politik, Sankt Augustin (ACDP) 07-001-930.

[19] Elisabeth Noelle-Neumann and Friedrich Tennstädt, *Rückblick auf die Bundestagswahl 1972*, January 15, 1973, unverzeichnet, Pressedokumentation, ACDP.

[20] Noelle-Neumann, "Spiral of Silence" (1974), 46. The *Jahrbuch für Demoskopie* published by the IfD is a mine of data. The archive of IfD in Allensbach contains approximately 300,000 questions, which are now stored electronically; Kepplinger, "Three Contexts," 48.

conservatism and fascism.[21] Underlying all this was a pervasive feeling among conservatives that they had been silenced.[22]

As early as 1965, Noelle-Neumann became aware of her own defensive position vis-à-vis the changing climate of public opinion when, for the first time, her students hissed at her use of the term "elite education" to describe the function of the university. Five years later, the very foundations of her convictions appeared to be under attack in the Federal Republic: traditional understandings of liberty and justice, democracy and peace, the idea of a free market economy, the concept of totalitarianism.[23] The willingness of the young to speak out, raise their voices, and "question things" (*hinterfragen*) stood in contrast to the quietism of earlier generations of students.[24] The confrontation with leftist students left many professors with lasting scars; this was certainly true for Noelle-Neumann. She would later recall her conflicts with radical students time and again. Classes were regularly interrupted, and in 1971, her institute at the University of Mainz was "occupied." The press reported that students and apparently a few members of the non-professorial teaching staff criticized Noelle-Neumann's "autocracy" and her use of her university position to acquire contracts for her IfD as well as her absenteeism due to health problems. They called for co-determination (*Mitbestimmung*) in setting the curriculum and for more "critical reading." The university rector refused to call in the police to deal with the occupiers and insisted that the conflict at the institute be settled internally; according to Noelle-Neumann, the rector even encouraged the students. No doubt, equally disheartening for her was that some of the more important newspapers and *Der Spiegel* sided with the students: *Die Zeit* went so far as to report that the students considered "their professor, in plain language, corrupt."[25]

---

[21] See the contributions by Martina Steber (chapter 14) and Anna von der Goltz (chapter 4) in this volume.

[22] In the United States, this feeling was expressed most clearly by Daniel Patrick Moynihan; Steven R. Weisman, ed., *Daniel Patrick Moynihan: A Portrait in Letters of an American Visionary* (New York, 2010), 238, 252.

[23] Elisabeth Noelle-Neumann, *Die Erinnerungen* (Munich, 2006), 267.

[24] Josef Kopperschmidt, "'So gar kein Volk des Wortes'? Vermutungen über das öffentliche Reden in Deutschland," in Martin Wengeler, ed., *Deutsche Sprachgeschichte nach 1945: Diskurs- und Kulturgeschichtliche Perspektiven* (Hildesheim, 2003), 301–315; Martin H. Geyer, "War over Words: The Search for a Public Language in West Germany," in Willibald Steinmetz, ed., *Political Languages in the Age of Extremes* (Oxford, 2011), 293–330.

[25] "Ein gewöhnlicher Streit," *Die Zeit*, January 22, 1971; "Ein Attest verbietet Streit mit Studenten," *Süddeutsche Zeitung*, January 8, 1971; "Noelle-Neumann, Pause im Fond," *Der Spiegel*, no. 6, February 1, 1971; Noelle-Neumann, *Erinnerungen*, 274–276.

Noelle-Neumann was not alone in interpreting student radicalism as a new version of totalitarianism. Marxist lingo was considered to be a new form of "newspeak." That Noelle-Neumann had used the "newspeak" of the Third Reich in her student days and in her doctoral dissertation on public opinion in the United States was to become an issue in Germany later in her life. In America, however, criticism of her had been voiced since the 1960s, and her critics became particularly loud when she was appointed to teach at the University of Chicago in the 1980s.[26] The references to *"schweigen"* (note the active form of the German verb, which is captured in English in expressions like being or keeping silent) during the Third Reich were highly contested, especially when students started to ask critical questions and attacked the silence of individual persons and the *"beschweigen"* – hushing – of the Nazi past. No doubt, this silence was to haunt a whole generation. Born in 1916, Noelle-Neumann belonged to the age cohort of the Munich student resistance group Die Weiße Rose, whose members had actually spoken out against the regime, quite unlike the great majority of their peers, and had been sentenced to death. At least in her memoirs, Noelle-Neumann left no doubt that she had been well informed about the mass killings of Jews in the east, not least because her husband Erich Peter Neumann had been a propaganda officer in the German army during the war.[27]

Explaining the Silence of Silent Majorities

The aforementioned 1973 article in the *FAZ* was the wider German public's first introduction to the spiral of silence. The year before, Noelle-Neumann had presented some of her ideas in a paper at a conference of the International Congress of Psychologists in Tokyo. Her presentation was apparently a huge success and paved the way for considerable inter-national academic recognition. In 1974, she presented her fully developed argument in an essay entitled "The Spiral of Silence: A Theory of Public

[26] Noelle-Neumann, *Erinnerungen*, 131–132.
[27] Unfortunately Noelle-Neumann never dealt with historical issues of silence in general and silence during the Nazi period in particular. For her own description of her past during this time, see Noelle-Neumann, *Erinnerungen*, 38–137, especially 137, about her "feeling of complicity," which, however, refers primarily to the German people. Leo Bogart, "The Pollster and the Nazis," *Commentary* 92 (1991): 47–49, and Christopher Simpson, "Elisabeth Noelle-Neumann's 'Spiral of Silence' and the Historical Context of Communication Theory," *Journal of Communication* 46 (1996): 149–173 had some influence; in many respects very deficient is Jörg Becker, *Elisabeth Noelle-Neumann: Demoskopin zwischen NS-Ideologie und Konservatismus* (Paderborn, 2013).

Opinion," which appeared in both German and English and which was subsequently expanded into a book.[28]

How is it possible that people are silent even if numerically in the majority? How is this silence related to the fact that representatives of minorities may at times not only be vocal but also convey the impression that their views are held by the majority and even come to determine majority opinion? What role do the media play in this process? These were the fundamental questions Noelle-Neumann posed. She found the answers in the processes of a spiraling of silence, whereby individuals and groups are silenced step by step and a new dominant opinion emerges amid the resulting silence. Building on earlier reflections, Noelle-Neumann developed her theory to explain this dynamic in a relatively short period between 1972 and 1974.

Quoting a myriad of authors from John Locke to the German sociologist Ferdinand Tönnies and relying on the results of opinion polls conducted by the IfD, Noelle-Neumann came to argue that most people avoid expressing their beliefs openly unless they are convinced that their environment supports them. In other words, individuals are driven by a "fear of isolation," a well-established and often-tested argument that she derived from social psychology research. Consequently, one of her hypotheses was that silence might be more comfortable for individuals despite the fact that they shared the viewpoint held by a majority; the crucial point is that this majority remains silent, thus creating the impression (as measured by opinion polls) that its members are in a minority. Conversely, "a minority that is convinced of its future dominance and is therefore willing not only to convey its views but also to confront a majority that doubts whether its opinion will stand the test of time and is therefore less willing to voice it has a great chance to see its opinion become the dominant one."[29] Those who perceive widespread support for their opinion voice it more often, thereby reinforcing their ideas in a way that makes popular support for such opinions appear stronger than it actually is. A critical point was that those who were insecure and undecided "jumped on the bandwagon," as Noelle-Neumann argued, drawing on the work of Paul Lazarsfeld; in other words, they were "running with the pack," a "situation [that] applies, more or less, to all mankind."[30]

[28] The Tokyo presentation became published as "Kumulation, Konsonanz und Öffentlichkeitseffekte," in Jürgen Wilke, ed., Öffentlichkeit als Bedrohung: Beiträge zur empirischen Kommunikationsforschung, 2nd ed. (Freiburg, 1979), 127–168.

[29] Noelle-Neumann, "Schweigespirale" (1977), 199.

[30] Noelle-Neumann, *Spiral of Silence* (1993), 6.

One might add that the expression "jumping on the bandwagon" has more positive connotations than its German equivalent, being a *Mitläufer* (fellow-traveler, sympathizer), which calls to mind a practice widespread during the Nazi era. *and in relation to communism*

Noelle-Neumann also drew on the famous social psychology studies Solomon E. Asch carried out in the early 1950s and Stanley Milgram built upon in the 1960s, which were part of a larger postwar debate on the "authoritarian character." She argued that, under social pressure, the fear of "social isolation" might motivate individuals to join majorities and to remain silent. Her controversial explanation of how this happened was quite original – to the point of ridiculousness in the eyes of some critics: each individual, she maintained, has a "quasi statistical organ," a sense that allows them not only to perceive but also to gauge the "climate of opinion" and thus majority and minority opinions.[31] Public opinion was therefore not an abstract variable that could be measured only by pollsters; individuals too had this ability. In fact, public opinion was "our social skin" (the subtitle of her book). A peculiar – and empirically hard to prove – assumption of hers was that people not only assess and develop a subjective sense of the "opinion climate," as social psychologists commonly argued at the time, but that this awareness shapes people's willingness to express their views.[32]

This "opinion climate" may refer to very different things: to small groups with their "groupthink," as other authors were to argue later, or to society at large. Noelle-Neumann's empirical data were collected through general surveys conducted in West Germany and through special surveys in which participants were asked whether they would speak out or remain silent on a controversial issue in conversation with a small group of strangers in a train compartment. The "quasi-statistical" sense could be activated in any local and social setting. However, Noelle-Neumann, the professor of communications, left no doubt that the mass media were highly influential regarding the general "opinion climate," a point crucially important for the debates of the 1970s. Against the academic

---

[31] Noelle-Neumann, *Spiral of Silence* (1993), 9. The Swiss sociologist Peter Atteslander spoke of a "modern 'sozial-dermatology,'" in "Die Schweigespirale: Eine neue Theorie der öffentlichen Meinung oder Quatsch mit wissenschaftlicher Soße?" *Bild der Wissenschaft* 9 (1980), 96–97, quote on 96.

[32] But are such questions that tap people's beliefs about what the general public thinks methodologically sound indicators for belonging to a majority or minority? Jörg Matthes and Andrew F. Hayes, "Methodological Conundrums in Spiral of Silence Research," in Donsbach et al., *The Spiral of Silence: New Perspectives*, 54–64, 56; see also Jacob Shamir, "Pluralistic Ignorance and the Spiral of Silence Meet," in ibid., 153–160.

mainstream in her field (although not against more critical authors at the time), she argued that modern media, particularly television, had a greater impact in shaping public opinion than traditional newspapers. She had first presented this argument in a speech she gave in 1969 at an event sponsored by ZDF, West Germany's second public television broadcasting network. As her onetime student and eventual successor at the University of Mainz, Hans Mathias Kepplinger, recalls, this argument put Noelle-Neumann at odds with academic theory. She broke a taboo by arguing that the media were anything but a negligible factor in shaping public opinion.[33] Her 1972 lecture "Return to the Concept of Powerful Mass Media" received great attention. For reasons that we will come back to later in this chapter, the press and television were to play an increasingly important role in her elaboration of the spiral of silence.[34]

Without reflecting explicitly on the American debate, the silence of the "silent majority" was the central theme of *Die Schweigespirale*. It was tantamount to a scholarly elaboration on Nixon's brief description in his November 3 speech, and there can be no doubt that vital aspects of Agnew's critique of the liberal press resonate in Noelle-Neumann's account of the influence of the media.[35] In fact, she attached great importance to the formulation of the term silent majority in the United States, as the (stylistically deficient) sentence quoted here shows: "It [the silent majority] was a reality in which they [the members of the silent majority] themselves had participated, although they were not fully conscious of it since it had not been explicitly labeled."[36] No doubt, Nixon would have agreed that he acted as a voice on behalf of the silent majority.

However, the case Noelle-Neumann made for the silent majority was very much in tune with the aforementioned critical perspective predominant in Germany: the silent majority was weak, passive, and easy to manipulate; one of her examples was – hypothetical – passengers in a train compartment who were asked whether members of the German Communist Party could become judges and who, when they sensed that they "lacked support from the media [on this issue], evolved into a silent

[33] Kepplinger, "Three Contexts," 49.

[34] Elisabeth Noelle-Neumann, "Der getarnte Elefant," in Wilke, *Öffentlichkeit als Bedrohung*, 115–126; Noelle-Neumann, "Spiral of Silence" (1974), 50f.; Kepplinger, "Three Contexts," 47–48.

[35] In her notes for her university seminar in the spring of 1969 she had stacked, apparently some time later, clippings of the media reaction to Agnew, Privatarchiv Prof. Dr. Elisabeth Noelle-Neumann, Piazzogna, Switzerland, Compactus 18, Seminar SoSe 1969. I thank Erich Ralph Schmidt for making these papers available to me. Further research in her archive might reveal more material.

[36] Noelle-Neumann, *Spiral of Silence* (1993), 23.

majority."[37] In such contexts, she would speak of the "powerlessness of a majority that does not express itself" and would refer to the recently invented "formula of the silent majority," meaning that "a silent majority alone can hardly exert pressure."[38] Noelle-Neumann maintained that people who were less educated and more heavily exposed to television were particularly prone to shifting their opinion. It is thus not surprising that she included James Bryce, a nineteenth-century British ambassador and scholar who had commented on the "fatalism of the multitude," as one of the first people to describe what would later be called the silent majority.[39] No doubt, this pejorative understanding of the masses also explains her misinterpretation, namely that "Vice President Agnew's *complaint* about the 'silent majority' became justifiably famous because it touched on a reality that many people felt."[40] This idea was based on the notion that the silent majority could not activate itself; instead it needed (opinion) leadership and direction. This argument was not altogether foreign to American ears. In the words of Daniel Patrick Moynihan, "the silent majority is silent because it has nothing to say."[41]

Noelle-Neumann's laboratory was contemporary Germany, focusing above all on events since the mid-1960s and, in particular, the 1972 election. Broad as the argument was in terms of its claims to represent a general theory, the empirical base of the argument was strikingly limited. It is hard to imagine Noelle-Neumann explaining how the spiral of silence worked in Nazi Germany or addressing Germany's postwar silence about its past, not to mention other issues of acquiescence in modern societies.[42]

More Than a Theory: Breaking the Spiral of Silence

If a "strategy of public opinion" were possible, a ZDF reporter asked Noelle-Neumann in 1974, what would it entail? Her answer to this

---

37 Noelle-Neumann, *Spiral of Silence* (1993), 201.

38 Noelle-Neumann, "Kumulation," 151; Noelle-Neumann, "Schweigespirale" (1977), 183.

39 Noelle-Neumann, *Spiral of Silence* (1993), 93. She also regularly cited Alexis de Tocqueville, however, not his critical remarks in *Democracy in America*.

40 Noelle-Neumann, *Spiral of Silence* (1993), 23 (italics added).

41 Moynihan to Nixon, November 13, 1970, quoted in Mason, *Nixon*, 116.

42 George Steiner, *Language and Silence: Essays on Language, Literature and the Inhuman* (London, 1967); Thomas Mathiesen, *Silently Silenced: Essays on the Creation of Acquiescence in Modern Society* (Winchester, 2004); Adam Jaworski, *The Power of Silence: Social and Pragmatic Perspectives* (Newbury Park, 1993); Lynn Thiesmeyer, ed., *Discourse and Silencing: Representation and the Language of Displacement* (Amsterdam and Philadelphia, 2003).

undoubtedly prearranged question was straightforward: first, there would be "the battle for public opinion." Then the party in question would have to mobilize its supporters and encourage them to speak out publicly. It had to make sure they were both heard and seen.[43] Making the silence of the supposedly silenced majority noticeable and speaking on its behalf was indeed the more practical aspect of her *Die Schweigespirale*. From the very beginning, the book was an attempt to explain public opinion theoretically and, at the same time, to apply its findings strategically. In fact, speaking publicly about a spiral of silence, how it worked and how it could be broken, was part of a strategy of creating visibility – with Noelle-Neumann herself playing a very prominent role in this media game. She always insisted that her job as a pollster and advisor was comparable to that of an "auditor," meaning that she only gauged, compared, and summarized public opinion but did not create it.[44] Yet she certainly did her part by raising issues and making certain things visible and others not. No doubt many German conservatives would have been jealous had they known how effectively and professionally Nixon's staff had organized the media campaign in conjunction with his aforementioned speech in 1969: this included the letters and telegrams that flooded the White House (not least thanks to prearranged special rates with AT&T), the page-long newspaper articles by supporters who spoke out for the silent majority, and the film by the U.S. Information Agency.[45]

In practical terms, this strategy was not directed toward an abstract silent majority but toward what appeared to be the lukewarm CDU rank-and-file and politically undecided middle-of-the-road voters. Politically, the Federal Republic was split between three major parties: the CDU/CSU, the SPD, and the FDP. All three had a large core of loyal voters, but the number of voters willing to switch their party preferences was increasing. The Social Democrats were making inroads with Catholics and women, two groups who had traditionally tended to support the CDU/CSU. With election participation jumping to over 90 percent of all eligible voters (as

43 Bundespresseamt, transcript of the TV Program *Fragen zur Zeit*, July 14, 1974, "Die Schweigespirale" Gespräch mit Prof. Elisabeth Noelle-Neumann, ACDP, Pressedokumention, Noelle-Neumann 1964–1976.

44 Noelle-Neumann, "Staatliche Kontrolle für Meinungsforscher," *Neue Ruhr-Zeitung*, August 15, 1969; see Kruke, *Demoskopie*, 149–161, 475–489; Thomas Mergel, *Propaganda nach Hitler: Eine Kulturgeschichte des Wahlkampfs in der Bundesrepublik 1949–1990* (Göttingen, 2010), 94–101.

45 Game Plan for the President's November 3rd Speech, Nixon Presidential Library, Vietnam National Security Council (NSC) Files. Vietnam Subject Files, Box 79, File Nr. 3: Notes for President's November 3, 1969 Speech.

opposed to registered voters in the United States) in the 1970s, the number
of those who were silent in the sense that they abstained from voting was
extremely small indeed. Consequently, the major parties found themselves
competing for the growing number of undecided or unaffiliated voters
without whom they could not hope to win an electoral majority.

The CDU/CSU suffered an electoral defeat in 1972 that was hefty and
shocking. For the first time since the founding of the Federal Republic,
the CDU/CSU was not the strongest party in the Bundestag. Breaking the
spiral of silence became a part of the CDU's overall electoral strategy.[46]
The new head of the party was Helmut Kohl, at the time minister president of Rhineland-Palatine, with whom Noelle-Neumann was on close
terms. Together with Kurt Biedenkopf, the new secretary general of the
party, Kohl promised to find a way out of the impasse and to modernize
the staid and stodgy image plaguing the party. A look through the party's
archival records reveals the emerging optimism and enthusiasm at the
time. Planning for the next election was conducted with great precision
on several levels.[47] First, efforts were made to reorganize and centralize
the party. Second, the fundamental overhaul of the party program, which
is so important to German parties (even if traditionally less so for the
CDU/CSU than for the SPD), was already on the agenda, but the work
was intensified and finally completed in 1977. This involved a reposi-
tioning of the party on major political, social, and economic questions.
Third, new emphasis was placed on social science expertise, not least
because there was a general feeling that not just the CDU but conservatives in general fell below the state of the art in contemporary theory.
Die Schweigespirale has to be seen in this larger context of new theoretical ambitions of conservatives in general and of Noelle-Neumann in
particular, the development of which unfolded quite independently in
new intellectual forums with many links to universities.[48] Fourth, market researchers invested considerable time in coming up with new campaign slogans and designing posters for the party. The new CDU leadership set up a group to reflect on the semantics of campaigns by using

---

[46] Frank Bösch, *Macht und Machtverlust: Die Geschichte der CDU* (Stuttgart and Munich,
2002); on the following, see also Kruke, *Demoskopie*.

[47] The following is based on the rich and readily available sources in the archive of the CDU
(ACDP), which cannot be treated here in detail. See also Bösch, *Macht*; Wulf Schönbohm,
*Die CDU wird moderne Volkspartei: Selbstverständnis, Mitglieder, Organisation und
Apparat 1950–1980* (Stuttgart, 1985).

[48] Nikolai Wehrs, *Protest der Professoren. Der „Bund Freiheit der Wissenschaft" in den
1970er Jahren* (Göttingen, 2014).

up-to-date research on language and language strategy (discussed further
below), compared to which the then widely read reflections on political
language by William Safire, an experienced PR man and speechwriter
for Nixon and Agnew, seemed almost old-fashioned (albeit much more
pleasant to read).[49] Fifth, great effort was made to mobilize the rank-
and-file membership and thus prevent a repeat of the obvious mistakes of
1972. Handouts were distributed on how to speak in public, on placing
bumper stickers on cars, and wearing campaign buttons – all steps aimed
at breaking the spiral of silence.[50]

That the business of public opinion research could also be to shape
public opinion was hinted at in IfD surveys, which spotlighted these strategies and made them a public issue. For example, IfD asked respondents
which party's bumper sticker was most likely to be found on a car parked
at the side of the road with its tires slashed. The answer is not difficult
to guess – and the hypothetical case became heatedly debated in public
(including in classrooms, as the author remembers).[51] Noelle-Neumann
liked to tell the story of a female student at the University of Mainz who
one day wore a Christian Democratic campaign button, although Noelle-
Neumann knew the student was not a party member. Asked why she did
this, the student said that she just wanted to find out what it felt like.
By the time Noelle-Neumann met her later in the day, the student had
taken the button off: "It was too awful," she said.[52] That was exactly the
point: to break the spiral of silence, it would be necessary to overcome
such pain and to put an end to such stigmatization.

In the 1976 election, judging by the results, the conservatives apparently did almost everything right. At least this was the tenor of the post-
election analysis provided by the IfD.[53] The CDU/CSU alliance had gained
in strength considerably. Unlike his predecessor four years earlier, the
Union's new lead candidate, Helmut Kohl, was apparently highly attractive to voters. Above all, the CDU/CSU had been successful in mobilizing party members and unaffiliated voters and had achieved the goal of

---

49 William Safire, *The New Language of Politics: A Dictionary of Catchwords, Slogans
    and Political Usage* (New York, 1972); see also Geyer, "War over Words."
50 Hauptabteilung Öffentlichkeitsarbeit, May 9, 1975, Mitgliedermobilisierung, ACDP
    07-001-11493.
51 Noelle-Neumann, *Spiral of Silence* (1993), 52, 54.
52 Noelle-Neumann, *Spiral of Silence* (1993), 4.
53 IfD, Bundestagswahl 1976. Ergebnis einer Nachwahl-Analyse im Überblick, 1977,
    Pressedokumentation ACDP; Peter Radunski, Kurze Auszüge wichtiger Thesen aus der
    Nachwahlanalyse des IfD, ACDP 07-001-17026.

breaking the spiral of silence. With 48.6 percent of the vote (1972: 44.9), the CDU/CSU had the largest block of seats in the Bundestag, but they were just shy of a majority; the SPD–FDP governing coalition under Helmut Schmidt thus remained in power.

Could the outcome not have been even better? Some in the CDU/CSU thought the parties could have won an outright majority and speculated that they had been hindered by the highly controversial campaign slogan "Freedom instead of socialism," which Noelle-Neumann had strongly backed.[54] The slogan was controversial and polarizing, even within the CDU. It could be and was indeed understood as juxtaposing the Social Democrats, who spoke for a "democratic socialism," and the Christian Democrats, who stood for freedom. In keeping with the CDU's older Cold War slogan of "Freedom or socialism," the new slogan was also framed within the logic of German–German division, in which the Federal Republic stood for freedom and the German Democratic Republic stood for a "communism that called itself 'socialism.'"[55] Undoubtedly, the slogan "Freedom instead of socialism" was meant to polarize. As Noelle-Neumann, sounding rather like Carl Schmitt, had argued during the campaign, the objective for the party was to "polarize and stake its ground in the election campaign."[56] Another point was equally important. IfD registered both long- and, especially, short-term shifts of opinion with respect to the attraction of "socialism," which was on the decline, and "freedom," which was on the rise. It was important that the CDU/CSU take advantage of this climate of opinion, she advised: a silent majority does not exert pressure, but "a noticeably growing [political] faction certainly does."[57]

Noelle-Neumann found yet another reason why the CDU/CSU was at a disadvantage. As she argued before and especially after the 1976 election, radio, television, and the print media were not favorable to the CDU/CSU in general and Helmut Kohl in particular. He appeared not

---

[54] Mergel, *Propaganda*, 268–270; Fritz Hermann, "Slogans und Schlagwörter," in Jochen Bähr et al., eds., *Sprachliche Kürze: Konzeptionelle, strukturelle und pragmatische Aspekte* (Berlin, 2007), 459–478; Martin H. Geyer, "Rahmenbedingungen: Unsicherheit als Normalität," in Martin H. Geyer, ed., *Geschichte der Sozialpolitik in Deutschland*, vol. 6, *Deutschland 1974–1982: Der Sozialstaat im Zeichen wirtschaftlicher Rezession* (Baden-Baden, 2007), 1–109, 48–49.

[55] Elisabeth Noelle-Neumann, "Eine Fall-Studie: Deutsche Bundestagswahl 1976," in European Society of Opinion and Market Research, ed., *Research for Decision Making*, vol. 1 (Amsterdam [1977]), 1–24, 9, ACDP, Pressedokumentation.

[56] IfD, Politische Berichte 1976: Freiheit oder Sozialismus, August 5, 1976, 10f., 16, ACDP.

[57] Noelle-Neumann, "Schweigespirale" (1977), 183.

only provincial but also clumsy. Underestimating this aspect of Kohl's public image was, she warned several months before the election, a "serious mistake by the CDU."[58] She and her colleague Mathias Kepplinger analyzed, among other things, the way Helmut Kohl was filmed and presented on television and correlated the television and press consumption of different social groups with their electoral behavior. Exposure to the – biased – media, which was more liberal and leaned further to the left than the electorate at large, allegedly led people not to choose Kohl even if they had originally held a favorable opinion of him.[59] What had happened? The "fear of isolation" had driven people to jump onto the bandwagon of the journalists.

Noelle-Neumann came to speak of a "dual climate" of opinion, of a divergence between the tone of media coverage and the views prevailing among individuals' families, friends, and colleagues. An actual numerical majority would not change the nature of media coverage, but media coverage would change the opinion of the actual numerical majority, the conclusion ran.[60] Accordingly, those most susceptible to such influence did not have a strong opinion to begin with, were less self-confident, and exposed themselves more intensely to television; in short, people of lower social status. As we have seen already, this critique of the strong impact of the media had been long in the making. Framed as a "dual climate of opinion," these arguments were integrated into *Die Schweigespirale*, as difficult as this part of the argument was and still is to verify or falsify. But, over the years, it has enlivened many radio and television discussions, been the focus of university seminars, and kept media scholars busy. Last but not least, it was also a strong argument for the introduction of commercial radio and television broadcasting in the Federal Republic.[61]

The Loss of Social Control

As far back as her inaugural lecture in Mainz in the mid-1960s, Noelle-Neumann argued that there was a close connection between "public opinion and social control," and she was to expand upon that theme for the rest of her life. She first came across the term "social control" in

---

[58] Noelle-Neumann to Kurt Biedenkopf, April 23, 1976, ACDP 07-001-11038.
[59] Noelle-Neumann, *Spiral of Silence* (1993), 159–167. This controversy cannot be dealt with here.
[60] Kepplinger, "Three Contexts," 48; Noelle-Neumann, *Spiral of Silence* (1993), 168.
[61] See chapter 13 by Frank Bösch in this volume.

the work of the American sociologist Edward A. Ross.[62] Linking social control and public opinion appears to have been a genuine idea of hers. As she emphasized, hers was a radically different understanding of public opinion than that which had been in common use since the 1960s. Unlike intellectuals such as Jürgen Habermas and a good part of the critical media public, she denigrated the importance of public debate, casting doubt on the significance of "rational discourse" in shaping public opinion and democratic decision-making. To "dare more democracy" would require the ideas and engagement of *mündige Bürger*, independent and sovereign citizens.[63]

Noelle-Neumann took an altogether different path. In the 1950s, she had first tried to write her habilitation with Max Horkheimer and Theodor Adorno in Berlin. Yet, she soon parted ways with them (or vice versa) and headed in a different direction. She found the ideas and arguments she sought in her eclectic reading of David Hume and John Locke, of Jean-Jacques Rousseau and Alexis de Tocqueville, which she bolstered with the experiments of Stanley Milgram and Solomon Asch. Instead of rational discourse and the empowerment of individuals, she came to stress pressures to conform and "conformity" in morale, behavior, language, and fashion. In fact, as Noelle-Neumann argued, this pressure to conform could pertain to all aspects of social life, and in this sense public opinion was an enduring pressure to conform to norms and thus was part of our "social skin."[64]

Her own survey data demonstrated a massive loss of "social control." This pertained foremost to values – law and order, sexual habits, patriotism – a diagnosis she no doubt shared with Richard Nixon and many other conservatives on both sides of the Atlantic. In the summer of 1975, she published an article entitled "Are We All Becoming Proletarians?" In terms of generating debate, it was an instant media

62 Elisabeth Noelle [sic], *Öffentliche Meinung und soziale Kontrolle* (Tübingen, 1966), reprinted as "Public Opinion and Social Control," in Donsbach et al., *The Spiral of Silence: New Perspectives*, 19–32.

63 Noelle-Neumann's arguments can be read as a rebuttal of Jürgen Habermas, *The Structural Transformation of the Public Sphere: An Inquiry into a Category of Bourgeois Society* (Cambridge, MA, 1991), which had been published in Germany in 1962; see also Craig Calhoun, *Habermas and the Public Sphere* (Cambridge, MA and London, 1992).

64 Noelle-Neumann, *Spiral of Silence* (1993), 230, and passim; see also Timothy K. F. Fung and Dietram A. Scheufele, "Social Norms, Spirals of Silence and Framing Theory: An Argument for Considering Cross-Cultural Differences in Media Effects Research," in Donsbach et al., *The Spiral of Silence: New Perspectives*, 131–152, 134.

success. Were Germans not losing their "bourgeois values," namely their work ethic and honesty, she asked. Were they becoming too keen on personal self-fulfillment in their lives? It was clear to Noelle-Neumann that social progress and the reform agenda of the SPD–FDP government were responsible for the decline of values in the Federal Republic. She followed up on this article with a continuous stream of books and articles, bursting with data compiled by the IfD documenting changing attitudes toward work, morality, education, and the welfare state.[65] These arguments were anything but foreign to Americans at the time. Without direct reference to the American sociologist Ronald Inglehart, Noelle-Neumann spoke of a "silent revolution." For her, that was not just a metaphor. The situation was "revolutionary," in fact, it was a "silent revolution" in Germans' values, and there can be no doubt that she did not use the terms merely as metaphors. Part and parcel of this ongoing transformation of values was a move away from established conceptions of patriotism and national identity.[66] But whereas Nixon had linked the silent majority and the issue of patriotism from the outset – in a follow-up to his "Silent Majority" speech, he proposed a campaign to waken patriotic feelings similar to the one carried out during World War II – Noelle-Neumann did not turn her attention to patriotism until the 1980s, well after the publication of *Die Schweigespirale*.[67]

Noelle-Neumann's arguments about fundamental shifts in values and social control were part of a larger discourse, as was the topic of control over language. This point was made by none other than the CDU's general secretary, Kurt Biedenkopf, at the 1973 party conference. Biedenkopf, a

---

[65] Elisabeth Noelle-Neumann, "Werden wir alle Proletarier?," *Die Zeit*, June 13/14, 1975; Elisabeth Noelle-Neumann, *Werden wir alle Proletarier? Wertewandel in unserer Gesellschaft* (Zurich, 1977); Elisabeth Noelle-Neumann and Burkhard Strümpel, *Macht Arbeit krank? Macht Arbeit glücklich? Eine aktuelle Kontroverse* (Munich, 1984); Daniel Bell, *The Cultural Contradictions of Capitalism* (New York, 1976); Michael Crozier and Samuel P. Huntington, *The Crisis of Democracy* (New York, 1975); Ronald Inglehart, "The Silent Revolution in Europe: Inter-Generational Change in Post-Industrial Societies," *American Political Science Review* 65 (1971): 991–1017; Ronald Ingelhart, *The Silent Revolution: Changing Values and Political Styles among Western Publics* (Princeton, 1977).

[66] Elisabeth Noelle-Neumann, "Die Lust an der Revolution erlosch. Es bleibt die Umwertung der Werte," *Die Zeit*, April 23, 1976; following up later on this debate were Warnfried Dettling and Werner Weidenfeld, "Die schleichende Krise der Republik," *Die Zeit*, July 14, 1978.

[67] Game Plan for the President's November 3rd Speech, 12–13; Elisabeth Noelle-Neumann and Renate Köcher, *Die verletzte Nation: Über den Versuch der Deutschen, ihren Charakter zu ändern* (Stuttgart, 1987).

lawyer by training who had worked for the chemical company Henkel and had served as the president of the University of Bochum, made a statement that became famous:

Language, dear friends, is not only a means of communication. As the conflict with the Left demonstrates, it is also an important means of strategy. What is occurring in our country today is a new type of revolution. It is the revolution of society by way of language... Instead of the forceful occupation of the citadels of state power, terms are being occupied [*werden die Begriffe besetzt*] by which the state governs, the terms with which we are describing our state order, our rights and duties, as well as our institutions. The modern revolution occupies them with meaning, which makes it impossible for us to live in this state.[68]

Cooked up by a newly established party planning group that dealt with the semantic dimension of political strategy, this position was an odd mixture of ideas from Friedrich Wilhelm Hegel – "If the realm of ideas has been revolutionized, reality cannot withstand it" – Herbert Marcuse, and the so-called extra-parliamentary opposition (Außerparlamentarische Opposition, or APO). If nothing else, the APO could be credited with having demonstrated that "major decisions are made first in the conceptual domain, in a revolutionizing of the realm of ideas," argued Gerd-Klaus Kaltenbrunner, who was at the time one of the most active and influential proponents of a new conservatism in Germany.[69]

Like many conservatives, Noelle-Neumann did not have to look far to identify agents of a silent revolution or of any other sort. She was convinced that small minorities and individuals could fundamentally alter society. This presented both a threat and an opportunity. Minorities "do not fear isolation or have overcome it" or are "willing to pay its price."[70] In *Die Schweigespirale*, the list of such "trailblazers" was long and ranged from "people who introduce new music" to figures such as Marc Chagall, Rainer Werner Fassbinder, Martin Luther, and Rachel Carson. Interestingly, she did not mention any political leaders.[71] No doubt she agreed

---

[68] For a detailed analysis and further references, see Geyer, "War over Words."

[69] Gerd-Klaus Kaltenbrunner, Zum Start der Serie „Initiative" [a new book series], 6, 8f., Privatarchiv Noelle-Neumann, Compactus 13, file Varia (including among other things Materialsammlung zum Vortrag Deutsche Bank: Haben wir einen neuen Konservatismus, May 16, 1974).

[70] Also for the following, Noelle-Neumann, *Spiral of Silence* (1993), ch. 17, 139 (quote).

[71] Rather excited about his findings, a research assistant of hers had unsuccessfully proposed to add the name of Adolf Hitler, about whom he presented page-long photocopies from *Mein Kampf*, Privatarchiv Noelle-Neumann, Compactus 11, no. 4.

with Kaltenbrunner, for whom the student movement and the APO stood
as proof that "not the masses but determined minorities... shape the
political form and the consciousness of a society."[72] Public opinion was a
matter of small elites. Even conservatives could be such trailblazers, such
as the outspoken Kaltenbrunner, if not the outspoken Noelle-Neumann
herself. The basis of this thinking was a decidedly elitist idea of the strong
individual but also of passive masses. The silent majority, in other words,
was made up of weak individuals who were in need of leadership.

The dystopian narrative of Noelle-Neumann's "silent revolution" was
the breakdown of this leadership, which was, after all, a leadership with
respect to public opinion. Culprits could be easily identified. One was
the Frankfurt School, which she considered the seedbed of the German left. But they were not the only ones responsible "for the cultural-
revolutionary movement starting in the mid-1950s" that she thought
had such a pernicious influence. In various contexts, she would recount
how "her ears had pricked up" as early as 1945, when her friend Carlo
Schmid, soon to become a well-known Social Democratic politician, had
noted that "one has to teach German youth to be disobedient." She had
no doubt that this had become the educational goal in Germany.[73]

Noelle-Neumann placed a great deal of blame on Adorno's study of the
authoritarian personality, which he and his collaborators had produced
during their exile in the United States.[74] Her attack on Adorno is interesting because the work of Asch and Milgram, which was so important
to her own work, lent itself to a critique of authoritarianism very much
like Adorno's critique of authoritarianism.[75] The author of this chapter
remembers having to watch at least twice (in history and religion class
in school) in the first half of the 1970s the documentary on Milgram's
frightening experiment on individuals' willingness to obey cruel orders.
Apparently, the film had been distributed by the educational film agency
of the – politically conservative – state of Baden-Württemberg. All of
this was part of civic education: a call *not* to "run with the pack" or "to

---

72 Kaltenbrunner, Zum Start der Serie, 9.
73 Noelle-Neumann, "Werden wir alle Proletarier?"; Noelle-Neumann, *Erinnerungen*, 139.
    See also Landestag der CDU-Frauenvereinigung in Mainz, June 21, 1980, 2, Privatarchiv
    Noelle-Neumann, Compactus 11, no. 2.
74 Theodor W. Adorno, *The Authoritarian Personality* (New York, 1950); Benjamin Beit-
    Hallahni, "Authoritarian Personality: Some Historical Reflexions," *Tel Aviver Jahrbuch
    für deutsche Geschichte* 23 (2004): 173–218; Noelle-Neumann, *Erinnerungen*, 139.
75 For a critical evaluation, see Gina Perry, *Behind the Shock Machine: The Untold Story
    of the Notorious Milgram Psychological Experiments* (New York, 2013).

jump on the bandwagon." This was encouragement to speak out and also remain critical of majorities – at a time when participation in discussions and the ability to voice one's own opinion became a civic duty.

This may also go far in explaining why it has been hard to replicate the assumptions of Noelle-Neumann in political settings similar to the ones in which she framed her theory. A study has shown that in California's conservative Orange County those holding minority political views did not lose the propensity to speak out over time. Authors of many other studies, some carried out in Germany, have come to similar conclusions. No doubt the same is true with respect to Noelle-Neumann's idea of "opinion leadership" at a time when the mass media have become increasingly competitive and pluralistic and have recently been enhanced by the upshot of decentralized social networks.[76]

Conclusion

The aim of this chapter is not to demonstrate the conceptual failings or possible uses of Noelle-Neumann's theory of the spiral of silence. By looking at the historical context in which they were produced, we can read Noelle-Neumann's writings on the spiral of silence in a different fashion. First of all, her theory can be understood as an academic interpretation of Nixon's utterances on the silent majority, in particular how silent majorities emerge. Second, although one may have doubts that conservatives were ever less inclined to articulate their views than other political groups, Noelle-Neumann offered recommendations on how to speak out against what appeared to many as a new liberal political and cultural hegemony and an ongoing "silent revolution" of social, political, and ethical values. Starting in the 1980s, all of this would be discussed under the heading "political correctness"; in Germany, that discussion focused in particular on the interpretation of the nation's past. The strong elitist impetus that can be seen in the work of Noelle-Neumann is typical of the German

---

[76] "It is almost impossible to truly test the theory of spiral of silence," argue Jörg Matthes and Andrew F. Hayes, "Methodological Conundrums," 63; Cheryl Katz and Mark Baldassare, "Using the 'L-Word' in Public: A Test of the Spiral of Silence in Conservative Orange County, California," *Public Opinion Quarterly* 56 (1992): 232–235. For a first round of debates, see Keith Sanders, Lynda Lee Kaid, and Dan Nimmo, *Political Communication Yearbook 1984* (Carbondale, IL, 1985); Dieter Fuchs, Jürgen Gerhard, and Friedhelm Neidhardt, "Öffentliche Kommunikationsbereitschaft. Ein Test zentraler Bestandteile der Theorie der Schweigespirale," *Zeitschrift für Soziologie* 21 (1992): 284–295.

context. It implied a distrust of the silent majority, which was thought to be weak, unreliable, easy to manipulate, and thus a not altogether positive point of reference. After all, the public opinion polls demonstrated that Germany's silent majority was far less conservative than many had hoped. Perhaps this point best characterizes the difference between West Germany and the United States. Nixon and Agnew appealed to the silent majority as a plebiscitary force on which the administration could rely. They thereby opened the floodgates for a powerful self-mobilization by those willing to identify themselves as members of the silent majority. By the end of the decade, Jerry Falwell would argue that the Christian right "might be the silent majority now," but "as the ranks of our Moral Majority swell into an army, we will be able to look at the politicians, eyeball to eyeball."[77] This sort of radical self-confidence was curiously absent among West German conservatives, who were otherwise not shy about attacking real or supposed spirals of silence.

77 Cited in David Snowball, *Continuity and Change in the Rhetoric of the Moral Majority* (New York, 1991), 61; Daniel K. William, *God's Own Party: The Making of the Christian Right* (New York, 2010); see also chapter 9 by Mark J. Rozell and Britta Waldschmidt-Nelson in this volume.

13

Campaigning against "Red Public Television"

Conservative Mobilization and the Invention of Private Television in West Germany

Frank Bösch

Germany's Christian Democrats have always seen themselves as the party of the silent majority – and they still do. In 2013, for instance, the general secretary of the Bavaria-based Christian Social Union (CSU) commented on same-sex marriage: "The Christian Democrats as a people's party [*Volkspartei*] have the duty to give the silent majority a voice against the 'screaming minority,' against the 'Zeitgeist' and 'lobbyists of particular groups.'"[1] In describing itself as a *Volkspartei*, the party emphasizes its claim to speak for the majority of the population and for all average Germans. The phrase "silent majority" has been used relatively infrequently by the Christian Democrats and has not figured prominently in German public discourse more generally. The first articles employing this phrase mostly referred to the United States and President Richard Nixon.[2] The phrase was only rarely used in reference to the Federal Republic in parliamentary debates and newspaper articles during the 1970s and 1980s. As my research in several digital databases suggests, it was most likely to be found in the conservative *Frankfurter Allgemeine Zeitung*.[3]

Nevertheless, there was a widespread belief that a silent majority did exist in West Germany, and this belief was closely linked to the rise of opinion polling. The use of polls in the media and by political parties

---

[1] "Die Union als Volkspartei hat die Aufgabe, der stillen Mehrheit eine Stimme zu geben gegen die schrille Minderheit," *Süddeutsche Zeitung*, March 11, 2013.

[2] See, for example, "Ehrt Amerika," *Frankfurter Allgemeine Zeitung*, November 17, 1969; "Das Schwergewicht," *Der Spiegel*, December 8, 1969.

[3] See, for instance, the debates in the Bundestag on April 4, 1981 (http://dipbt.bundestag.de/doc/btp/09/09032.pdf) and May 28, 1982 (http://dipbt.bundestag.de/doc/btp/09/09104.pdf).

began to increase much later than it did in the United States – not until the 1960s. In this decade, many critical liberal media outlets used polls to argue that the majority did not support the conservative positions of the governing Christian Democrats. After 1968, especially during the Social Democratic governments of Willy Brandt and Helmut Schmidt in the 1970s, it was the other way round. Now the conservatives used polls to prove that the Social Democrats, social movements, and the media did not represent the majority of the people. Conservatives increasingly stressed the distinction between "published opinion" and "public opinion."

The conservatives' contention that the press was leaning toward the left had a long tradition in Germany that went back to the imperial era. Christian Democrats such as Chancellor Konrad Adenauer argued along these lines in the 1950s as well.[4] However, the belief that the media, and especially television, was dominated by the left and influenced public opinion against the views of the majority acquired a new dimension in the 1970s. Conservatives maintained that a coalition of political magazines like *Der Spiegel* and public television broadcasters played a decisive part in helping the Social Democrats win power in 1969 for the first time since the founding of the Federal Republic. This increased the conservative perception that media were responsible for the changing majorities. The Christian Democratic media expert Christian Schwarz-Schilling, for example, detected an "occupation of the media by the left and ultra-left."[5] Some of his party colleagues attacked the well-known public broadcaster Westdeutscher Rundfunk (WDR) as "the house of Mao" and denounced its employees as supporters of left-wing terrorists.[6] As each broadcaster in the Federal Republic was monitored by a Rundfunkrat, a governing board made up of representatives of the government, the parliamentary parties, churches, trade unions, and other groups, that charge was far-fetched. The boards split into political camps, and conservative and Catholic representatives voiced opposition to broadcasters' policies. Campaigns

---

[4] Frank Bösch, "Das Politische als Produkt. Selbstbeobachtungen und Modernisierungen in der politischen Kommunikation der frühen Bundesrepublik," in Habbo Knoch and Daniel Morat, eds., *Kommunikation als Beobachtung: Medienwandel und Gesellschaftsbilder 1880–1960* (Munich, 2003), 229–248. For an account from the perspective of a party insider, see Karl-Günther von Hase, *Adenauer und die Presse* (Düsseldorf, 1988).

[5] Speech by Schwarz-Schilling on the CDU/CSU media day, November 7–8, 1978, published as "Okkupation der elektronischen Medien durch Linke und Ultralinke," *Media Perspektiven* 11 (1978): 791–805, here 794.

[6] Josef Schmidt, "Intendant Klaus von Bismarck und die Kampagne gegen den WDR," *Archiv für Sozialgeschichte* 41 (2001): 349–382, here 372–373.

against the so-called *Rotfunk*, "red broadcasting," mobilized Christian Democrats in many elections during the late 1970s. The theory of the *Schweigespirale*, the "spiral of silence," put forward by the prominent pollster Elisabeth Noelle-Neumann in the 1970s lent scholarly credence to such campaigns.[7] Noelle-Neumann, along with fellow researchers Hans Kepplinger and Renate Köcher, seemed to have proven empirically that the majority of West German journalists belonged to the left and misrepresented and manipulated opinions through distorted reporting.[8] Due to the fact that West German viewers could choose between only three programs, it was argued, a few left-wing television journalists enjoyed immense political power.

This theory and the public campaigns against various so-called left-wing public broadcasters supported the Christian Democratic goal to open the way for commercial broadcasting in the Federal Republic. In the second half of the 1970s, the fight for commercial television became a major issue for the Christian Democratic Union (CDU). Its leaders believed that the party would be able to win elections in the 1980s only if commercial broadcasting were introduced – but of course they did not make this argument publicly.[9] One could therefore argue that the introduction of commercial television in Germany was the political result of the conservatives' belief that their voters and the silent majority were being manipulated by public broadcasters. This chapter analyzes this important aspect of conservative mobilization and the debate that culminated in the start of commercial broadcasting in West Germany in 1984.[10] *— After the CDU/CSU had won an election*

Conservative Mobilization in the 1970s

The CDU and its Bavarian sister party, the CSU, won all national elections in West Germany from 1949 until 1969, and a CDU chancellor headed the West German government during that period. The party was directed

---

7 Elisabeth Noelle-Neumann, *Die Schweigespirale: Öffentliche Meinung – unsere soziale Haut* (Munich, 1980).

8 Hans Mathias Kepplinger, ed., *Angepasste Aussenseiter. Was Journalisten denken und wie sie arbeiten* (Freiburg, 1979); Renate Köcher, *Spürhund und Missionar – eine vergleichende Untersuchung über Berufsethik und Aufgabenverständnis britischer und deutscher Journalisten* (Munich, 1985).

9 See Schwarz-Schilling in Fraktionsprotokoll CDU, November 6, 1979, 19, 23, Archiv für Christlich-Demokratische Politik, Sankt Augustin (hereafter ACDP), VIII-001-1059/1.

10 The examples presented here are discussed in more detail in Frank Bösch, "Zwischen Technikzwang und politischen Zielen: Wege zur Einführung des privaten Rundfunks in den 1970/80er Jahren," *Archiv für Sozialgeschichte* 52 (2012): 191–210.

mainly from the Federal Chancellery until the 1960s. It was poorly organized, and its members were hardly involved in decision-making processes. Consequently, the party only rarely had debates on its campaign
platforms and, until the mid-1960s, comparatively few members or full-
time staff. Election campaigns represented the most important moments
of mobilization. Conservative mobilization was organized less by party
personnel than by associations and interest groups, such as the Farmers'
League, gun clubs, and German expellees from Eastern Europe.[11] Neither
the CDU nor the CSU was a conservative party in the true sense of the
term. Especially in the Catholic regions where their roots lay, Christian
Democrats opposed liberal free market economics. The party was more
liberal, in a cultural sense, in Protestant urban areas.

Around 1970, the CDU/CSU changed fundamentally: it became a party
with a strong grassroots organization. Five developments might explain
this. First of all, the CDU lost the Chancellery to the Social Democrat
Willy Brandt in 1969. They also lost elections in major states, including North-Rhine-Westphalia. They thus decided to strengthen the party
leadership and to identify policy alternatives in response to the Social
Democrats' numerous reform initiatives. Second, with the emergence of a
culture of public debate, fostered mainly by left-wing alternative groups,
in the wake of 1968, the Christian Democrats decided to establish their
own opinion journals, and in 1968 they held their first general discussion
on the party's platform. Such discussion would be considerably expanded
in the 1970s. Third, the emergence of new political groups and social
movements, particularly on the left, at the end of the 1960s compelled
the CDU to try to increase its membership, which it did with great success. Fourth, the Brandt government enacted a number of policies that
spurred conservative mobilization: Brandt's *Ostpolitik* and rapprochement toward the German Democratic Republic (GDR) moved anticom-
munists to take action, and conservative Christians rallied in opposition
to reforms of family policy and the decriminalization of abortion. Fifth,
and most central to this chapter, the 1960s saw increased political polarization of public opinion and the media. Leading newspapers and magazines, such as *Der Spiegel, Stern,* and *Die Zeit,* openly supported Willy

---

[11] For a more detailed account, see Frank Bösch, *Macht und Machtverlust: Die Geschichte der CDU* (Stuttgart, 2002); Frank Bösch, *Das konservative Milieu: Vereinskultur und lokale Sammlungspolitik in ost- und westdeutschen Regionen (1900–1960)* (Göttingen, 2002).

Brandt, and others, such as *BILD*, *Quick*, and *Frankfurter Allgemeine Zeitung*, explicitly turned against him.[12] The television broadcaster ZDF supported the positions of the CDU/CSU, whereas ARD, West Germany's first public broadcaster, began voicing criticism of the CDU/CSU on some of its programs, particularly *Panorama*, in the 1960s.[13] By 1970, the CDU/CSU had come to believe that the left shaped public discourse and the media, and the parties' leaders therefore sought to regain their public voice.

At first glance, the Federal Republic does not appear to have experienced a conservative mobilization similar to the one in the United States in this period. It did not see the emergence of the strong grassroots movements fighting for tax cuts or on behalf of religious beliefs that became increasingly important in the United States over the course of the 1970s. I would nevertheless argue that Christian Democracy and the conservative milieu as a whole used the crisis quite successfully as a chance to mobilize their supporters.[14] In contrast to the United States, however, this mobilization took place primarily within the party itself, which can be explained by the strong role of parties in parliamentary democracies with proportional representation. Party membership grew rapidly, passing the one million mark by 1970, and soon a quarter of all members were actively engaged in party activities. The creation of a professional party staff stabilized support at the grassroots level. Policy debates and the establishment of party-affiliated magazines and think tanks fostered the development of new ideas that helped modernize the CDU.

The Christian Democrats' effort at mobilization was a response to the left as well as an integral part of heightened political activism more generally in the Federal Republic. Because party leaders cannot easily influence levels of activism and membership rates, this broad Christian Democratic commitment must be understood as an independent reaction from below. Moreover, West Germany also saw individual conservative

12 Daniela Münkel, *Willy Brandt und die „Vierte Gewalt": Politik und Massenmedien in den 50er bis 70er Jahren* (Frankfurt am Main, 2005).

13 Gerhard Lampe, *Panorama, Report und Monitor: Geschichte der politischen Fernsehmagazine 1957–1990* (Konstanz, 2002).

14 Frank Bösch, "Die Krise als Chance: Die Neuformierung der Christdemokraten in den siebziger Jahren," in Konrad Jarausch, ed., *Das Ende der Zuversicht? Die Strukturkrise der 1970er Jahre als zeithistorische Zäsur* (Göttingen, 2008), 288–301; Axel Schildt, "Die Kräfte der Gegenreform sind auf breiter Front angetreten. Zur konservativen Tendenzwende in den Siebzigerjahren," *Archiv für Sozialgeschichte* 44 (2004): 449–479.

protests on the streets and in the media, such as rallies after 1973 against the liberalization of abortion laws.[15]

The campaigns against supposedly left-leaning broadcasters investigated in this chapter must thus be understood as part of a broader mobilization. This mobilization resulted in large measure from the Christian Democrats' belief that the party could no longer set the terms of public debate and would not be able to do so again on its own. They responded by increasingly pinning their electoral hopes on the media, which represented a shift from earlier political campaigns. Traditional conservative networks, such as the farmers' and the expellees' associations, became less important in the 1970s. Television emerged as the decisive opinion-shaping medium in the consumer society of the Federal Republic.

Media Techniques, Politics, and the Market

To abolish the Weimar and Nazi-era system of governmental control, the Western Allies modeled West German public broadcasting on the British model during the postwar occupation.[16] It was based on funding through fees and independence from the government. The Germans soon altered the system and partially curbed broadcasters' independence by giving the political parties influence on supervisory bodies. As a result, the *Weltanschauung* of regional broadcasters increasingly corresponded to the political majorities in their home regions. A more conservative outlook prevailed in the consistently Christian Democratic states in the Federal Republic's south than that in Social Democratic-controlled regions like Bremen and Hessen. Chancellor Konrad Adenauer tried to establish a pro-government commercial television broadcaster in the late 1950s. This attempt, resisted by the states and questioned by the churches, ultimately failed when the Federal Constitution Court ruled that the limited availability of broadcast frequencies justified the continuation of the public broadcasters' monopoly.[17] The small number of broadcasters, the court

---

[15] Jana Ebeling, "Religiöser Straßenprotest? Medien und Kirchen im Streit um den § 218 in den 1970er Jahren," in Frank Bösch and Lucian Hölscher, eds., *Jenseits der Kirche: Die Öffnung religiöser Räume seit 1945* (Göttingen, 2013), 253–284.

[16] On the history of radio in the Federal Republic, see Peter J. Humphreys, *Media and Media Policy in West Germany: The Press and Broadcasting since 1945* (New York, 1990), 239–292.

[17] This attempt is not discussed in this chapter because it has been well researched. See Rüdiger Steinmetz, *Freies Fernsehen: Das erste privat-kommerzielle Fernsehprogramm in Deutschland* (Konstanz, 1996).

explained, could not ensure the kind of pluralism provided by the print media and thus only public broadcasting would guarantee the involvement of all parts of society. As a result, a new nationwide public broadcaster was established in 1963, the Zweites Deutsches Fernsehen (ZDF). Its rather conservative outlook reflected the balance of power in Bonn at that time.

When cable television opened up the possibility of more channels for West German viewers in the mid-1970s, the Christian Democrats argued even more determinedly in favor of commercial television and radio. They initially based their arguments on technology. Christian Schwarz-Schilling, who became the CDU's spokesperson on media policy in 1975, stressed that media technology had created a new situation that required a legal and regulatory framework "based on the market economy."[18] In 1981, the Federal Constitutional Court ruled that private television stations were legal under the condition that plurality was regulated. In 1986, it opened the way for easing the regulations on private broadcasters, provided that the public broadcasters were meeting the public's needs.

The Christian Democrats' campaign for commercial television and radio appeared at first glance to center on technology. Its political core soon became evident in the public debates, however, and, as a consequence, the Social Democratic Party (SPD) argued against the reforms. The Social Democrats reasoned that technological developments should not determine political decisions.[19] This explains why the SPD started lengthy experiments with the new cable technology, internally estimating that this test phase would take up to ten years.[20] Chancellor Helmut Schmidt stressed that the decision whether to allow commercial cable television could not be based on technological arguments because increasing the number of stations would "greatly influence social relationships" and could "affect the substance of our democratic life."[21] Two visions of modernity clashed in this debate: whereas the CDU presented itself as the party of technological progress, the Social Democrats claimed to be the party of morality dedicated to protecting family life and

---

[18] Schwarz-Schilling, "Okkupation," 795.

[19] See the speech delivered by Volker Hauff in *Aktuelle Stunde*, November 7, 1979; reprinted in *Das Parlament*, November 17, 1979, 4.

[20] Vorlage des SPD-Präsidiums, 2.12.1979, Archiv der sozialen Demokratie, Bonn (hereafter AdsD), PV-Bestand Mappe 334.

[21] Helmut Schmidt in the Bundestag, May 1979, 154. Sitzung, Stenograph. Berichte, 12262.

education.[22] Believing that the popular press was dominated by right-wing publishers who would also dominate private broadcasting, the Social Democrats thought they would have no chance of influencing public opinion in a world with commercial television and thus fervently defended the public broadcasters' monopoly. The political left saw a particular threat posed by the print media controlled by Axel Springer, including the country's most widely read tabloid (*BILD-Zeitung*) as well as by the rather conservative regional papers.

After Helmut Schmidt's reelection in 1976, there was a major political mobilization against the existing broadcasting system. The Christian Democrats explained their defeat by blaming the supposedly left-leaning television broadcasters and left-wing journalists who did not represent the "true" opinion of the people. CDU leader Helmut Kohl's advisor Elisabeth Noelle-Neumann was particularly influential in advancing the argument that most members of the public did not voice their true opinions – their support for the CDU/CSU – because the media marginalized them by suggesting that they were in the minority.[23] A study by Hans Mathias Kepplinger that argued that Helmut Kohl was usually depicted from a low, unfavorable angle on public television added support to such views, and it captivated party leaders. Such arguments about the impact of allegedly negative media coverage largely ignored the fact that the CDU actually came close to winning an absolute majority of votes in 1976 as it achieved its second best result at the polls ever. The Christian Democrats failed to win control of the government only because the FDP and SPD agreed to form a coalition. Consequently, the CDU believed that far more than half of the electorate – the silent majority – supported its position during the 1970s.

Leading Christian Democrats became convinced that they could no longer win elections without commercial television. At a party meeting in 1979, Schwarz-Schilling argued, "This issue is going to decide how we are going to be able to campaign in the federal elections of 1984 and 1988 and how we will be perceived in people's living rooms. And this will be crucial in determining the outcome of these elections."[24] Without commercial television, he insisted, the SPD would "win the power struggle of the

---

[22] Peter M. Spangenberg, "Der unaufhaltbare Aufstieg zum dualen System? Diskursbeiträge zur Technikinnovation und Rundfunkorganisation," in Irmela Schneider and Christina Bartz, eds., *Medienkultur der 70er Jahre* (Wiesbaden, 2004), 21–39, here 23.

[23] See chapter 12 by Martin H. Geyer in this volume.

[24] Schwarz-Schilling in Fraktionsprotokoll CDU, November 6, 1979, 19, ACDP VIII-001-1059/1.

1980s."[25] Accordingly, the Christian Democrats were eager to increase their influence on journalists with the public broadcasters by founding associations for party-affiliated journalists and creating directories of like-minded journalists for use in filling open positions.[26] Kohl in particular thought about media influence in terms of personnel: "We do not want to engage in journalist bashing, but we want to put people in power who will not forget where they came from."[27]

The conservative press supported this Christian Democratic campaign against "red broadcasting." The tabloid *BILD-Zeitung*, which sold four million copies a day, attacked supposedly leftist television reporting on a regular basis, claiming that it was financed by taxpayers' money. At the same time, *BILD* and other newspapers published series of articles on the benefits that commercial television had brought in the United States, Britain, and Luxembourg.[28] *BILD*'s support for commercial broadcasting was influenced by the hopes of its parent company, the Axel Springer Verlag, to enter the television business. Trade associations also protested the public broadcasters' allegedly critical take on business, taking note, for instance, of how often rich people were depicted as criminals in thrillers.[29]

Despite these efforts to sway public opinion, polls showed that the majority of the population was not really interested in commercial broadcasting or cable television. Two-thirds of the public said in 1979 that they would not be interested in additional commercial channels. Even only one-third of CDU/CSU supporters backed commercial television. Moreover, only 19 percent of the respondents were willing to pay more to receive a larger number of channels.[30] That fewer households than

[25] Ibid., 23.

[26] "Bis auf den Süddeutschen Rundfunk haben wir in allen ARD-Anstalten und im ZDF (ausgenommen ist der Süddeutsche Rundfunk, hier gibt es nur 4 Mitglieder der CDU) Freundeskreise gegründet... Aufgabe der Freundeskreise ist u.a. die Erzeugung eines Solidaritätsgedankens Gleichgesinnter," zudem Kontakte und Austausch; Entwurf Fischer Vorlage CDU-Bundespräsidium, Eingang, June 21, 1977, ACDP 01-824-225. Cf. the invitation to "Mitglieder des Freundeskreises der CDU in der Deutschen Welle," Einladung CDU Bundesgeschäftsstelle, March 5, 1979, ACDP 01-824-225.

[27] Protocol CDU-Bundesvorstand, October 9, 1978, ACDP 07-001.

[28] See the series of articles published under the title "Die Wahrheit über das Privat-Fernsehen," *Bild am Sonntag*, December 2, 1979, December 16, 1979, December 23, 1979.

[29] Knut Hickethier, *Geschichte des deutschen Fernsehens* (Stuttgart, 1998), 322.

[30] Data from Infratest PPP No. 221, November 15, 1979; cf. with data from Allensbach: Alfred-Joachim Hermanni, *Medienpolitik in den 80er Jahren: Machtpolitische Strategien der Parteien im Zuge der Einführung des dualen Rundfunksystems* (Wiesbaden, 2008), 225–226.

expected subscribed to cable service in the 1980s stands as further evidence that the privatization of television was first and foremost an elite project with political objectives and not a bottom-up initiative of a silent majority. Thus, the defenders of commercial television claimed to speak for the people as well as for those people who did not want to have it in the first place.

It should be noted that the liberal Free Democratic Party (FDP) seemed to lack a clear position in this debate. Through most of the 1970s, the Free Democrats condemned the parties' influence on public broadcasters – mainly because of their own lack of influence – but they also spoke out repeatedly against commercial broadcasting and commercials on regional channels. Only in late 1979 did the party take a firm stand on the issue of commercial broadcasting; its proposed "guidelines for new media" would allow private broadcasters to operate in the Federal Republic but only under the supervision of the public broadcasters.[31] The FDP's 1980 campaign platform stated, "Private non-commercial channels should be allowed" if the advertisements and number of channels were limited.[32] The FDP's cautious backing for commercial broadcasting was not a factor in the collapse of its coalition with the SPD in 1982; not until 1984, after it had joined forces with the CDU in the Bundestag and the first private broadcasters were already on the air, did the FDP decide to follow the CDU's line on broadcast policy.

The public broadcasters' monopoly was one of the cornerstones of the postwar order. With their campaign against public television, the conservatives undermined the postwar consensus in the late 1970s. A radical step in that direction came when the Christian Democratic state governors Gerhard Stoltenberg (of Schleswig-Holstein) and Ernst Albrecht (of Lower Saxony) announced that their states were pulling out of the regional broadcaster, Norddeutscher Rundfunk (NDR). Both federal states claimed that the Social Democratic state of Hamburg was turning the shared broadcasting station in a left-wing direction, although the other northern states were governed by Christian Democrats. More generally, the call for privatization and deregulation became louder in the Federal Republic, as in other Western European countries, during the

[31] Bericht über interne Gespräche der Parteigeschäftsführer von Egon Bahr im SPD-Parteipräsidium, November 12, 1979, AdsD, 3.95 Mappe 123. SZ 3.12.1979; Günter Verheugen, "Der Rundfunkhörer darf nur eins, zahlen," *Frankfurter Rundschau*, April 2, 1980.

[32] Hermanni, *Medienpolitik in den 80er Jahren*, 87.

1980s. It went hand in hand with a rhetoric that stressed that the market would solve the perceived problems of the public sector. Commercial television was presented as efficient and consumer-friendly, delivering what people really wanted to see free of charge, and public broadcasting was portrayed as inefficient, lavish, and elitist.

Supporters of commercial television called particular attention to plans to involve newspaper publishers in broadcast supervision, thereby reinforcing the impression that commercial television was about supporting pluralism of opinion rather than advancing the economic interests of corporations. The words "private" and "commercial" were often avoided in favor of the more elusive phrase "new media." The fact that the expansion of broadcasting promised significant profits for the new broadcasters – as could be observed quite early in the case of the British private broadcaster ITV – never came up in discussions.

It should be noted that the Christian Democrats argued for creating a tightly regulated media market. They often emphasized that their policies differed from the neoliberal initiatives of Ronald Reagan and Margaret Thatcher. In the case of media policy, they supported only limited privatization. No influential Christian Democrat demanded the complete privatization of broadcasting, that is, the abolition of public broadcasting; rather, they supported the coexistence of public and private broadcasters. The Christian Democrats demanded strict supervision and licensing, which they held up as one example (of many) of how greatly their policies differed from their more market-oriented counterparts in the United States.[33]

The Social Democrats lost the battle over commercial television. They did manage, though, to get some regulations on advertisements and monopolistic influence passed. They finally embraced commercial broadcasting. The party even bought stocks in some radio stations but did not try to influence the content of their programming.

Changing Value Systems within the Parties

Historians have typically cast the history of the 1970s in Western Europe and the United States in terms of three broad, interconnected developments. First, the 1970s are often seen as a decade of crises and decline, of

---

[33] As already argued in a CDU paper (Fraktion und Partei, Klein/Schwarz-Schilling), March 24, 1977, *Media Perspektiven* 3(1977): 155–170, 161.

stagnation and the abandonment of innovative ideas for building a better future. Second, the 1970s were marked by the efforts of left-leaning liberals and a variety of social movements to bring about social reforms or changes in values, including the liberalization of sexual norms. Third, the liberal pursuit of reforms spurred the rise of new conservative movements, not only in the United States but also in several Western European countries.[34]

This case study offers a slightly different view. The conservative campaign against public broadcasting networks constructed a crisis, but it went hand in hand with a profoundly new vision, and indeed a fundamental reform followed. The Christian Democrats' campaign not only was based on conservative values but also supported television channels whose programming, which included soft porn, shows with high levels of violence, and many American imports, was fundamentally at odds with its own value system.

The debate and the rhetoric employed reveal how the traditional values of the parties changed. The Christian Democrats adopted many positions that had typically been held by the Free Democrats and the Social Democrats. The Christian Democrats had traditionally presented themselves as the defenders of the family/ and of German national identity. They were against the display of sexuality in public and critical of mass culture and cultural pluralism. In the debate on commercial television, however, roles were reversed. Leading Christian Democrats had turned into supporters of greater pluralism. Echoing the arguments of defenders of civil liberties and freedom of the press, they maintained that the introduction of commercial television "would be the only way to reestablish a plurality of opinion because public networks are no longer able to live up to their social responsibility" because they lacked balance in their programming and were "agitating like missionaries."[35]

This "balance" was to be brought about by "new independent institutions" in the private sector. At the same time, the Christian Democrats associated the new media technology with the promise of democracy. According to Schwarz-Schilling, the prospect of "individual

---

[34] See Thomas Borstelmann, *The 1970s: A New Global History from Civil Rights to Economic Inequality* (Princeton, 2012); Hartmut Kaelble, *The 1970s in Europe: A Period of Disillusionment or Promise?* GHI London Annual Lecture (London, 2009), 18. See also the debate "The 1970s and 1980s as a Turning Point in European History?" *Journal of Modern European History* 9:1 (2011): 8–26.

[35] Speech printed in *epd*, December 11, 1976, AdsD ZASS III. Cf. articles in *Welt*, November 30, 1976; *Westfälische Rundschau*, November 30, 1976.

communication" would expand individual choice.[36] The "monopoly" of the public broadcasters was to be replaced by diversity. These claims rested on the assumption that the free market would be incorruptible and non-partisan: consumers, not politicians, would decide what broadcasters offered. Private providers were also presented as a more economical and more efficient answer to an existing problem. Accusing individual public broadcasters of running up debt and mismanagement, the Christian Democrats presented commercial broadcasting as a freebie for the public, which allowed them to portray themselves as the party that stood up for deprived citizens.

In the debate on private broadcasting, we can see signs of the transformation that West German conservatism underwent during the 1970s: its shift toward more market-oriented policies and move away from its traditional preoccupation with moral issues. With their turn toward liberal free market policies, the Christian Democrats even risked a conflict with the churches. West German conservatives had long been prejudiced against American culture, especially American commercial television programs. Now, they no longer saw such shows as a threat to national identity and instead promoted them as positive examples.

The Social Democrats, by contrast, now espoused traditionally conservative views. Four conservative elements can be identified in their reasoning. First, the Social Democrats warned that commercial television would destroy the consensus on values within German society, endanger families and morality, and harm children. They repeatedly pointed to expectations that commercial broadcasting would bring an increase in the amount of sex and violence shown on television.[37] The entire discourse on violence and addiction was connected to the private media market.[38] In many respects, the Social Democrats shared the arguments put forward by the churches and even tried to form a coalition with them.[39] In particular, they shared the churches' concern about the prohibition of advertising on Sundays. However, the CDU eventually allowed advertising on Sundays

---

[36] Schwarz-Schilling in Bundestag, June 27, 1980, 227.Sitz., Sp. 18450.

[37] See Helmut Schmidt's speech, "Medienpolitische Fachtagung der SPD," in Dokumentation FR, November 30, 1979, 12; Klose at the Hamburg media days, printed in *Vorwärts*, July 5, 1979, 31.

[38] Christina Bartz, "Kabelfernsehen: soziale Integration oder Desintegration? Ökonomische und medizinische Antworten auf eine Fragestellung," in Irmela Schneider et al., eds., *Medienkultur der 70er Jahre* (Wiesbaden, 2004), 50–51.

[39] Entwurf Dohnanyi Protokoll Sitzung SPD-Medienkommission 19.12.1985, AdsD, NL Peter Glotz, Ordner Medienpolitik I; also FUNK-Korrespondenz 11.10.1985.

against the wishes of the churches by pointing out that the advertising market would move abroad and the Federal Republic would be left out.[40] The CDU/CSU also ignored the argument about the threat to families – even though family policy had always been a key pillar of its political program.

Second, the SPD predicted a loss of programming quality, arguing that the multiplication of broadcasters would result not in diversity but rather in uniformity across the networks. With this argument, the Social Democrats clothed the traditional cultural pessimism of the *Bildungsbürgertum*, the educated middle class, in a left-wing guise. They were convinced that advertisers would want to work with the largest media companies – corporations such as Bertelsmann, Springer, and Leo Kirch – and that would lead to greater concentration in the media industry. To avert that development, the SPD advocated antitrust limitations to preserve competition in broadcasting.[41]

Third, the SPD championed the "protection of the nation" on almost nationalistic and protectionist lines by arguing that Germany had to be protected from American television series, "foreign commercialization," and "international media multinationals."[42] When privatization could no longer be delayed in 1984, the party demanded quotas on imported series and movies for "the protection of national and European identity and the tradition of culture and language as well as the protection of the local and European movie and film production industry and its employees."[43] At least half of the programs should be German or European productions; for movies the quota was 60 percent, of which half had to have been produced in German. Although conservatives had long sought to protect German high culture from dumbing down by foreign, particularly American, movies, the CDU/CSU opposed such quotas, knowing that the new commercial broadcasters, such as SAT.1, would subsist mainly on American movies.

Fourth, the SPD detected a grave political danger. Helmut Schmidt warned that "great power of political influence will fall into

---

[40] "Antwort Bernhard Vogel auf das Medien-Monitum der beiden Kirchen," *Media Perspektiven* 1 (1985): 59–60.

[41] Anlage Dieter Stammler zu TOP 5a Protokoll Sitzung 13.3.1986, AdsD, NL Peter Glotz, Ordner Medienpolitik I.

[42] Medienpolitisches Aktionsprogramm 16.2.1984, AdsD, NL Peter Glotz, Ordner Medienpolitik IV; Entschließung Vorsitzenden SPD-Fraktionen 27/28.9.1984, in ibid., Ordner Medienpolitik V.

[43] SPD-Medienreferat 12.9.1985, AdsD, NL Peter Glotz, Ordner Medienpolitik I.

unsupervised and unsupervisable hands" and, elsewhere, that private broadcasting was "the ground in which dictators dig into people's souls."[44] By the 1980s, the Social Democrats were no longer invoking the specter of Baron Alfred Hugenberg, the right-wing press baron of the Weimar era, to warn of the dangers of concentration in the media industry as they had in the 1960s: contemporary figures such as Axel Springer and Leo Kirch apparently sufficed as bogeymen. Nonetheless, they feared conservative dominance of print and broadcast media and worried that the situation for expressing "opinions critical of the valorization of capital" would become hopeless.[45] The SPD thus tried to strengthen public access television, not least local and municipal channels.

In short, both parties believed that television affected the character of German society and would continue to do so. The 1970s could be labeled as the decade of television because so many politicians believed that the influence of television reached into every fiber of German society. Despite their clear turn toward free market liberalism, the Christian Democrats still held to their traditional conservative position, which could be called the "politics of depoliticization." The conservatives argued that politics and, in particular, debates on controversial issues should not be conducted in public view. This went hand in hand with the belief that the majority of Germans held conservative values and would simply be misled by political debate and a critical media. Indeed, commercial television has encouraged the depoliticization of the public in recent decades.

Examples from Abroad

The Christian Democrats' campaign obviously had some similarities to the conservative mobilization against public broadcasting in the United States. Of course, the media system and cultural role of public broadcasting was very different in the Federal Republic. In the United States, commercial television, "free TV," had been seen as a democratic right from the invention of broadcasting, and public television was introduced as a supplement to support education, minorities, and communities.[46] Beginning in the late 1960s, American conservatives criticized public

---

[44] Quoted in *Spiegel*, December 1, 1979, 21–22. See also Hartmut Soell, *Helmut Schmidt: 1969 bis heute: Macht und Verantwortung* (Munich, 2008), 802.

[45] Anlage Dieter Stammler zu TOP 5a Protokoll Sitzung 13.3.1986, AdsD, NL Peter Glotz, Ordner Medienpolitik I.

[46] Michele Hilmes, *Only Connect: A Cultural History of Broadcasting in the United States* (Boston, 2007), 200–201.

broadcasters as left wing in increasingly strong terms. While campaigning for the presidency, Richard Nixon called public television "a bas-
tion of cultural elitism" that catered to privileged liberals at taxpayers'
expense.[47] Such charges in the name of the silent majority continued in
the early 1980s. Ronald Reagan's supporters called public television a
bulwark of Democratic liberals," and conservative organizations like
Accuracy in Media called it a "left-leaning antenna."[48] Reagan, acting
on that belief, cut the support for public broadcasting (Public Broadcasting Amendments Act) and commercialized it while at the same time
deregulating the commercial television market.[49]

In Britain, there was no similar debate about the public broadcaster,
the BBC, which still enjoyed a good reputation. Conservative criticism
began to grow, however, after the election of Margaret Thatcher. In late
1979, the police seized a BBC report about the Irish Republican Army
(IRA), and some Tories charged journalists for the BBC news program
"Panorama" with supporting terrorism. However, this led to an outcry
in parliament and the media. In the 1980s, BBC reports on the IRA and
Sinn Fein remained a subject of conservative complaint, and Thatcher
scrutinized the political balance of the BBC.[50] Nonetheless, only a small
group of Tories in parliament demanded more commercial channels.[51]

Starting in the late 1970s, the West German media reported frequently
about commercial television in other countries. Such reports provided
examples, both positive and negative, for the debate on commercial television and figured prominently in the political parties' public campaigns.
West German reporting focused above all on commercial television in
Great Britain, Luxembourg, Italy, and, of course, the United States. Reference to foreign commercial broadcasting was supposed to underline the
inevitability of the media reform. Prominent Christian Democrats argued

---

47 Laurean Ouellette and Justin Lewis, "Moving Beyond the 'Vast Wasteland': Cultural
    Policy and Television in the United States," in Robert C. Allen et al., eds., *The Television
    Studies Reader* (New York, 2004), 52–65, here 58.
48 B. J. Bullert, *Public Television: Politics and the Battle Over Documentary Film* (New
    Brunswick, NJ, 1997), 57–58.
49 William Hoynes, "Public Television and the Culture Wars," in James L. Nolan, ed., *The
    American Culture Wars: Current Contests and Future Prospects* (Charlottesville, VA,
    1996), 61–88, esp. 63–65.
50 Peter Walters, "The Crisis of 'Responsible' Broadcasting: Mrs. Thatcher and the BBC,"
    Parliamentary Affairs 42 (1989): 380–398, here 392; Jean Seaton and James Curran,
    Power Without Responsibility: The Press, Broadcasting, and New Media in Britain
    (New York, 2005), 208.
51 Andrew Crisell, *An Introductory History of British Broadcasting* (London, 2002), 84–
    86.

that Germany "could not be a green island in a world of cable TV, satellites, and copying technology."[52] "Satellite TV will come simply because other countries... will shoot satellites into space."[53] Such references to globalized markets were taken up to prove the urgent need for a different system and privatization. Otherwise, it was argued, Germany would lose its advertising market as well as many jobs and tax revenues if commercial programming in German was broadcast via satellite from Britain or Luxembourg.[54] This reasoning emphasized the inevitability of commercial television in a globalized world and was thus supposed to remove the issue from political debate.

Italy became the most negative example of a liberal media market in the West German public debate.[55] The Christian Democrats did not intend to have a free television and radio market as in the United States or especially in Italy, where more than a thousand small local broadcasters had sprung up after a reform enacted in 1976 and now presented a mix of political programs, erotica, and astrology shows. The fact that almost all small broadcasters in Italy had run up deficits and were fighting for survival provided left liberals in Germany with another argument against privatization. German conservatives also considered Italy's private television sector a negative example, above all because of its "anarchic" local diversity. They had deep reservations about giving air time to local political groups that ranged from the far left to the far right and to social groups such as homosexuals and feminists. Only rarely did German advocates of bottom-up broadcasting invoke the Italian example as a model.[56]

At the end of the 1970s, some Christian Democrats euphorically praised the Luxembourg-based commercial broadcaster RTL (Radio Télévision Lëtzebuerg). Its radio programs in German, English, and French had long been available to audiences in several neighboring countries. RTL had been regarded as a rather dull commercial television station up until that time, even among conservatives. Now leading Christian Democrats such as Hans Hugo Klein identified RTL as a "qualified program of an internationally respected while privately organized TV station," and Christian Schwarz-Schilling described it as a "successful,

[52] Manuscript of speech by Schwarz-Schilling, June 21, 1979, ACDP 01-824-232.
[53] Quoted in Hermanni, *Medienpolitik in den 8oer Jahren*, 80, 103.
[54] Quoted in Hermanni, *Medienpolitik in den 8oer Jahren*, 79, 104.
[55] *Spiegel*, October 28, 1979, 191–193; *Quick*, February 21, 1980.
[56] In a more positive vein, Siegfried Zielinski, "Warum kein 'Radio DGB?,'"*Die Neue*, November 29, 1979.

high-class role model."[57] Given that the introduction of RTL into the German broadcasting system was supposed to open the way for other private broadcasters, this elation was not surprising; however, it was quite unexpected to hear a member of the educated middle class such as Schwarz-Schilling heap praise on RTL.[58]

American television offerings came in for reevaluation in the Federal Republic during the debate on privatization. For the Social Democrats, the left-liberal press, and the public broadcaster ARD, American television continued to stand as evidence of the dangers of commercial broadcasting. They argued that it was dumbing down the content of its offering and increasingly showed violence, quiz programs, and talk shows.[59] The American model was also held up as proof that costs would soar for West German viewers, who could expect to pay as much as DM 80 to DM 120 for monthly cable television subscription fees. High-quality films, opponents of commercial broadcasting charged, would thus be accessible only to the affluent.[60] Above all, the Social Democrats saw U.S. commercial television as a threat to families and children. As Social Democrat Hans-Ulrich Klose argued, "In America, children are often 'switched off' by 'switching on' TV. Television replaces kindergarten."[61] The left-liberal press reported that American pre-schoolers were watching television eight hours a day, which resulted in social isolation and reduced learning capacity.[62] Highlighting the welfare of children to appeal to Christian Democratic voters, the Social Democrats put forward a quite conservative argument against commercial television. Christian Democratic politicians and right-leaning media outlets such as the *BILD-Zeitung*, on the other hand, praised the fact that American television was closer to the people, allowing for the audience to influence the program, and even applauded

---

[57] Speech by Schwarz-Schilling, printed in *epd*, December 11, 1976, AdsD ZASS III; *Welt*, November 30, 1976.

[58] Schwarz-Schilling was born into a family of musicians. He studied history and East Asian culture and linguistics, earning his doctorate in 1956 with a dissertation on Asian history.

[59] Compare, for instance, the interview with Hans-Ulrich Klose, *Die Neue*, May 19, 1979; Schmidt, "Medienpolitische Fachtagung der SPD," in Dokumentation FR 30.11.1979, 12; similarly an American journalist on the morning program *Internationaler Frühschoppen*: Sendung 26.8.1979; Wilhelm Roth, "Konzentration wird nicht verlangt," *Frankfurter Rundschau*, January 24, 1980.

[60] Bernd Leptihn, "Zu teure neue Medienwelt," *Hörfunk, Film und Fernsehen* 4 (1980): 9–16; *Spiegel*, August 7, 1978, and March 9, 1981, 63–72. "Vorlage der ARD in Anhörung Landtag NRW Jan. 16/17, 1980," *Media Perspektiven* 1 (1980): 34–39.

[61] Interview Klose, *Neue Ruhr Zeitung*, August 4, 1979.

[62] *Spiegel*, December 17, 1979, 46, 53; *Spiegel*, February 11, 1980, 39.

American political programming.[63] Many leading Christian Democrat politicians visited commercial television stations in the United States and praised the quality of their programming.[64]

The Christian Democrats wanted to have a regulated dual system like the one in Britain: only a few broadcasters should be allowed, and licensing and strict supervision would be used to regulate the market and maintain standards.[65] Unlike in Britain, however, the supervisory committee would be staffed by representatives of the political parties.[66] Only public broadcasting officials and some Social Democrats detected a decline of standards in British television and emphasized the reduction of minority programming and the explosion of costs because of the competition.[67]

Commercial Television and the Politics of Depoliticization

In the famous Orwellian year of 1984, private broadcasting began in Germany. What was the outcome of this important reform? The Christian Democrats had little to fear when West Germany's first private broadcasters went on the air in that year. Viewers of PKS's inaugural broadcast were welcomed by the network's executive director, Jürgen Doetz, the former spokesman for the well-known CDU politician Bernhard Vogel. Several times each day, PKS presented "FAZ-Nachrichten," a news show based on the reporting of the conservative daily *Frankfurter Allgemeine Zeitung*. More generally, the influence of publisher Axel Springer and media entrepreneur Leo Kirch seemed to guarantee that conservative influence would be felt within the private broadcasting industry.

Although some commercial broadcasters did become important supporters of the CDU, notably SAT.1, the main result of West Germany's broadcast reform was not an increase in conservative news programming

---

[63] "Die Wahrheit über das Privat-Fernsehen," *Bild am Sonntag*, December 2, 1979.

[64] See, for instance, Los Angeles Consulate to Federal Foreign Office, July 12, 1983; Bericht Hans H. Klein/Benno Erhard über die USA-Reise vom 31.7.–15.8.1982, Embassy Washington to Federal Foreign Office, July 26, 1984, ACDP 01-824-181; Bericht Fuchs/Vorsitzende ZDF-Fernseh-Rats über die USA-Reise vom 26.5.–6.6.1981, 17.9.1981, ACDP 01-824-181.

[65] Schwarz-Schilling, "Okkupation," 795. Similarly his speeches of April 27, 1979 and November 17, 1979.

[66] "Schwarz-Schilling auf dem Medienkongreß der hessischen CDU," *Hessen-Kurier*, November 1977. See also his debate with Hans Bausch, the general manager of the broadcaster Süddeutscher Rundfunk, *Spiegel*, February 11, 1980, 39.

[67] See ZDF broadcast "Noch mehr Fernsehen," August 27, 1979; Hans Bausch, October 15, 1979, SWR.

but rather the depoliticization of viewing audiences, especially younger viewers who generally preferred the offerings of private broadcasters. If the Christian Democrats had hoped that commercial television would help silence the younger generation, they were also victims of their own success as they saw their popular base shrink as a result of the depoliticization of German society. Commercial television also contributed to greater pluralism as the role of media events in integrating society declined. With the introduction of commercial television, West Germany's left as well as its conservative middle class became more silent.

14

Talking in Europe

The CDU/CSU, the British Conservative Party, and the Quest for a Common Political Language in the 1960s and 1970s

Martina Steber

In October 1973, representatives of the Scandinavian conservative parties, the British Conservative Party, the West German Christian Democrat Union (CDU) and Christian Social Union (CSU), the Austrian People's Party (ÖVP), and several smaller European center-right parties met for a short conference during the British Conservative Party Conference at Blackpool. These "inter-party conferences" were well established by this time. They had been set up in the mid-1960s to provide a European forum for parties excluded from the European Union of Christian Democrats (EUCD), which had been established in 1965 as the successor to the Nouvelles Équipes Internationales (NEI).[1] The NEI had played an important role in the process of European integration in the late 1940s and 1950s, providing a forum for senior politicians from the founding member states of the European Communities to meet to negotiate a common line on key issues. After the NEI had fallen into stagnation in the early 1960s, the EUCD was founded to provide a rejuvenated platform for the European center-right. West Germany's Union parties served as a crucial link between the EUCD and the excluded Northern European conservative parties, and the CDU in particular been lobbying hard for their

---

[1] See Wolfram Kaiser, "Deutschland exkulpieren und Europa aufbauen. Parteienkooperation der europäischen Christdemokraten in den Nouvelles Equipes Internationales 1947–1965," in Michael Gehler, Wolfram Kaiser, and Helmut Wohnout, eds., Christdemokratie in Europa im 20. Jahrhundert (Vienna, Cologne, Weimar, 2001), 695–719; Michael Gehler and Wolfram Kaiser, "Transnationalism and Early European Integration: The Nouvelles Equipes Internationales and the Geneva Circle 1947–1957," Historical Journal 44:3 (2001): 773–798.

inclusion in the European party network since the mid-1950s. With
Britain's accession to the European Community (1973-2020) (EC) in 1973, the integration of its Conservative Party became a pressing issue for the EUCD,
at least in German eyes. Resistance to that step was strong, however.
Despite years of negotiations, in the end North European and other conservative parties were denied membership. This was due, as this chapter
will show, above all to linguistic incompatibility.

The story of the formation of the center-right in an integrated Europe
provides an opportunity to explore the hitherto unconsidered role of language in the process of European integration and in the development
of European conservatism in the second half of the twentieth century.
Whereas the history of conservatism in Europe is usually told from a
nation-centered perspective, this chapter will focus on the transnational
side of the story, taking account of international cooperation, networking, and the transfer of ideas and policies.[2] As we will see, the history of
conservatism in Western Europe during the 1960s and 1970s was characterized by a push toward Europeanization driven by the EC's move
toward expansion and closer integration of its member states.[3] Although
international conservative elite networks, especially of the 1940s to the
1960s, have recently been the focus of research,[4] and although the cooperation of Christian Democrat parties in the NEI, EUCD, and the European
People's Party (EPP) has been widely discussed,[5] not much light has been

---

[2] Transatlantic party cooperation between European conservative parties and the Republican Party is a largely unexplored field. An exception, focused on the history of elec-
tioneering, is James Cooper, "'Superior to Anything I Had Seen in the States': The
'Thatcherisation' of Republican Strategy in 1980 and 1984," *Journal of Transatlantic
Studies* 11:1 (2013): 1–21.

[3] For the concept of "Europeanization" see Ulrike von Hirschhausen and Kiran Klaus
Patel, "Introduction," in Martin Conway and Kiran Klaus Patel, eds., *Europeanization
in the Twentieth Century: Historical Approaches* (New York, 2010), 1–18; Reiner Mar-
cowitz, "Historicising Europeanisation: An Introduction," in Matthieu Osmont et al.,
eds., *Europeanisation in the 20th Century: The Historical Lens* (Brussels, 2012), 15–26.

[4] Philip Mirowski and Dieter Plehwe, eds., *The Road from Mont Pèlerin: The Making of
the Neo-Liberal Thought Collective* (Cambridge, MA, 2009); Johannes Großmann, *Die
Internationale der Konservativen: Transnationale Elitenzirkel und private Außenpolitik
in Westeuropa seit 1945* (Munich, 2014); Valérie Aubourg, "Organizing Atlanticism:
The Bilderberg Group and the Atlantic Institute, 1952–1963," in Hans Krabbendam and
Giles Scott-Smith, eds., *The Cultural Cold War in Western Europe, 1945–1960* (London,
2003), 92–105; Thomas W. Gijswijt, *Uniting the West: The Bilderberg Group, the Cold
War and European Integration, 1952–1966* (Heidelberg, 2007); Vanessa Conze, *Das
Europa der Deutschen. Ideen von Europa in Deutschland zwischen Reichstradition und
Westorientierung (1920–1970)* (Munich, 2005).

[5] See, e.g., Gehler, Kaiser, and Wohnout, *Christdemokratie in Europa*; Michael Gehler
and Wolfram Kaiser, eds., *Transnationale Parteienkooperation der europäischen*

shed on the linkages between the British and Scandinavian conservative parties and their counterparts in the rest of Western Europe.[6] This chapter will begin to fill this gap and will also elaborate on the reasons for this historiographical lacuna. Because of its significance for European politics and its intensity, the cooperation between the CDU/CSU and the British Conservative Party will be the focus here.

The ever more intense process of European integration provided a platform for dialogue among conservatives in Europe: the European communicative space literally possessed a conservative layer. For this dialogue to succeed in the multilingual context of the European Communities, conservatives needed a common political language and, above all, shared political concepts, even if certain aspects of those concepts might be stressed more heavily than others in the differing national contexts. Hence when conservatives talked with each other in Europe, they were constantly negotiating the meaning of concepts.

At Blackpool in 1973, the parties gathered there decided to establish a "joint translation unit" to make party documents available in French, English, and German. One of the tasks of the projected translation unit would be the "evolution of a standard inter-language terminology."[7] Politicians active on the European level apparently saw a pressing need for a common pool of shared concepts. Whether the translation unit ever saw the light of day is doubtful. Funds were notoriously scarce, and the luxury of translation could be provided by the national parties' own translating staff, if necessary.

The problem of finding a shared terminology for conservatives in the EC was thus left unaddressed. A common language, or rather a pool of shared concepts, nevertheless emerged but always remained contested. That the EC employed a multitude of official languages further

---

Christdemokraten. Dokumente 1945–1965 (Munich, 2004); Thomas Jansen, *Die Entstehung einer Europäischen Partei: Vorgeschichte, Gründung und Entwicklung der EVP* (Bonn, 1996); Wolfram Kaiser, *Christian Democracy and the Origins of European Union* (Cambridge, 2007); Michael Gehler and Wolfram Kaiser, "Toward a 'Core Europe' in a Christian Western Bloc: Transnational Cooperation in European Christian Democracy, 1925–1965," in Thomas Kselman and Joseph A. Buttigieg, eds., *European Christian Democracy: Historical Legacies and Comparative Perspectives* (Notre Dame, IN, 2003), 240–266.

[6] An exception is Karl Magnus Johansson, "The Alliance of European Christian Democracy and Conservatism: Convergence through Networking," in Wolfram Kaiser and Peter Starie, eds., *Transnational European Union: Towards a Common Political Space* (London, 2005), 131–149.

[7] Bodleian Library, Oxford, Conservative Party Archive (CPA), IDU 30/3, Minutes of an interim meeting, Blackpool, October 10, 1973.

complicated the situation: national traditions of meaning were of course stored in the concepts and gave them specific connotations in their national contexts.[8] The history of European integration has therefore always also been the history of a battle over words. This is very much true for the history of European conservatism, as this chapter will demonstrate. It is informed by the history of concepts approach that developed from Reinhart Koselleck's pioneering studies and has subsequently been enriched by the history of discourse and the history of communication. In recent years, international comparison and transfer have become fruitful areas of research, above all into the history of colonialism.[9]

The story of center-right parties, embodying different traditions of European conservatism, meeting on the European level, and starting to talk to each other, is the story of the quest for a common political language. This chapter will examine this quest and its political implications.

Party Cooperation and the Challenge of Political Language

The problem of language in European center-right politics particularly challenged the British Conservatives. Britain succeeded in joining the EC only in 1973 under the Conservative government of Edward Heath.[10] The United Kingdom was a latecomer to the institutions of the European club and had to adapt to them before it could contemplate trying to shape them. This also implied that British Conservatives first had to speak the political language already spoken in center-right circles in the EC if they wanted to influence debate. And that proved to be difficult.

The Conservatives had regarded themselves as the party of Europe from the late 1940s and pressed hard for Britain's integration into the

---

[8] See, e.g., Reinhart Koselleck, *Futures Past: On the Semantics of Historical Times* (Cambridge, MA and London, 1985).

[9] See Kathrin Kollmeier, Begriffsgeschichte und Historische Semantik, Version 2.0, in Docupedia-Zeitgeschichte, 29.10.2012, http://docupedia.de/zg/Begriffsgeschichte_und_Historische_Semantik_Version_2.0_Kathrin_Kollmeier?oldid=85045 (accessed June 17, 2014); Willibald Steinmetz, "Vierzig Jahre Begriffsgeschichte – 'The State of the Art,'" in Heidrun Kämper and Ludwig Maximilian Eichinger, eds., *Sprache – Kognition – Kultur. Sprache zwischen mentaler Struktur und kultureller Prägung* (Berlin, 2008), 174–197; Margrit Pernau, "Whither Conceptual History? From National to Entangled Histories," *Contributions to the History of Concepts* 7:1 (2012): 1–11.

[10] John D. Young, "The Heath Government and British Entry into the European Community," in Stuart Ball and Anthony Seldon, eds., *The Heath Government 1970–1974: A Reappraisal* (London, 1996), 259–284; for an overview see Ben Patterson, *The Conservative Party and Europe* (London, 2011); Nick Crowson, *The Conservative Party and European Integration since 1945: At the Heart of Europe?* (New York, 2007).

economic and political structures of the Communities.[11] Toward that end, the Conservatives tried to associate themselves with existing alliances of center-right parties and establish close ties with like-minded parties on the Continent.[12] The CDU was key to the Conservatives' strategy. Beginning in the mid-1950s, they sought contacts with West Germany's Christian Democrats, first on an individual basis and then more formally through institutionalized meetings and exchanges involving politicians, activists, and party staffers to discuss policies, strategy, and tactics. Both parties regarded this multidimensional exchange as highly valuable, and each was the other's closest foreign partner.[13] From the CDU's perspective, contacts with the British Conservatives complemented its support for British EC membership,[14] offered an alternative to the Franco-German axis, loosened the grip of the Southern European Christian Democrats, and provided a forum to discuss liberal approaches to economic and social policy. Tellingly, the CDU's bilateral cooperation with the Democrazia Cristiana Italiana was much more limited.[15] The 1970s in particular saw intensive cooperation between the CDU and the Conservative Party. It was no coincidence that both parties were in opposition at the time – excluded from international governmental channels, they put particular value on party contacts – and had entered periods of far-reaching transformation following the ascent of Helmut Kohl and Margaret Thatcher to the leadership of their parties in 1973 and 1975, respectively.[16] The

---

[11] See Jim Buller, "Conservative Statecraft and European Integration in Historical Perspective," in Kai Oppermann, ed., *British Foreign and Security Policy: Historical Legacies and Current Challenges* (Augsburg, 2012), 70–93.

[12] See Crowson, *The Conservative Party*, 188–196.

[13] See the extensive collections on party cooperation in the Conservative Party Archives, Bodleian Library, Oxford (CPA), the Archiv für Christlich-Demokratische Politik, Sankt Augustin (ACDP), and the Archiv für Christlich-Soziale Politik, Munich (ACSP).

[14] For German policy toward British EC membership see N. Piers Ludlow, "Constancy and Flirtation: Germany, Britain, and the EEC, 1956–1972," in Jeremy Noakes, Peter Wende, and Jonathan Wright, eds., *Britain and Germany in Europe 1949–1990* (Oxford and New York, 2002), 95–112, and Stephen Wall, *The Official History of Britain and the European Community*, vol. 2, *From Rejection to Referendum, 1963–1975* (London and New York, 2013).

[15] See Carla Masala, "Die CDU und die Democrazia Cristiana Italiana, 1949–1969. Eine schwierige Beziehung," *Historisch-Politische Mitteilungen* 3 (1996): 145–162.

[16] See Frank Bösch, "Die Krise als Chance. Die Neuformierung der Christdemokraten in den siebziger Jahren," in Konrad H. Jarausch, ed., *Das Ende der Zuversicht? Die siebziger Jahre als Geschichte* (Göttingen, 2008), 296–309; Robert Saunders, "'Crisis? What Crisis?': Thatcherism and the Seventies," in Ben Jackson and Robert Saunders, eds., *Making Thatcher's Britain* (Cambridge, 2012), 24–42; Richard Vinen, *Thatcher's Britain: The Politics and Social Upheaval of the 1980s* (London, 2009), 60–100.

cooperation between the Conservatives and the CDU on the European
level was both a result and an intensification of these bilateral contacts.

What did these two parties, anchored in very different political traditions, think that they might have in common? During the 1960s and
1970s, party leaders and experts saw both pragmatic and ideological
reasons to cooperate. First, the parties were neither socialist nor liberal
in terms either of their membership in European party alliances or of
their place in the political spectrum at home. Second, it was assumed, the
parties shared a bundle of core convictions. The first decades of cooperation between the parties were a time of reciprocal recognition and
discovery. Evelyn Emmet, external relations officer of the Conservative
Party, confessed that in their endeavor to "rethink" their policies after the
devastating loss of power in 1964, the Conservatives had "been struck
by how often our own ideas coincide with what we know of Christian
Democrat thinking."[17] The parties' curiosity about one another during
the 1960s and 1970s was spurred in large measure by programmatic
insecurity. Each party lost its long-held parliamentary majority, and profound social and cultural changes were sweeping away traditional conservative certainties. During these decades, West Germany witnessed a
profound secularization and liberalization of Christian Democratic and
conservative thought. That process resulted in the amalgamation of those
traditions and the birth of a reformulated conservatism oriented toward
European and American models. In Britain during this period, the Conservative Party was struck by deep inner divisions over ideology that were
only partially resolved under Thatcher's leadership.[18]

The assumption that the parties shared central convictions required
proof in theory and in practice. Shared convictions first had to be identified, and then concepts to express them had to be found. As long
as those concepts were part of the parties' established vocabularies or
could be integrated into them, this process proceeded smoothly. The
two parties could agree on their shared belief in concepts such as "market," "competition," and "family" even if those concepts carried different connotations in their political lexicons. These shared political concepts provided the basis for cooperation between the parties, and they

[17] ACDP, 07-001-11226, Evelyn Emmet to Konrad Kraske, October 18, 1966.
[18] For an overview of party history see Frank Bösch, *Macht und Machtverlust: Die
Geschichte der CDU* (Stuttgart and Munich, 2002); John Ramsden, *The Winds of
Change: Macmillan to Heath, 1957–1975* (London, 1996); John Ramsden, *The Mak-
ing of Conservative Party Policy: The Conservative Research Department since 1929*
(London, 1980).

reassured politicians on both sides of the Channel of their common ideological aims. The concept of freedom is the best example of the unifying effect of shared concepts on the European level. But concepts also had the capacity to divide, as the debate on the concept of conservatism itself shows.

The Political Glue of "Freedom"

"Freedom," a key term in the West's Cold War rhetoric, became the central concept in communications between British and West German conservatives.[19] From the very beginning of their cooperation, the CDU and the Conservative Party could reassure themselves of their common pursuit by invoking "freedom." When the Conservative Party was represented at a CDU party conference for the first time in 1958, Conservative MP Peter Smithers received "enthusiastic applause" when he told his German colleagues, "As members of the C.D.U. and of the Conservative Party we share a common belief in the value of a free society, in which the state is the servant, and not the master of its citizens"[20] The Conservative Party's recently published program "Onward in Freedom" also made a great impression at the CDU conference.[21] Eugen Gerstenmaier, the deputy chairperson of the party and the leading representative of its Protestant wing, took up the slogan at the close of his address to the conference, calling on his party to proclaim together with "England's Conservatives in shared belief and hope . . . : Onwards, friends, onwards in freedom!"[22] Naturally, the Cold War framed the conservative enthusiasm for freedom. "Free Europe" had to be defended externally against the Soviet Union and the Warsaw Pact, German and British conservatives were convinced, and internally against the threat of socialism embodied in the Federal Republic by the Social Democrats and in Britain by the

---

[19] On the influence of the Cold War on political language, see Willibald Steinmetz, ed., *Political Languages in the Age of Extremes* (Oxford, 2011). For rhetorical analyses of the Cold War, see Martin J. Medhurst, Robert L. Ivie, Philip Wander, and Robert L. Scott, *Cold War Rhetoric: Strategy, Metaphor, and Ideology* (East Lansing, MI, 1990); Paul A. Chilton, *Security Metaphors: Cold War Discourse from Containment to Common House* (New York, 1996).

[20] CPA, COB 64/2, Peter Smithers, [Address to the CDU conference 1958], 19.9.1958; 8. Bundesparteitag der CDU, Kiel, 18.–21.9.1958 [Niederschrift], ed. CDU-Bundesgeschäftsstelle, Bonn [1958], 39 (in German).

[21] See CPA, COB 64/2, C.D.U. Annual Conference – Kiel, 18.–21.9.1958 [Report by Peter Smithers].

[22] Ibid., 108.

Labour Party. The CDU and the Conservative Party each saw itself as the main political force standing up for freedom in its home country.

The impetus behind conservative cooperation, thus, was antisocialism. Antisocialism functioned as a glue, especially during the highly polarizing debates both countries experienced during the 1970s.[23] This was the context for intensified party cooperation: center-right parties thought it was high time to counter the influence of socialist European networks, above all the Socialist International, by means of a strong alliance of their own. The concept of "freedom" became the rallying cry of conservative cooperation in Western Europe. It was the central term in a tightly structured political vocabulary directed entirely against a single opponent: "socialism." In conservative political language, socialism denoted all political manifestations left of the center, from social democracy to Eurocommunism.[24] The latter was a source of particular alarm to conservatives between 1976 and 1979.[25]

It also tended to define [by virtue] the conservatives' opponent)

"The socialist challenge" was a major topic on the agenda of an interparty conference in 1974. The CSU representative introduced the topic by analyzing the "nature of socialism" for which he used a catchy metaphor: like Janus, it "has two faces, Social Democracy and Marxism."[26] As the communist East threatened Western Europe from without, the West European left undermined free society from within. Following this logic, British and West German conservatives saw the Cold War as a struggle that also had to be fought at home in domestic economic and social

---

[23] For conservative mobilization in the 1970s see Axel Schildt, "'Die Kräfte der Gegenreform sind auf breiter Front angetreten'. Zur konservativen Tendenzwende in den Siebzigerjahren," *Archiv für Sozialgeschichte* 44 (2004): 449–478; Massimiliano Livi, Daniel Schmidt, and Michael Sturm, eds., *Die 1970er Jahre als schwarzes Jahrzehnt: Politisierung und Mobilisierung zwischen christlicher Demokratie und extremer Rechter* (Frankfurt am Main, 2010); Anna von der Goltz, "A Polarised Generation? Conservative Students and West Germany's '1968,'" in Anna von der Goltz, ed., *"Talkin' 'Bout My Generation": Conflicts of Generation Building and Europe's 1968* (Göttingen, 2011), 195–215; Nikolai Wehrs, *Protest der Professoren: Der Bund Freiheit der Wissenschaft in den 1970er Jahren* (Göttingen, 2014); Jackson and Saunders, *Making Thatcher's Britain*.

[24] See Nikolas R. Dörr, Eurokommunismus als Teil der historischen Kommunismusforschung, Version 1.0, in Docupedia-Zeitgeschichte, 6.1.2014, http://dx.doi.org/10.14756/zzf.kok.2.235.V1.

[25] For the EDU see ACSP, Sammlungen, Europäische Demokratische Union, Eurokommunismus, Bulletin 5, beschlossen am 20.7.1979. For the CDU and CSU's positioning see Nikolas R. Dörr, "Die Auseinandersetzungen um den Eurokommunismus in der bundesdeutschen Politik 1967–1979," *Jahrbuch für Historische Kommunismusforschung* (2012): 217–232, esp. 224–228.

[26] CPA, IDU 30/3, Inter-Party Conference 1974, Minutes, May 19, 1974.

policies. In 1976, Margaret Thatcher told a CDU party conference that Europeans ultimately had a choice between only two political philosophies, the "Marxist-Socialist" philosophy and "the philosophy of the Christian Democrats and Conservatives." Thatcher put "freedom" at the center of her vision for Europe's center-right and won her audience over by ending her speech with several lines in German.[27] This dichotomy was effectively encapsulated in the CDU's campaign slogan for the Bundestag election that year: "Freedom instead of socialism." Certainly not uncontroversial in the CDU, it thrilled the British party leader so much that she promised Helmut Kohl to integrate it into her rhetorical repertoire.[28] The slogan had been insisted upon by the party's right wing as well as by the CSU and its leader, Franz Josef Strauß, who had long favored a political vocabulary centered on stark oppositions and clear-cut dichotomies. Congratulating Thatcher on her election victory in 1979, Strauß underlined their close association in their "common struggle against Socialist totalitarianism... in the European battle between popular front [*Volksfront*] and freedom."[29] Indeed, with their strong antisocialist focus, Strauß and Thatcher spoke a very similar political language during the 1970s.

Marching under the banner of "freedom," the antisocialist front employed a rhetoric reliant on an "either/or" structure that categorically ruled out compromise. CDU secretary general Kurt Biedenkopf, one of the masterminds behind the CDU's ideological reinvention of the 1970s,[30] warned the delegates to the European Union of Women's Conference in 1977 that Eurocommunism was becoming stronger than ever. "Free society" had to be defended unyieldingly, Biedenkopf claimed, and he strongly advised his female audience to "[d]ebate not with the idea of compromise, but with the idea of thrashing it out."[31] It was this conviction that was at the bottom of the strategy of "occupying terms" that Biedenkopf had set out for his party in 1973.[32] It similarly shaped Thatcher's rhetorical

[27] Margaret Thatcher, Speech to Christian Democratic Union Conference, May 25, 1976, http://www.margaretthatcher.org/document/103034 (accessed June 16, 2014).

[28] CAC, THCR 2/6/1/21, Margaret Thatcher to Helmut Kohl, July 9, 1976.

[29] ACSP, NL Strauß Büro PV: 12970, Franz Josef Strauß to Margaret Thatcher, May 4, 1979.

[30] For an overview of the programmatic renewal see Bösch, "Die Krise als Chance."

[31] Churchill Archive Centre (CAC), THCR, 2/6/1/23, CDU, Büro für Auswärtige Beziehungen, Address by Professor Biedenkopf before the General Assembly of the European Union of Women (EUW) in Turku (Finland), 11.8.1977, November 1977.

[32] 22. Bundesparteitag der CDU Deutschland, Hamburg, 18.–20.11.1973 [Niederschrift], ed. Bundesgeschäftsstelle, Bonn [1973], 61–62; for the CDU strategy of "occupying terms" see Martin H. Geyer, "War over Words: The Search for a Public Language in

style. The prophets of the Old Testament, Thatcher famously maintained at an election rally in Wales in 1979, did not preach consensus; rather, they had left their homes, imbued with fervent faith and a clear vision, prepared to pursue their goals to their last breath.[33] The clarity that was a defining trait of Thatcher's oratory rested on adamant antisocialism and a highly charged political vocabulary.

European conservatives believed that socialists were undermining freedom at the European level too, and, accordingly, "freedom" was adopted as the guiding concept of conservative policy on Europe. The conservative stress on "freedom" in Europe found its nucleus in the European Democrat Union (EDU), which was established as a more visible successor to the inter-party conferences and rather constrained alternative to the EPP in 1978. "[W]ith the forming of the EDU we have started a new chapter in the history of freedom in Europe," Thatcher wrote to Josef Taus of Austria's ÖVP, the first president of the EDU.[34] At the EDU's founding conference, she voiced her conviction that it was "the threat which Marxism brings against freedom" that had led the participating parties to join forces.[35]

This conservative closing of ranks against socialism followed after a self-conscious turn from pragmatism to a more ideologically inspired style of politics. At a meeting in 1975, leaders of Europe's conservative parties agreed "that a renewal and revival of interest in basic ideas is necessary. The main decisions for the present and future of a free society in the European democracies cannot be taken on the basis of day-to-day pragmatism. Only a dynamic and convincing identification with the lasting values of liberty and the dignity of man will guarantee an open and democratic society."[36] Conservative pragmatism alone was not considered sufficient for confronting the challenges of the 1970s: European conservatives longed for conservative ideology.

This belief also lay behind the internal debates on basic values and policies that the CDU, CSU, and the Conservative Party conducted

West Germany," in Steinmetz, *Political Languages*, 293–330; for a critical analysis of the notion of "occupying terms" see Frank Liedtke, Martin Wengeler, and Karin Böke, eds., *Begriffe besetzen. Strategien des Sprachgebrauchs in der Politik* (Opladen, 1981).

[33] Margaret Thatcher, Speech to Conservative Rally in Cardiff, 16.4.1979, http://www.margaretthatcher.org/document/104011 (accessed June 16, 2014).

[34] CAC, THCR, 2/6/1/23, Margaret Thatcher to Josef Taus, April 26, 1978.

[35] Margaret Thatcher, Speech to European Democratic Union, April 24, 1978, http://www.margaretthatcher.org/document/103663 (accessed June 17, 2014).

[36] CPA, IDU 30/3, Party Leaders' Conference, Klesheim Palace, Salzburg, September 8–9, 1975.

during the 1970s. The CDU backed antisocialism at the European level but, on account of internal resistance to strict antisocialism and the party's flirtation with the Northern European conservatives, at the same time counterbalanced it with other conservative tropes.[37] The party differentiated itself semantically in part by aligning the concept of freedom with other central terms in the conservative political vocabulary. In a 1973 speech to the EUCD, Richard von Weizsäcker had espoused the idea of *verantwortete Freiheit*, "freedom in responsibility." Freedom, Weizsäcker argued, is "not only individualism but also active neighborliness [*praktizierte Nachbarschaft*], not only emancipation but also commitment, and not only ideological pluralism but also the acceptance of the moral and normative order on which society is based. Freedom and responsibility are therefore inseparable."[38] The concept of "responsibility" was an integral part of conservative language in both Germany and Britain, as was the conjunction of "freedom" and "responsibility." Weizsäcker's differentiation therefore was entirely in line with conservative political language in stressing the distinction between a conservative and a liberal understanding of "freedom." His plea for "freedom in responsibility" was delivered before the EUCD conference, where skepticism toward the integration of North European Conservative parties prevailed. Nonetheless, the belief in "freedom" was pivotal for Christian Democrats and Conservatives alike, despite disagreements over the handling of Eurocommunist parties and social policy.[39] By drawing on this concept, Weizsäcker's speech intended to bring unity to the conservative camp, which, he claimed, was an absolute necessity for defending "freedom and solidarity" in a Europe threatened by socialism.

The distinctive bipolarity of political language was not affected by such semantic balancing acts. When high-ranking CDU and Conservative Party policy analysts met for one of their regular workshops in February 1979, they focused on the "Menace of European Socialism to the social market economy in Europe," a topic suggested by the CDU. The bipolarity of conservative political language structured their discussion of social and

---

[37] See, e.g., the interview with Peter Radunski, in Michael Gehler, Marcus Gonschor, Hinnerk Meyer, and Johannes Schönner, eds., *Mitgestalter Europas: Transnationalismus und Parteiennetzwerke europäischer Christdemokraten und Konservativer in historischer Erfahrung* (Sankt Augustin and Berlin, 2013), 93–148, here124–126.

[38] ACSP, Sammlungen, EUCD, XIX. Kongress der EUCD, Bonn, 7.–9.11.1973, Richard von Weizsäcker, Die Christliche Demokratie – für den Fortschritt in Freiheit und Solidarität.

[39] For the conflict between CDU/CSU and Democrazia Cristiana Italiana see Dörr, "Auseinandersetzungen," 224–225.

economic policy. Their agenda gives a vivid impression of the antithetical semantics that had developed:

1. Free competition versus dirigistic restraints.
2. Structural changes as a result of adjustment processes in the market versus socialist models of regulated economy and control of investment.
3. Integrated family policy versus exclusively job-oriented women's liberation.
4. Social welfare as a means to safeguard individual freedom versus socialist regulation of the citizen.[40]

Party cooperation reinforced and invigorated the process of semantic polarization that characterized the CDU/CSU and Conservative Party in the 1970s and transferred it onto a European level.

"Freedom" was the key term in the political language of the CDU, the CSU, and the Conservative Party in the 1970s. "Freedom" literally bundled a whole set of antisocialist concepts that shaped center-right policies in Europe during the 1970s. By the end of the decade, conservative rhetoric increasingly appeared to offer a viable approach for overcoming the "Eurosclerosis" many saw afflicting the European Community as well as the economic stagnation besetting the national economies of the EC member states. The hardening of positions in the Second Cold War also nurtured the antisocialist concept of freedom.[41] It was no coincidence that the Single European Act, which cut the Gordian knot of Eurosclerosis in 1986, echoed the conservative political language of freedom.[42] At the same time, however, that language could also be turned against the European project: in Thatcher's anti-European rhetoric of the late 1980s, the socialist threat to freedom emanated from the reformed institutions of the EC. Conservatives, she stressed again and again, would stand up for "a free Europe" but would not tolerate "a Socialist super-state in Brussels which submerges our identity and snuffs out our sovereignty."[43]

[40] CPA, IDU 28/5, Conservative Research Department, Sandy Walker, CDU Researchers, February 2, 1979.
[41] See Philipp Gassert, Tim Geiger, and Hermann Wentker, eds., *Zweiter Kalter Krieg und Friedensbewegung. Der NATO-Doppelbeschluss in deutsch-deutscher und internationaler Perspektive* (Munich, 2011).
[42] See Kenneth Dyson and Kevin Featherstone, *The Road to Maastricht: Negotiating Economic and Monetary Union* (New York, 1999).
[43] See, e.g., Margaret Thatcher, Speech to Scottish Conservative Conference, May 12, 1989, http://www.margaretthatcher.org/document/107663 (accessed June 17, 2014).

"Conservatism" and the Fight over Linguistic Incompatibility

If the concept of freedom enabled center-right parties with very different traditions to cooperate, the concept of conservatism had exactly the opposite effect. With Britain's accession to the European Economic Community (EEC), the place of the British Conservatives in center-right party alliances had to be clarified once and for all. The problem had remained unresolved for more than a decade by then. The main reason for this political deadlock was the resistance of the Italian, Belgian, and Dutch Christian Democrat parties to the integration of the North European conservatives into the EUCD. Their problem was a problem of words, or, more precisely, a problem with a single word: "conservative." The discussion of what "conservative" actually meant had kept the European center-right parties busy during the 1960s and 1970s. This debate illustrates plainly how deeply conceptual questions influenced the integration process.

Even though their European credentials were not called into question, the British Conservatives and their Scandinavian counterparts learned their party names did not carry the same positive associations throughout the Continent that they enjoyed at home. To a certain degree this also held true for the CDU. In the language of the Federal Republic, "conservative" as a political term belonged to an array of concepts discredited by National Socialism.[44] For the dominating Catholic founding fathers of the Union parties, nothing seemed to be more abstruse than to pick up the epithet "conservative"; they considered themselves as "Christian." That was much less the case, however, for those in the CDU who regarded themselves as heirs to the North German, mainly Protestant conservative tradition. For them, the label "conservative" had positive connotations; it was associated with the conservative resistance groups involved in the July 20, 1944, plot against Hitler and was epitomized by Eugen Gerstenmaier, who had participated in the oppositional Kreisauer Kreis.[45] After the last conservative parties with roots in the Weimar Republic dissolved in the late 1950s and were integrated in the

---

[44] For the special linguistic situation of the Federal Republic see Georg Stötzel, "Der Nazi-Komplex," in Georg Stötzel, Martin Wengeler, and Karin Böke, eds., *Kontroverse Begriffe: Geschichte des öffentlichen Sprachgebrauchs in der Bundesrepublik Deutschland* (Berlin, 1995), 355–382; Tillmann Bendikowski and Lucian Hölscher, eds., *Political Correctness: Der sprachpolitische Streit um die nationalsozialistischen Verbrechen* (Göttingen, 2008).

[45] See Daniela Gniss, *Der Politiker Eugen Gerstenmaier 1906–1986* (Frankfurt am Main, 2005).

CDU,[46] the concept lost some of its political distinctiveness and was subsequently taken up by CDU/CSU politicians of all stripes as one element in the party's self-description. That the label "Christian" lost some of its appeal in the secularizing 1960s also spurred the search for semantic alternatives.[47] Eventually, the Union parties came to see themselves as a *Volkspartei*, a "people's party," that encompassed "liberal," "social," "conservative," and "Christian" elements: the exceptionally difficult semantic situation of political language in the Federal Republic is readily evident in this amalgamation of conceptual labels. The meaning of "conservative" in this context was restricted to an attitude toward change that regarded change as justified only if an established practice no longer worked or stood in opposition to Christian beliefs.

In the open semantic situation of the early 1960s, the Union parties' strengthening of contacts with the British Conservatives could play a part in helping to refashion the concept of conservatism in a liberal sense. In a short address to the 1964 CDU party conference, Evelyn Emmet, the external relations officer of the Conservative Party, felt it necessary to explain the political meaning of the term "conservative" in the British context. "For us," she said, "it means to preserve the best, so that in the present we can build on it for the future. Surely, most important in this is the Christian faith, and here . . . we wholeheartedly agree with the CDU."[48] Unsurprisingly, the CDU politicians most heavily committed to the bilateral contacts in the 1960s belonged to the Protestant, liberal, and North German wing of the party. In British conservatism, they saw a merger of liberal and conservative thinking that could serve as a model for the CDU. Conservative West German Catholics, by contrast, were still rather oriented toward France or Southern Europe. This basic conflict within the Union parties had led to the deep split in foreign policy ideas between "Gaullists" and "Atlanticists" in the 1950s and 1960s.[49]

This pattern loosened in the early 1970s, when a new generation of CDU/CSU politicians took over and German–British party cooperation had become firmly established. As we have seen, a set of shared

46 See Frank Bösch, *Die Adenauer-CDU: Gründung, Aufstieg und Krise einer Erfolgspartei 1945–1969* (Stuttgart and Munich, 2001), 174–194.

47 For the context see Thomas Großbölting, *Der verlorene Himmel: Glaube in Deutschland seit 1945* (Göttingen, 2013), 120–130; and his contribution to this volume (chapter 10).

48 CPA, COB 88/2, Evelyn Emmet, Report on the CDU Party Conference, Hanover 1964, n.d.; quote in German, my translation.

49 See Tim Geiger, *Atlantiker gegen Gaullisten: Außenpolitischer Konflikt und innerparteilicher Machtkampf in der CDU/CSU 1958–1969* (Munich, 2008).

antisocialist beliefs was crucial in this regard. The change in attitude among conservative German Catholics was exemplified by Franz Joseph Strauß, who admired British conservatism and did his utmost to promote cooperation between the CSU and the Conservative Party. According to Weizsäcker, Strauß saw himself as a "German Thatcher."[50] The crucial problem of harmonizing the traditions of conservatism and Christian Democracy was repeatedly described in this period as a problem of terminology, not of substance.[51] That reflected the acute consciousness of language in West German and British conservative circles during the 1960s and 1970s.[52] The conservatives' increased European and global involvement certainly contributed to this, as did the general feeling among conservatives that the left had seized control over language.

Although the Union parties did integrate the term "conservative" into their vocabulary, conservatism remained a difficult concept for them – not least because the 68ers had basically equated the concept with fascism. The CDU eventually adopted the tag *Partei der Mitte* – "party of the center" – to describe itself in order to avoid conceptual pitfalls arising from Germany's Nazi past.[53] In Italy and the Benelux countries, by contrast, the center-right parties could not integrate the concept of "conservatism" into their vocabularies. The politicians at the top of the Christian Democrat party organizations, especially the Italians, remained firm in their rejection of the North European conservatives, branding them un-Christian and reactionary,[54] and they were also worried about the domestic impact of a Christian Democratic–Conservative alignment on the European level at a time when they relied on coalition partners from the

[50] Richard von Weizsäcker, *Vier Zeiten: Erinnerungen* (Berlin, 2002), 245.

[51] See, e.g., Kai-Uwe von Hassel, "The Swinton Lecture 1972: Conservatism and Christian Democracy in Europe," *Swinton Journal* 18:3 (1972): 14–26; CPA CCO 3/7/19, European Union of Christian-Democrat and Conservative Students, Tom Spencer, Memorandum on the name "Conservative," December 26, 1971; IDU 30/3, The Problems of Inter-Party Links for the Conservative Party, August 8, 1975 ("Despite many years of explanation the reactionary connotation of the word 'Conservative' in various European countries continues to elicit hostile reaction. It is not generally understood that the Party by no means relies on exclusively middle class support and that it must attract substantial working class support in order to win power").

[52] Willibald Steinmetz, "Some Thoughts on a History of Twentieth-Century German Basic Concepts," in Stefan-Ludwig Hoffmann and Kathrin Kollmeier, eds., Roundtable: Geschichtliche Grundbegriffe Reloaded? Writing the Conceptual History of the Twentieth Century, *Contributions to the History of Concepts* 7:1 (2012): 87–100, here 99–100; Geyer, "War over Words."

[53] See, e.g., CDU-Bundesparteitag 1973, 370–371.

[54] See, e.g., ACDP, NL Bruno Heck, I 022 101/2, Mariano Rumor to Bruno Heck, April 2, 1966.

left.[55] During the EUCD presidency of the Italian Mariano Rumor (1965–1973), the doors to the Christian Democratic European club were essentially closed to the North European conservatives.[56] For the British, the ongoing continental "obsession . . . about Conservatism as such" was indeed difficult to grasp.[57]

The British Conservatives lobbied relentlessly for the conservative cause, and the CDU/CSU supported them in the endeavor.[58] A detailed paper on the principles of the Conservative Party was prepared for the inter-party conference at Vienna in 1971. It was widely distributed among like-minded parties on the Continent. The Conservatives sought to convey the impression that they were a Christian party of the center that "vigorously eschew[ed] rigid doctrine of the radical type." Pursing a "*via media*" between Liberal individualism and socialist collectivism, correcting by commonsense [the socialists'] doctrinaire follies," they held to "moderation in all things" and policies of "distinctly religious and ethical inspiration."[59] "Every opportunity must be taken," an internal memorandum of May 1975 stressed, "to explain to those parties, having reservations about the Conservative Party, that British Conservatism is moderate, modern and broadly based."[60] William Whitelaw, then party chairman, appealed to his counterparts at the inter-party conference some months later to open the door to the Conservative Party, which, he explained, could not change its name to incorporate the word "Christian" even if it wanted to and even though it upheld Christian principles.[61]

[55] See, e.g., CPA, CCO 20/15/11, International Inter-Party Relations with Special Reference to Europe, October 31, 1970. For the Italian Democrazia Cristiana and its policy of "apertura a sinistra" in the 1960s and 1970s see for an overview Hans Woller, *Geschichte Italiens im 20. Jahrhundert* (Munich, 2010), 269–323; and Agostino Giovagnoli, *Il Partito Italiano: La Democrazia Cristiana dal 1942 al 1994* (Rome and Bari, 1996).

[56] For Mariano Rumor's EUCD presidency see Francesco Malgeri, "The Italian Presence in the Christian Democrat International: Aspects and Personalities," in Jean-Dominique Durand, ed., *Christian Democrat Internationalism: Its Action in Europe and Worldwide from Post World War II until the 1990s* (Brussels, 2013), 187–200, here 193–200.

[57] CPA, CCO 20/32/1, Meeting on Links with Like-Minded Parties in Europe, December 10, 1962.

[58] See, e.g., ACDP, 07-001-11226; 07-001-11479; 07-001-12095; NL Bruno Heck, I 022 101/2; Douglas Hurd, *Memoirs* (London, 2003), 245–247; Margaret Thatcher, *The Path to Power* (London, 1995), 340–347.

[59] CPA, CCO 20/15/11, Some working principles of the British Conservative & Unionist Party, 1971.

[60] CPA, IDU 30/3, The Problems of Inter-Party Links for the Conservative Party, August 8, 1975.

[61] Ibid.; Party Leaders' Conference, Klesheim Palace, Salzburg, September 8–9, 1975.

The British peculiarity, where the Christian churches were not exclusively linked with one party as in the Christian Democrat countries on the Continent, complicated the European situation even further. For the British Conservatives, integrating "Christian" in the party's name was inconceivable. Here lay the conceptual boundaries of the British conservative vocabulary. Whereas West German bridge-builders had to explain to what extent Christian Democracy was based on conservative principles, Conservatives had to explain to what extent conservatism was based on Christian beliefs. This conceptual incompatibility made the search for a name for the successor organization to the informal inter-party conferences rather difficult. As a result of the ongoing resistance of the Italian, Dutch, and Belgian parties, the North European conservatives were not invited to join the European People's Party upon its founding in 1976.[62] Although the Northern Europeans' courtship of the Italian, Dutch, and Belgian Christian Democrats had been in vain, the alliance with the parties of the inter-party conference, including the CDU, CSU, and the Austrian ÖVP,[63] had deepened, and found its expression in the ensuing founding of the European Democrat Union, EDU, in 1978.[64] Its name speaks volumes: it accentuated the concept of "democracy," which the British and West German center-right parties tried to occupy amidst the political polarization of the 1970s, and it avoided "the terms Christian, People's Party or Conservative," as a memo on a preparatory meeting noted.[65]

The founding of the EDU would have been inconceivable without the two decades of West German–British cooperation that had preceded it.

---

[62] See Thomas Jansen, *The European People's Party: Origins and Development* (Basingstoke, 1998), 61–67; for the conflicts over the name of the EPP see Steven Van Hecke, "The Fractious Foundation of the European People's Party," in Durand, *Christian Democrat Internationalism*, 173–184, here 178–179.

[63] For the ÖVP's very lively commitment to European center-right party cooperation see Michael Gehler and Johannes Schönner, "Transnationale christdemokratische Parteienkooperationen in Europa 1965–1989. Der Beitrag österreichischer Ideen und Initiativen," *Demokratie und Geschichte. Jahrbuch des Karl-von-Vogelsang-Instituts zur Erforschung der Geschichte der christlichen Demokratie in Österreich* 11:12 (2007/2008): 271–318.

[64] For the EDU see Andreas Khol, Lars Tobisson, and Alexis Wintoniak, *Twenty Years European Democrat Union 1978–1998* (Vienna, 1998), the interesting volume of interviews by Gehler, Gonschor, Meyer, and Schönner, *Mitgestalter*, and Johansson, "Alliance"; for the complicated foundation history of the EPP and EDU see Jansen, *Entstehung*, 97–110, and Mark Speich, *Kai-Uwe von Hassel: Eine politische Biographie* (Bonn, 2001), 451–475.

[65] CAC, THCR 2/6/1/23, Note on Meeting of Christian Democrat and Conservative Parties, held in London, February 12–13, 1976.

Not only had party leaders and officials got to know each other and establish relationships of trust, they had also learned to understand each other's political language. They were thereby able to work around their conceptual differences and develop a body of shared concepts. This was the precondition for cooperation on the European level. It is no coincidence that the parties that so vehemently opposed the integration of the Northern European conservatives lacked this experience.

The conceptual negotiations on the European level also affected conservative political language at the national level. A letter to Margaret Thatcher from her parliamentary private secretary, Adam Butler, written in February 1977 shows how far internal considerations about the problems of the term "conservative" could proceed in this context. The letter suggested a change of the party name. "The two 'ingredients' we need are Democrat and National," Butler argued. "Whilst I think it would be difficult at one stroke to drop Conservative altogether, and wrong, the adoption of the name 'The National Democratic Conservative Party' would allow a gradual transition to National Democrats, and this abbreviation would gain more ready usage in Europe."[66] What his party leader made of this, we do not know, but that Butler's suggestion was buried in the files speaks volumes.

Obviously, talking in Europe was a delicate endeavor. National traditions of conceptual meaning could not easily be set aside, nor was it easy to establish a common terminology. In the case of the term "conservative," the attempt to do so ended in failure. In the end, it was not the British conservative political terminology that was adopted at the European level but rather that of the Continental Christian Democrats. This had far-reaching consequences for the institutional structure of the center-right in Europe. Two separate parliamentary groups were established in the European Parliament in 1979, the EDU and EPP. They worked independently of each other during the 1980s, and the British were not at the table when the EPP conducted negotiations during the lead-up to the Single European Act.[67] The two parliamentary groups merged in the 1990s, but their differences on the purpose of the European Union only grew more pronounced. In 2009, the Northern European conservatives finally felt compelled to withdraw from the EPP.[68] The self-exclusion of British Conservatives from

[66] Ibid., Adam Butler to Margaret Thatcher, February 8, 1977.
[67] See Karl Magnus Johansson, "Party Elites in Multilevel Europe: The Christian Democrats and the Single European Act," *Party Politics* 8:4 (2002): 423–439.
[68] See Johansson, "Alliance," esp. 133–135; Pascal Fontaine, *Herzenssache Europa: Eine Zeitreise 1953–2009: Geschichte der Fraktion der Christdemokraten und der*

the European project was preceded by their exclusion from center-right party networks. Semantic transfer had failed spectacularly.

Merely an Episode?

Was the history of German and British center-right party cooperation within the European networks of the 1960s and 1970s merely an interesting episode that ultimately had no real impact? This chapter, opening a new perspective on the recent history of European conservatism, has argued that there was more to this cooperation than events might suggest.

The history of cooperation among European center-right parties has hitherto been written in terms of an established terminology that distinguishes between Christian Democrats and conservatives. However, as this chapter has shown, the presumed incompatibility of Christian Democratic and conservative thought and politics in Europe was the result of semantic and political conflicts within the European center-right in the 1960s and 1970s, when language was in flux, party ideology was questioned, and new alliances were taking shape. In addition to shedding new light on the trajectory of British participation in the process of European integration, this episode serves as a reminder to historians of the need to scrutinize their own analytical concepts. Ultimately, it leads to the crucial question of how the history of European conservatism from the 1960s onward can be understood. It surely casts doubt on the widely held view that European conservatism is a predominantly Northern European, if not exclusively Anglo-Saxon, phenomenon. Crucially, to understand the development of conservatism in Europe in the second half of the twentieth century, an analytical, genuinely historiographical concept of conservatism is vital. It constitutes an essential requirement for European as well as for transatlantic comparison.

The history of cooperation between the CDU/CSU and Conservative Party shows the complexity of European conservatism both as a body of thought and as a political movement, and it highlights the difficulties that attempts to harmonize the different stands of conservatism in Europe faced. In the end, friction could only be camouflaged, even in the case of

Europäischen Volkspartei im Europäischen Parlament (Brussels, 2009), 293–297, 386–389; from a political science perspective Markus Wagner, "The Right in the European Parliament since 1979," *Perspectives on European Politics and Society* 12:1 (2011): 52–67.

the impassioned invocation of "freedom." Any attempt to define European conservatism must therefore be elastic enough to do justice to the plurality of conservatism. This will be a major task for future research.

The episode in the history of European center-right party cooperation explored in this chapter underlines the role of politics in general and political language in particular in the transformative period of the 1970s,[69] when European conservatives developed an antithetical vocabulary of a highly pointed nature which increasingly gained currency and would shape politics in the 1980s. It further demonstrates the extent to which the Cold War framework influenced conservative political language in this decade. European integration and the Cold War were indeed entangled,[70] and this proves especially true for the 1970s, a decade which has wrongly been seen as stagnant in terms of European integration.[71] In the realm of networking, intellectual exchange, and party politics, the 1970s certainly witnessed closer integration. The political push to further Europeanization reinforced the political polarization that marked national political cultures of the 1970s, and as it was burrowed into political language, it had long-term effects. "What's in a name?" Adam Butler had asked Margaret Thatcher rhetorically in the late 1970s, quoting William Shakespeare and clearly assuming that the answer was not much.[72] This chapter aptly demonstrates that as historians we need to object vehemently.

[margin note: *Though the EC added three members plus Greece 1981*]

[margin note: *The Tories used the "National" label for their coalition in 1931–45 project*]

[69] For an economic reading of the 1970s and the profound transformations that began in this decade see Niall Ferguson, Charles S. Maier, and Erez Manela, eds., *The Shock of the Global: The 1970s in Perspective* (Cambridge, MA, 2010); Anselm Doering-Manteuffel and Lutz Raphael, *Nach dem Boom: Perspektiven auf die Zeitgeschichte seit 1970* (Göttingen, 2008); Jarausch, *Das Ende der Zuversicht?*; Thomas Raithel, Andreas Rödder, and Andreas Wirsching, eds., *Auf dem Weg in eine neue Moderne? Die Bundesrepublik Deutschland in den siebziger und achtziger Jahren* (Munich, 2009).

[70] N. Piers Ludlow, "European Integration and the Cold War," in Melvyn P. Leffler and Odd Arne Westad, eds., *The Cambridge History of the Cold War*, vol. 2, *Crises and Détente* (Cambridge, 2010), 179–197.

[71] Convincingly critical toward the stagnation thesis are Franz Knipping and Matthias Schönwald, eds., *Aufbruch zum Europa der zweiten Generation: Die europäische Einigung 1969–1984* (Trier, 2004).

[72] CAC, THCR 2/6/1/23, Adam Butler to Margaret Thatcher, February 8, 1977.

PART VI

CULTURES OF CONSERVATISM

15

Goodbye to the Party of Rockefeller

How a Decidedly "Un-Silent Minority" Pushed the GOP to Embrace Antifeminism

Stacie Taranto

New York State, especially the New York City area, was a key intellectual and political center of liberal and radical feminism in the 1960s and 1970s. At that time, the Democratic Party had growing feminist representation within it. This was especially true in New York State, where politicians such as U.S. Congresswomen Bella Abzug (D-Manhattan) and Shirley Chisholm (D-Brooklyn) garnered a lot of press coverage. The state's Republican Party was then a Manhattan-based organization dominated by Governor Nelson Rockefeller's personal fortune, top-down leadership, and generally moderate politics. Rockefeller Republicans, as they were called, supported most feminist initiatives, such as the state's abortion reform law in 1970.[1]

After New York's legislature legalized abortion in 1970, a conservative "family values movement" formed across the state as hundreds of women, most of them housewives, organized against this and other feminist-backed proposals. The movement was anchored in the four expanding

---

[1] T. Norman Hurd and Gerald Benjamin, eds., *Rockefeller in Retrospect: The Governor's New York Legacy* (Albany, 1984); Joseph F. Zimmerman, *The Government and Politics of New York State* (Albany, 2008); Jo Freeman, "Who You Know vs. Who You Represent: Feminist Influence in the Democratic and Republican Parties," in Mary Katzenstein and Carol Mueller, eds., *The Women's Movements of the United States and Western Europe: Feminist Consciousness, Political Opportunity and Public Policy* (Philadelphia, 1987), 215–244; Catherine E. Rymph, *Republican Women: Feminism and Conservatism from Suffrage through the Rise of the New Right* (Chapel Hill, 2006); Mark Stricherz, *Why the Democrats are Blue: Secular Liberalism and the Decline of the People's Party* (New York, 2007); Richard Norton Smith, *On His Own Terms: A Life of Nelson Rockefeller* (New York, 2014); Timothy J. Sullivan, *New York State and the Rise of Modern Conservatism* (Albany, 2008).

and ever more important suburban counties outside of New York City: Nassau and Suffolk Counties on Long Island, Rockland County to the north and west of the city, and Westchester County, directly north of the Bronx. The women were new to electoral politics and feared that feminists were out to destroy so-called traditional nuclear families like theirs.

Prior to 1970, these antifeminist suburban women were largely apolitical but generally leaned toward the Democratic Party. Most of them had been born in the late 1920s and early 1930s. They grew up in working-class neighborhoods in New York City. Their families revered President Franklin D. Roosevelt and his New Deal, which had helped them weather the Great Depression. Some of their mothers were forced to work outside of the home to supplement tight family budgets during the lean Depression-era and wartime years. Some of these women were Jewish, such as Annette Stern from the Bronx who settled in Westchester County; others were Protestant, with a smattering of Mormons upstate. Most, however, belonged to New York's large and politically significant Catholic population, which comprised 36 percent of the state's residents by the 1970s.[2] The vast majority of Catholic women had attended parochial schools and still went to mass as adults. They watched their church – through papal encyclicals that filtered down to the local level – support various civil rights and social justice measures for racial minorities and the poor. These causes were promoted by the national Democratic Party in the women's lifetimes, especially in the 1960s with President Lyndon Johnson's Great Society reforms. Following the dictates of the church and party that they had grown up with, most women praised the Civil Rights Act of 1964, the Voting Rights Act of 1965, and Johnson's attempts to end poverty, including its racialized forms.[3]

But much of this support was theoretical and far removed from the women's everyday lives as homemakers in suburban New York. They

[2] Jane Gilroy, interview by author, October 27, 2007, New York, NY, tape recording; Theresa Anselmi, interview by author, December 4, 2007, Pearl River, NY, tape recording; Phyllis Graham, interview by author, June 13, 2011, Port Jefferson, NY, tape recording; Adam Welinsky to Jimmy Carter, "The Northern Campaign and the Catholic Problem," Memorandum, Undated 1976, 1–27, Catholic Strategy (1) Folder, Box OA 12450, Morton Blackwell Files, Archives, The Ronald Reagan Presidential Library, Simi Valley, CA.

[3] Edward P. DeBerri and James E. Hug, with Peter Henriot and Michael J. Schultheis, *Catholic Social Teaching: Our Best Kept Secret*, 4th ed. (Maryknoll, NY, 2003), 45–49, 54; Richard Ryan, "Why Not Follow This Leader – Discover Yourself," *Tablet Magazine*, February 13, 1975, 3M, microforms, The New York Public Library, Astor, Lenox, and Tilden Foundations, New York, NY (hereafter: NYPL).

moved with their upwardly mobile husbands and young children to the suburbs of New York City in the late 1950s and early 1960s. Many families took advantage of cheaper, mass-produced housing and federally backed mortgages and education benefits for male veterans. These opportunities lifted their families into the middle class and made it easier for them to subsist on a single male-earned income as the women raised children at home full time. In the process, their families moved from racially heterogeneous working-class urban enclaves to nearly all-white, red-lined suburbs where there was little racial strife to put their political beliefs to the test. The exclusivity of their new communities ensured that the version of the family that they later rallied to protect looked a lot like their own white, middle-class, traditional male-breadwinner families.[4]

Most women paid very little attention to political issues prior to abortion becoming legal in New York State in 1970. As the antiwar and various civil rights and liberation movements unfolded across the country in the 1960s, most women were exposed to them only remotely through television and other media. They were, as future antifeminist organizer Annette Stern noted, "interested primarily in husband, children, and home."[5] They voted indiscriminately for both major parties based on superficial issues or simply mimicked what their husbands did. Neither party embraced feminism in a significant way at first, which spurred the women's political apathy. To them, politics revolved around issues that had little direct relevance in their lives, such as foreign policy and taxation.[6]

[4] Jonathan Rieder, *Canarsie: The Jews and Italians of Brooklyn Against Liberalism* (Cambridge, MA, 1985); Kenneth T. Jackson, *Crabgrass Frontier: The Suburbanization of the United States* (New York, 1987); Margaret Fitton, interview by author, December 4, 2007, Pearl River, NY, tape recording; Jane Gilroy, interview by author, October 27, 2007, New York, NY, tape recording; Theresa Anselmi, interview by author, December 4, 2007, Pearl River, NY, tape recording; Phyllis Graham, interview by author, June 13, 2011, Port Jefferson, NY, tape recording; U.S. Commerce Department and Bureau of the Census, *1970 Census of Population: Volume I*, Part 34, Section 1 (Washington, DC, 1974), 34–72; Stricherz, *Why the Democrats are Blue.*

[5] Annette Stern, interview with Phyllis Graham, Part II, Undated 1976, *Eagle Forum Presents* (hereafter: *EFP*), digitized MP3 recording, the personal collection of Phyllis Graham.

[6] Jane Gilroy, interview by author, June 4, 2011, Merrick, NY, tape recording; Theresa Anselmi, interview by author, June 7, 2011, West Nyack, NY, tape recording; Margaret Fitton, interview by author, June 7, 2011, West Nyack, NY, tape recording; Phyllis Graham, interview by author, June 13, 2011, Port Jefferson, NY, tape recording; Annette Stern, interview by author, July 18, 2011, telephone, tape recording.

The Equal Pay Act became law in 1963

Nor was the increased visibility of feminism in the early 1960s, with its focus on equal pay, seen as a threat. Jane Gilroy, a founder of New York State's Right to Life Party, remembered that she and her likeminded neighbors in suburban Long Island "said 'yes' for equal work and equal pay."[7] Many like Gilroy were full-time homemakers in the early 1960s when the first Equal Pay Act passed, but their more modest upbringings made them sensitive to the fact that, as Annette Stern argued, "many women have to go to work, and that is why . . . equal pay is so essential."[8] They believed that women with young children should work only out of economic necessity, as some of their mothers had been forced to do; in these cases, women ought to be able to provide as well as possible for their families. Either way, a woman's top priority was her family.

Then the nature of politics changed in ways that awakened women like Stern and Gilroy from their political slumber. Just as their families finally had attained their version of the American dream – one that was predicated upon suburban home ownership and a single male breadwinner's salary – feminists formed groups like the National Organization for Women (NOW) and expanded their platform. Stern and others watched in dismay as, for example, self-proclaimed dissatisfied housewife and writer Betty Friedan, from a nearby suburb in Rockland County, encouraged alternate possibilities for women in her groundbreaking book *The Feminine Mystique.*[9] 1963 When feminists advocated for greater educational and work opportunities for all women, including economically secure ones, homemakers like Annette Stern felt devalued. From their perspective, letting women choose between homemaking or working outside of the home implied that the former was not as valuable as Stern and others believed. First-generation homemakers, in particular, felt their prize being undercut. Echoing their Catholic leaders, Jane Gilroy and others equated legal abortion with state-sanctioned murder and agonized over women evading their maternal responsibilities. The women went on to defeat a state-level Equal Rights Amendment (ERA) mandating full legal equality for men and women in 1975. They worried that if feminists passed the ERA and their broader agenda, the United States would devolve into the Soviet Union, where women were compelled to work outside of the home and daycare was subsidized by the state. Clearly delineated sex roles, in

Oh no! Not subsidized day care!

---

[7] Jane Gilroy, interview by author, October 27, 2007, New York, NY, tape recording.

[8] Annette Stern, interview with Phyllis Graham, Part II, Undated 1976, *EFP*, digitized MP3 recording, the personal collection of Phyllis Graham.

[9] Betty Friedan, *The Feminine Mystique* (New York, 1963).

their view, were not just good for the family: they were the basis for a moral and successful capitalist America. Once feminist movements had succeeded in making "the personal political," suburban women started to pay attention and organize in opposition.[10]

This chapter focuses on New York State from 1970, when abortion was legalized there, through the elections of 1980, a span of ten years when feminists and an emerging conservative family values movement competed side by side to define the family. These mostly Catholic, middle-class, white women living in the four suburban counties outside of New York City presented themselves as part of a silent majority that refused to surrender to bipartisan political support for dangerous feminist reforms. In reality, they were a very vocal minority of no more than a thousand activist women in a state of more than eighteen million people. But the women reached thousands more at the polls, which helped them forge a new, more conservative politics in New York State that was centered on nuclear families, heterosexual marriage, and traditional gender roles. As the women began taking an active role in politics, they saw the Democratic Party of their youth moving in the opposite direction as it embraced feminist reforms. The women formed their own political organizations and eventually aligned their movement with conservatives in the Republican Party.[11]

As they worked from kitchen tables, marched on the state capitol, and organized political campaigns, these self-declared "average suburban housewives" caught the eye of the right wing of New York State's Republican Party. By 1980, a quarter of all votes in New York came from the four populous suburban counties where many antifeminist women lived. Nassau, Suffolk, Rockland, and Westchester counties became a bellwether section of the state: candidates who carried those counties typically won the race. Tapping into the antifeminist politics that was anchored in these counties was an especially enticing proposition for conservative Republicans looking to increase their influence beyond their small, mostly rural base upstate. The election results in 1980, which

[handwritten margin note: Had she lived, Betty Anger Francis might have joined these women]

[10] Jane S. De Hart, "Gender on the Right: Meanings Behind the Existential Scream," *Gender and History* 3:3 (Autumn 1991): 256; Jane Gilroy, interview by author, June 4, 2011, Merrick, NY, tape recording; Theresa Anselmi, interview by author, June 7, 2011, West Nyack, NY, tape recording; Margaret Fitton, interview by author, June 7, 2011, West Nyack, NY, tape recording; Phyllis Graham, interview by author, June 13, 2011, Port Jefferson, NY, tape recording; Annette Stern, interview by author, July 18, 2011, telephone, tape recording; Freeman, "Who You Know."

[11] *1970 Census of Population: Volume I*, Part 34, Section 1, 34–36.

brought conservative Republicans to power across New York, underscored the women's successful partnership with the right wing of the
Grand Old Party (or GOP, as the Republican Party is often called). By
1980, conservative downstate antifeminists dominated Republican politics in New York State as liberal, urban pro-feminist Rockefeller Republicans became a minority faction within the party – a rich illustration of
trends that reshaped the GOP nationally during the 1970s.[12]

This case study builds on several histories of the rise of political conservatism in postwar America, including recent works on women and gender.
Most scholars have explored how race and the Cold War shaped liberalism's decline and conservatism's rise in the decades after World War II.[13]
Thinking about these concerns alongside gender and women refines our
analysis. Few historians have examined gender – sociologists, political
scientists, and journalists have done a better job of doing so – and even
fewer scholars have focused on ordinary women operating at the grassroots level.[14] In recent years, a handful of historians have drawn attention
to the crucial role of women activists at the grassroots level in the anticommunist New Right of the 1950s and 1960s. Most of these works focus on
America's Sunbelt region, where such appeals were popular because the
region's economy was based on Cold War-related defense manufacturing.
Scholars have shown, for example, how middle- and upper-middle-class
white women assumed a maternal, home-centered identity as they, ironically, entered the male-dominated public sphere to rid America of an
alleged communist menace. Other women minimized the importance of

---

[12] Frank Lynn, "Suburbs' Power Mirrored in Tally of GOP Victors," *New York Times*,
November 9, 1980; Zimmerman, *The Government and Politics of New York State*.

[13] See, for example, John A. Andrew, *The Other Side of the Sixties: Young Americans for
Freedom and the Rise of Conservative Politics* (New Brunswick, NJ, 1997); Mary C.
Brennan, *Turning Right in the Sixties: The Conservative Capture of the GOP* (Chapel
Hill, 1995); Lisa McGirr, *Suburban Warriors: The Origins of the New American Right*
(Princeton, 2001); Rick Perlstein, *Before the Storm: Barry Goldwater and the Unmaking
of the American Consensus*, 1st ed. (New York, 2001); Gregory L. Schneider, *Cadres
for Conservatism: Young Americans for Freedom and the Rise of the Contemporary
Right* (New York, 1999); Robert O. Self, *American Babylon: Race and the Struggle for
Postwar Oakland* (Princeton, 2003).

[14] See, for example, Susan Faludi, *Backlash* (New York, 1991); Pamela Johnston Conover
and Virginia Gray, *Feminism and the New Right: Conflict Over the American Family*
(New York, 1983); Rebecca E. Klatch, *Women of the New Right: Women in the Political
Economy* (Philadelphia, 1987); Tanya Melich, *The Republican War Against Women:
An Insider's Report from Behind the Lines* (New York, 1996); William Saletan, *Bearing
Right: How Conservatives Won the Abortion War* (Berkeley, 2003); Judith Stacey, *In
the Name of the Family: Rethinking Family Values in the Postmodern Age* (Boston,
1996); Kristen Luker, *Abortion and the Politics of Motherhood* (Berkeley, 1984).

gender in their anticommunist work, although the fact that they were
homemakers with more time to organize than men undergirded their
political activism.[15]

A comparable gender analysis of political conservatism in the 1970s
is warranted. In that decade, concerns about communism, smaller government, and taxes intersected with new worries provoked by the rise
of modern feminism. By the mid- to late 1970s, suburban women in
New York sensed that their taxpayer dollars were going into expensive, feminist-backed government programs that threatened the nuclear
family – an institution that many felt was a necessary bulwark against
communism since Soviets did not live in traditional families with women
staying home. These developments made conservative Republicans'
promises to lower taxes, decrease the size of government, and fight communism take on new resonance when positioned as a means to save the
traditional nuclear family from a dangerous feminist onslaught.

Analyzing New York State broadens our understanding of the New
Right in America. Conservatism was not exclusively a Sunbelt phenomenon: it also resonated in suburban areas of the North, a fact rec-
ognized by contemporary conservative Republican political strategists.[16]
Historians have not adequately analyzed the rise of conservatism in the
Northern suburbs. Instead, most studies about the North are racial backlash narratives set in urban areas such as Boston, Philadelphia, and New
York City.[17] But just as America's political center shifted in the postwar era from the urban Northeast to the more suburban Sunbelt, New
York State's center of political gravity shifted from New York City to
the surrounding suburbs. Furthermore, New York's strong history of
both feminist and antifeminist campaigns – as well as the clear division
between the liberal and conservative factions of its Republican Party –
make the state, as opposed to a Sunbelt location, ideal ground to assess

---

[15] See, for example, Michelle Nickerson, *Mothers of Conservatism: Women and the Postwar Right* (Princeton, 2012); Mary C. Brennan, *Wives, Mothers, and the Red Menace:
Conservative Women and the Crusade Against Communism* (Boulder, CO, 2008); Paige
Meltzer, "Maternal Citizens: Gender and Women's Activism in the United States, 1945–
1960," PhD dissertation, Brown University, 2009.

[16] See, for example, Kevin P. Phillips, *The Emerging Republican Majority* (New Rochelle,
NY, 1969); Richard M. Scammon and Ben J. Wattenberg, *The Real Majority* (New
York, 1970).

[17] See, for example, Ronald P. Formisano, *Boston Against Busing: Race, Class, and Ethnicity in the 1960s and 1970s* (Chapel Hill, 1991); John T. McGreevy, *Parish Boundaries:
The Catholic Encounter with Race in the Twentieth-Century Urban North* (Chicago,
1996); Rieder, *Canarsie*.

how the conservative family values movement shifted the politics of the
Republican Party to the right.

* * *

In order to understand the dramatic migration of New York State's
Republican Party to the right and away from feminist positions over
the course of the 1970s, one must first understand the composition of
the state's GOP at the beginning of the decade. Nelson Rockefeller, who
had been serving as governor since 1959, exercised very tight, top-down
control over the state's Republican Party, which had very few strong
county-level organizations. He oversaw every aspect of party operations
and often doled out money from his family fortune to local Republican
clubs and candidates. Rockefeller's base of support was in New York
City and the surrounding suburbs – in places such as wealthy Westchester County, where his family estate was located. There was an opposing
bloc of conservative Republican leaders in the more rural counties upstate
led by State Senate Majority Leader Warren Anderson, but during Rockefeller's tenure, their power was minimal. The dominance of moderate
Republicans in New York State was not an anomaly: moderates were in
control of the party throughout most of the country. Memories of Barry
Goldwater's spectacular loss in the 1964 presidential election were still
fresh, and Richard Nixon's conservative rhetoric as a candidate hardly
matched his more moderate policy positions as president.[18] When President Gerald Ford assumed office in the wake of the Watergate scandal,
he asked Rockefeller to be his vice president. The governor accepted, but
little changed back in New York while he was serving in Washington
(1974–1977). Rockefeller's key allies in New York ensured that the state
party remained under his all-encompassing influence.[19]

Moderate Republicans embraced key elements of the modern women's
liberation movement(s) in New York, particularly calls to decriminalize
abortion from both liberal and radical feminist factions. Abortion in
New York, as in other states, had been illegal in almost all circumstances
since the nineteenth century. In the early 1960s, reformers – most of

---

[18] Joan Hoff, *Nixon Reconsidered* (New York, 1994).
[19] Zimmerman, *The Government and Politics of New York State*; Malcolm Wilson, "The
Man and Public Servant," in T. Norman Hurd and Gerald Benjamin, eds., *Rockefeller
in Retrospect: The Governor's New York Legacy* (Albany, 1984), 25; Wolfgang Saxon,
"Bernard Kilbourn, 81, Republican State Chairman," *The New York Times*, July 7,
2005; Smith, *On His Own Terms*; Sullivan, *New York State and the Rise of Modern
Conservatism*.

them men from the legal and medical professions or members of certain progressive religious communities – began lobbying for liberalization. Feminists soon embraced access to legal abortion as a core woman's right, which inspired countless politically unaffiliated women as well as activists in social welfare and good government groups to get involved as reform efforts gained momentum at the end of the decade. Rockefeller's Republicans guided the final abortion reform bill through the state legislature in Albany. Republican Assemblywoman Constance Cook, who was a member of the preeminent liberal feminist group NOW, led the GOP's efforts to do so. Supportive Democrats could not do so because, with little representation upstate, they were in the minority in the Assembly and Senate. The Democrats' base was downstate, and even there it was split: heavily Jewish and African American districts supported legal abortion, while Catholic ones did not. The abortion bill therefore had to be ushered through the state legislature by moderate Republicans who were in the majority of both houses and who, like Cook and Rockefeller, equated legal abortion with the GOP's historic embrace of personal liberty and small government.[20]

Reform efforts were aided by the fact that opponents in the state were very thinly organized, if at all, in the years before 1970. Most of the women who later mobilized against legal abortion were occupied with small children and family life at the time. Those paying attention to the abortion debates in Albany in 1968–1970 typically were made aware of the issue by Catholic priests and church organizations. Some women took buses to Albany from their parishes to try to persuade lawmakers not to legalize abortion; others attended local church forums designed to highlight the issue. Far more women believed that common sense would prevail in the capital and elected to do nothing as the bill was being debated. Few could imagine lawmakers approving what they and their Catholic leaders viewed as state-sanctioned murder; their time, the women felt, would be better spent at home. At the time, most Catholic leaders in the state were busy lobbying for a bill that would have enabled perpetually underfunded parochial schools to receive taxpayer funding. Once the abortion bill passed in 1970,

[20] Constance Cook, interview by Ellen Chesler, 47–50, Interviews by Kathryn M. Moore Collection, #21-32-2360, Division of Rare and Manuscript Collections, Cornell University Library, Ithaca, NY (hereafter Cornell); Bonnie Eissner, "Constance Cook: Engineering Abortion Law Reform in the New York State Legislature, 1968–1970," undergraduate honors thesis, Cornell University, 1994, 36–37, Cornell; Lawrence Lader, *Abortion II* (Boston, 1973).

however, the church's priorities shifted dramatically. The church went on to lead the religious opposition to legalized abortion in New York. Elsewhere in the country, by contrast, Evangelical Christians, who were not numerous in New York State, were on the forefront of the anti-abortion movement.[21]

Opponents were spurred on by the fact that Rockefeller had signed the most expansive abortion reform law in the nation. Between 1967 and 1970, sixteen states legalized abortion in some form through either legislation or judicial review. New York's law went the furthest by allowing abortion for any reason through the twenty-fourth week of pregnancy, and thereafter only if the expectant woman's life were at risk. The procedure had to be performed by a doctor, with the woman's permission, but there was no residency requirement as in other states. New York soon became a haven for those seeking safe and legal abortions in the years before the U.S. Supreme Court legalized the procedure at the federal level in 1973. As the number of legal abortions in the state increased, a female-led, suburban-based, anti-abortion movement gathered force in New York.[22]

The women were motivated to organize against legal abortion (and feminism more broadly) by two principal factors. Above all, they, like Catholic leaders, believed that the procedure killed living babies and children – much like their own, whom they were raising full time. A second attendant concern was that legal abortion would allow women to avoid their divinely inspired highest calling in life: motherhood. The women were convinced that in promoting legalized abortion, feminists were sounding the death knell for the traditional nuclear family, which revolved around procreation and prescribed gender roles. Feminism seemed to be the most serious threat to this vision of the family, but movements for

---

[21] Constance Cook, interview by Ellen Chesler, 47, Interviews by Kathryn M. Moore Collection, #21-32-2360, Cornell; Richard Perez-Pena, "'70 Abortion Law: New York Said Yes, Stunning the Nation," *The New York Times*, April 9, 2000; Lader, *Abortion II*, 135–146; Margaret Fitton, interview by author, December 4, 2007, Pearl River, NY, tape recording.

[22] Fred P. Graham, "Abortions: Moves to Abolish All Legal Restraints," *The New York Times*, November 16, 1969, Folder 267, Box 26, Counsel's Office – Subseries 4, Record Group (hereafter: RG) 15, Nelson A. Rockefeller Gubernatorial Papers (hereafter: NARGP), Rockefeller Family Archives, The Rockefeller Archive Center, Sleepy Hollow, NY (hereafter: RFA, RAC); "Abortion," Memorandum, September 1974, 3, Folder 51, Box 6, New York Office Vice Presidential Series 1974–1977 – Vice Presidential Confirmation Hearings 1974, RG 26 Nelson A. Rockefeller Vice Presidential Papers (hereafter: NARVP), ibid.; Jane E. Brody, "Abortion: Once a Whispered Problem, Now a Public Debate," *The New York Times*, January 8, 1968.

gay and lesbian liberation were also regarded as dangerous. Taking their
cues from national antifeminist organizations such as Phyllis Schlafly's
Eagle Forum, the women often conflated gay and lesbian rights with feminism as a means to discredit the latter. To be sure, gays and lesbians
offended the women because same-sex relationships did not conform to
the heterosexual marital relation at the center of nuclear family life. Still,
the political movements behind gay men and lesbians seemed far less
threatening because they did not have as many legislative successes in
New York in the 1970s as feminists did, beginning with the abortion
reform law. As a result, opposition to legal abortion and other related
feminist goals was at the core of the women's conservative "family values" activism.[23]

Most women found it difficult to speak out at first, but with politics
converging upon what they deemed most important – home and family –
they summoned the will to do so. As Margie Fitton, a homemaker and
mother of ten children from Rockland County who joined the state's
anti-abortion movement, explained: "You didn't do that...you didn't
make scenes and go picketing. That was for hippies, and it was a very
difficult thing for people like us to get used to."[24] For many Americans like
Fitton, protest was no longer associated with marches in the early 1960s
for causes that they respected, such as civil rights for African Americans
in the Jim Crow South. By 1970, protest had become associated with
sensational televised images of antiwar demonstrations, student unrest,
and rioting in urban communities like the ones the women had grown up
in. Nor could Fitton and her allies – as the conversation moved beyond
equal pay – relate to women, including fellow homemakers and mothers,
who joined feminist groups like NOW and took to the streets to remake
the home and American society as much as the workplace. Like many
people who identified with the so-called silent majority of Americans,

[23] Annette Stern, interview by author, July 18, 2011, telephone, tape recording; Theresa
Anselmi, interview by author, June 7, 2011, West Nyack, NY, tape recording; Mar-
garet Fitton, interview by author, June 7, 2011, West Nyack, NY, tape recording; Jane
Gilroy, interview by author, June 4, 2011, Merrick, NY, tape recording; Phyllis Schlafly,
"IWY: A Front for Radicals and Lesbians," *The Phyllis Schlafly Report* 11, no. 1, sec-
tion 2, August 1977, 1, Schlesinger Library, Radcliffe Institute for Advanced Study,
Harvard University, Cambridge, MA (hereafter: SL); Erica J. Ryan, "Red War on the
Family: Sex, Gender, and Americanism, 1919–1929," PhD dissertation, Brown Univer-
sity, 2010; Fred Fejes, *Gay Rights and Moral Panic: The Origins of America's Debate
on Homosexuality* (New York, 2008).

[24] Margaret Fitton, interview by author, December 4, 2007, Pearl River, NY, tape recording.

[marginal annotation, top right: Because it contradicted the subordinate status of legal + differential status the women claimed themselves]

Fitton was reluctant to enter the political fray.[25] Yet she and a very vocal minority of hundreds of women across New York decided to speak out to benefit the anti-abortion cause.

By claiming public space, Fitton and other anti-abortion activists hoped to insert their viewpoint into public discourse; theirs was a perspective from women more accustomed to private domestic life who rejected legal abortion and modern feminism so vehemently that they had no choice but to break their silence and mobilize in a populist fashion.[26] As Ellen McCormack, an activist who went on to run for president of the United States on an anti-abortion platform, frequently noted, "If things have gotten so bad that a housewife from Merrick [Long Island]" gets involved in politics, "then it's time for a change."[27] McCormack's declaration underscored her status as an outsider in politics as well as her authority as a housewife on matters related to the family and home. Feminists had been working to make "the personal political" by showing that the public political sphere and the home-centered private sphere were not in fact separate entities, as the vast majority of political actors, including maternalist feminists of earlier generations, long had maintained. By the 1970s, many feminists argued, for instance, that who does the dishes at home was related to the fact that women had fewer opportunities in the paid workforce, and that choices about reproduction were not merely private ones. Doing so opened the door for women like McCormack, whose identities were firmly rooted in the private domestic sphere, to enter the public political sphere to save their home and families from what they saw as antifamily feminist policies.[28]

[marginal annotation, left: Populist invocation of crisis which had worried a group of older women going]

[marginal annotation, left: To preserve the private, allegedly apolitical sphere]

[25] Pete Hamill, "The Revolt of the White Lower Middle Class," *New York*, April 14, 1969 (http://nymag.com/news/features/46801); "Man and Woman of the Year: The Middle Americans," *Time*, January 5, 1970 (http://content.time.com/time/magazine/article/0, 9171,943113,00.html).

[26] Theresa Anselmi, interview by author, December 4, 2007, Pearl River, NY, tape recording; Margaret Fitton, interview by author, December 4, 2007, Pearl River, NY, tape recording; Matthew D. Lassiter, *The Silent Majority: Suburban Politics in the Sunbelt South* (Princeton, 2006), 1–19.

[27] "Anti-Abortion Candidate for President," *The New York Times*, November 30, 1975; clipping in Binder Volume I: 1972 through December 1975 Binder, 126, The Ellen McCormack Presidential Campaign Papers (hereafter: EMP BI), The Dr. Joseph R. Stanton Human Life Issues Library and Resource Center, Our Lady of New York Convent, Bronx, NY (hereafter: SHLL).

[28] Sonya Michel and Robyn Rosen, "The Paradox of Maternalism: Elizabeth Lowell Putnam and the American Welfare State," *Gender and History* 4 (1992): 367–370; Donald T. Critchlow, *Phyllis Schlafly and Grassroots Conservatism: A Woman's Crusade* (Princeton, 2005).

McCormack and others pursued a multifaceted strategy to bring about the repeal of New York's pioneering abortion law. First, they helped form the New York State Right to Life Committee (RTLC), which lobbied legislators in Albany to overturn the law. Anticipating a long struggle, they also tried to weaken the law with restrictive ordinances until it could be overturned outright. Other women created the New York State Right to Life Party (RTLP) and began running supporters in local elections to highlight the abortion issue. The RTLP was a vehicle for running anti-abortion advocates for political office, while the RTLC, for tax purposes, was exempt from endorsing or promoting candidates: two different tactics and organizations, both appealing to the same type of women. The "right to life" moniker in both groups' names reflected their maternal focus on the unborn fetus's (or as they saw it, baby's) right to live over the opposing side's belief that a pregnant woman had the right to choose a safe, legal abortion.[29]

To build their movement, these previously apolitical women used the suburban infrastructure that surrounded them. The RTLC and RTLP relied on, for example, the expanding infrastructure of the Catholic Church, which after the Vatican II reforms of the mid-1960s had created several parish-level groups designed to energize the laity. They also exploited civic organizations and neighborhood networks. By tapping into these local groups, the women could channel people into anti-abortion activism on the grassroots level. Neighborhood coffee klatches became potential spaces to recruit volunteers and solicit donations for various antifeminist causes, as did the busy shopping centers, local parks, Little League games, and civic and religious groups. The message of the feminist threat to families was used to turn previously apolitical, family-oriented spaces into centers of political activity and fundraising.[30] Although anti-abortion activists enjoyed limited political success – none of their candidates won office, and Governor Rockefeller vetoed the bill to overturn the abortion reform law that they pushed through the state legislature in 1972 – their efforts created a passionate new type of conservative politics focused on women and the family.[31]

[29] Sarah Dubow, *Ourselves Unborn: A History of the Fetus in Modern America* (Oxford, 2010).

[30] "Housewives, $5,000 Beat ERA," *Newburgh News*, December 3, 1975, the personal collection of Virginia Lavan Taylor; Lisa Cronin Wohl, "The ERA: What the Hell Happened in New York?" *Ms.*, March 1976, 92, 96.

[31] Constance Cook, "Statement on Donovan Crawford, Unrevised from the Record," Press Release, May 9, 1972, 1–6, 1972 L. Abortion Reference Folder, Box 86, Constance Cook

Anti-abortion activism was a launching point for many women into the fight over the state ERA in 1974–1975. With the federal ERA at a standstill by the mid-1970s, feminists hoped that adding an Equal Rights Amendment to the state constitution would cover women in New York until the federal constitution could be amended. In order to do so, voters would need to approve the state ERA in a ballot referendum. Opponents of the ERA at both the state and federal level feared that the amendment would compel homemakers to enter the paid workforce to become equal with men, while their children became wards of the state. In essence, they worried that by offering women the same legal rights as men, the state would be mandating the same expectations for women and men. Feminists often countered with dense legal explanations. They noted, for instance, that the Thirteenth Amendment to the U.S. Constitution that had outlawed slavery would prevent homemakers – or anyone else – from being channeled into the workforce against their will. But that argument did little to calm the fears of many first-generation homemakers who hoped to avoid the same fate as their own working mothers.[32]

As the women and their allies rallied against the state ERA, their tactics again were molded by the suburban experience. They formed a statewide opposition group named Operation Wakeup, which mobilized nearly a thousand women. The group, based in the New York City suburbs, vowed to "wake up" New Yorkers to the supposed threats posed by the state ERA. The Wakeup women soon organized their communities on the grassroots level – talking to other parents at the dentist's office, raising the topic at mothers' groups, and reaching out to local civic, religious, and ideologically aligned anti-abortion groups. In other words, their desire to organize in the first place (to save their allegedly imperiled lifestyles from a feminist threat) as well as the political tactics that they

Papers, #2881, Cornell; Fred Corota to Governor Nelson A. Rockefeller, Memorandum, May 10, 1972, Folder 750, Box 71, Counsel's Office – Subseries 4, RG 15 NARGP, RFA, RAC; Alan F. Guttmacher, MD, "Memorandum on Conference with Governor Rockefeller," December 20, 1972, Folder 407, Box 39, ibid.; The Office of Governor Nelson A. Rockefeller, Press Release, May 5, 1972, Folder 51, Box 6, New York Office Vice Presidential Series 1974–1977 – Vice Presidential Confirmation Hearings 1974, RG 26 NARVP, ibid.; William E. Farrell, "Assembly Votes to Repeal Liberalized Abortion Law," *The New York Times*, May 10, 1972; Alfonso A. Narvaez, "Abortion Repeal Passed By Senate, Sent to Governor," *The New York Times*, May 11, 1972; Lader, *Abortion II*, 196–207.

[32] State of New York, Senate, New York State Equal Rights Amendment Debate, Bill No. S. 2824, transcript, microfilm (May 21, 1975): p. 5290–5322, 5414–5415, 5475, 5454–5455, 5581, Senate Records Office, Capitol Building, Albany, NY (hereafter: SRO).

deployed to do so – coffee klatches, bake sales, and the like – reflected how suburban and domestic the women's lives had become in the past decade or more.[33]

Only a paltry three million New Yorkers (in a state of eighteen million people) participated in the ERA ballot referendum, but thanks to the votes and activism of women like those in Wakeup, it did not pass. A postmortem on the election based on interviews with thousands of New Yorkers concluded that the state ERA's failure hinged on the votes of women aged eighteen to fifty-nine, particularly suburban Catholic women energized by issues such as abortion: in short, Wakeup's core constituency. Opponents were helped by the fact that in this off-year election, there were only referenda and no contested races on ballots in New York City, an area of strength for ERA proponents. Led by suburban women, roughly 1.3 million people (43 percent) voted for the state ERA and 1.7 million (57 percent) against it. In the suburbs right outside of New York City where most opposition leaders lived – spanning Nassau, Suffolk, Rockland, and Westchester counties – the state ERA was defeated by majorities ranging from 52 to 61 percent. Since these were very densely populated counties, the state ERA's defeat there was more impactful than its failure in less populous, traditionally conservative counties upstate, where it lost by as much as 72 percent in some places. Driven by fears of dangerous feminist encroachment upon traditional nuclear families like theirs, the women had proven their strength at the ballot box, forming a potentially decisive swing vote that conservative Republicans later sought to win.[34]

After the state ERA's defeat, conservative family values activists in New York fixated on two federally funded initiatives with strong feminist

---

[33] "Ambitious Project," *Operation Wakeup Newsletter*, Undated, ERA Opposition Arguments US and NYS incl. Schlafly Folder, Box 1, Karen S. Burstein Women's Issues Files (hereafter: Burstein Files), New York State Archives, Cultural Education Center, Albany, NY (hereafter: NYSA); Judy Klemesrud, "As New York Vote on Equal Rights Nears, Two Sides Speak Out; Pro Con," *The New York Times*, September 18, 1975; De Hart, "Gender on the Right" 254–256; State of New York, Senate, New York State Equal Rights Amendment Debate, Bill No. S. 2824, transcript, microfilm (May 21, 1975): p. 5290–5322, 5414–5415, 5475, 5454–5455, 5581, SRO.

[34] "Erie County LWV Asks Why," *New York State Voter* (Summer 1976): 2, Humanities and General Research Room, NYPL; Martha Weinman Lear, "You'll Probably Think I'm Stupid," *The New York Times Magazine*, April 11, 1976, 30–31, 108; Wohl, "The ERA: What the Hell Happened in New York?," 92; Linda Greenhouse, "Defeat of Equal Rights Bills Traced to Women's Votes," *The New York Times*, November 6, 1975; Betsy Ruechner, "ERA Defeat Pinned on Women," *Democrat and Chronicle*, November 6, 1976, the personal collection of Virginia Lavan Taylor.

overtones: the meetings for the National Commission on the Observance of International Women's Year (IWY) in 1977 and the White House Conference on Families (WHCF) in 1980. They felt that these efforts suffered from two fatal flaws. First, these initiatives provided a platform for feminists who advocated objectives – such as lesbian rights, government-funded childcare, and legal abortion – that threatened the traditional family and its prescribed gender roles. One WHCF workshop even proposed an expanded definition of the family to include any group bound by "bonds of affection, mutual support, and commitment which will enable adults and/or children to grow and develop into creative and productive people."[35] Second, both initiatives placed taxpayer dollars in the direct service of this supposedly antifamily feminist agenda.

This new preoccupation with how tax dollars were spent helped women who had grown up identifying as Democrats later find a comfortable home in the Republican Party. Many women historically viewed Rockefeller's GOP as an out-of-touch party that catered to the wealthy. Even worse, the GOP's conservative wing called to mind Herbert Hoover ignoring their working-class urban neighborhoods during the Great Depression. But as the women's political consciousnesses were awakened in the 1970s, Republican calls for smaller government and lower taxes came to mean less money for objectionable, taxpayer-funded programs like the IWY and WHCF. Republican language about individual rights was recast in terms of parents' or homemakers' rights, with Operation Wakeup and similar groups worrying about feminists corrupting their children with divergent values in taxpayer-funded public schools. In this way, the GOP and its adherence to low taxes and small government attracted women who hoped to save the heterosexual traditional nuclear family.[36]

This migration toward Republican ideology was magnified by the fact that many women were ready to leave the Democratic Party by the 1970s. The so-called New Politics coalition that emerged within the Democratic Party in the late 1960s, along with the internal McGovern-Frasier

35 The White House Conference on Families, *Summary of State Reports*, vol. 1 (Washington, DC, 1980), 129.
36 Phyllis Graham, "Taxation," June 11, 1977, *EFP*, digitized MP3 recording, the personal collection of Phyllis Graham; Phyllis Graham, "In The Name of Education," Part II, September 19, year unknown, 1976–1979?, ibid.; Rosalind Pollack Petchesky, "Antiabortion, Antifeminism, and the Rise of the New Right," *Feminist Studies* 7:2 (Summer 1981): 207; Marjorie J. Spruill, "Gender and America's Right Turn," in Bruce Schulman and Julian E. Zelizer, eds., *Rightward Bound: Making America Conservative in the Seventies* (Cambridge, MA, 2008), 72.

Commission that met from 1969 to 1972, had helped transform the party from a working-class, urban Catholic, machine-driven organization into a more liberal, secular one led by college-educated professionals, including feminists. As Ellen McCormack, a founder of the New York State Right to Life Party who grew up as a working-class Catholic Democrat in New York City, once said: "Instead of [metaphorically] distributing hats," as the Democratic social welfare programs of the New Deal and Great Society had aimed to do, by the 1970s, party leaders were more apt to support proverbially "cutting off heads" by backing legal abortion.[37]

McCormack even ran in the primaries for the Democratic presidential nomination in 1976 to try to show party leaders how widespread anti-abortion sentiment was among traditionally Democratic Catholics in the North, one of the party's core constituencies for the past half century at least. Her campaign hoped that by winning a sizable number of votes, it could persuade party leaders to adopt anti-abortion (and more generally antifeminist) policies. In the end, McCormack only netted a mere 3–5 percent of the popular vote in the twenty-one states that she competed in – hardly the results she expected. Instead, in 1976, the first presidential election year after *Roe v. Wade*, the Democratic Party responded to its growing feminist caucus by including support for legal abortion in its platform for the first time.[38]

McCormack and her allies viewed their campaign as a vehicle to express the will of the silent majority of Americans that the press seemed fixated on in the late 1960s and 1970s.[39] As one of McCormack's leaflets declared, "Behind the front page [headlines] of the libbers and the liberals . . . [m]illions like you . . . make the country go, day in and day out. We know you're there and we know you believe in the traditional values, as Ellen does."[40] Despite actively embracing this largely constructed label on the campaign trail, McCormack and her allies were not silent; nor did the 267,590 popular votes that they won nationwide prove that a

---

37 Ellen McCormack, "March for Life" (speech given at the March for Life Rally, New York, NY, July 11, 1976), Volume III: May 1976 through 2004, Plus Appendix Binder, The Ellen McCormack Presidential Campaign Papers (hereafter: EMP BIII), SHLL.

38 Stacie Taranto, "Ellen McCormack for President: Politics and an Improbable Path to Passing Anti-Abortion Policy," *Journal of Policy History* 24 (2012): 263–287; Robert J. Spitzer, *The Right to Life Movement and Third Party Politics* (New York, 1987), 89; Stricherz, *Why the Democrats are Blue*, 4–9.

39 Hamill, "The Revolt of the White Lower Middle Class;" "Man and Woman of the Year."

40 PLAC, "The Next President of the United States?" *Indiana Harmonizer*, November 16, 1975, EMP BI, SHLL.

majority of Democrats and other primary voters felt as they did about abortion.[41]

McCormack's campaign did, however, undercut the contemporary conventional political wisdom that longtime (Catholic) Democratic voters were a silent and malleable lot who could be wooed over to the conservative wing of the GOP as the Democratic Party continued to shift leftward to embrace feminism and related movements.[42] Her presidential primary bid revealed that rather than merely switching parties in the voting booth, some people – led by women like McCormack, people who later would be called Reagan Democrats – first aired their concerns across the nation and tried to reform the Democratic Party from within. Much of what McCormack said as a Democratic contender about abortion in particular (and nuclear families and heteronormative gender roles in general) echoed what the most famous antifeminist from that era, Phyllis Schlafly, said as she and other conservative Republicans seized power from the more liberal Rockefeller wing of the GOP that supported feminist reforms such as legal abortion. McCormack's candidacy reveals that similar antifeminist activism emerged on the Democratic side, too, as secular liberals took control of the party's infrastructure and marginalized lower- and middle-class northern Catholics. Much like their church leaders, McCormack and other traditional Democrats supported the social welfare measures of the New Deal and Great Society but rejected the party's embrace of abortion rights and other tenets of the new feminism.[43]

McCormack's campaign and others like it prompted conservative GOP bosses like Joseph Margiotta on Long Island to partner with family values women to seek greater power within New York's Republican Party. Party chairmen had little influence under Nelson Rockefeller, let alone conservative ones like Margiotta in the downstate suburban region where Rockefeller lived. But the deeply entrenched networks that the women had built from the grassroots up, coupled with Rockefeller's complete withdrawal from state politics in 1977 until his death in 1979, later allowed county-level GOP chairmen like Margiotta to have real power in the state party. When this occurred, a new conservative Republican power bloc arose in the suburbs that the women had organized – one that became

[41] Ellen McCormack, "Voter Pamphlet Statement," Undated, Vol. 1: 1972 through December 1975 binder, EMP BI, SHLL.

[42] Phillips, *The Emerging Republican Majority*; Scammon and Wattenberg, *The Real Majority*.

[43] Critchlow, *Phyllis Schlafly*; Saletan, *Bearing Right*; Stricherz, *Why the Democrats are Blue*.

far more influential than the stalwart conservative bloc upstate, owing to the greater population density and media influence in the New York City area. In addition to supporting anti-abortion and related measures, Margiotta and his allies won support in the downstate suburbs by, for example, calling for lower taxes, which many women backed to defund feminist initiatives or as a means to keep more money in families' pockets to prevent mothers from having to enter the paid workforce during the recessionary 1970s. The prospect of a tax cut was no doubt enticing to husbands too, especially as Nassau, Suffolk, Rockland, and Westchester counties had some of the highest property taxes in the country.[44]

A combination of these factors led incumbent Senator Jacob Javits, the longest-serving U.S. senator in New York State's history, to lose his primary bid in 1980 to a little-known conservative Republican town supervisor from Long Island, Al D'Amato, who went on to win the general election. As he campaigned across the state, Javits acknowledged that he was a more liberal Republican in Rockefeller's mold who supported feminist goals such as legal abortion and the ERA. But the political climate had changed, and Javits lost his primary race in 1980 to D'Amato, owing to everything from the flailing economy to Javits's support for feminist reforms (and the links that many women drew between, for example, lower taxes and saving the nuclear family from feminist perversion). Ellen McCormack and her Right to Life Party cross-endorsed D'Amato, as is allowed in New York State. D'Amato's votes on the RTLP line surpassed his overall margin of victory in the general election; this fact led McCormack and her allies to claim (somewhat dubiously) that D'Amato would not have won without their backing.[45]

As the GOP's suburban-based right wing gained ascendency, it set the stage for Ronald Reagan's victory in 1980 in a state that, the *New York Times* noted, had "once [been] the most arid political terrain" for his conservative politics.[46] In 1976, Rockefeller was pressured by the

[44] Smith, *On His Own Terms*; Sullivan, *New York State and the Rise of Modern Conservatism*; Wolfgang Saxon, "Bernard Kilbourn, 81, Republican State Chairman," *The New York Times*, July 7, 2005; Thomas P. Ronan, "Party Workers Don't Live on Pay," *The New York Times*, August 14, 1977; Frank Lynn, "G.O.P. Presidential Race Shaping Up in New York," *The New York Times*, February 6, 1979.

[45] Frank Lynn, "Right to Life Party Shows Its Strength: Qualifies for Future Ballot Line – May Get Liberals' No. 4 Spot," *The New York Times*, November 10, 1978; Frank Lynn, "Suburbs' Power Mirrored in Tally of GOP Victors," *The New York Times*, November 9, 1980; Zimmerman, *The Government and Politics of New York State*.

[46] Maurice Carroll, "Conservatives Give Reagan Line on the New York Ballot," *The New York Times*, September 16, 1980, Folder 24, Box 2, Series 2, Conservative Party of New

party's right wing to remove his name as vice president from Ford's ticket. Despite this snub, Rockefeller ensured that Reagan was barely competitive in New York that year by locking up nearly all of the state's delegates at the Republican National Convention for Ford. Four years later, however, Reagan made winning electorally rich New York a priority. He announced his candidacy in New York City and appointed several people in the state to prominent positions in his campaign, including Long Island native Bill Casey as his campaign manager. As Al D'Amato solidified his RTLP and Conservative Party cross-endorsements in 1980, Reagan sought to do the same. His campaign was convinced that winning votes on the Conservative and RTLP lines would be needed in a tight race with President Jimmy Carter. New York's Conservative Party quickly endorsed him, but the RTLP dragged its feet because Reagan supported abortion in cases where it was necessary to save the life of a pregnant woman and had signed California's abortion reform law as governor in 1967, a decision he later regretted.[47]

Reagan's campaign continued to pursue the RTLP's cross-endorsement throughout the spring and summer of 1980 before falling short, although it appeared not to have mattered in the end. Frustrated by the RTLP's indecision, Roger Stone, Reagan's Northeast regional coordinator, tried to minimize the RTLP women's importance by telling the press that with or without their cross-endorsement, Reagan would win anti-abortion voters in New York – an opinion shared by most anti-abortion advocates in the state and around the nation. The RTLP leaders retaliated by telling fellow Long Islander Bill Casey, Reagan's campaign manager, that the RTLP would no longer negotiate with Roger Stone but only with Casey or, preferably, Ronald Reagan himself. As a testament to the RTLP's demonstrated ability to deliver votes in the all-important suburbs of New York City, Reagan personally called Ellen McCormack. But the RTLP decided to cling to principle and ran McCormack on its line in 1980 instead. Despite the obstinacy of the RTLP, Reagan won the four populous suburban counties outside of New York City, where groups like Wakeup and the RTLP were strongest, and with them, New York State.[48]

York State Records, M. E. Grenander Department of Special Collections and Archives, University Libraries, University at Albany, State University of New York, Albany, NY.
47 Ibid.
48 Frank Lynn, "Right to Life's Political Dilemma," *The New York Times*, July 20, 1980, Right to Life Party Folder, Carton 8, NARAL Records, SL; Ellen McCormack to Right to Life Party State Committee, July 29, 1980, the personal collection of Richard Bruno; Richard Bruno, interview by author, April 8, 2008, Piermont, NY, tape recording.

Exit polling showed that the votes of married white women aged forty-five to sixty-four had been central to Reagan's victory in the state – the same demographic that had organized these suburban areas around traditional family values, as well as a coveted demographic that reliably goes to the polls in any given election.[49] The women hastened the GOP's shift to the right by, ironically, working alongside the feminists whom they opposed to reframe politics around issues related to women and the family. The RTLP founders and their allies on the grassroots level in New York were not ambitious political types like Phyllis Schlafly, a woman who long had taken an interest in conservative Republican politics. Most women were raised as working-class Democrats and were disinterested in electoral politics. As they reached adulthood, they were most concerned with full-time homemaking, tending to children, and adapting to life in the suburbs. When politics seemed to converge with their homes and families, the women entered the political arena. Conservative Republican calls for more muscular anticommunism, lower taxation, smaller government, and individual rights had previously seemed foreign to these homemakers and their allies. In the wake of second-wave feminism and related movements, however, these demands were reimagined as the means to stymie dangerous taxpayer-backed feminist initiatives and privilege parents' and homemakers' rights over government intrusion – and in so doing, preserve the traditional division of roles and responsibilities within families like their own. This was an attractive proposition for women beset by new opportunities outside of the home and potential setbacks for male breadwinners in the anemic economy, all of which threatened to upend the domestic arrangements they had built their lives around.

But these suburban women were much more than a silent majority of voters who abandoned their Democratic roots after being lured in by the rhetoric and policy prescriptions of conservative Republicans. In New York in the 1970s, a vocal minority of women had voiced their concerns and organized a coveted statewide swing vote based in the four suburban counties that could decide the fate of elections there. It was they who lured the likes of conservative Republican boss Joseph Margiotta, U.S. Senator Al D'Amato, and even Ronald Reagan to their side, not the other way around. To be sure, longtime activist women such as Phyllis Schlafly at the national level and several well-heeled conservative religious organizations also had a hand in moving the GOP to embrace "family values."

[49] Frank Lynn, "Anti-Abortion Groups Split on Reagan's Candidacy," *The New York Times*, June 22, 1980.

But we cannot discount the contributions of northern (mostly Catholic) women who were new to politics and operated at the grassroots level in the years before 1980. In New York, these overlooked political actors demonstrated that people like them (notably married women aged forty-five to sixty-four who reliably went to the polls) would pull the lever for policies and politicians that would not, as they saw it, compel home-makers into the paid workforce, kill babies, or make it easier to evade motherhood. This moved conservative Republicans to begin discussing ideas such as limited government and lower taxation through the lens of heterosexual nuclear family rights. The women expanded upon and pro-moted these links through the organizations that they had built from the ground up like the New York State Right to Life Party – in turn making core conservative Republican demands more palpable to other women who saw themselves as everyday housewives primarily focused on their (traditional nuclear) families and homes. *The NYSRLP cit rep. still exists. lost ballot access in 2002*

This partnership in New York between antifeminist women in the downstate suburbs and the GOP's previously marginal right wing reshaped state politics and made it possible for conservatives to triumph over the more liberal, urban, pro-feminist Rockefeller faction of the party. Rather surprisingly, this shift occurred in what had been Nelson Rocke-feller's backyard and a political stronghold for both moderate Republi-canism and feminism. In these ways, conservative family values activists were crucial in the migration of political power toward the right and into the suburbs in the 1970s. The women considered here helped construct feminism as "antifamily" while modeling an attack on liberalism that has become a staple of statewide and national politics.

The NY GOP whimatly became much less competive statewide - it lost the Legislature in recent yrs) and last won a statewide election I believe 2002

16

Pornography, Heteronormativity, and the Genealogy of New Right Sexual Citizenship in the United States

Whitney Strub

Whatever else it was quiet about, the so-called silent majority talked incessantly about sex. From pornography and the floodtides of filth, to the Equal Rights Amendment and the symbolic death of traditional gender roles at the door of the unisex bathroom, from reproductive rights and the final dislodging of sex from procreation, to the queer menace of LGBT visibility and demands for equality, the silent majority and the New Right fought tooth and nail against this onslaught of challenges to tradition. A sizable body of historical scholarship has shown how sexuality played a central role in the rhetorical molding of an imagined silent majority composed primarily of middle-class white voters, positioned in contrast to the sexual revolution, feminist activism, and gay rights movements of the era.[1]

Yet the sexual politics of the New Right were not merely reactive. Rather, the New Right's vision of sexual citizenship was a brilliant recasting of already prevailing Cold War frameworks, reconfigured into newly partisan lines that collapsed liberalism into libertinism and claimed the mantle of the "normal." The New Right's notion of sexual citizenship

[1] The American New Right has been the focus of an outpouring of recent historical scholarship. For works that highlight the role of sexuality in New Right politics, see, among others, Janice Irvine, *Talk About Sex: The Battles over Sex Education in the United States* (Berkeley, 2002); Daniel Williams, *God's Own Party: The Making of the Christian Right* (Oxford, 2010); Darren Dochuk, *From Bible Belt to Sunbelt: Plain Folk Religion, Grassroots Politics, and the Rise of Evangelical Conservatism* (New York, 2010); Whitney Strub, *Perversion for Profit: The Politics of Pornography and the Rise of the New Right* (New York, 2011); Robert Self, *All in the Family: The Realignment of American Democracy since the 1960s* (New York, 2012).

built on existing disciplinary projects but co-opted them in the name of a new ritualized performance of proper heteronormativity, calibrated to deny social inclusion to those beyond its provinces. In this chapter, I use pornography as a window into the layered construction of this silent majoritarian regime while also tracing some of its contours, particularly the ways in which antigay sentiment pervaded and colored conservative discourse even when homosexuality was not the immediate referent.

Scholars often understand heteronormativity as the various mechanisms through which heterosexuality and its dominant institutions (marriage, monogamy, procreation, etc.) are produced as seemingly the natural order of things rather than an outcome of contested sexual politics. Examining the New Right serves to remind us that while we often reduce the project of heteronormativity to the mere naturalization of sexual hierarchies, it is as well a constant and ongoing disciplining of heterosexuality, too, and it is in many ways through the lens of the demonized queer or the uncontained libidinal fervor of smut that the New Right brought into better focus its decent body politic. There was always something queer about smut, and something pornographic about homosexuality; these parallel yet intersecting lines acted as boundaries of the permissible. In teasing out these links, I would also like to hint at some of the mechanisms that mobilized New Right sexual politics that have yet to receive sustained attention, such as the counter-empiricist epistemology and the affective and performative aspects of the New Right in these years that drew particular sustenance from their oblique invocations of race.

While a sizable body of sociological, legal, and theoretical work engages with the notion of sexual citizenship, we might profitably define it simply as that sense of belonging or inclusion that accompanies membership in a public.[2] Between the late 1960s and the early twenty-first century, the New Right asserted a hetero-supremacist vision of sexual propriety, defined through marriage and procreation. It meanwhile ostensibly depoliticized this framework through its absorption into an ahistorical normality that fixed an idealized vision of 1950s white, middle-class nuclear families as the standard-bearers of *the* American family. It is

Central texts here are Brenda Cossman, *Sexual Citizens: The Legal and Cultural Regulation of Sex and Belonging* (Stanford, 2007); Lauren Berlant, *The Queen of America Goes to Washington City: Essays on Sex and Citizenship* (Durham, NC, 1997); and David Bell and Jon Binnie, *The Sexual Citizen: Queer Politics and Beyond* (Cambridge, 2000). See also Scott Lauria Morgensen, "Settler Homonationalism: Theorizing Settler Colonialism within Queer Modernities," *GLQ: A Journal of Lesbian and Gay Studies* 16:1–2 (2010): 105–131.

precisely that axiomatic notion of normalcy that projects like queer theory seek to destabilize, but they run against deeply entrenched national belief structures – beginning, in this case, with postwar liberalism.

Not merely complicit, postwar liberalism had actively and aggressively enforced the restrictive boundaries of Cold War sexual politics. Though David Johnson has shown that the Lavender Scare, a multi-decade federal war on queerness, began as a Republican effort, it instantly amassed uncontested bipartisan support that allowed it to flourish as a seemingly ambient backdrop through the 1950s and 1960s, imagined as something separate from the political sphere if only because its politics were so presumptively universal.[3] As police raided, entrapped, blackmailed, beat, and sexually assaulted queer Americans, as psychiatry deemed them pathological and the media presented queerness as a lurid spectacle of perversity, *(white)* federal housing policy assiduously promoted the image of procreative heterosexual nuclear families as the legitimate denizens of the burgeoning suburbs on every level from booster literature to zoning plans, as Clayton Howard has shown.[4]

None of this was linked to anything that would have been understood as conservative at the time. What Margot Canaday labels the Straight State and its expansive bureaucracies constitute an integral part of modern liberalism.[5] From Arthur Schlesinger's *Vital Center* (1949) to John F. Kennedy's carefully orchestrated phallic politics, the liberal Cold War order was fundamentally premised on procreative heterosexuality and hegemonic gender norms as central components of the national project.[6] Further, the notion of sexuality as a private matter rather than public concern carried little weight in the Cold War era; even as heterosexual families sought refuge in single-family houses and bomb shelters, inscribing a clear barrier between the public and private spheres, there was no parallel queer private sphere. Not until the early twenty-first century, in the Supreme Court case *Lawrence v. Texas* (2003), would consensual gay adult sexuality in private space win legal validation; in the preceding

The just – When democratic society was [?] what – Marxist – Leninist. Counterpart. socially [?]

3   David Johnson, *The Lavender Scare: The Cold War Persecution of Gays and Lesbians in the Federal Government* (Chicago, 2004).

4   Clayton Howard, "Building a Family Friendly Metropolis: Sexuality, the State, and Postwar Housing Policy," *Journal of Urban History* 39:5 (2013): 933–955.

5   Margot Canaday, *The Straight State: Sexuality and Citizenship in Twentieth-Century America* (Princeton, 2009).

6   Robert Dean, *Imperial Brotherhood: Gender and the Making of Cold War Foreign Policy* (Amherst, 2003); Elaine Tyler May, *Homeward Bound: American Families in the Cold War Era* (New York, 1988).

decades, national public interest superseded individual civil rights claims. Even the American Civil Liberties Union (ACLU) came to defend queer rights only in the second half of the 1960s after intense pressure from its more progressive branches.[7]

When a sensationalized comic-book panic emerged in the early 1950s, it came not from sanctimonious moralists but rather from Doctor Fredric Wertham, a progressive psychiatrist who was sensitive to the demeaning primitivization of people of color in the comics and emphatically pushed for school desegregation. Yet when it came to sexuality, non-normative practice and identity served as his central demonology. At a time when homosexuality was being linked to communism through their shared undermining of the monolithically imagined American family, Wertham's analysis of Batman and Robin as queer perverts insidiously corrupting American youth reinforced the linkage; Wertham's 1954 magnum opus *Seduction of the Innocent* was marked by a gay panic in which all roads, from sadomasochism to fetishes, led ultimately back to homosexuality.[8]

Likewise, when comics gave way to pornography as the locus of collective sexual anxiety in the mid-1950s, again liberals led the way. The key architect of the porn panic, which grew immediately out of the comics crusade, was again a liberal, Democratic Senator Estes Kefauver of Tennessee. A staunch New Dealer, a relative racial progressive, and also a media-savvy politician with presidential aspirations, Kefauver held hearings on the national smut problem in 1955. Kefauver's assistants had coached and vetted their witnesses in private correspondence beforehand, and experts such as psychotherapist Benjamin Karpman and Washington, DC, vice squad officer Roy Blick performed well, linking pornography to sex crimes, juvenile delinquency, and more: as Blick testified, porn caused "kids who are just at the age that they should know right from wrong to become perverts and homosexuals."[9]

Significantly, this analysis so precisely anticipates the rhetoric of the New Right that the two eras are historically inseparable. The popular liberatory narrative of the sexual revolution highlights important

---

[7] *Lawrence v. Texas*, 539 U.S. 558 (2003). On the ACLU and sexuality, see Judy Kutulas, *The American Civil Liberties Union and the Making of Modern Liberalism, 1930–1960* (Chapel Hill, 2006); Leigh Ann Wheeler, *How Sex Became a Civil Liberty* (New York, 2013).

[8] Andrea Friedman, "Sadists and Sissies: Anti-Pornography Campaigns in Cold War America," *Gender and History* 15:2 (2003): 201–227.

[9] *Juvenile Delinquency (Obscene and Pornographic Materials). Hearings before the Committee on the Judiciary*, U.S. Senate (Washington, DC, 1955); also Strub, *Perversion for Profit*, 19–30.

moments like the Food and Drug Administration's (FDA) approval of the birth control pill, the scaling back of obscenity law, the abandonment of *in loco parentis* doctrine at colleges and universities, and increasing premarital cohabitation and gay and lesbian visibility. But another trajectory undergirds that triumphalist narrative, running unbroken from 1950s moral panics to those of the 1970s. This layer of the history of American sexuality rests on reasserted boundaries, and inchoate anxieties channeled into official forms. The contrast can be jarring; in 1967, the year the Supreme Court struck down miscegenation laws in *Loving v. Virginia*, opening the door to interracial heterosexual marriage, that same famously liberal Warren Court also consigned Canadian immigrant Clive Michael Boutilier to deportation after a decade in the United States – for having a "psychopathic personality," which the Court accepted as a description of homosexuality.[10]

Not every expression of antigay sentiment was so blatant. Take, for instance, the 1962 antiporn short film *Perversion for Profit* by the Cincinnati-based group Citizens for Decent Literature (CDL). Reporter and narrator George Putnam surveys the ravages of smut, listing moral decay, illegitimate births, venereal disease, and more. But the recurring apex of moral horror is homosexuality, invoked repeatedly throughout the film. Physique magazines can pervert even "normal" men, while young boys are easier targets yet, and Putnam warns us of "your daughter, lured into lesbianism," too. In this constellation of heteronormative concerns, unleashed sexuality collapsed as if by queer inevitability into homosexual perversion, a slippery slope of sexual degeneration.[11]

Indeed, CDL discourse reflected the pervasive centrality of revulsion to queerness in antiporn activism. Again in their 1965 film *Printed Poison*, CDL lingered on images of physique magazines and queer pulp fiction, and across the decade spokesmen for the group resorted to homosexuality as a moral trump card in denouncing smut. Founder Charles Keating warned that pornography allowed innocent teens to "enter the world of lesbians, homosexuals, sadists, masochists, and other deviates" in his stock speech. The threat of converting "decent" youth into perverts and degenerates remained a staple of CDL's antiporn arguments, as when

[10] On the Supreme Court's boundary maintenance during the sexual revolution, see Marc Stein, *Sexual Injustice: Supreme Court Decisions from Griswold to Roe* (Chapel Hill, 2010). On the sexual revolution see Beth Bailey, *Sex in the Heartland* (Cambridge, MA, 1999), and David Allyn, *Make Love, Not War: The Sexual Revolution, an Unfettered History* (Boston, 2000).

[11] *Perversion for Profit* (Citizens for Decent Literature, 1962).

[Handwritten margin notes: "I think 1954 y 1960"; "Interracial marriage was widely unpopular in 1967, and for a long time after"; "Larry Flynt who also from Cincinnati. new"; "Even though pornography tends to be straight"; "As in the Keating Five, the renders he tried to bribe"]

Southern California CDL Executive Director Raymond Gauer lectured on
"The Pornographic Conspiracy" in 1962. "It is a fact," Gauer intoned,
"that our homosexual population today, per capita, is greater than it has
ever been in the history of our country." Until he became an antiporn
activist, Gauer explained, he had thought that "if you were a homosexual
or any other type of pervert, you were born that way." Only through
prolonged exposure to smut and its effects had he learned "that this is
a trait that can be acquired and you acquire this through the things you
do and the people you hang around with and stuff that you read" – a
somewhat vague etiology of perversion, but one that firmly grounded
opposition to pornography in revulsion toward homosexuality. Helping
Gauer secure credibility, it also resonated effectively with the governing
psychiatric consensus of the time, which understood homosexuality as a
curable affliction.[12]

Among the changes of the 1960s was the emergence of an army of
social scientists who decisively refuted all of this. First Alfred Kinsey,
then William Masters and Virginia Johnson, helped spawn legions of
sexologists, who examined everything from juvenile arrest records to
penile responses to porn. The conclusion, and overwhelming consensus,
was that sexually explicit materials caused none of the harms opponents claimed; rather, America's paltry public discourse on sexuality,
which encouraged ignorance and anxiety, was the problem. Conservative
sexual politics were often approached as a reaction-formation to social
change. These conclusions, backed by ten volumes of empirical research,
formed the basis of the 1970 report of the President's Commission on
Obscenity and Pornography, the result of three years of investigation
by dozens of teams of psychologists, psychiatrists, sociologists, and legal
scholars.[13]

12 *Printed Poison* (Citizens for Decent Literature, 1965); Charles Keating, "Typical CDL
    Talk," n.d. (1962), box 2, Published Material, Youth Protection Committee Records,
    Utah Historical Society, Salt Lake City; "A Typical CDL Talk Delivered By Ray P.
    Gauer," September 14, 1962, ibid. Homosexuality had initially been understood as a
    congenital condition ("inversion") in the late nineteenth century, but by midcentury that
    theory had been superseded by one that saw it as a result of psychosexual maladjust-
    ment. Jennifer Terry, *An American Obsession: Science, Medicine, and Homosexuality
    in Modern Society* (Chicago, 1999).
13 *The Report of the Commission on Obscenity and Pornography* (New York, 1970); on
    the Kinsey reports, see Miriam Reumann, *American Sexual Character: Sex, Gender,
    and National Identity in the Kinsey Reports* (Berkeley, 2005); on Masters and Johnson,
    Thomas Maier, *Masters of Sex: The Life and Times of William Masters and Virginia
    Johnson, the Couple Who Taught America How to Love* (New York, 2009).

Yet this report went unheeded. Rather, denunciations greeted it: from the Senate, which voted 60–5 against it; from the press, which mocked it ("an unscientific piece of tripe," declared the Fort Wayne *News-Sentinel*); from President Nixon, who linked it to moral anarchy; and from within the commission itself, where Charles Keating delivered a blistering minority report saturated with exclamation marks and anecdotal evidence of pornography's moral harms, such as migrant Puerto Ricans working on a fur farm who "changed from rather manly, decent people to rapists being obsessed with sex, including many deviations," when they were suddenly exposed to smut.[14] Moral outrage and indignation superseded empiricist social science in providing the proper interpretive frame for American sexuality.

Parable replaced data, as Richard Nixon offered his own explanation in October 1970: "The Commission contends that the proliferation of filthy books and plays has no lasting harmful effect on a man's character. If that were true, it must also be true that great books, great paintings, and great plays have no ennobling effect on a man's conduct. Centuries of civilization and 10 minutes of common sense tell us otherwise."[15] This argument, illogical as it was, would be echoed repeatedly in the decades that followed, not least by Supreme Court Chief Justice Warren Burger.

Indeed, Burger made a grand contribution to this commonsense epistemology in several important cases of the early 1970s. After a few initial stumbles in the form of failed nominations, Nixon was able to reshape the Supreme Court through four new appointments in swift succession, abruptly bringing the famed liberalism of the Court under Chief Justice Earl Warren to a halt. As soon as Nixon's appointments reached critical mass, with the support of sexually conservative Byron White, they overhauled obscenity doctrine in a series of 1973 cases, enacting a retrenchment that made standards more conservative. In *Paris Adult Theatre I v. Slaton*, Chief Justice Burger issued his most openly counter-empirical claim, brushing aside the momentous body of research contained in the ten volumes of the Commission on Obscenity and Pornography's technical reports, and instead privileging the dissenting minority report of Reverend Winfrey Link and Father Morton Hill, founder of the Catholic activist group Morality in Media, whose career ran almost precisely

---

[14] Strub, *Perversion for Profit*, 130–136.
[15] Richard Nixon, "Statement about the Report of the Commission on Obscenity and Pornography," October 24, 1970, American Presidency Project, http://www.presidency.ucsb.edu/ws/?pid=2759.

parallel (temporally and rhetorically) to the efforts of Mary Whitehouse to "clean up" British television and culture, as chronicled elsewhere in this volume by Bill Schwarz (chapter 7) and Lawrence Black (chapter 17). Their report, based on no discernible research beyond anecdotal testimony, "indicates that there is at least an arguable correlation between obscene material and crime." That was enough for Burger, and in fact remains the epistemological underpinning of contemporary American obscenity doctrine in the twenty-first century.[16]

"At least arguable" thus superseded empirically tested as the formula for ascertaining social harm in obscenity doctrine. Meanwhile, the performative aspects of New Right sexual citizenship found a particularly good, or at least eager, actor in Nixon, who denounced the perceived sexual excesses of the 1960s with the same fervor he had brought to opposing communism and red-baiting liberals early in his political career.[17] Indeed, while directly linking pornography to communism by 1970 would reek too much of right-wing extremist John Birch Society claims of earlier years, Nixon cannily accused pornography of promoting anarchy – he used the word three times in his denunciation of the 1970 commission report. His rising rhetoric hailed the silent majority as a decent majority, defining it through the contrast of its basic sexual normality and restraint. While "the warped and brutal portrayal of sex in books, plays, magazines, and movies, if not halted and reversed, could poison the wellsprings of American and Western culture and civilization," he warned, decent citizens resisted. "Mothers and fathers by the tens of thousands have written to the White House and the Congress," he had already declared in 1969, implicitly staking his majority's claim to decency on the routing of sexuality into its ordained procreative role. "They resent these intrusions into their homes, and they are asking for federal assistance to protect their children against exposure to erotic publications."[18]

He even considered physically enacting their fight. H. R. Haldeman's diary records a plan, tantalizing but never undertaken, for Nixon to attend

---

[16] *Paris Adult Theatre I v. Slaton*, 419 U.S. 49 (1973).

[17] Greg Mitchell, *Tricky Dick and the Pink Lady: Richard Nixon vs. Helen Gahagan Douglas – Sexual Politics and the Red Scare, 1950* (New York, 1998).

[18] Richard Nixon, "Special Message to the Congress on Obscene and Pornographic Materials," May 2, 1969, American Presidency Project, http://www.presidency.ucsb.edu/ws/index.php?pid=2032. Nixon did not yet have to contend with organized feminism's engagement with pornography, a movement that would develop in the United States only after the controversies surrounding the film *Snuff* in 1976; see Strub, *Perversion for Profit*, 213–255.

a play with nudity in New York City (probably *Hair* or *Che*), for the sole purpose of storming out in anger midway through.[19] Obsessed with manipulating the media, Nixon also fixated on the performance of sexual decency. As the Nixon archives reveal, the first note on pornography from the new president in 1969 read, "What can we do to get some publicity on this?" Even as the commission found no harm in smut, Nixon staffers in the spring of 1970 suggested "very visible raids on the pornography shops" located in the "near vicinity of the White House" in order to "demonstrate an immediate concern on the part of the President." The raids were carried out – and indeed, focused largely on homosexually themed materials.[20]

By this period, liberals had largely moved beyond Cold War sexual politics. Among the Democratic presidential candidates during these formative years of the New Right, none showed any meaningful commitment to either sexual revolution or the values Nixon associated with his invented silent majority; in 1972, George McGovern and the Democratic platform began hinting at greater inclusion of gays and lesbians, while Jimmy Carter's infamous *Playboy* interview on the eve of the 1976 election suggested a broadly libertarian approach to sexuality.[21] Yet if liberalism moved forward, it did so meekly, moving away from the sexual politics of the past without ever renouncing or even substantively engaging them. In the face of strong outrage, liberals were apt to acquiesce rather than fight, as witnessed in the congressional denunciations of the pornography report, where conservatives led the way but liberals quietly followed, with few exceptions (McGovern being one, in that case). The result was a ceding of sexual values understood simply as American in the very recent past to new partisan contours in which the New Right could claim them for itself.

[Handwritten margin note:] "I have looked in my heart" – The letters are, line, broadly supportive of LGBT rights

[Handwritten note at bottom:] The right claimed sexual normalcy for itself and still does

[19] H. R. Haldeman, *The Haldeman Diaries: Inside the Nixon White House* (New York, 1994), 43.

[20] Richard Nixon, handwritten note on Alexander Butterfield's Memorandum for the President, March 12, 1969, box 1, folder: Presidential Handwriting, March 1–15, White House Special Files-Staff Members and Office Files-Presidential Office Files, Richard Nixon Archives, National Archives and Records Administration, College Park, MD; Nixon, "Special Message to the Congress on Obscene and Pornographic Materials," May 2, 1969, American Presidency Project, http://www.presidency.ucsb.edu/ws/? pid=2032.

[21] On McGovern and gay rights, see Bruce Miroff, *The Liberals' Moment: The McGovern Insurgency and the Identity Crisis of the Democratic Party* (Lawrence, 2007), 215–218; on Carter, see Williams, *God's Own Party*, 133–158, and Strub, *Perversion for Profit*, 185–187.

Liberals had no wellspring of public sentiment to draw on that ran nearly as deep as that of the New Right. The affective elements of New Right sexual politics have been powerfully analyzed by sociologist Janice Irvine, whose book *Talk About Sex* examines battles over sex education as sites where politics and emotion combined to form a discourse largely impervious to classical models of rational debate.[22] Again on that front, both antigay and antiporn language constituted central threads in the affective and discursive tapestry of activism against public school sex education. This same matrix resurfaced when Anita Bryant took the latent heteronormativity of American politics writ large and translated it into an overtly homophobic, partisan New Right project with her "Save Our Children" crusade against gay rights in Miami-Dade County, Florida, in 1977. Bryant took her cues from Nixon's approach to smut. Decent heterosexual families, she contended, were on the defensive against what her very book subtitle called "the threat of militant homosexuality." Militant, to Bryant, was simply *out in* gay life – that is, in her language, *flaunting* homosexuality by making it publicly visible. Language was carefully employed to generate maximum disgust, and Bryant constantly referenced child pornography as if gay men possessed a monopoly on it.[23]

Bryant's antigay campaign was hardly subtle in its lineage, nor sophisticated in its blunt linkages between gay men, pornography, and child molestation. But the antigay foundations of antiporn positions manifested less transparently in the parallel social scientific work of her ideological ally Victor Cline, a University of Utah psychologist. A well-published scholar, Cline dissented from the prevailing social scientific consensus that porn could not be directly linked to antisocial behavior. In numerous books and articles, Cline countered that exposure to porn did, in fact, lead to sexually deviant behavior. Though national media outlets frequently cited Cline and his work, few paused to parse his semantics; not only did Cline include rape and sexually aggressive behavior in his definition of deviance, he also added adultery, non-monogamy, and homosexuality. Even progressive feminist activists of the late 1970s continued to invoke Cline in their arguments against porn, showing how deeply sutured into antiporn rhetoric antigay positions remained – even if sometimes without the knowledge of the speakers. Indeed, the feminist antiporn movement

[22] Janice Irvine, *Talk About Sex: The Battles over Sex Education in the United States* (Berkeley, 2002).

[23] Anita Bryant, *The Anita Bryant Story: The Survival of Our Nation's Families and the Threat of Militant Homosexuality* (Grand Rapids, 1977).

that developed in the late 1970s sometimes showed striking affinities with New Right politics. As their feminist critics in the so-called sex wars of the 1980s would accuse, antiporn feminists relied on a gender politics that implicitly reinscribed Victorian norms of women as sexually pure victims of male desire; meanwhile, movement leaders Andrea Dworkin and Catharine MacKinnon actively collaborated with the Reaganite Meese Commission in the mid-1980s, an investigative body that began its work with a mandate to arrive at antiporn conclusions and was to take antigay stances repeatedly.[24]

Meanwhile, as Gillian Frank has recently shown, race was also embedded in Bryant's "Save Our Children" efforts in multiple and fundamental ways. In a literal, material sense, activist energy from preceding and ongoing efforts against school desegregation by busing was channeled directly into antigay activism. Ideologically, both campaigns centered on the imperiled, implicitly white child in need of protection against "forced busing" or the figure who became central to Bryant, the gay teacher out to recruit and pervert.[25] In uncovering this, Frank also points toward a broader genealogy, as racialized tropes migrated freely in the late 1960s onto sexual terrains. That this happened through key New Right pioneers like Senators Strom Thurmond (R-South Carolina) and Jesse Helms (R-North Carolina), and evangelical Moral Majority leader Jerry Falwell, was no coincidence. By the late 1960s, for instance, Falwell's position that Martin Luther King, Jr. was a communist dupe was no longer tenable, and the shift to sexual politics provided a necessary escape route from an otherwise dead end of racism on which such figures had built their careers.[26]

The roots of this shift are visible as far back as the late 1950s, as the Supreme Court under Earl Warren, having ended formal segregation in the mid-1950s, began relaxing obscenity standards. An

---

[24] Victor Cline, *Where Do You Draw the Line? An Exploration into Media Violence, Pornography, and Censorship* (Provo, 1974); on Cline and feminists, see Strub, *Perversion for Profit*, 236; on the feminist antiporn movement, see Lisa Duggan and Nan Hunter, *Sex Wars: Sexual Dissent and Political Culture* (New York, 1995), and Carolyn Bronstein, *Battling Pornography: The American Feminist Anti-Pornography Movement, 1977–1986* (New York, 2011).

[25] Gillian Frank, "'The Civil Rights of Parents': Race and Conservative Politics in Anita Bryant's Campaign against Gay Rights in 1970s Florida," *Journal of the History of Sexuality* 22:1 (2013): 126–160.

[26] On these key figures, see Nadine Cohodas, *Strom Thurmond and the Politics of Southern Change* (Macon, 1994); William Link, *Righteous Warrior: Jesse Helms and the Rise of Modern Conservatism* (New York, 2008); Williams, *God's Own Party*.

increasingly nationalized obscenity regime provided fertile ground for the
expansion of states' rights-oriented arguments about federalism. In 1959,
for instance, Mississippi senator James Eastland presented a Supreme
Court ruling overturning New York's ban on a film of *Lady Chatterley's
Lover* as a "mortal blow to the power of a State to maintain within its borders minimum standards of decency and morality." Eastland obliquely
nodded toward his racial concerns as he warned that the Court might
move in similar directions with regard to "bigamy, or sodomy, or miscegenation." Aligning himself with fellow segregationists such as South
Carolina's Strom Thurmond and Georgia's Herman Talmadge, Eastland
proposed a constitutional amendment that would bar the Supreme Court
from hearing cases involving "public policy questions of decency and
morality." Such matters, which in Eastland's view touched on questions
of racial propriety, would, in line with the states' rights agenda, remain
state concerns.[27]

The proposed amendment failed, but it showed how an already racialized states' rights agenda could seamlessly evolve into an ostensibly moral
platform, albeit one in which race and sexuality remained fused. Throughout the 1960s, conservative politicians performed this conversion, shifting from race to sexuality in ways that carried affective, connotative, and
legal traces of the fading segregationist past. James Kilpatrick, a Virginia
journalist, had championed massive resistance against school desegregation. In the early 1960s, he turned his attention to *The Smut Peddlers*,
as his 1960 book labeled them. Kilpatrick engaged in an extensive legal
survey of obscenity law. His index did not include *Brown v. Board of
Education*, segregation, or much evident carryover from the recent past.
Yet *The Smut Peddlers* concluded with a tribute to the obscenity doctrine of Justice John Marshall Harlan – who had not played much of
a meaningful role in the Court's obscenity debates but whose proposed
doctrine resonated quite precisely with states'-rights federalism. "The federal authority is thus attenuated," Kilpatrick warmly noted of Harlan's
doctrine, leaving little ambiguity as to the broader legal implications.[28]

In Memphis, late 1960s mayor Henry Loeb, a Spiro Agnew fan who
had built his career largely on opposition to black civil rights claims in

[27] Quotes from Whitney Strub, *Obscenity Rules: Roth v. United States and the Long
Struggle over Sexual Expression* (Lawrence, 2013), 209.

[28] James Jackson Kilpatrick, *The Smut Peddlers* (New York, 1960), 263. Anders Walker
has reached similar conclusions about Kilpatrick in "'A Horrible Fascination': Segregation, Obscenity, and the Cultural Contingency of Rights," *Washington University Law
Review* 89 (2012): 1017–1203.

The anti-porn campaign was a proxy war w/ the Warren Court

the late 1950s, spearheaded a local war on porn that likewise trafficked in coded racial tropes. Most blatantly, the local police director, Frank Holloman, who described pornography as "a concerted and planned campaign to destroy the morals of our young people" at an antiporn rally, went on to claim that Memphians "don't have to accept the rulings of the Supreme Court." The allusion to massive resistance was unmistakable in a city still divided along racial lines. Goldwaterite city councilman Robert James, joining the attack to condemn the presence of Philip Roth's notoriously sexual novel *Portnoy's Complaint* (1969) in the local public library, claimed "the City shouldn't have to buy it – just for a minority group that is depraved enough to read it," again using language that, in its specific local historical context, carried inescapable connotative baggage. Mayor Loeb, using broader terms that nonetheless inescapably signified his allegiances, simply observed in 1969, "This country has to turn back to some kind of morality." Turning back, to a simpler era of presumed social order, again contained unstated corollaries about the social changes of the 1960s, among which race relations could not but loom large.[29]

These subtextually racialized moral tropes carried into the 1970s, proving transportable, as antigay and Jim Crow traces converged within the rhetoric of opposition to the Equal Rights Amendment (ERA). The ERA, which overwhelmingly passed both houses of Congress with broad bipartisan backing in 1972 before heading to individual states for ratification, *And may still* would have formally instilled gender equality in the U.S. Constitution. It quickly became a site of mobilization, however, for conservatives opposed to what they saw as its destabilization of traditional gender roles. In North Carolina, anti-ERA activists coined the unique neologism "desexegregation" to point to the threats of a ratified ERA – suggesting it would do for gender what *Brown v. Board* had done for race. Meanwhile, the conservative women's movement against the ERA, spearheaded by Illinois activist Phyllis Schlafly, warned that the amendment would "legalize homosexual 'marriages,'" as Schlafly put it in her 1977 book *The Power of the Positive Woman*. That homophobia provided a central source of modern antifeminist political formations was further on display in conservative women's resistance to International Women's Year in 1977; in

The ERA proved unnecessary for that; the Supreme Court handed down Obergefell v. Hodges in 2015

[29] John Clark, "Loeb and Holloman Point to Indifference on Smut," Memphis *Press-Scimitar*, October 2, 1969; Lloyd Holbeck, "100 Picket Adult Center After Antismut Meeting," Memphis *Commercial Appeal*, October 3, 1969; Robert James to Marjorie Weber, July 31, 1969, Robert James Papers, box 8, folder: Pornography/Obscenity Correspondence, Memphis-Shelby Public Library; "Loeb Calls for Decency At Library," *Press-Scimitar*, July 11, 1969.

Indiana, among numerous other states, opponents labeled the year's conferences a "$5 million Lesbian Bash," with one leader instructing readers to "start looking under the rug" where "ERA's Lesbian and Communist promoters have swept their dirt."[30]

Anti-empiricist traditionalist epistemology paralleled racial matters on other fronts too, of course. As Matthew Lassiter has shown, the silent suburban majority who fueled the rise of modern conservatism rejected sociological analyses of institutionalized inequalities and group behavioral patterns, preferring the ahistorical elegance of individualized, market-based explanations for the persistence of middle-class white privilege and residential segregation. The New Right's rejection of sexual science thus played into the hands of this movement, consolidating a broader questioning of the empiricist social science that undergirded the liberal administrative state.[31]

These trends reached their zenith in Jesse Helms's antigay activism of the late 1980s. Like Falwell and many other key Southern figures in the movement, a longtime opponent of African American civil rights until that stance became untenable in the wake of 1960s civil rights advances, Helms had found new political sustenance in the various moral positions of the 1970s and 1980s, supporting civil rights legislation for the first time when it applied to unborn fetuses.[32] Vocal homophobia marked Helms's political stances of the 1980s, and his two efforts to censor homosexuality from the body politic, each labeled the Helms Amendment, represent high-water marks of New Right sexual backlash. As he displaced race through reactionary sexual politics, he found pornography in homosexuality and queerness in the obscene.

Most famously, in his 1989 war against the National Endowment for the Arts (NEA), Helms considered homoeroticism inherently obscene

[30] Donald Mathews and Jane Sherron De Hart, *Sex, Gender, and the Politics of ERA: A State and the Nation* (New York, 1990), 172; Phyllis Schlafly, *The Power of the Positive Woman* (New Rochelle, NY, 1977), 90; Erin Kempker, "Battling 'Big Sister' Government: Hoosier Women and the Politics of International Women's Year," *Journal of Women's History* 24:2 (2012): 144–170, quoted at 160. Schlafly also warned of "homosexual 'marriage'" in the top headline of her *Phyllis Schlafly Report*, September 1974 (thanks to Gillian Frank for sharing this with me). For a powerfully researched account of Schlafly that nonetheless omits this side of her political argument against the ERA, see Donald T. Critchlow, *Phyllis Schlafly and Grassroots Conservatism: A Woman's Crusade* (Princeton, 2005).

[31] Matthew Lassiter, *The Silent Majority: Suburban Politics in the Sunbelt South* (Princeton, 2006).

[32] William Snider, *Helms and Hunt: The North Carolina Senate Race, 1984* (Chapel Hill, 1985).

and would have prevented any federal funding for such material on those grounds. The Reagan administration had already declared war on porn, embodied most visibly in the 1986 report of the Attorney General's Commission on Pornography. To this, Helms added a distinctly antigay twist. Though only a weakened version of his original hardline proposal passed Congress, the Helms Amendment nonetheless proved a potent symbolic battle cry. In the ensuing moral uproar, criminal charges were filed against the director of the Cincinnati Contemporary Art Center for displaying the photographs of respected gay artist Robert Mapplethorpe – one of Helms's most infamous targets.[33]

It was Helms's crusade against explicit safer-sex education, however, that inflicted the greatest harm. Two years before the NEA battles, but less closely watched by the mass media, Helms fought for a gag order against Centers for Disease Control funding of any materials that "promote, condone, or encourage homosexual activities."[34] Since the Reagan administration remained indifferent to the AIDS crisis, grassroots activist groups such as Gay Men's Health Crisis had filled the federal void with their own frank, explicit comics and short videos designed to promote condom use by integrating it, graphically, into broader gay consciousness. Public health officials achieved virtual unanimity in endorsing these tactics, but the Helms Amendment brought an immediate end to federal funds for them, even as HIV transmission and AIDS fatalities proliferated.[35] Though a protracted court struggle finally resulted in a lift on the gag order in the 1990s, the elimination of an undeniably effective preventive educational tactic at a moment of epidemic catastrophe ensured the Helms Amendment's causal role in the perpetuation of the AIDS crisis.[36]

The threads of recent history echoed through the Helms debates. Even the language the senator used – "We have got to call a spade a spade," an aphorism using a word that doubled as a derogatory term for African Americans – could hardly fail to carry racial baggage, given his lengthy

---

[33] Museum director Dennis Barrie beat the charges; see Richard Meyer, "The Jesse Helms Theory of Art," *October* 104 (Spring 2003): 131–148.

[34] Helms Amendment, quoted in Jessica Tourk, "Controlling Expression: The Stagnant Policy of the Centers for Disease Control in the Second Decade of AIDS," *Cardozo Arts and Entertainment Law Journal* 13 (1993): 596–917.

[35] Douglas Crimp, "How to Have Promiscuity in an Epidemic" (1987), reprinted in his *Melancholia and Moralism: Essays on AIDS and Queer Politics* (Cambridge, MA, 2002), 43–81.

[36] On AIDS education efforts, explicitness, and effectiveness, see Cindy Patton, *Fatal Advice: How Safe-Sex Education Went Wrong* (Durham, NC, 1996).

Whitney Strub

history of insensitivity and hostility to black equality.[37] The conflation of homosexuality and obscenity perpetuated a well-established linkage. Tellingly, Helms's prioritizing of moralism over public health won the backing not only of all of his overtly homophobic Republican colleagues but also of the overwhelming majority of Democrats – only two in the Senate voted against it. Democrats had not led the antigay charges of the 1980s, but neither did they offer meaningful resistance to them, unable to advance a sexual politics that went beyond the abstractions of the liberal rights agenda and into the messy complications of graphic gay sexuality and vectors of HIV transmission. Indeed, many of the most outspokenly antigay New Right Republican leaders were precisely the ghosts of the Cold War Democratic past. The heteronormative liberal sexual politics that underwrote the emergence of the New Right platform thus remained intact well into the purported culture wars of the 1980s.[38]

As such, the New Right's exclusionary sexual citizenship proved a dynamic force despite its reactionary qualities, absorbing, reconfiguring, and redeploying racial and sexual normativities in new formations as old ones fell into obsolescence. Confronting a liberalism committed to fundamentally similar sexual hierarchies, the New Right capitalized on the contradictions of consensus American values. Although the Democratic Party, socially liberal if decreasingly so on many other policy fronts, rarely showed the vindictiveness of many New Right moral crusades, liberals never offered a robust, affirmative sexual politics that celebrated difference or questioned the structuring institutions of American sexuality. In several telling moments of the 1990s, such as the 1996 Defense of Marriage Act or the sweeping Communications Decency Act the same year, New Right politicians led the charge, but Democratic President Bill Clinton ultimately signed the legislation.

Even as sexual citizenship expanded in the wake of the fraught culture war years of the 1980s and 1990s, slowly welcoming LGBT citizens so long as they entered through such gatekeeping institutions as marriage or the military, the longstanding disciplinary projects of heteronormativity were reinforced through these normalizing structures. The legacies that linked Cold War homophobia and Jim Crow segregation to the Helms Amendments concealed themselves well, and it has required the

---

37 Edward Koch, "Senator Helms's Callousness Toward AIDS Victims," *The New York Times*, November 7, 1987.

38 James Davison Hunter, *Culture Wars: The Struggle to Define America* (New York, 1991).

theoretically driven naming practices of queer theory and critical race studies to begin their excavation.[39] Yet outside the academy, the very silence of the silent majority haunts modern sexual politics; as LGBT rights are articulated through assimilation into dominant institutions, more complicated historical questions are held at bay by a national triumphalist narrative. Much like the almost immediate banishment of antimiscegenation laws from national collective memory in the wake of *Loving v. Virginia* documented by historian Peggy Pascoe, the homophobic politics that undergirded modern conservatism for four decades – and that went almost wholly unchallenged by liberals until the very recent past – seem slated for omission from national memory (unless revived by the Trump administration, which appears plausible as this volume goes to press).[40] Should this silence prevail, with this memory will go the chance to interrogate the intersecting logics that formed modern sexual citizenship in the United States and also the ability to resist the inevitable new regimes of sexual normativity that stand open to political exploitation in the continued absence of a rigorous national dialogue on sexuality.

[39] The naming of "homonormativity" by Lisa Duggan in *The Twilight of Equality? Neoliberalism, Cultural Politics and the Attack on Democracy* (Boston, 2003) was one crucial moment in the twenty-first-century genealogy of sexual politics; another significant intervention came through Jasbir Puar's linking of "homonationalism" to the "War on Terror"; *Terrorist Assemblages: Homonationalism in Queer Times* (Durham, NC, 2007).

[40] Peggy Pascoe, *What Comes Naturally: Miscegenation Law and the Making of Race in America* (New York, 2009), 287–314.

1968 and All That(cher)

Cultures of Conservatism and the New Right in Britain

Lawrence Black

In the annals of British conservatism, 1968 is best remembered for the contretemps between Conservative Party leader Edward Heath and his shadow cabinet colleague Enoch Powell – a clash as much of styles as over race and immigration. Radicalism dominates histories of 1968 and "1968" rapidly became a synonym for its aspirations. The year is pivotal in Geoff Eley's epic history of the European left, even in the United Kingdom where, excepting Northern Ireland, cultural outweighed political upheaval. For Conservatives, 1979, when Margaret Thatcher triumphed in the general election, was more like their 1968.[1]

But the rise of the New Right was not all about Thatcher, and to privilege one moment can simplify a more involved process. Nor were Conservatives just reactive to 1968 – as if a New Right emerged in the 1970s to replace a discredited Keynesianism and social democracy, neatly culminating in 1979. True, many of conservative disposition were profoundly agitated by "1968," feeding the febrile 1970s. But the New Right contributed to this shift from what were perceived as the liberal, permissive 1960s to a resurgent conservatism prior to the 1970s' economic crisis. A similar transition in the United States saw President Reagan elected in 1980. In both, the New Right fashioned a new popular political appeal. This was more than anticommunism or abstruse market economics. They mobilized support in appeals to homeowners, taxpayers, and consumers that couched a moral critique of social liberalism and state bureaucracy in

---

[1] Geoff Eley, *Forging Democracy: A History of the Left in Europe, 1850–2000* (Oxford, 2002), ch. 21; Christian Caryl, *Strange Rebels: 1979 and the Birth of the 21st Century* (Cambridge, MA, 2013).

a candid, commonsense style, and they often employed non-institutional techniques to make those appeals.[2]

Conservatives were then part of the mix in 1968, but the emergent New Right was itself a mix of activists, intellectuals, think tanks, neoliberals, authoritarians, libertarians, Eurosceptics, and marginal dead ends.[3] Conservatism had always been a medley of voices to judge by recent research that warns against rooting around in the party's past with an eye only for proto-Thatcherism.[4] Tempting as it is to write about the left and right as if there were agreed borders, if the focus is political culture as a whole, then how they related, competed, with each other and in the wider culture, is key. The analogies to be found on the right with the radical sense of 1968 recommend this approach. This is not to overlook differences but to avoid using a received, normative definition of politics that misses the very redefinitions of "the political" instigated around 1968. Whilst acknowledging a more conservative 1960s, this chapter also contends conservatism was ruptured in quite recognizably 1960s, even "1968," ways.[5]

Burgeoning research on the New Right has focused on transnational economic ideas, think tanks, and policy.[6] This can focus on elite areas at the expense of grassroots activism, political styles and cultures – on just official conservatism rather than broader conservatism of manner, lifestyle or values. As Matthew Grimley suggests, historians might assess Thatcherism not just by what it achieved but by what it represented, by its rhetoric as well as legislation. That the New Right repertoire was more than the geopolitics of the Cold War and political economy of

---

[2] Lawrence Glickman, *Buying Power: A History of Consumer Activism in America* (Chicago, 2009), 275–279; Martin Durham and Margaret Power, "Transnational Conservatism: The New Right, Neoconservatism and Cold War Anti-Communism," in Martin Durham and Margaret Power, eds., *New Perspectives on the Transnational Right* (Basingstoke, 2010).

[3] Ben Jackson, "The Think Tank Archipelago: Thatcherism and Neo-liberalism," in Ben Jackson and Robert Saunders, eds., *Making Thatcher's Britain* (Cambridge, 2012), 43–61.

[4] Kit Kowol, "The Lost World of British Conservatism: The Radical Tory Tradition 1939–51," DPhil, Oxford University, 2014.

[5] Lawrence Black, *Redefining British Politics: Culture, Consumerism, Participation, 1954–70* (Basingstoke, 2010); David Farber and Jeff Roche, eds., *The Conservative Sixties* (New York, 2003).

[6] Jackson and Saunders, *Making Thatcher's Britain*; Philip Mirowksi and Dieter Plehwe, eds., *The Road from Mont Pèlerin: The Making of a Neoliberal Thought Collective* (Cambridge, MA, 2009); Rachel Turner, *Neo-liberal Ideology: History, Concepts, Policies* (Edinburgh, 2008); Daniel Stedman Jones, *The Masters of the Universe: Hayek, Friedman and the Birth of Neoliberal Politics* (Princeton, 2012).

neoliberalism was clearer in the United States, where the religious right and culture wars raged. But it was an integral part of Thatcherism's currency too, which was not just about economics, not simply neoliberal, more a hybrid.[7] Thatcherism was not a purely New Right entity, and nor was the New Right always so new.[8] The New Right's cultural preferences, whilst strongly held, coexisted with a more conventional, traditional conservatism – that often outweighed it in party circles and in popular estimation and that it also frequently exhibited. This chapter interrogates cultures of conservatism in the Young Conservatives (YCs), the Conservative Party's youth wing; Swinton College, the party's stately home-cum-cadre education center; and censorious Christian moralist Mary Whitehouse's campaigns against permissiveness. It contextualizes these by comparison with the American New Right and the invocations of a "silent majority" popularized by President Nixon.

What's Wrong with Politics?

Kenneth Minogue complained in a 1968 festschrift for Michael Oakeshott that too much conservatism since 1789 had been "little more than a timid appeal to caution."[9] That was wishful thinking, and it is not hard to recognize "1968" (in its usual radical sense) on the right: student and grassroots activists protesting for participation, fighting cultural politics, taking on established power, international, and ideologically assertive in style. For Tony Judt, "the 1960s were the great age of Theory," and Conservatives, no less than anyone else (if more surprisingly, given their reputed aversion to soul-searching), were posing eschatological questions.[10] Swinton College's 1968 forum on "Intellectuals and Conservatism" initiated "a debate that was to become all too familiar in the 1980s, but which was already being addressed by Conservatives." For its protagonists, this was a battle for the party's soul, between traditions that regarded each other as more liberal or social democratic than conservative.[11] YCs pressed for inner-party democracy

---

[7] Matthew Grimley, "Thatcherism, Morality and Religion," in Jackson and Saunders, *Making Thatcher's Britain*, 78–79; Beatrix Campbell, *The Iron Ladies: Why Do Women Vote Tory?* (London, 1987), 99; Anna Marie Smith, *A New Right Discourse on Race and Sexuality, Britain 1968–90* (Cambridge, 1995).

[8] Its ready use of fear in campaigning against opponents was age-old.

[9] Kenneth Minogue, "Revolution, Tradition and Political Continuity," in Preston King and B. C. Parekh, eds., *Politics and Experience* (Cambridge, 1968), 307.

[10] Tony Judt, *Postwar* (London, 2007), 398.

[11] Richard Cockett, *Thinking the Unthinkable: Think-Tanks and the Economic Counter-Revolution, 1931–83* (London, 1995), 192–196.

and a voice in policymaking – contributing to the undermining of deference during the 1960s. Whitehouse made the personal political (to borrow a key slogan of the women's movement) by focusing on TV's domestic intrusion. Her campaigns mobilized a mostly female, middle-aged grassroots against the cultural and media establishment. Her central claim was that TV viewers, as taxpayers and consumers, had a democratic right to influence public broadcasting, and she expected this would end sexual, violent, and un-Christian BBC programming. Powell's and Whitehouse's claims to be speaking for people marginalized by the radical 1960s found some credence in opinion polls. A 1969 *New Society* Opinion Research Centre Survey found most were uneasy about "liberal" law reforms and large majorities felt that there was "too much publicity given to sex" and were "too many colored immigrants in Britain."[12]

Conservatives had appealed to a silent majority in the 1920s, alerting them to raucous Labour supporters as evidence of the party's unfitness to govern.[13] But when the New Right sought to mobilize a silent majority from the 1960s, it was raucous. During industrial disputes, most visibly the Grunwick strike at a North London film processing lab from 1976, unofficial conservative groups like the National Association for Freedom cut their teeth in resisting union recognition. After capital punishment was abolished in 1969, Conservative retentionists turned to mass petitions, whereas abolitionists had based their case on "informed opinion." Chris Moores found that RAGE's (Ratepayers against the Greenham Encampments) campaigns against the women's peace camp in the 1980s focused on its local economic impact and the lifestyle and sexuality of the protesters. But its tactics and rhetoric were too confrontational to garner support from Conservatives and undermined its claim to be voicing residential, community concerns.[14]

Whilst the right invoked a silent majority, the idea of a "silent revolution" simultaneously emerged in the work of Ronald Inglehart and offered succor to reformers. Inglehart argued that economic well-being was driving an underlying generational shift from traditional institutions and material politics toward issues of the environment, gender equality, and quality of life. This offered an explanation of Conservatism's

[12] Paul Barker, "Facing Two Ways: Between the 60s and 70s," *New Society* 14:374 (November 27, 1969), 847–850.
[13] Jon Lawrence, *Electing Our Masters* (Oxford, 2009), 124.
[14] Thomas Wright, "Arguing for the Death Penalty: Making the Retentionist Case in Britain, 1945–79," MA dissertation, University of York, 2010; Chris Moores, "Rage against the Obscene: Opposition to the Greenham Encampments and Thatcherism in 1980s Britain," *History Workshop Journal* 78 (2014).

post-material interests and fractious character in this period, as the
authority of the party fell (something Thatcherites exploited).[15] Either
way, the politics of the silent were noisily contested.

Conservatives questioned the political status quo well before the mid-
1970s economic crisis. In 1968, Thatcher uncompromisingly criticized
consensus as "an attempt to satisfy people holding no particular views."
She preferred "to have a philosophy and policy which because they are
good appeal to a sufficient majority." Thatcher's speech picked up the
dissenting zeitgeist to ask *What's Wrong with Politics?* She did not name
Whitehouse but noted how "television" was "radically influencing the
judgments we have to make about events and . . . politicians." Accounting
for why people "doubt the future of the democratic system" and "distrust
the politicians," she felt "criticism of politics is no new thing." Among
the causes she identified for why the present discontent "runs . . . deep
here and abroad" were how "the rapid spread of higher education has
been to equip people to criticize and question almost everything" and to
"stop . . . there instead of going on . . . to arrive at new beliefs or reaffirm
old ones." And there was "too much government" – here Thatcher cited
Powell's tenure as health minister (1960–1963) in what was a popular
way for politicians on the right to distance themselves from Powell after
his 1968 "Rivers of Blood" speech. By contrast with this criticism of
a New Right icon, she praised the leadership of Benjamin Disraeli, the
nineteenth-century Conservative leader, whose "one nation" tradition
Thatcherism usually shunned. As for Daniel Cohn-Bendit, the Franco-
German student radical, she was amazed he had "been awarded a degree"
on the grounds that "his past work . . . had posed a series of most intelligent questions." Thatcher "would have been happier had he also found
a series of intelligent answers."[16]

Young Conservatives

The YCs' claim to be the free world's largest political youth organization
was confirmed by opponents and comics who mocked the organization
as a middle-class marriage bureau. Certainly, the YCs reproduced Conservative values, in a large extended family (by 1965, although smaller
than at its late 1940s peak, its membership was still four times that of any

[15] Ronald Inglehart, "The Silent Revolution in Europe: Intergenerational Change in Post-
industrial Societies," *American Political Science Review* 65:4 (1971): 991–1017, and
The Silent Revolution: Changing Values and Political Styles among Western Publics
(Princeton, 1977).
[16] Margaret Thatcher, *What's Wrong with Politics?* (London, 1968).

competitor). They were neither notably young (thirty was the upper age limit) nor especially political, preferring a lifestyle of dances, tennis, car rallies, and beauty contests to direct activism on the party's behalf. A quiet presence – measured, conformist – YCs were a mainstay of middle-class, suburban civic life and a resource for routine politics, the foot soldiers of many local associations. They were a career breeding ground from which ninety Members of Parliament (MPs) had emerged by 1970 – all of them male.[17]

Lord Woolton, party chairman at the YCs' creation in 1946, explained they were insistent on their own activities and semi-detached from the party. This meant YCs could drift from political activity once they turned thirty, married or pursued careers.[18] By the later 1960s several factors contrived to politicize the YCs. Their social activities were curtailed by growing commercial competition and newer tastes. After the return to opposition in 1964 did not offset falling membership, the McLeod Report (1965) argued for a smaller, more active membership. The expansion of universities bolstered the Federation of Conservative Students (FCS, as the Federation of University Conservative and Unionist Associations was renamed in 1967) at the YCs' expense. Conservative local election gains between 1965 and 1969 meant 600 YCs became councilors.[19] Finally, there was the spirit of 1968, to which YCs not only reacted but contributed. The Greater London YCs' (GLYCs) 1969 pamphlet *Set the Party Free* featured Powell and McLeod. It denounced the party as "patrician, hidebound and undemocratic" and its Central Office (borrowing the depiction of King George III in Walter Bagehot's *The English Constitution*) as a "consecrated obstruction." They demanded rule changes to open the organization up and allow YC influence over policy and candidate selection. These YCs were vociferous, not loyal and deferential – in manner they hardly seemed conservative. The mood of *Democratory* (the London reformers' magazine) spread.[20] "We YCs, sitting in our dream world of dances, cheese and wine parties... have the cheek to sneer at long-haired university students who protest," complained a Birmingham YC in 1968. "Let's protest, let's be heard, let's not conform."[21]

---

[17] Black, *Redefining British Politics*, ch. 4.
[18] Earl of Woolton, *The Memoirs of the Rt. Hon. the Earl of Woolton* (London, 1959), 358.
[19] *Tomorrow* (June 1971), 1; *Looking Right* (Summer 1969), 31. *Tomorrow*, Conservative Party Archive (CPA), Bodleian Library, Oxford CPA/Pub/139-1-6, *Impact* CPA/PUB144/4; *Looking Right*, British Library.
[20] GLYCs, *Set the Party Free* (London, 1969).
[21] *Looking Right* (Autumn 1968), 36.

Similar tensions and aims were to be found in the 1960s amongst the Young Americans for Freedom, as John Andrew's study demonstrates.[22] YCs mostly expressed antipathy toward drugs and skepticism about lowering the voting age to eighteen. They discussed homelessness (albeit in the environs of stately homes like Swinton) and reported they were motivated by the intolerance of Marxist campus opponents.[23] The point was that YCs were part of, not apart from, 1968. Combining support for popular culture with criticism of state intervention, as they had done over "pirate" radio in the 1960s, they campaigned against the restrictions on late night and outdoor concerts in the 1972 Night Assemblies Bill. This won coverage in the *New Musical Express* and, in working against their own government, signaled the demise of YCs' deference.[24]

Factionalism grew even though schism had been "foreign to the tradition" of the YCs.[25] Monday Club neoconservatives (critics of Prime Minister Harold Macmillan's Europe, empire, and immigration policies) complained about pro-European, socially liberal groups like Pressure for Economic and Social Toryism (PEST, forerunner of the Tory Reform Group) and the "long-haired yahoos" of the Greater London YCs (GLYCs). Acronyms proliferated, like Peter Walker's Campaign for the Urban Renewal of the Environment (CURE), which piqued the harderline right.[26] The YCs were Common Market cheerleaders, close to the Conservative and Christian Democratic Youth Community and the West German Junge Union.[27] The GLYCs were notably paternalist, winning a 1972 UN Youth Association prize for a plan to limit family size that advocated local authority provision of vasectomies.[28] The GLYCs gradually inched away from Powell, and the YCs reconciled with the party hierarchy, with figures like Roger Boaden (national organizing secretary, 1967–1973) and David Hunt (YC national chair and British Youth Council chair in 1972) awarded MBEs. In truth, YCs were divided on social

---

[22] John A. Andrew III, *The Other Side of the Sixties: The Young Americans for Freedom and the Rise of Conservative Politics* (New Brunswick, NJ, 1997).

[23] Alan Craig, "Conservatives and Campus Protests," *Impact* (Winter/Spring 1968–1969), 16–17.

[24] *Tomorrow* (April 1972), 1, 8; (July 1973), 4–5; YC Management Committee minutes (June 10, 1972), CPA CCO (Conservative Central Office) 506/19/7.

[25] *Conservative Agents Journal* (March 1973), 12–13.

[26] *Tomorrow* (April 1972), 4–6; (June 1972), 2, 8.

[27] *Tomorrow* (May 1973), 8; Conservative and Christian Democratic Youth community reports, CPA CCO4/10/324–329.

[28] *Tomorrow* (November 1972), 8; GLYC population report, CPA CCO4/10/322.

issues. A 1970 survey found 73 percent favored abortion for all, but half opposed the abolition of censorship.[29]

This demonstrates that their politicization did not mean the YCs had become rowdy Thatcherites-in-waiting or neoliberal ideologues. Nor had their social bonhomie or casual sexism been extinguished. A 1971 YC silver jubilee party in London's Café Royal spilt into Trafalgar Square, with dancing in bow ties and ball gowns. In 1972, they chartered a Boeing 707 to observe Nixon's reelection. In 1974, they campaigned against the Bolshoi Ballet in London.[30] Discussing the first election with votes for eighteen-year-olds, the Bridgewater by-election in March 1970, *Tomorrow* noted that the first elector aged eighteen was YC Trudy Sellick. She was pictured and applauded as "the early bird," which took the author "back to my favourite subject, women."[31]

But commentators noted a change. In 1968, one party agent reflected that the YCs were "losing the image ... of a movement which ran the best dances and had the prettiest girls ... but didn't know the first thing about politics." Another agent noted how YCs "give less attention than they used to the proper organization of social events."[32] In 1973, Nicholas Scott MP, a former YC national chairman, mused on an infamous semi-clad, wine-drinking image published in *Crossbow* in 1967 and concluded "today's YCs are more radical, more trenchant, more 'hard' in their political attitudes."[33]

As a largely social group, the YCs were relatively style-conscious. Articles in *Impact* in the mid-1960s covered "all the gear" modeled by Miss YC. Male YCs assumed the garb of their elders: blazers or sober suits enlivened by YC ties. But by the later 1960s this was fusing with fashionable trends, "cavalry twills and paisley cravats" were "all the rage."[34] Occasional goatees and instances of "studied dishevelment" appeared, and Clive Landa, the GLYC chair, shocked the 1972 party conference by addressing them, in a sign of self-confidence, in a T-shirt. Still, in 1970 *Crossbow* mused on how "the insecurity of the Tory student" was heightened "by an insistence on dress standards that would not have looked out of place at court, sometime towards the end of the

[29] *Tomorrow* (November 1972), 1; (January 1973), 3; (May 1974), 2; (August 1970), 2.
[30] *Tomorrow* (February 1971), 3; (June 1972), 1; (September 1974), 4–5; Management Committee minutes (June 10, 1972) CPA CCO 506/19/7.
[31] *Tomorrow* (May 1970), 3.
[32] *Conservative Agents Journal* (September 1968), 3; (July 1969), 18.
[33] Nicholas Scott, "Have the YCs Really Changed?," *Crossbow* (January 1973), 24–27.
[34] "All the Gear," *Impact* (Autumn 1964), 10–11; Elizabeth Wilson, "All the Rage," *New Socialist* (November–December 1983), 26.

last century."[35] This portends Malcolm Bradbury's classic 1970s campus novel *The History Man*, where blazer-wearing student George Carmody receives the full force of radical sociologist Howard Kirk's ideological certainty.[36]

The Miss YC contest was a centerpiece of social life, the winner dancing with the party leader and very much a public face of the party. In 1967, the National Advisory Committee had agreed to end it, on grounds of cost, but this was rapidly overturned.[37] By 1971, the West Midlands, Greater London, and Eastern regions had voted against continuing the contest. Mike Rouse, the new editor of *Tomorrow*, sounded more like the feminists who disrupted the Miss World pageant in London in 1970 when he derided Miss YC as "an unseemly cattle show," which "reduces certain girls to objects to be leered at" and felt "the time has come to put the sash in the drawer, pawn the crown." Its abolition was "common sense" – it had become "irrelevant" to proper politics.[38] If there was a whiff of feminism here, it was of the type that saw fit to issue a party report in 1969 entitled *Fair Shares for the Fair Sex*. But its passing was a wrench for many. The final Miss YC, Pat Gaywood, who was secretary of the West Lancashire Monday Club (Miss GLYC, by contrast, was a fervent Common Marketeer), felt it provided good publicity and averred, "although I'm married I'm far too interested in politics to disappear." Others felt Rouse would be better off "in Women's Lib."[39] Competitions continued in some regions, advertisements for YC-branded ties saw them draped over naked women, and in 1977 pro-Thatcher T-shirts proclaiming "Put a woman on top" won coverage in *The Sun*.[40]

The FCS stole the YCs' thunder. Organized in universities rather than constituencies, the FCS had a different social base and culture than the YCs. By 1973, the YCs and FCS shared regional organizers, and when Thatcher became leader, the post of party youth director was abolished.

[handwritten margin notes:]
The '70s saw this style return to the mainstream etc.
Beauty contests became a topic of feminist activism from 1968
Subject of the film Misbehaviour, starring Keira Knightley, Greta Gerwig, ... Jessie Buckley
1975

35 *Crossbow* (January 1973), 26; Tom Spencer, "Any Chance of a Demo?," *Crossbow* (October–December 1970), 36–38.

36 Malcolm Bradbury, *The History Man* (London, 1975).

37 YC National Advisory Committee (NAC) minutes (June 10, July 1, 1967), CPA CCO 506/19/6.

38 *Tomorrow* (June 1971), 6; (March 1973), 1; Management Committee (September 18, 1971) CPA CCO 506/19/7; Eley, *Forging Democracy*, 370.

39 Tim Bale, *The Conservatives since 1945* (Oxford, 2012), 151; *Tomorrow* (June 1971), 4; (August 1971), 6.

40 *Tomorrow* (February 1972), 2; (May 1973), 4; YC NAC minutes (March 12, 1977) CPA CCO 506/19/7.

YC numbers fell, but between 1974 and 1978 FCS branches tripled and membership hit 160,000.[41] Even so, this was less than the college Democrats and Republicans in the United States. Powell was an FCS hero, telling their 1968 conference, "it is your duty as students to question and be skeptical – even cynical – about the beliefs, ideas and attitudes... accepted by the older generation."[42] By the 1980s, the FCS were "libertarian louts" (a right counterpart to Labour's so-called loony left), demanding the death sentence for Nelson Mandela and equating anything left wing with the KGB. They were a thorn in the Thatcher government's side, siding with the Ulster Unionists (Powell was by then an Ulster Unionist MP) in opposing the 1985 Anglo-Irish agreement, which gave the Irish government an advisory role in Northern Ireland's government. After charging former Prime Minister Macmillan of collusion with Stalin, the FCS was closed down in 1986.[43]

Journalist Jo-Anne Nadler, whose parents met in the YCs, contrasts her sleepy Wimbledon YC branch, where politics were lightly worn, to the world of the FCS. Here a craving for certainty meant opinions were deemed "sound" according to their fidelity to sacrosanct ideological texts. Like the 1950s YCs, they were parodied but for their doctrinal manner and tastes. Where the YCs had been restrained, assured, part-and-parcel of civic life, the 1980s "Tory Boys" reveled in their shock value. So whilst Wimbledon YCs campaigned against "video nasties" with the local MP, on principle FCS libertarians opposed the regulation of drugs, prostitution, or pornography. Nadler recognized this as more than a generational conflict because there was a mix of stiffly suited Monday Club diehards, fogeyish YCs, and neoliberals whose "slovenliness" aped the left and "punctured the old school tie pretensions of their traditional colleagues." In 1998, symptomatic of an aged, electorally weakened party, the YCs were closed down.[44]

Swinton

Since 1948, the party's college for training MPs, activists, and agents had been housed in Lord Swinton's bespoke castle in rural northern

[41] *Tomorrow* (January 1973), 3; YC NAC minutes (December 13, 1975) CPA CCO 509/16/7; Bale, *Conservatives since 1945*, 194.

[42] Craig, "Conservatives and Campus Protests," 16.

[43] Stephen Howe, "Libertarian Louts," *New Statesman* (February 24, 1989), 23.

[44] Jo-Anne Nadler, *Too Nice to be a Tory* (London, 2004), 68–71.

England. It indulged many Conservatives' penchant for stately homes, country sports, and a social order associated with these. It was part of conservatism's public image. Macmillan was regularly pictured pheasant shooting at Swinton. Heath used it for policy weekends, escaping the hothouse of Westminster.[45]

By the later 1960s, like the YCs, Swinton's sedate lifestyle was fraying. Its remoteness encouraged a non-metropolitan atmosphere, outside the day-to-day control of the party, much like another feeder of the New Right, St. Andrews University. The emergence of a New Right cadre in the bucolic idyll of Swinton, a paradigm (almost cliché) of traditional conservatism, hints at the limited degree of change in the New Right, and that it was not alien to existing party culture. In line with Ewen Green's history of Conservatism, it wasn't that Swinton had no ideology before the New Right. But it had been one that had emphasized flexibility and a conservative sensibility to adapt to change – less doctrinal in form and content. Newer tutors, like Stephen Eyres, came to Swinton from St. Andrews. He later became secretary of the anti-Heath Selsdon Group. As a tutor from 1965, John O'Sullivan relaunched the *Swinton Journal* with an invitation to Powell to critique the Conservative governments from 1951 to 1964. By 1970, O'Sullivan declared the paternalist "one nation" Tory tradition to be "floundering as helplessly as whales stranded by a receding tide." O'Sullivan went on to advise Thatcher and took various editorial roles at *National Review*, the leading magazine of the New Right in the United States. Powell was already a Swinton regular, enjoying its mix of ideas, debate, and escape from urban life.[46]

In summer 1968, Swinton debated "Intellectuals and Conservatism." During that debate, Richard Cockett writes, economic liberals exhibited the ideological fervor of "their doppelgängers on the New Left," and in their "rhetoric of self-determinism, classlessness and meritocracy... worked with the grain of the 1960s." Arthur Seldon, cofounder of the free market think tank the Institute of Economic Affairs, told how he voted Liberal and how his business sales background could "often offend" Conservative audiences. Conservatives needed principles, not just personnel or policies, to offer a real alternative. As an example he (like Thatcher) criticized Powell's health ministry for failing to free up

[45] Lawrence Black, "Tories and Hunters: Swinton College and Landscape of Modern Conservatism," *History Workshop Journal* 77 (2014).
[46] Ewen H. H. Green, *Ideologies of Conservatism* (Oxford, 2002); *Swinton Journal* (Summer 1965); (Spring 1970), 32.

competition. But other debaters warned "against an over-emphasis on dogma" in favor of "the Conservative tradition of pragmatism."[47]

For all Swinton's New Right output, among Thatcher's first acts as party leader in 1975 was to close it. This was partly due to cost, but it also marked her desire to degentrify the party, to limit the influence of high Tory grandees and the patrician influence exemplified by Swinton. Personally, this was not her milieu – the world of country sports and a culture of assumed power seemed at odds with her rhetoric. She shared Seldon's qualms at elite Conservative unease with commerce and stood firm against those who emotionally lamented Swinton's end.[48] It also showed parties were less needy of a mass membership in an era of mass communication, less keen to reproduce their own identities than to reach beyond these.

To attach to moderate elites

One of Swinton's pet projects, under Principal Reginald Northam, had been to cultivate trade union support by captivating union activists in the surroundings of Swinton and assessing their potential as candidates. But Northam more often seemed impressed with their shortcomings. By the later 1960s, as Tim Bale notes, Trade Union Advisory Committees had withered away, the victims of "social snobbery and antipathy" that Swinton embodied. After Swinton and under Thatcher, trade union membership and electoral support (if not candidacies) increased.[49] – *Partly one meaning ble of council-house privatization*

Swinton's closure hardly banished such instincts from conservatism: rather, Thatcher's self-confidence liberated them in wider conservative life, making it hard to degentrify the party. "Sloane Rangers" – dubbed by style commentators Ann Barr and Peter York in their million-selling 1982 book as a portmanteau of London's wealthy Sloane Square residents and the Lone Ranger (though Sloanes were as likely to ride a 4x4 Range Rover in town and country) – flourished as upper-middle-class, aspiring-aristocratic chic. A Sloane was a "dog in disguise," instinctively, not intellectually conservative (they admired Thatcher, but she "does go on"); working for, socializing within, and marrying into the party. York noted these entitled urban residents flocked to the country, field sports, preindustrial heritage, and the City of London. The City was preferable to industry or commerce, promising "brass without muck," lucre without undue effort or filth. The City's elite "private" school ethos, until

The contemporary equivalent might be Starbucks

---

[47] Richard Cockett, "The New Right and the 1960s: The Dialectics of Liberation," in Geoff Andrews, Richard Cockett, Alan Hooper, and Michael Williams, eds., *New Left, New Right and Beyond* (Basingstoke, 1999), 98; Cockett, *Thinking the Unthinkable*, 344–350.

[48] Black, "Tories and Hunters."   [49] Bale, *Conservatives since 1945*, 194–195.

1986's deregulation of financial markets (the "Big Bang"), distinguished Sloanes from "Yuppies," a more conspicuously Thatcherite type (suburban, newer money). There were even "Young Fogeys," ostentatiously tweedy and retro.[50]

Historians were even to be found arguing that the cultural penchant for aristocratic ruralism over Victorian industry accounted for British economic decline. Martin Wiener's thesis appealed to Thatcherite modernizers (if not its implication that the state might offset this anti-entrepreneurialism or echoes of New Left theories of Britain's incomplete bourgeois revolution). Wiener felt Thatcher's biggest battle might be less the trade unions or public spending than this cultural propensity among parts of its newly confident middle-class support.[51] The City and government were close, and City winnings were often ploughed into rural pursuits, as if Toryism could not be detached from its origins as a "country" party. Nadler – a self-styled Thatcherite, urban, meritocratic, squeamish about blood sports and "people whose houses smell of dogs" – found herself awed by a trip stag hunting in 2001.[52] The Countryside Alliance, mobilized against New Labour's anti-hunting legislation, held considerable sway over the post-1997 Conservatives. David Cameron's privileged background attached a rural-elite aspect to his identity. The public association of Conservatism with such lifestyles was reinforced by a prominent MP during 2009's "expenses scandal" claiming for clearing his moat. Conservatism seemed apt to reproduce what Thatcherism wanted to reject and, indeed, blamed for national decline.

Not that the association was entirely toxic. Interest in heritage was hardly the preserve of Sloanes; it resonated nationally. Gentrification could be urban, young, and post-industrial, and even Thatcherites recognized the commercial appeal of traditional forms of heritage. If early 1980s poshness reacted against trade union 1970s Britain, the late 2000s variant was also at odds with the villains of the economic downturn, post-"Big Bang" bankers. Traditional landed aristocracy, stripped of real power, seemed reassuring, to judge by the trans-political appeal – to liberals and conservatives alike – of the TV series *Downton Abbey* or Harry Potter's boarding school. York updated the Sloane handbook; Barbour jackets, Hunter wellington boots, and the "ecosloane" (or "Hackney

---

[50] Ann Barr and Peter York, *The Official Sloane Ranger Handbook* (London, 1982), 10–11, 22, 150–151; Susanne Lowry, ed., *Young Fogeys Handbook* (Littlehampton, 1985).
[51] Martin Wiener, *English Culture and the Decline of the Industrial Spirit, 1850–1980* (Cambridge, 1981), 166.
[52] Nadler, *Too Nice to be a Tory*, ch. 11.

farmer," named after a newly fashionable London borough and denoting the hip mix of heritage, country, and city) emerged, if still relying more on patronage than skill.[53] The New Right did not shed all traditional right associations. The key point was that this culture was not just defensive or nostalgic but quite modern and popular and tied Thatcherism to a mainstream, broader conservatism. ⌐mixing neoliberalism into a broader coalition

In the political unconscious of conservatism, the landscape, lifestyle, and elite aura of Swinton remained potent and hints at limits to Thatcherism's agency to refashion conservatism. If there was something English to Swinton culture, in form it was less distinctive. In the hinterlands of the American New Right, a "preppy" culture, not dissimilar to Sloanes in its demographic, flourished.[54] ⌐ Here Michael J. Fox Alex Keaton, ct

[margin notes, right side:] The genteel image merged with the hipster in the mold of (Cameron's social-liberal) project (not his unk → was on ct-school emel)

Whitehouse

On the periphery of formal conservatism was Mary Whitehouse's National Viewers and Listeners' Association (NVALA). From 1963, it protested against sex, violence, and blasphemy on BBC TV and the liberal, secular bent of 1960s society. If the Campaign for Nuclear Disarmament (CND) was the left's conscience, Whitehouse was the right's. She voiced a visceral unease at the pace and trajectory of change: coalescing those perturbed at their church's impotent response or at conservatism's complicity and Heath's 1965-75 stand disregard of this sphere. ⌐ Heath a fairly wholeheartedly bachelor

Here was a more authoritarian strain of the New Right, and a populist one, according to Whitehouse's assertions of the millions supporting her. An "Iron Lady" before Thatcher, she was, like the U.S. Republicans' 1964 presidential candidate Barry Goldwater, "extreme in the cause of moderation," charismatic, articulate, and, in her own terms and time, a failure. Parallels are suggestive with Phyllis Schlafly, "the sweetheart of the silent majority," who like Whitehouse emerged as a public figure in the early 1960s and campaigned against equal rights, homosexuality, abortion, and pornography (among other issues) with a skeptical eye on her own party's elite. Schlafly and Whitehouse highlight the significant role of women in the early New Right and not only in providing a moral revival.[55] It was tempting to mock Whitehouse as backward-looking, but

[margin notes, right side:] ⌐ Though I think she turned to these issues in the 70s

53 Andy Beckett, "Tory Chic: Return of Poshness," *The Guardian*, December 16, 2009.
54 Lisa Birnbach, ed., *The Official Preppy Handbook* (New York, 1980).
55 Campbell, *Iron Ladies*; Carol Felsenthal, *The Sweetheart of the Silent Majority* (New York, 1981); Lisa McGirr, *Suburban Warriors: The Origins of the New American Right*

DIY protest was the essence of the "sixties," and she was media savvy. NVALA's prolific letter writing made campaigning accessible, and its public petitions prefigured Internet campaigning.[56]

By 1970, NVALA, taking its cue from Nixon, cast itself as "the voice of the silent millions." It was not "a noisy pressure group representing a tiny minority, but... an awakening democracy conscious of its power and responsibility."[57] This claim was based on the numbers signing petitions, not its membership (ca. 7,000 in 1968, larger in the 1970s). The NVALA were loud and confrontational. "Silence means assent," "Don't moan, phone!" were among its slogans. For Whitehouse, the enemy was the metropolitan, secular, liberal establishment in the media, culture, and politics. The NVALA was firmly provincial (she had been a neighbor-but-one of Powell's in Wolverhampton) and took on the assured tones of the knows-best BBC and well-meaning liberals. Whitehouse was undeferential in her haranguing of high-profile figures and institutions, despite wishing a restoration of due deference to established authority. Her intolerant, vitriolic tone put her beyond the pale of official conservatism but squarely among the middle-class "respectable rebels" of the grassroots small retailer and taxpayer revolts of the 1970s.[58]

Whitehouse less reflected moral unease than inflamed it, spotting permissiveness in pop music, satire, film, theater, drugs, poetry, science fiction. The NVALA's campaign was animated by culture and values, not material concerns. It had no need of academic research to detail what it instinctively knew were the damaging effects of such culture. In this period, the New Left has traditionally been seen as the creative force behind cultural politics, but they were not its preserve. In 1960, Stuart Hall (then a schoolteacher, like Whitehouse) wrote of how "sexual sensation" was "seducing our consciousness... corrupting moral standards, encouraging a weak, flaccid, self-indulgence... Sex has become the universal salesman... on the hoarding, the television screen... Capitalism which emerged with the Methodist Sunday School and the gospel of work, now offers a week in Monte Carlo."[59] The NVALA would also have concurred with the New Left's "TV supplement," which

(Princeton, 2001); Donald T. Critchlow, *Phyllis Schlafly and Grassroots Conservatism: A Woman's Crusade* (Princeton, 2005).

56 Black, *Redefining British Politics*, ch. 5.   57 *Viewer and Listener* (Summer 1970), 1.
58 Roger King and Neill Nugent, eds., *Respectable Rebels: Middle Class Campaigns in Britain in the 1970s* (London, 1979).
59 Stuart Hall, "The Supply of Demand," in E. P. Thompson, ed., *Out of Apathy* (London, 1960), 82.

saw in "every programme . . . some view of life, some implicit or explicit social or moral attitude" and "worried about the sheer volume of television . . . dealing with violence or with the implied virtues of materialism."[60]

In another overlap with 1960s radicals, Whitehouse fused the personal and political, much as she desired to preserve the border and felt it was a pity TV had forced itself into the private home. Whitehouse was no feminist, but her politics inhabited a related sphere. In 1970, the advertising trade journal *Campaign* (itself born in 1968) asked commentators to express "What I think about advertising." Alongside denizens of the left like Raymond Williams, Joan Robinson, and Jill Tweedie, Whitehouse argued it "degraded women."[61] A longstanding opponent of depictions of sex and violence, she forged an unholy alliance with feminists – anathema in all other respects to both parties – to campaign against pornography in the late 1970s. "Right on, Mary," they chanted as she debated with the head of *Playboy* UK.[62]

As the historian of sexuality Jeffrey Weeks has acknowledged, NVALA campaigns had a definite "appeal to the inarticulate . . . far from being a crank . . . there was something deeply representative about Mrs. Whitehouse."[63] The volume of letters she received attested to this. Playwright Dennis Potter, one of her arch-enemies, admitted she was "standing up for all the people with ducks on their walls who have been laughed at and treated like rubbish by the sophisticated metropolitan minority."[64] Yet her "belief that public opinion was fundamentally behind the moralists" could falter. In 1971, NVALA regretted how "history has been shaped by a tiny minority" and "the 'misty millions' go where they are led."[65] To this end, besides popular mobilization, Whitehouse increasingly turned to litigation, the police, and the state. A petition against child pornography led to the 1978 Protection of Children Act. The 1981

---

[60] "TV Supplement," *New Left Review* 7 (1961), 43.

[61] Winston Fletcher, *Power of Persuasion: The Inside Story of British Advertising, 1951–2000* (Oxford, 2008), 94, 99.

[62] Mary Kenny, "Was Mrs. Whitehouse Right" and "In Defence of Mary Whitehouse," *The Spectator*, February 12, 1977 and June 7, 2010; David Holbrook, "Mary Whitehouse," *Political Quarterly* 51:2 (1980): 154–156; Mary Whitehouse, *Quite Contrary* (London, 1994), chs. 9, 17; Eley, *Forging Democracy*, 374.

[63] Jeffrey Weeks, *Sex, Politics and Society: The Regulation of Sexuality since 1800* (Harlow, 1981), 277–281.

[64] Ben Thompson, ed., *Ban this Filth! Letters from the Mary Whitehouse Archive* (London, 2012), 173.

[65] Weeks, *Sex*, 281.

Indecent Displays Act and 1988 Broadcasting Standards Commission
were weaker than she hoped.

Keith Joseph lauded Whitehouse in an infamous 1974 speech and
Thatcher made her a CBE in 1980, but despite such recognition, differences between Whitehouse and Thatcherism remained. Thatcher saw
the state as a cause of Britain's crisis and was chary of turning to it to
remedy the nation's moral welfare. These were matters of the heart or
individual self-discipline. Thatcher's governments wanted to roll back the
1960s but did not repeal its "permissive" legislation, despite her support
for the death penalty. And it is hard to hear Whitehouse in the decision
to knight the editor of *The Sun* or to license cable TV. The governments
did promote Christianity and restrict information about homosexuality
in schools, and one of Thatcher's first acts was to increase police pay. Her
very first was to quote St. Francis of Assisi as she entered No. 10, and she
was apt to invoke religion as a template for commonsense decency.[66] That
she wanted to do more suggests the limits to Thatcherism, and its contradictions – wanting to restore law and order, not question everything,
but so abrasively iconoclastic itself.

As the BBC campaign faltered, Whitehouse widened her aims, part of
a global turn to religious zealotry in the 1970s.[67] She backed the evangelical Festival of Light, founded by a missionary who returned from India
to find the United Kingdom in moral decay. In 1973, the Festival and
NVALA organized a Petition for Public Decency, amassing 1.35 million
signatures. The Festival's tactics were demos-cum-mass rallies and pop
festivals. The majority attending were young – 90 percent of the 25,000
at the Northern Festival of Light in Manchester were under twenty-five.
Its pamphlets detailed confiscations and prosecutions of retailers who
sold pornography. But the question whether this was revealing or reviv-
ing Britons' Christianity vexed organizers. For many involved with the
Festival, combatting permissiveness did not necessarily mean turning to
Jesus; they might be informed by Christianity but were not religious in
the churchgoing sense. The Festival arose in part because of the official
church's organizational decline. That Amy Whipple suggests the Festival

---

[66] Grimley, "Thatcherism, Morality and Religion"; Raphael Samuel, "The Tory Party at
Prayer," *New Statesman*, January 28, 1983, 8–9.
[67] Michael Tracey and David Morrison, *Whitehouse* (London, 1979), ch. 10; Caryl, *Strange
Rebels*; Andrew Preston, "Christian America's Response to the Years of Upheaval"
and Ayesha Jalal, "Islam's Contemporary Globalization, 1971–79," in Niall Ferguson,
Charles Maier, Erez Manela, and Daniel Sargent, eds., *The Shock of the Global* (Cambridge, MA, 2010), 306–318, 319–336.

was "too Christian" to generate popular or political momentum to mobilize support in the same way the Moral Majority formed in the United States in 1979 did, tells us much about Whitehouse's fortunes too. The votes and finance of the American religious right were vital resources – that might have made Whitehouse more successful in channeling the call for decency toward political ends.[68]

Thatcher's appeals to Christian heritage and Victorian values were conscious that Britons were not rabidly practicing – unlike Whitehouse (who thought Britons were or should be), and unlike those political scientists who, like her allegedly clear-cut ideology, saw in Thatcherism's doctrinal encryptions a "crusade."[69] The historical association between the Tory Party and the Church of England was weaker. What Raphael Samuel calls the "degentrification of the party," promoted in closing Swinton and evident in the YCs' lack of deference, also meant the cloth no longer commanded such reverence among Tories. Thatcher viewed the Church of England skeptically, seeing it as an institution staffed, like the BBC, by liberal do-gooders inclined to criticize her government's policies. Like Whitehouse, she was often disappointed by Anglican bishops. They rowed with her over Sunday shop opening, nuclear weapons and urban poverty, the Falklands memorial service (where Thatcher was "spitting blood"), and after her "Sermon on the Mound" (as the press dubbed her 1988 address to the Church of Scotland General Assembly). Organizational decline meant Thatcher could appeal across religions. As Matthew Grimley argues, her appeal "was to a 'silent majority' who no longer attended church, but who... had some folk memory of religious stories, and symbols, and who remained susceptible to Christian morality." And this constituency was large. Thatcherism thus "benefitted from, and contributed to, the decline of religious authority" – rather as she exploited popular discontent with the political status quo, and critiqued the alleged moral rot initiated in the 1960s, whilst profiting from its appeals to the self and individualism.[70]

---

[68] Amy Whipple, "Speaking for Whom? The 1971 Festival of Light and the Search for the 'Silent Majority,'" *Contemporary British History* 24:3 (2010): 319–339; Thompson, *Ban this Filth!*, 280–281; Callum Brown, *The Death of Christian Britain* (London, 2009).

[69] Ivor Crewe and Donald Searing, "Mrs. Thatcher's Crusade: Conservatism in Britain, 1972–86," in Barry Cooper, Allan Kornberg, and William Mishler, eds., *The Resurgence of Conservatism in Anglo-American Democracies* (Durham, NC, 1988); Eliza Filby, *God and Mrs. Thatcher* (London, 2015).

[70] Samuel, "Tory Party at Prayer"; Grimley, "Thatcherism, Morality and Religion," 92–94.

New Times?

British Conservatism's renewal by the end of the 1970s, as Bruce Schulman argues for the United States, owed much to the "vitality of 1960s
reform efforts: drawing on their example, conservatives constructed their
own grassroots organizations, developed a powerfully resonant anti-
institutional, anti-bureaucratic message, and... even embraced activist
government."[71] But compared with its U.S. counterpart, the New Right
in Britain made less social and cultural headway. Religion was nowhere
near as significant in Britain as in the United States: the Conservatives
never had to fear, as Barry Goldwater feared for the Republicans, that
the religious right might overrun the party. British New Right culture
was less distinct from the "old right," and where it was more strident,
struggled to gain traction in wider society. Despite the New Right's interest in non-economic issues, liberal, secular trends in Britain were barely
reversed. There was nothing like the cultural backlash Jefferson Cowie
identifies in country music or 1979's "disco demolition" – opposing the
liberal establishment by celebrating purportedly traditional working-class
values, and with which some Republicans tried to inveigle themselves.
Punk and Thatcher both spat at the status quo, but not in harmonious
ways – never mind the political consensus! Nor, despite Thatcher being
a grocer's daughter and her liking for Marks & Spencer, was there anything like Wal-Mart, blending free market business practice with appeals
to traditional Christian values.[72] Some commentators detect authoritarian and consumerist strains in popular culture prefiguring Thatcherism,
but the evidence is equivocal. Sloanes and the heritage cult for country
living *could* have conservative valence but in some ways were at odds
with Thatcherism – revealing its limits, not its hegemony. The tabloid
media sided with and were cultivated by Thatcherism, but affected less
of a change in popular attitudes than some tabloids claimed and many
politicians assumed.[73]

---

[71] Bruce Schulman, "The Empire Strikes Back: Conservative Responses to Progressive
Social Movements in the 1970s," *Journal of Contemporary History* 43:4 (2008): 699;
Andrew, *The Other Side of the Sixties*.

[72] Jefferson Cowie, *Stayin' Alive: The 1970s and the Last Days of the Working Class* (New
York, 2010), 167–173, 321–324; Bethany Moreton, *To Serve God and Wal-Mart: The
Making of Christian Free Enterprise* (Cambridge, MA, 2010); Joe Moran, *Queuing for
Beginners* (London, 2007), 156.

[73] Lawrence Black, "An Enlightening Decade? Histories of 1970s' Britain," *International
Labor and Working-Class History* 82 (2012): 178–184; James Thomas, *Popular Newspapers and the Labour Party in British Politics* (London, 2005), ch. 4; James Curran
and Ivor Gaber, *Culture Wars: The Media and the British Left* (Edinburgh, 2005).

Does this mean the "silent revolution" held out against the "silent majority"? Not entirely. The modernizing, liberalizing trajectory Inglehart assumed of post-material politics was belied by Whitehouse's campaigns, the American religious right (and some strains of environmentalism). But even in the United States, Schulman contends, the progressive "cultural agenda of... social movements – demands for recognition and representation... proved to be more successful than their radical socioeconomic objectives." The New Right, in short, won economic arguments but fewer cultural ones.[74] Bill Clinton and Tony Blair were the results of this. Cockett suggests this reinforced the British New Right's prioritization of economic freedom. Cockett mistakes a lack of political traction for lack of interest – it wasn't that the New Right lacked its own culture or interest in matters cultural, but when they did approach less economic spheres they tended toward older-school morality, unwilling to countenance the choice they so valued in economic life. This contradiction between economic liberalism and cultural conservatism meant the New Right neglected the legacy of the 1960s and limited its own impact. Because culture, as the 1960s, Inglehart, and this chapter insinuate, matters.[75]

The transatlantic comparison has its limits – civil rights and welfare states saliently – though difference discloses much. Matthew Lassiter has argued that to ascribe the rise of the Republican right to a suburban, white, Southern anti-civil rights strategy misses the national spread of this style of middle-class, silent majority politics.[76] Conversely, Thatcherism's penetration both into the national culture and electorally was thinner, more regional, and lost longstanding support in Scotland and among younger women.[77] Hall has argued, "Thatcherism... put down deep roots in the traditional, conventional social culture of English society," but so far as moral retrenchment and degentrifying conservatism went, this does not seem the case.[78] Its roots were often of the traditional, extant conservative type that Thatcher wanted to pull up or question. There was not the religious base for the backlash many Thatcherites wanted. In the

---

[74] Schulman, "The Empire Strikes Back," 699.

[75] Cockett, "The New Right," 99, 104.

[76] Matthew Lassiter, "Suburban Strategies: The Volatile Center in Postwar American Politics," in Meg Jacobs, William Novak, and Julian Zelizer, eds., *The Democratic Experiment: New Directions in American Political History* (Princeton, 2003), 327–349.

[77] Richard Finlay, "Thatcherism, Unionism and Nationalism" and Laura Beers, "Thatcher and the Women's Vote," in Jackson and Saunders, *Making Thatcher's Britain*, 165–179, 113–131.

[78] Stuart Hall, *The Hard Road to Renewal: Thatcherism and the Crisis of the Left* (London, 1988), 91.

end, Thatcherism hardly challenged privilege, whilst regretting that the declining authority of party did not enable them to go further. This suggests that Thatcherism was not that new, lacked the resources to remake, or was assimilated by inherited Conservative cultures.

In its unrestrained manner and style (as much as content), the New Right was distinctive. They asserted it was what they knew that was their chief quality, where Conservatives had assumed it was who they were. The YCs vividly illustrate change here. Whilst not hegemonic over popular attitudes in the wider society, there is little doubt Thatcherism reframed political debate and language.[79] The argument here notes the evident restraints as well, and its cultural approach indicates limits to the degree of change involved in Thatcherism. It could not remake Conservatism in its own ideal image, much less the nation. But we should also remember the political right had plenty to say in 1968. The shift between the 1960s and Thatcherism was less dramatic than commonly supposed by a language of eras. These were not quite or always the "New Times" that Thatcherites and their critics alleged.[80]

---

[79] Louise Phillips, "Hegemony and Political Discourse: The Lasting Impact of Thatcherism," *Sociology* 32:4 (1998): 847–867.

[80] Stuart Hall and Martin Jacques, eds., *New Times: The Changing Face of Politics in the 1990s* (London, 1989).

Afterword

Winners and Losers

Michael Kazin

To analyze a political movement, the first questions one should ask are the most obvious ones: what did it win, what did it lose, and why. This splendidly wide-ranging collection of essays makes clear that, on both sides of the Atlantic, right-wing activists shed their self-doubts and defensiveness in the 1960s and 1970s and began to develop a vital alternative to the social democratic consensus that had held sway since the end of World War II – even under such moderate conservative leaders as Dwight Eisenhower, Harold Macmillan, and Konrad Adenauer. The New Right began to assemble coalitions of students, intellectuals, and rising politicians and made sharp critiques of both cultural libertinism and Keynesian economics.

The "silent majority" activists appealed to was hardly a majority, but those who identified with that term would no longer be silent. On both continents, almost half a century later, their ideological descendants have become a sizable and dynamic force in political life. But the New Right neither initiated a new political era nor was able to slow, much less halt, the wave of libertarian expression and desire – promoted by both the mass and left-wing media – that kept building in strength during the decades following World War II.

Conservatives in the long 1960s struggled to adapt to the same changes in structures and ideologies that were spurring the growth of the New Left they vehemently opposed. Gradually but surely, "advanced capitalist" societies were moving away from a reliance on manufacturing to jobs in the service and clerical sectors. In part to fill such positions, higher education was booming. For the first time in history, millions of people were free to spend their late teens and part of their twenties living with one another in settings that encouraged thinking about political and cultural issues as well as a questioning of gender roles and sexual mores their elders often scorned and yet some also envied. Peoples of African, Latin American, and Middle Eastern descent were demanding equal rights and opportunities on both sides of the Atlantic. Finally, the long and largely shared prosperity of the postwar years – the Great Compression, as historians now call it – stirred utopian yearnings for a "post-materialist" society that might do away with poverty and drudgery, at least in Europe and North America. A radical left that had once focused on class inequality now shifted a good deal of its energy to fighting racism and imperialism – and tended to view the avidity of consumers as a new kind of alienation.[1]

Conservatives resisted the challenge to institutions and modes of behavior they cherished. To them, protests from the left seemed unruly and destructive to the social order. Thus, Frank Meyer, an editor of the U.S. magazine *National Review*, condemned civil rights demonstrators and the liberal politicians who supported them for "depriving private citizens of the protection of their property; of enjoining under threat of federal armed power, the police power from preserving order in our communities." Thus, in Britain, Mary Whitehouse led a campaign against rampant "permissiveness" promoted by "the metropolitan, secular, liberal establishment."[2] These responses seemed to affirm that, as the political scientist Samuel Huntington wrote in an influential 1957 essay, conservatism was largely a "situational" ideology, "arising out of a distinct but recurring type of historical situation in which a fundamental challenge is directed at established institutions and in which the supporters of those institutions employ the conservative ideology in their defense."[3]

But such an ideology, while capable of mobilizing citizens against specific threats for limited stretches of time, could not create a durable movement. For that to happen, conservatives needed to articulate a set of normative appeals and a program, passionately articulated alternatives to liberalism (American-style) and social democracy that might be as disruptive in their own way as the changes they abhorred. They learned

---

[1] For a summary of these changes, see Eric Hobsbawm's classic interpretation of the postwar "Golden Age" in his *The Age of Extremes: A History of the World, 1914–1991* (New York, 1994), 257–343.

[2] Frank Meyer, "Principles and Heresies," *National Review*, June 18, 1963, 496; Lawrence Black, "1968 and All That(cher): Cultures of Conservatism and the New Right in Britain," chapter 17 in this volume.

[3] Samuel Huntington, "Conservatism as an Ideology," *American Political Science Review* 51 (June 1957): 455.

how to organize powerful coalitions that offered a vision of a different future instead of simply asserting the virtues of a vanishing past.

Such a strategy was most fully developed in the United States. Wealthy donors set up foundations and think tanks to promulgate the merits of "free enterprise" and the tyrannies of welfare programs and trade unions. They subsidized a new generation of conservative intellectuals whose work challenged left-wing verities in such fields as economics, political theory, and the law.[4]

At the same time, a growing Christian right forged a partnership with corporations and politicians who opposed the regulatory state and the influence of organized labor. The fast-growing Southern Baptist Convention and interdenominational groups like the Moral Majority and the Christian Coalition turned "family values" into both a critique of feminism and gay rights and an ideal that should guide national policy. They also lauded giant firms like Wal-Mart for endorsing their views and, in turn, castigated the secular state for promoting dependence and weakening the self-reliant spirit. In 1980, this Christian–corporate alliance helped sweep Ronald Reagan into the White House. Writes the historian Seth Dowland, "Voters had come to understand the phrase family values to mean standing against liberal reforms that would weaken the roles and responsibilities of mothers, fathers, and children."[5]

In Western Europe, conservative activists were unable, and usually unwilling, to forge a similar partnership rooted in a version of Christian ethics and individual self-reliance. Church attendance there kept declining during the postwar era, particularly in majority Protestant nations, and the right-to-life movement, so central to "movement conservatism" in the United States since the 1970s, failed to gain many followers in Britain, West Germany, or Scandinavia. Thus, most conservatives in Europe attacked the secular left in a language of "freedom" and "antisocialism" that was almost entirely devoid of religious references. Absent the mobilizing élan of the American right's normative appeals, parties on the European right lost ground to their social democratic rivals during the late 1960s and 1970s. In the United States at the same time, politicians who appealed to "the silent majority" were throwing liberals on the defensive. It is telling that the only Democratic presidents elected between

---

[4] See, among other works, Jane Mayer, *Dark Money: The Hidden History of the Billionaires Behind the Rise of the Radical Right* (New York, 2016); Steven Teles, *The Rise of the Conservative Legal Movement* (Princeton, 2009).

[5] Seth Dowland, *Family Values and the Rise of the Christian Right* (Philadelphia, 2015), 179.

the mid-1960s and Barack Obama over half a century later were Southern Baptists.[6] *(Carter + Clinton (and almost Bush, I think))*

Bush!! was actually Methodist

Yet American conservatives were no more able to create a new common sense about their core ideas than were their counterparts across the Atlantic. As president, Ronald Reagan made occasional statements about outlawing abortion and curbing gay rights. But he did not urge Congress to take action on either issue and was far more passionate about toppling the Soviet empire and cutting income taxes – matters that united more voters than divided them. What is more, neither he nor Prime Minister Margaret Thatcher, who took power in Britain in 1979, dismantled the welfare states whose "creeping socialism" they both railed against. Few citizens in either nation, whatever their ideology or voting habits, were eager to give up state benefits that made their lives more secure.

The influence of right-wing populists in the late 1960s and early 1970s who sought to capitalize on racial and ethnic resentments was more enduring. Take the examples of George Wallace in the United States and Enoch Powell in Britain. During the late 1960s, both men seemed to be spearheading a revolt of silent majorities of white citizens fearful that racial minorities were endangering their status and privileges.

The former governor of Alabama, Wallace ran for president in 1968 on an independent ticket and drew large crowds both in his own region and in white working-class communities in the North. His tough defenses of "law and order" and "neighborhood" public schools capitalized on widespread resentment against black militancy. But he also belittled the hypocrisy of elite liberal whites who sent their own children to private schools and "bureaucrats" and "theoreticians" who tried to foist "absurd blueprints" on ordinary people.[7]

That same year, Powell, an MP from the West Midlands and the shadow defense secretary of the Conservative Party, gave a speech that attacked immigration to his nation from its former colonies in vitriolic and colorful terms. He charged, "We must be mad, literally mad to be permitting" thousands of people whose race and culture clashed with

---

[6] Even though not all of them were such devout believers as Jimmy Carter, whose private life was beyond reproach even to the most conservative Republican critics, in sharp contrast to his younger counterpart Bill Clinton. On the language of conservative parties in Europe, see chapter 14 by Martina Steber in this volume.

[7] For these quotes and those of Powell, see Michael Kazin and Stephane Porion, "George Wallace and Enoch Powell: Comparing the Politics of Populist Conservatism in the US and the UK" (forthcoming).

those of most native-born citizens. A classicist by training, Powell went on to translate a line from Virgil's *Aeneid:* "As I look ahead, I am filled with foreboding. Like the Roman, I seem to see the River Tiber foaming with blood."

Neither Powell nor Wallace reaped much political benefit from the furious controversies they aroused. The British press excoriated Powell as a shameful racist, and he was dismissed from the shadow cabinet. Although polls showed that most voters agreed with his warnings and he received a torrent of sympathetic mail, Powell's moment in the spotlight was his last – even though he continued to serve in the House of Commons for almost twenty more years. Wallace received over 13 percent of the vote for president in 1968 and was running a strong race for the Democratic nomination in 1972. But that May, he was shot by a would-be assassin and gradually faded from national prominence.[8] *Though he had made much shifts as governor on Alabama, moderating his hostility to Black people*

The two men had, however, touched a nerve in the body politic on both sides of the Atlantic. In the United States, conservative Republicans became adept at evoking, in racial code, the "middle Americans" who felt condescended to by a liberal elite above them and besieged by violent black criminals below. Democrats who protested were thrown on the defensive on issues of civil rights and remained there into the twenty-first century. In Britain and on the Continent, a similar populist back-lash against dark-skinned immigrants, *as Eastern Europeans* allegedly coddled by the "elitist bureaucrats" at the European Commission in Brussels, became a permanent fixture of partisan conflict. It was a key factor in the rising vote totals won by the Front National in France, the Freedom Party in Austria, and the People's Party in Denmark – and, more recently, the United Kingdom Independence Party. *– Reform and the Brexiteers are its descendants in effect*

* * *

So the new conservatives who emerged in the 1960s and 1970s made history but not quite as they pleased. They and their ideological progeny won some victories, although no lasting ones, and lost some battles, although none that activists on the right have conceded. The popularity of libertarian ideas helps explain this ambivalent legacy. As the theorist Mark Lilla argued in 1998, the cultural "revolution" of the 1960s in

---

[8] Powell left the Conservative Party in 1974 and was elected MP as an Ulster Unionist. See also Bill Schwarz, "The Silent Majority: How the Private Becomes Political," chapter 7 in this volume.

private life seriously eroded traditional standards of morality and gender hierarchy and has not been reversed. Yet, by the 1990s, "free market" or "neoliberal" economics had largely replaced Keynesian ones as the dominant mode of thought in that critical field, if not always the best guide to the policies of state. Its ideas were more contested in Western Europe, where Social Democrats remained a major force, than in the United States or the United Kingdom. But Eastern Europeans who, after the downfall of the Soviet bloc, turned older books by Friedrich Hayek and Milton Friedman into bestsellers suggested that an intellectual corner had been turned. According to Lilla, the result of the libertarian triumph was thus "a morally lax but economically successful capitalist society." The obvious fact that millions of those who live in such places rarely get to enjoy that success has so far not shaken the exponents of free market thinking.[9]

On the other hand, the enduring popularity of the welfare state, and of cultural freedom, has made it impossible for right-wing parties to win enduring majorities. Since the 1970s, Republicans and Democrats in the United States have traded control of the national government, as have Tories and Labour in Britain, the Socialists and the main center-right party (under different names) in France, and the Social Democrats and Christian Democrats in Germany. More recently, citizens frustrated and enraged by the deep recession and its aftermath have organized independent parties and insurgencies within established ones. But, at this writing, none has come close to toppling the system they view as hopelessly corrupt and ineffective.

Meanwhile, "the silent majority" continues to resonate in right-wing political discourse. Donald Trump revived (2017-21) it during his 2016 campaign for the Republican presidential nomination. The arrogant, bigoted mil-lionaire's performance alarmed many veterans of the conservative move-ment. But with a huge margin among white working-class voters, he narrowly defeated Hillary Clinton in the general election. Few voters probably knew, or recalled, that the only U.S. president ever to resign in disgrace had popularized the term in a speech defending a war that would end in total defeat. The idea that masses of ordinary people seethe for years, in private, about their discontents until a movement or a man

---

[9] Lilla was writing about the United States but his point, with some caveats, applies to Europe as well. Mark Lilla, "A Tale of Two Reactions," *New York Review of Books*, May 14, 1998; Paul Dragos Aligica and Anthony John Evans, *The Neoliberal Revolution in Eastern Europe: Economic Ideas in the Transition from Communism* (London, 2009).

emerges to give voice to what they had been repressing has long been a powerful trope among rebels both on the right and the left. We should not be surprised that it keeps returning.[10]

[10] On the grumbling about Trump's campaign among conservative intellectuals in the United States, see Thomas Edsall, "Can This Really Be Donald Trump's Republican Party?," *The New York Times*, December 16, 2015 (http://www.nytimes.com/2015/12/16/opinion/campaign-stops/can-this-really-be-donald-trumps-republican-party.html?action=click&pgtype=Homepage&clickSource=story-heading&module=opinion-c-col-right-region&region=opinion-c-col-right-region&WT.nav=opinion-c-col-right-region).

Actually, he lot the popular vote

Index